Against the grain

MANCHESTER
1824
Manchester University Press

Against the grain

The British far left from 1956

Edited by
Evan Smith and Matthew Worley

Manchester University Press

Published by Manchester University Press
Oxford Road, Manchester M13 9NR, UK
and Room 400, 175 Fifth Avenue, New York, NY 10010, USA
www.manchesteruniversitypress.co.uk

Distributed in the United States exclusively by
Palgrave Macmillan, 175 Fifth Avenue, New York,
NY 10010, USA

Distributed in Canada exclusively by
UBC Press, University of British Columbia, 2029 West Mall,
Vancouver, BC, Canada V6T 1Z2

British Library Cataloguing-in-Publication Data
A catalogue record for this book is available from the British Library

Library of Congress Cataloging-in-Publication Data applied for

ISBN   978 07190 9590 0   hardback

First published 2014

The publisher has no responsibility for the persistence or accuracy of URLs for any external or third-party internet websites referred to in this book, and does not guarantee that any content on such websites is, or will remain, accurate or appropriate.

Typeset in Sabon 10.5/12.5
by Carnegie Book Production, Lancaster
Printed in Great Britain
by CPI Group (UK) Ltd, Croydon, CR04YY

Contents

List of contributors

Ian Birchall was a member of International Socialism/Socialist Workers Party from 1962, active as a trade unionist and in campaigns against war and racism, formerly a lecturer at Middlesex University and is now an independent writer and translator. He is a member of the editorial board of *Revolutionary History* and author of *The Spectre of Babeuf* (1997), *Sartre Against Stalinism* (2004) and *Tony Cliff: A Marxist for His Time* (2011).

Paul Blackledge is professor of political theory and UCU branch secretary at Leeds Metropolitan University. He is author of *Marxism and Ethics* (2012), *Reflections on the Marxist Theory of History* (2006) and *Perry Anderson, Marxism and the New Left* (2004).

Sue Bruley is a reader in modern history at the University of Portsmouth. Her work includes *Women in Britain Since 1900* (1999), *The Women and Men of 1926: The General Strike and Miners's Lockout in South Wales* (2010) and the book of her Ph.D. thesis, *Leninism, Stalinism and the Women's Movement in Britain 1920–39*, which has recently been reissued.

Phil Burton-Cartledge lectures in sociology at Derby University, and regularly blogs about the far left (among other things) at http://averypublic sociologist.blogspot.co.uk. His Ph.D. thesis looked at the life histories of Trotskyist activists, paying particular attention to their radicalisation and how they remained committed to revolutionary socialist politics.

John Callaghan is professor of politics and contemporary history at the University of Salford. He is the author of *The Far Left in British Politics* (1987), *Socialism in Britain since 1884* (1990) and *The Retreat of Social Democracy* (2000).

Rich Cross has written about the British, European and US left for *Contemporary Politics, Twentieth Century Communism, Science & Society* and *Communisme* and on the culture and practice of anarchist punk for *Socialist History, Music and Politics* and *Freedom*. His doctoral thesis was a study of the decline and demise of the British Communist Party. He works as an academic librarian and is currently researching a book on the history of anarcho-punk.

Mark Hayes is a senior lecturer in politics and criminology at Solent University, Southampton. He has published on a wide variety of subjects including Irish Republicanism, Ulster loyalism, anti-fascism, and the New Right in Britain. He is currently working on a book about fascism and the extreme right in Britain and was an active member of both Anti-Fascist Action and Red Action.

Celia Hughes is assistant professor of British History in the department of English, Germanic and Romance Studies at the University of Copenhagen. Her study of the socio-cultural milieus of Britain's New Left cultures in the late 1960s will be published by Manchester University Press in 2015. 'Young Lives on the Left: Sixties Activism and the Liberation of the Self' examines the relationship between activist subjectivities and the shaping of Britain's New Left cultures in the late 1960s. She is currently working on a study of the subjectivities of pro-feminist men in 1970s and 1980s Britain.

Lawrence Parker lives and works in London. His book, *The Kick Inside: Revolutionary Opposition in the CPGB, 1945–91*, was published in 2012.

Andrew Pearmain is a political historian, whose recent book, *The Politics of New Labour*, offered a Gramscian analysis of British Labourism. He is also a national expert on HIV/AIDS social care and is a contributing editor to *Arena Homme Plus*.

David Renton is a barrister at Garden Court chambers, author of several books about fascism and anti-fascism and was previously a member of the national steering committee of Unite Against Fascism (2003–6).

Evan Smith is a vice-chancellor's postdoctoral research fellow in the School of International Studies at Flinders University, South Australia. He has written widely on the post-war history of the Communist Party of Great Britain, anti-racism/fascism and the politics of 'race'. He is currently conducting a comparative research project of the communist parties in Britain, Australia and South Africa between 1920 and 1960.

Satnam Virdee is professor of sociology at the University of Glasgow and founding director of the Centre for Research on Racism, Ethnicity and Nationalism (CRREN). His research focuses on the study of anti-racist collective action and the relationship between racism, nationalism and the socialist left. His book *Racism, Class and the Racialized Outsider* will be published in 2014.

Graham Willett is a recovering academic who researches gay and lesbian history. His current project is an examination of the origins and diffusion of homosexual politics in the British world in the 1950s and 1960s. He is an honorary fellow in the school of historical and philosophical studies at the University of Melbourne, Australia.

Matthew Worley is professor of modern history at the University of Reading. He has written widely on British politics, including the Communist Party of Great Britain, and is a co-editor of the *Twentieth Century Communism* journal. He is currently working on a study of the relationship between politics and youth culture, from which an article on the influence of the far left (and far right) on British punk was published in *Contemporary British History* in 2012.

Acknowledgements

The editors would like to thank the contributors for the time they gave to produce this book. Thanks, too, to those who refereed the chapters herein and particularly Ian Birchall, Mark Perryman and David Lockwood for their comments on the introduction. The support provided by Keith Flett and the London Socialist Historians Group, especially with regard to the workshop held at the Institute of Historical Research in 2012, is also very much appreciated.

Abbreviations

ACF	Anarchist Communist Federation
ACMLU	Action Centre for Marxist-Leninist Unity
ACORD	Action Campaign to Outlaw Racial Discrimination
AEU	Amalgamated Engineering Union
AFA	Anti-Fascist Action
AFB	Anarchist Federation of Britain
ANC	African National Congress
ANL	Anti-Nazi League
APEX	Association of Professional, Executive and Computer Staff
AUEW	Amalgamated Union of Engineering Workers
AWA	Anarchist Workers' Association
BNP	British National Party
BRS	*British Road to Socialism*
C18	Combat 18
CARD	Campaign Against Racial Discrimination
CARF	Campaign Against Racism and Fascism
CATP	Campaign Against Tube Privatisation
CDRCU	Committee to Defeat Revisionism for Communist Unity
CND	Campaign for Nuclear Disarmament
CPB	Communist Party of Britain
CPB (M-L)	Communist Party of Britain (Marxist-Leninist)
CPC	Communist Party of China
CPGB	Communist Party of Great Britain
CPSA	Civil and Public Servants Association
CPSU	Communist Party of the Soviet Union
CPUSA	Communist Party USA
CR	consciousness-raising
CWI	Committee for a Workers International

DAM	Direct Action Movement
EC	European Community
EDL	English Defence League
FI	Fourth International
FLN	National Liberation Front (Algeria)
GLC	Greater London Council
HnH	Hope not Hate
ILP	Independent Labour Party
IMG	International Marxist Group
INLA	Irish National Liberation Army
IRA	Irish Republican Army
IRSP	Irish Republican Socialist Party
IS	International Socialists
IWA	Indian Workers' Association
IWCA	Independent Working Class Association
JCC	Joint Committee of Communists
JVP	People's Liberation Front (Sri Lanka)
LCG	Libertarian Communist Group
LLY	Labour League of Youth
LMHR	Love Music Hate Racism
LPYS	Labour Party Young Socialists
LSA	London Socialist Alliance
LSE	London School of Economics
M-L	Marxist-Leninist
NAAR	National Assembly Against Racism
NATO	North Atlantic Treaty Organisation
NCP	New Communist Party
NEC	National Executive Committee
NF	National Front
NLF	National Liberation Front (Vietnam)
NLR	*New Left Review*
NUJ	National Union of Journalists
NUM	National Union of Mineworkers
NUPE	National Union of Public Employees
NUS	National Union of Students
NUT	National Union of Teachers
ORA	Organisation of Revolutionary Anarchists
PCI	Italian Communist Party
RA	Red Action
RAR	Rock Against Racism
RCP	Revolutionary Communist Party
RMT	Rail, Maritime and Transport Union

RSL	Revolutionary Socialist League
SA	Socialist Alliance
SGUC	Socialist Green Unity Coalition
SLL	Socialist Labour League
SLP	Socialist Labour Party
SML	Scottish Militant Labour
SP	Socialist Party
SPG	Special Patrol Group
SR	Socialist Review
SRG	Socialist Review Group
SSP	Scottish Socialist Party
StWC	Stop the War Coalition
SWF	Syndicalist Workers Federation
SWG	Socialist Workers Group
SWP	Socialist Workers Party
TASS	Technical, Administration and Supervisory Section
TGWU	Transport and General Workers Union
TUC	Trades Union Congress
UAF	Union Against Fascism
UCU	University and College Union
ULR	*Universities and Left Review*
UPW	Union of Post Office Workers
USSR	Union of Soviet Socialist Republics (former Soviet Union)
VSC	Vietnam Solidarity Campaign
VSO	Voluntary Service Overseas
WF	Workers' Fight
WLM	Women's Liberation Movement
WRP	Workers Revolutionary Party
WV	*Women's Voice*
YCL	Young Communist League
YS	Young Socialists

Introduction

The far left in Britain from 1956

Evan Smith and Matthew Worley

In 1972, Tariq Ali, editor of the radical newspaper *Black Dwarf* and leading figure in the International Marxist Group (IMG), wrote in the introduction to his book, *The Coming British Revolution*:

> The only real alternative to capitalist policies is provided by the revolutionary left groups as a whole. Despite their smallness and despite their many failings, they represent the only way forward.[1]

At the time, the British left appeared in the ascendancy. The momentum of its counterparts on the European continent seemed to have stalled in 1968–69, but the left in Britain continued to experience what Chris Harman called a 'British upturn'.[2] A surge in industrial militancy and wider political (as well as cultural) radicalism had benefited the British left in terms of membership, activism and the awareness of radical ideas. Struggles and campaigns such as the defeat of Harold Wilson's anti-union legislation, the mobilisation of the labour movement against Edward Heath's Industrial Relations Bill, the explosion of left-wing activism in the universities, the beginnings of the women's liberation and gay rights movements (amongst many others) all served to hearten Ali and others across the broad contours of the left. For a brief moment it seemed as if the foundations of capitalist Britain were being undermined. Indeed, the oil crisis of 1973 provided a further shockwave in the period after Ali's book was published.

And yet, within a short while, the fortunes of the British left began to fall as sharply as they had risen. Certainly, by the end of the 1970s, the far left's forward march, which had been gathering pace since the political eruptions of 1956 (Nikita Khrushchev's 'secret speech', the Soviet invasion of Hungary, the collapse of the British imperial system after the Suez crisis), seemed – in the words of Eric Hobsbawm – to have 'halted'.[3]

Thereafter, the British far left continued to debate how best to react to the changes in the political, economic and social landscape that occurred under Margaret Thatcher and New Labour. In so doing, it realigned itself, fractured and evolved as new struggles emerged to test preconceptions and continually thwart the expected 'breakthrough'. Whatever way you shape it, the revolution did not come around. Nevertheless, the far left played its part in shaping what remains an ongoing historical epoch, challenging social mores and providing a dissenting voice within the British body politic.

Locating the 'left'

The term 'the left' in British politics is open to different interpretations. It is often refined by various adjectives to discern differing degrees of militancy or radicalism. In more mainstream politics, the term is used to describe the Labour Party and the trade union movement, as well as those on the periphery of Labour such as associated with *Tribune* and the *New Statesman*. In Gerald Kaufman's edited collection on the British left from the mid-1960s, Llew Gardner distinguished between the 'orthodox left' (who accepted the Labour Party as the party of reform) and the 'fringe left' (whom he described as a 'hotch-potch of self-styled Marxists, frustrated revolutionaries and inveterate malcontents').[4] Kenneth O. Morgan's history of the British left places the Labour Party at the centre of left-wing politics since the late nineteenth century, but argues that the ideas and policies of Labour have tended to be more progressive than socialist.[5] Even within the Labour Party, there are those who identify as left wing and those who do not; several groups within the party, such as the *Tribune* group, the Socialist Campaign Group and the Chartist Group self-identify themselves as left wing in some way or other.

Many critics of Labour have argued against such interpretation. The 'left', therefore, has often been used to define groups outside the Labour Party – that is, groups, parties or movements deemed more revolutionary or overtly socialist than Labour. Given such ambiguity, 'the far left' is typically used to distinguish between Labour and those such as the Communist Party of Great Britain (CPGB) or the various Trotskyist groups to have emerged in Britain from at least the 1960s. In his 1987 book, John Callaghan used the term 'far left' to describe the 'Leninist left' of the CPGB, the Socialist Workers Party (SWP), IMG, Militant and the Workers' Revolutionary Party (as well as their many off-shoots).[6] In the introduction to David Widgery's edited collection of primary sources on the left in Britain, Peter Sedgwick described an 'independent left' which incorporated the intellectuals of the New Left, the social movements of the late 1950s and early 1960s (primarily the Campaign for Nuclear Disarmament: CND), and 'sectarian' political groups such as the CPGB and the Club/Socialist Labour League (SLL). Sedgwick wrote that the high time of this 'independent left' was from 1956 to 'roughly 1970', but suggested that the late 1960s and early 1970s saw an 'independent left' overtaken by a 'revolutionary left' that comprised the International Socialists and IMG.[7] Within these far-left groups, the Communist Party's Betty Reid wrote that the CPGB made 'no exclusive claim to be the only force on the left', but dismissed its rivals as 'ultra-left'; that is, Trotskyist, anarchist, syndicalist or those who 'support the line of the Communist Party of China'.[8]

In this collection, we have chosen to use the term 'far left' to encompass all of the political currents to the left of the Labour Party. This includes the CPGB and the Trotskyist left, but also anti-revisionist and anarchist groups, intellectuals and activists centred on particular journals (such as *New Left Review* for example), and those engaged in progressive social movements. Some may dispute the currents we have included – many anarchists would argue that they share little with the communist/Leninist left – but, as the collection will show, there has tended to be much cross-over between the various political currents of the far left since the mid-twentieth century.

Outlining the history of the British far left

The year 1956 may be seen as representing 'year zero' for the British left. Eric Hobsbawm described the impact thus:

> There are two 'ten days that shook the world' in the history of the revolutionary movement of the last century: the days of the October Revolution ... and the Twentieth Congress of the Communist Party of the Soviet Union (14–25 February 1956). Both divide it suddenly and irrevocably into a 'before' and 'after' ... To put it in the simplest terms, the October Revolution created a world communist movement, the Twentieth Congress destroyed it.[9]

Prior to 1956, the CPGB had dominated the political field to the left of the Labour Party. The party had grown out of the unification of several socialist groups in 1920 and gradually built itself as *the* radical alternative to Labour. The only real competition came from the Independent Labour Party (ILP), whose disaffiliation from Labour in 1932 cast it adrift from the political mainstream. Although sectarianism served, at times, to limit the CPGB's appeal, the 1930s saw it greatly expand in influence, buoyed by its leadership role within the National Unemployed Workers' Movement, its anti-fascist stance (sending volunteers to fight in the Spanish Civil War and mobilisations against Sir Oswald Mosley's British Union of Fascists), and its campaigns for peace in Europe. Such advance was halted by its opposition to the war effort between September 1939 and June 1941, during which it followed Moscow's lead in defining the Second World War as 'imperialist'. Come Hitler's invasion of the Soviet Union, however, and the Union of Soviet Socialist Republics' (USSR) part in the allied war effort, the CPGB claimed its highest membership figure in 1942 (56,000).

Initially, at least, the CPGB appeared to maintain its advance at the end of the war. The 1945 election saw the CPGB win two parliamentary seats (Willie Gallacher in West Fife and Phil Piratin in Stepney/ Mile End), following which 215 communist councillors were elected at a municipal level.[10] Simultaneously, the party began to suffer in the face of the anti-communist hysteria that came with the onset of Cold War. Even then, its promotion of a parliamentary road to socialism and a future Communist-Labour alliance ensured that it maintained a foothold in the British labour movement. A trade union presence proved key to the longevity of the CPGB and its survival between the events of 1956 and the 'British upturn' ten years later.

Trotskyism and left-communism developed as two oppositional currents in the Communist Party during the 1920s and 1930s, but it was not until the post-war period that British Trotskyism really emerged as an alternative left-wing movement to the CPGB. The genesis of post-war British Trotskyism can be traced back to the Revolutionary Communist Party (RCP), which contained all of the subsequent leading figures of the Trotskyist movement and held the position of the official British representative of the Fourth International between 1944 and 1949. The RCP made some headway in the rank and file of the trade unions, particularly by supporting strikes when the CPGB was still promoting cooperation with the government, as well as in the anti-fascist activism against Mosley's newly formed Union Movement. However, the RCP soon split over questions concerning entrism within the Labour Party and how the Fourth International should view the 'People's Democracies' of Eastern Europe. By 1956, Gerry Healy's The Club (soon after the SLL) was the main Trotskyist group in Britain, with the others being relegated to discussion groups or journals in this period.

Such alignments across the British left would change in 1956. Khrushchev's denunciation of the 'cult of personality' that arose around Stalin and admission that crimes had been committed during Stalin's reign had a major impact on the CPGB. While many party members wanted a discussion over the CPGB's uncritical support for the Soviet Union, the leadership sought to quash any frank and open debate, particularly amongst the rank and file at branch or district level. As a result, some members – including E. P. Thompson and John Saville – were moved to publish mimeographed material to reach others dissatisfied with the leadership's approach. Soviet intervention in Hungary later the same year only exacerbated matters, leading to some 8,000 people leaving the CPGB between February 1956 and February 1958.

The trajectory of those who left the CPGB varied. As several authors have pointed out, this was the beginning of a British 'New Left' that sought to combine socialism with humanism and democracy. Divorcing themselves from party politics, Thompson and Saville started *The New Reasoner* in 1957, which alongside Stuart Hall's *Universities and Left Review* became the focal point of the first wave of the New Left. By the early 1960s, a number of people who had been involved in left-Labour circles had come into contact with these new journals and began two new ventures that solidified the left's realignment in the period before '1968': the *New Left Review* (edited firstly by Stuart Hall, then Perry Anderson) and the *Socialist Register* (edited by Saville and Ralph Miliband). What further galvanised the New Left in Britain was the rise of single-issue social movements that brought a younger generation of activists into contact with the left, the most predominant of which was CND. Although most of the leftist parties eventually supported CND, the campaign showed that political activism could be mobilised outside of party structures (or their front groups).

In terms of Trotskyism, the SLL benefited somewhat from the mass exodus from the CPGB in 1956. A small number of erstwhile CPGB activists joined Healy's group, including the historian Brian Pearce, Ken Coates, the Scottish trade unionist Lawrence Daly and the *Daily Worker* journalist Peter Fryer, who had been in Budapest at the time of the Soviet invasion. Few if any of those who joined the SLL from the CPGB were sudden converts to orthodox Trotskyism. Because of this, perhaps, the SLL proved unable to hold onto many of these defectors for long and Trotskyist recruitment soon turned its attention to the youth wing of the Labour Party.

Peter Sedgwick's description of the period between 1956 and 1968 as providing a 'record of a political adolescence' is particularly apt in regard to the far left.[11] The time roughly between the election of Harold Macmillan's Conservative government (1959) and the Seamen's strike of 1966 was one of transition, with several Trotskyist and anti-revisionist groups in incubation ready to emerge in the next decade. After the catastrophes of 1956, the CPGB refocused its efforts on creating a 'mass party' which promoted closer ties with the trade unions and the Labour left in a 'broad left alliance'. By 1964, the party had made up the 8,000 members it had lost less than a decade before. Two years later, and the party's links to the trade union movement proved integral to the founding of the Liaison Committee for the Defence of Trade Unions that played such an influential role in the campaigns against Harold Wilson's industrial relations reforms between 1966 and 1969. Even so, the CPGB's shift towards a parliamentary road to socialism and 'broad left alliance' disappointed some in the party who sought inspiration in the Chinese Communist Party's promotion of anti-revisionism. Thus, Britain's first Maoist group was formed by Michael McCreery in 1961: the Committee to Defeat Revisionism for Communist Unity (CDRCU). In 1963, the CDRCU formally broke from the CPGB.

The Trotskyist left, meanwhile, tended to remain inside the Labour Party for the first half of the 1960s. In 1964, the entrist group that existed around the leadership of Ted Grant and Peter Taaffe started producing a newspaper, *Militant*, recruiting inside the Labour Party Young Socialists (LPYS) for 'the tendency'. The IMG also started as a group on the Labour left, gathered around *The Week*. Over the course of 1965–68, however, the activists behind the paper transformed into a political group that joined with other Trotskyists, 'soft' Maoists and left libertarians to produce *Black Dwarf*. By contrast, the Socialist Review Group – founded by Tony Cliff – emerged outside the Labour Party in 1968 as the International Socialists (IS), with a monthly theoretical journal called *International Socialism* and a weekly paper, *Industrial Worker*, that eventually became known as *Socialist Worker*.

Indeed, '1968' marked a moment of transformation for the British far left. A multitude of international events – such as the uprising in France in May 1968, the emergence of the civil rights movement in Northern Ireland, the campaigns of the Students for a Democratic Society in the United States, the 'Prague Spring' in Czechoslovakia – not to mention domestic campaigns against the recommendations of the Donovan Report into industrial relations and Enoch Powell's 'rivers of blood' speech, spurred many (young) people into activist politics. Most significantly, perhaps, the Vietnam War and the Vietnam Solidarity Campaign (VSC) served to alter the composition of the British far left. As Martin Jacques wrote in *Marxism Today*, the two major effects of the Vietnam War in Britain were to change 'the international outlook of large sections of British youth', especially with regard to imperialism and socialism, and to inform attitudes towards 'the nature of British capitalism and the forms that revolutionary struggle at home might take.'[12]

The CPGB, of which Jacques was an Executive Committee member, was not among the major beneficiaries of the radicalism fostered by the VSC. With Tariq Ali in a leadership position within the VSC, so the IMG rose to some prominence, while the IS also made headway amongst the anti-war movement and the student radicals. Infamously, Healy's SLL (soon to become the Workers' Revolutionary Party: WRP) boycotted the anti-Vietnam War demonstrations, distributing a leaflet titled 'why the Socialist Labour League is not marching' at Grosvenor Square in October 1968.[13] At this moment, there seemed to be a contrast between the groups that benefited from the radicalism of the late 1960s and the ideas being simultaneously developed on the New Left. The *New Left Review* can be read as an indication of the Marxist theory that grew out of this era (and the worldwide spread of radicalism), with an enthusiasm for non-conformist communists such as Althusser, Marcuse, Poulantzas and Gramsci (and not necessarily the idea of Trotsky). But while these ideas were important for the development of the left in the 1970s, those associated with *New Left Review* had little impact on the practical politics of the period. Despite Trotsky not being read to the same extent as structural Marxists, it was the Trotskyist groups 'on the ground' that benefited membership-wise.

Whatever the ideological underpinning, the 'British upturn' and the fight against Edward Heath's industrial relations reforms saw the far left grow in confidence and optimism. For the CPGB, the industrial struggles and its presence inside the trade union movement made the late 1960s and early 1970s appear as an 'Indian summer',[14] with Roger Seifert and Tom Sibley recently stating (perhaps controversially) that the party's 'most successful achievement was its contribution to the trade union radicalism' of this era.[15] Both the IMG and the IS grew exponentially in size, though this brought its own problems. For the IMG, the inter-party alliance that existed around *Black Dwarf* broke down as the IMG pushed for a more formalised youth wing and emphasised the leadership role of the student movement. In due course, *Red Mole* replaced *Black Dwarf* as the IMG paper. By 1970, the IS had also started to push for more formal leadership over the disparate movements that had emerged out of 1968. Greater links between the new social movements, the student movement and the trade unions (particularly the rank and file) were seen as essential to further political activism. This, subsequently, has been described as a 'turn to class', but the IS' growth (and fear of Cliff's over-optimism about recruiting factory workers) led to heated debate within the group. The end result was the expulsion in 1975 of key personnel, such as Jim Higgins and Roger Protz, with some suggesting that the loss of such experienced members marked the end of the libertarian and democratic IS and the beginning of a slow march towards Leninist suffocation.[16]

Arguably, it was the electoral victory of Labour in 1974 that signalled the end of the left's forward momentum, with Labour and the Trades Union Congress (TUC) settling on a 'social contract' to deal with inflation and limit the outbreaks of industrial action. For most of the late 1960s and early 1970s, the labour movement and the left seemed to be pulling in the same direction. The 'social contract', however, drove a wedge between the leadership of the trade unions, who supported Labour, and a left that opposed putting the brakes on industrial militancy. Coupled with the economic downturn sparked by the Oil crisis of 1973, the political and socio-economic landscape changed and the left's strategy of confrontation served to isolate it from large swathes of the trade union movement. By the time the 'Social Contact' ran its course at the end of the 1970s, so the relationship between the labour movement and the left had all but fractured.

The result, taken generally, was strategic realignment across much of the left. In the CPGB, a number of party members began to question the tangible gains made by such a focus on industrial strategy and 'broad left alliances', especially if the Labour left and trade union leadership were willing to sacrifice them for political expediency. By concentrating on industrial militancy, the critics argued, the CPGB had discouraged other groups of people from joining or getting involved in activist politics. Accordingly, calls to reform the CPGB programme, *The British Road to Socialism*, were manifest by the party congress in 1977.

For the IS/SWP, too, the 'betrayal' of the TUC demonstrated that alliances with the leaders of the labour movement were ineffective. In its place, the party promoted the mobilisation of the trade union rank and file ('rank-and-filism') to present the IS/SWP as a workers' party committed to support the localised strikes that grew out of the economic crisis of the 1970s. Simultaneously, the IS/SWP saw new avenues of mobilisation emerging that related to the economic crisis – amongst the unemployed via the Right to Work campaign, and through anti-fascist activism aimed at a buoyant National Front. The latter, of course, facilitated the launch of Rock Against Racism (RAR) in 1976 and the Anti-Nazi League (ANL) in 1977.

The fortunes of these single issue movements, particularly the ANL (the biggest social movement since the CND), pushed the SWP to prominence on the left. By contrast, the IMG's investment in the student movement (as well as the new social movements) saw their influence begin to slip away during the mid-to-late 1970s. Though it continued to exist into the 1980s, it became the Socialist League in 1982; an entrist group within the Labour Party that published *Socialist Action*. Militant, meanwhile, slowly gained influence within the local levels of the Labour Party.

It is worth noting that on the fringes of the far left, Maoism and anti-revisionism also experienced a brief fillip in the 1970s. Probably the most successful Maoist organisation was the Communist Party of Britain

(Marxist-Leninist) (CPB (M-L)). Established by Reg Birch, a member of the CPGB and Amalgamated Engineering Union (AEU), the CPB (M-L) grew out of concern over the CPGB's 'reformism' and the party's unwillingness to support Birch against Hugh Scanlon in an AEU election. As a result, the CPB (M-L) had a strong base in the AEU, with Birch's election to the TUC leadership in 1975 giving the party a certain gravitas in comparison with comparable leftist groups. Other Maoist sects emerged in the 1970s, but most only gathered a handful of members. Nor did the Maoists make significant inroads into the new social movements, though some influence was evident among students and, importantly, within South Asian communities in Britain.[17] The main criticism aimed at the Maoist groups by the other sections of the left was that they used impenetrable Marxist-Leninist jargon to propose political strategies not suited to the United Kingdom. Student-peasant alliances and guerrilla warfare, for example, did not tend to translate very well. By the end of the 1970s, Maoism in Britain had more or less faded into obscurity.

At the opposite end of the anti-revisionist spectrum, the pro-Stalin section of the CPGB that had remained in the party despite its moves away from Stalinism broke in 1977 in protest against the revised *British Road to Socialism*. Led by Sid French and the Surrey District of the CPGB, these pro-Stalinists formed a New Communist Party (NCP) that peaked in the late 1970s before going into decline in the 1980s. Thereafter, a section of the NCP's youth wing decided to re-enter the CPGB in the early 1980s under the auspices of *The Leninist*, which in turn became involved in further factional disputes before being expelled in the mid-1980s.

In hindsight, the election of Margaret Thatcher in May 1979 may be seen as a watershed moment in British politics that coincided with a period of turmoil across the British far left. Alongside Stuart Hall's 'The Great Moving Right Show', Eric Hobsbawm's 'The Forward March of Labour Halted?' (published in *Marxism Today* in late 1978) captured the mood amongst reformers in the CPGB, recognising – as it did – that Thatcherism represented a fundamental shift in British politics and that traditional Labour strategies had reached an impasse. Reformers in the CPGB believed that the party and Labour left had to work together to encourage the non-conventional Labour Party supporter to become involved in leftist politics and align against what became the Thatcherite hegemony. For many of these reformers, who started to group around *Marxism Today* and the ideas of Eurocommunism, the struggles of the CPGB had to incorporate a pro-actively *ideological* dimension rather than the defensive and primarily economic industrial struggles of the late 1960s and 1970s. Schisms had already emerged after the 'broad democratic alliance' was incorporated into the CPGB programme in 1977, but the splits solidified and grew after an article in *Marxism Today* by Tony Lane criticised the practices of the trade unions under Thatcherism. The editorial board of the *Morning Star* was generally staffed by supporters of the party's existing industrial strategy (connected to Mick Costello, the Industrial Organiser) who used the paper to attack the ideas being promoted in *Marxism Today*. Amidst much recrimination, splits and division, the party moved closer to its endgame.

In the SWP, Tony Cliff confronted a similar problem to that presented by Hobsbawm – what was to be learnt from the decline of *organised* industrial militancy and the rise of more *sporadic* industrial action of the late 1970s? Cliff's analysis was that it reflected a 'downturn' in the industrial struggle, which he envisioned as a relatively short-term problem (in contrast to Hobsbawm's long-term diagnosis). Equally, Cliff showed concern that initiatives like RAR and the ANL had reached people outside the conventional structures of the left but had not really served to benefit the SWP in terms of recruitment.[18] Sales of the *Socialist Worker* did rise during the early 1980s, to 31,000 in 1984–85.[19] But this may have been due more to the confrontational politics of Thatcherism than any lasting appeal of the SWP/RAR/ANL. Certainly, by the time that the SWP recognised Thatcherism to be far more of a genuine threat than first anticipated (particularly as experienced by the miners' strike of 1984–85), it had lost the initiative on many fronts to Militant and, in some areas, the revived anarchist movement.[20]

The first of these, Militant, had slowly built its base within the Labour Party, primarily through the LPYS. By the early 1980s, a significant number of its members (officially 'supporters') held positions of influence in local branches and on Labour councils. The breakthrough came in 1982–83, when Militant gained control of Liverpool City Council and used its influence to foster local resistance to Thatcher's monetarist policies. Between 1982 and 1987, Liverpool was – along with Sheffield City Council and the Greater London Council – one of the primary sites of council opposition to the Conservatives.

Militant was further buoyed by the election of two of its 'supporters' as Labour MPs in 1983; Terry Fields in Liverpool and Dave Nellist in Coventry. Such successes pushed Militant to the fore of the opposition to Thatcher while also causing considerable distress to the Labour Party. The result was a protracted struggle first signalled in 1982 with the expulsion of *Militant*'s editorial board from Labour. On Neil Kinnock's becoming Labour leader following the 1983 electoral defeat, moreover, so the 'witch-hunt'[21] began in earnest, with a major purge of Militant supporters occurring in 1986 and expulsions continuing thereafter.

Despite this, Militant's influence at a municipal level meant that it was particularly well placed to take part in opposing the infamous 'poll tax', which from 1987 facilitated a major reform of how local tax rates were calculated, with the burden of the reforms impacting heavily upon those in lower socio-economic areas. Though by no means the only group involved in resisting the tax, Militant was often the public face of the revolt, with Nellist and Tommy Sheridan both jailed for taking part in non-payment protests. The crescendo of the anti-poll tax movement was the 'Poll Tax riot' of April 1990, which proved significant in destabilising Thatcher's premiership. When she resigned six months later, the initiative of the British left seemed to be with Militant, though this would again prove but a short-lived illusion of potential breakthrough.

The anarchist movement also came to the fore in the poll tax protest. The British anarchist movement of the 1980s had two main prongs, which sometimes overlapped but often worked in isolation: anarcho-punks borne out of milieus that existed around bands such as Crass; and Class War, a more militant anarchist group with its roots in Wales. The anarcho-punks emerged in the late 1970s and mobilised around issues such as pacifism, animal rights and squatting. As the Cold War began to 'heat up' in the early 1980s, so anarchists became heavily involved in campaigns against nuclear weapons, particularly the United States' use of the United Kingdom as an arms base. On the back of this, anarchists were prominent in the demonstrations against the Falklands War of 1982.

Class War began in 1983 and rejected the pacifism of the anarcho-punks, becoming involved in political activism at the fringes of industrial disputes, often in confrontation with the police.[22] Both sets of anarchists were involved in Stop the City demonstrations between 1983 and 1985, but Class War became the primary anarchist group of the late 1980s. Class War mixed publicity in the mainstream press, community activism and appeals to youth culture (such as the Bash the Rich tour of 1987) to promote their political agenda. Though membership remained small, its public profile and publication – *Class War* – gained a much larger circle (estimated to be in the thousands) of sympathetic supporters. By the early 1990s, Class War also engaged into anti-fascist activism in loose cooperation with Anti-Fascist Action.

As all this suggests, the far left changed significantly through the 1990s. Most importantly, the CPGB voted to dissolve itself in 1991, with the collapse of the Eastern Bloc and Soviet Union underpinning its decision. Already, in 1989, the influence of those writing in *Marxism Today* had led to *The British Road to Socialism* giving way to the *Manifesto for New Times*. The latter was criticised for its argument that the 1980s–1990s had ushered in a new era of 'post-fordism' and its alleged deviation away from the centrality of class-based politics. Thereafter, a section of party

reformers forged the Democratic Left as a left-wing pressure group/
think-tank, while the title of the CPGB was eventually taken up by those
around *The Leninist*. A Communist Party of Britain (CPB) had already
been formed by party traditionalists in 1988, after the *Morning Star*
divorced itself from the old CPGB but retained links to the trade union
movement. As for *Marxism Today*, though undoubtedly an influential
left-wing journal in the 1980s, it could not survive without the CPGB and
closed in December 1991. Although some have accused *Marxism Today*
and the *Manifesto for New Times* of helping to create New Labour, this
is vehemently denied by its key writers, such as Martin Jacques and Stuart
Hall. Certainly, as Andrew Gamble noted, Hall 'delivered a passionate
denunciation of New Labour ... refusing to recognise it as in any sense
a legitimate exponent of the new politics which he had advocated in the
1980s'.[23]

The SWP fared rather better, retaining its membership levels as the
CPGB declined. Indeed, the SWP was able to portray itself as a ready
alternative – an independent and recognisable party with a widely read
(in terms of the far left) newspaper and distinct ideology. The return
of the ANL in response to the rise of the British National Party (BNP)
also tapped into the heritage of the SWP and gave the party presence.
Militant, on the other hand, was somewhat encumbered by the successes
of the 1980s. An internal debate raged over whether the Labour Party still
represented the interests of the working class and whether the opportunity
had presented itself to break away and become an independent organisation. The Scottish wing of Militant parted ways with Labour in April
1991, while the 1991 congress saw a split in the main British party. The
majority of Militant members, led by Peter Taaffe, favoured becoming
an independent political party; the minority, led by Ted Grant and Alan
Woods, chose to remain inside Labour. The majority thus formed Militant
Labour, who continued to publish *Militant*; the minority formed the
International Marxist Tendency. In 1997, Militant Labour became the
Socialist Party of England and Wales (usually referred to as the Socialist
Party, but not to be confused with the Socialist Party of Great Britain),
the second-largest organisation on the British left after the SWP. *Militant*
became *The Socialist*.

As the far left realigned in the early 1990s, so the novelty of 'New
Labour' and the desire to overturn 18 years of Conservative rule made the
Labour Party under Tony Blair an attractive option for many. By 1999,
however, just two years after the landslide Labour election of 1997, such
appeal began to fade as many drawn to Labour became disillusioned with
a number of the government's policies and actions. This disillusionment
was exacerbated by two international events in 1999, which the far left

endeavoured to capitalise on: the anti-globalisation demonstrations in Seattle and the Blair-backed North Atlantic Treaty Organisation (NATO) airstrikes in Kosovo.

The anti-globalisation movement of the late 1990s and early 2000s was a diverse phenomenon that has been written on extensively.[24] The movement was characterised by a lack of centrality and its autonomous nature, with smaller groups embracing new technologies to organise a range of activities from mass demonstrations to acts of 'culture jamming' that involved smaller groupings or even individual activists. The movement tended to be portrayed in the popular press as a violent and unruly 'mob', primarily in relation to the rallies organised at events held by supra-national organisations such as the World Trade Organisation, G8 and International Monetary Fund. Taken generally, anarchists and non-aligned activists formed the basis of the anti-globalisation movement, though the organised left – hesitant at first – responded enthusiastically.

Alongside anti-globalisation, the British left (primarily the SWP) campaigned against NATO airstrikes on Serbian forces in Kosovo, a military operation prominently coordinated by Tony Blair as part of a strategy of humanitarian intervention. Many on the left opposed NATO's operations in the Balkans and viewed military intervention for humanitarian purposes as an oxymoron. But as the campaign brought the left into similar circles as Serbian nationalists, so the schisms occurred. The SWP was accused of knee-jerk anti-Americanism, and the party's embrace of (electoral) alliances with single issue pressure groups led also to concern that more sustainable party building was being neglected for short-term political point-scoring. Despite this, the 'War on Terror' and the anti-Muslim backlash that occurred in Britain saw the SWP further develop its strategy. The party was a key player in the anti-war movement that appeared after 11 September 2001. The Stop the War Coalition included the SWP's John Rees and Lindsay German among its leadership (alongside representatives from Labour, the CPB and CND) and worked closely with the Muslim Association of Britain to develop a campaign against NATO involvement in Afghanistan and Iraq. Claiming to be Britain's biggest mass movement ever,[25] Stop the War led a sustained campaign against the proposed invasion of Iraq and, in February 2003, over a million people marched in London to oppose military intervention in the Middle East. Although the campaign proved unsuccessful in preventing war, it presented a public presence to many who were dissatisfied with New Labour's enthusiastic participation in the 'War on Terror'. The SWP further capitalised on this resentment by forming Respect with expelled Labour MP George Galloway, who became renowned for his appearing before the US Senate regarding his alleged ties to Saddam Hussein. Respect contested the 2005 general election on a progressive platform, focusing on those who opposed the wars in Afghanistan and Iraq, as well as disillusioned Labour voters.

For a left-wing party, Respect did well. Galloway won Bethnal Green and Salma Yaqoob narrowly missed out on a seat in Birmingham. Subsequent council elections saw Respect record victories in Birmingham and London. Somewhat predictably, however, tensions between SWP supporters in Respect and George Galloway, particularly over Galloway's political style, led to a breakdown between the two groups. The SWP left Respect to form the Left List for the 2007 local elections, though proved unable to regain the footing it had in the early 2000s.

In some ways, the SWP's policy of alliance and emphasis on single-issue politics has led to resentments similar to those felt within the CPGB by the mid-1970s. Despite protestations from the SWP leadership that membership figures remained healthy, the party has more recently been characterised by a series of splits, expulsions and resignations over issues of direction, organisation and procedure. As things stand, the Socialist Party remains the second-largest far-left organisation in Britain and has established itself to a certain degree within the trade union movement, particularly in Unite. But neither it nor any other party of the left can really claim to have taken advantage of the political vacuum opened up by the decline of New Labour or the schism within the SWP.

More importantly, perhaps, the global economic crisis would appear to contain much potential for the revolutionary left. The evident failure of neo-liberal capitalism has led many to take to the British streets in opposition to the austerity measures of the Conservative-Liberal Democrat coalition, not to mention the widespread anger at 'the system' displayed by the riots that broke out across Britain in August 2011. The revolutions across the Arab world, as well as the Occupy movement, suggest people remain willing to challenge the status quo. The current wave of political activism certainly seems more sustained and localised than that of the late 1990s and early 2000s. Despite this, the far left in Britain has to date seemed only to react to such protest. The left has in no way claimed the debate over the cause of the financial crisis, nor shown a leadership role in moving beyond it. The Occupy movement that made camp outside St Paul's Cathedral in London was a space where the left had to tread carefully, with many involved wary about 'Trots' coming into the movement with notions of vanguardism. Similarly, if the left can claim a presence at demonstrations called against public-sector cuts, pension policy and student fees, then these have tended to be mobilised by institutions such as the TUC or the National Union of Students (NUS) rather than the clarion calls of the left.

The history of the far left in Britain suggests such limitations do not necessarily mean decline. Rather, the initiative – or impetus – tends to shift to different groups and different areas of struggle. One of the constant features of the British far left is its oscillation between periods of unbridled enthusiasm and periods of profound pessimism, both of which may be seen in the left's current analysis of the prevailing socio-economic and political climate.

The need for a history of the British far left

The purpose of this collection is to explore the role of the far left in British history from the mid-1950s until the present. It is not supposed to be a straightforward and all-encompassing narrative of the left during this period. Rather, it hopes to highlight the impact made by the far left on British politics and society. Even if the parties themselves have not been successful in ushering in the socialist revolution, they have still had a profound effect upon the political landscape in the second half of the twentieth century, particularly through the social movements that emerged since the 1950s. The chapters in this collection, for the most part, do not concentrate on individual parties or groups, but look at wider left-wing movements such as Trotskyism, anti-revisionism and anarchism, or at those political and social issues where the left sought to stake its claim. Taken as a whole, the collection should demonstrate the extent to – and ways in – which the far left has weaved its influence into the political fabric of Britain.

Little history has been written on the British far left in recent years. Since the dissolution of the CPGB in 1991, a flourish of studies emerged to examine aspects of communist history.[26] Two books and two edited volumes have also been produced on cultural, social and personal themes within the party history.[27] Of these, however, only two are dedicated solely to the post-war era (by John Callaghan and Geoff Andrews respectively), alongside one edited collection on the reminiscences of party activists after 1991 and a study of the CPGB and *Marxism Today*'s influence on New Labour.[28] That does not mean research is lacking, only that the various journal articles and book chapters written on the subject have tended to be more limited in scope.

Nor has the increase in communist histories been extended to the rest of the far left. John Callaghan's two books from the mid-1980s, *The Far Left in British Politics* and *British Trotskyism*, remain the authorative scholarly works on the subject, though both focus only on a section of the far left.[29] In 1976, SWP member David Widgery produced *The Left in Britain*, which collected primary source articles into a single volume dedicated to the period from 1956 to 1968. This was criticised (perhaps unfairly) by Ken Coates for 'attempting to incorporate all of the post-1956 British New Left under the hegemony of the International Socialists'.[30] Ted Grant, a founding member of Militant who remained in the group's entrist rump after the split with what became the Socialist Party, produced a history of British Trotskyism. But this ends in 1949 with the break-up of the Revolutionary Communist Party, leaving the history of the British Trotskyism since 1949 to a lengthy epilogue by Rob Sewell.[31] Other surveys from the 1970s and 1980s exist, predominantly written by journalists keen to portray the far left as a threat to democracy or a mirror image to the far right.[32] Michael Crick, too, published two books on Militant in the 1980s as the controversy over the group's entrism within the Labour Party came to a head.[33]

Beyond these surveys, the main source of information on the post-war British left comes from the biographies and autobiographies of party members. In 1994, Peter Taaffe published *The Rise of Militant*, though Coates' criticism of Widgery's book could also be made here with the substitution of Militant for the IS.[34] Tony Cliff, leader of the IS/SWP until his death in 2000, had his autobiography published posthumously. This, essentially, was a history of the party, though containing less detail about the SWP in the 1980s and 1990s.[35] A more robust and detailed biography of Cliff was published in 2011 by Bookmarks, the SWP's publishing house, written by long-time IS/SWP member Ian Birchall.[36] Indeed, Birchall had also written the history of the party in a pamphlet form in 1981. More controversially, a biography of Gerry Healy, the original 'guru' of British Trotskyism and leader of the SLL/WRP, appeared in the 1990s.[37] This has been criticised as a hagiography to a cult leader who preyed on female party members. Usefully, therefore, Bob Pitt (a former WRP member) serialised a more critical account of Healy in *Workers' News* in the early 1990s, which was subsequently published in full (with amendments) on the webpage of *What Next?* in the early 2000s.[38]

As things stand, the history of the left's more esoteric strands has barely been written. Tom Buchanan has produced a history of the British left's relationship with China since the 1920s, which includes substantial material on Maoism in Britain.[39] The history of the anti-revisionists and 'left' communists in the CPGB has also been documented by Lawrence Parker in his book *The Kick Inside* (2012), while Will Podmore of the CPB (M-L) produced a biography of Reg Birch in 2004, published by the party's own press.[40] At the other end of the British left, probably the most comprehensive account of anarchism in Britain is Benjamin Franks' *Rebel Alliances* (2006), but David Goodway has likewise written a history on left-libertarian thought in Britain that examines the space between anarchism and socialist humanism.[41] Two autobiographies by leading figures of the anarchist movement, Ian Bone of Class War and Stuart Christie, have also been published in the early 2000s, charting the varying strains of anarchism from the 1960s to the 1980s.[42]

As editors of this collection, we hope that the chapters included in this book reveal new episodes in the history of the British far left. The collection is separated into two parts – movements and issues. The first looks at particular strands of the far left in Britain since the 1950s; the second at various issues and social movements that the left engaged (or did not engage) with, such as women's liberation, gay liberation, anti-colonialism, anti-racism and anti-fascism. In many ways, this separation might seem arbitrary because there is significant cross-over between the two parts. Most of the chapters focus on events of the 1960s and 1970s, when the British far left was at its height, but a significant number look at the rise of the far left in the 1940s and 1950s and some extend in the 1980s and 1990s, when the far left's influence had dissipated.

The collection starts with John Callaghan's chapter on how the wider British left, in the Labour Party and amongst the intelligentsia, encountered Trotskyism between the 1930s and 1960s. While most chapters in this collection deal only with the politics of the far left, Callaghan reminds us that Trotsky's writings on the Soviet Union and the rise of fascism in Germany, unlike his more polemical work on the Fourth International and similar matters, reached a much broader audience, many of whom were critical of the Soviet Union but sympathetic to ideas of socialism. Reception of Trotsky's ideas by the Labour left, as well as by writers such as George Orwell and Bertrand Russell, was often an entry-point for those who eventually joined the far left. Following on, Paul Blackledge examines the political effectiveness of the New Left in Britain in the aftermath of 1956. Blackledge explores how the New Left broke with the democratic centralism of the CPGB and became involved in single issue social movements such as CND. However, he suggests that its avoidance of practical political organisation meant the New Left faded in the early 1960s, lying dormant until the radicalism of '1968'. In complementary fashion, Celia Hughes examines how the political awareness provoked by the New Left in the late 1950s transformed into practical political activism via involvement in CND and other social movements during the early-to-mid-1960s prior to the arrival of the VSC and '1968'.

The final chapters of the 'movements' part each address different strands of left-wing organisation in the post-war era. Firstly, Phil Burton-Cartledge outlines the histories of the two largest Trotskyist groups on the British far left: the IS/SWP and Militant/SP. He shows that both organisations have fluctuated between centralism and attempts to engage with broader social movements – with both strategies bringing mixed (and often diminishing) results. Secondly, Lawrence Parker explores the anti-revisionist currents that flowed through the CPGB from at least the 1950s, feeding into both Maoist and ultra-Stalinist groups that almost inevitably splintered from the party before its dissolution in 1991. Thirdly, Andrew Pearmain looks at another dissident group within the CPGB, the 'Smith Group', which was a secretive faction in the 1970s opposed to the political outlook of the party leadership but detached from the more well-known Gramscian/Eurocommunist dissidents. In so doing, Pearmain demonstrates that the opposition groups inside the CPGB were more varied than much of the previous literature takes into account. Lastly, Rich Cross analyses the anarchist resistance to Thatcherism in the 1980s and how anarchist groups, such as those linked to Crass, Class War or Stop the City were able to find political spaces to exploit when other section of the British far left were in retreat from the Thatcherite onslaught.

The issues with which the far left engaged with forms the second part of the book. This begins with Sue Bruley's account of the experiences of women in the far left from the late 1960s to the early 1980s. Using oral history, Bruley illustrates how the women's liberation movement inspired political activism but that the far left groups were reluctant to embrace feminist politics beyond the superficial level. Not dissimilarly, Graham Willett describes the relationship between the far left and gay liberation during the 1960s and 1970s. As Willett argues, homosexuality was a taboo subject for many on the left, thought of as a bourgeois deviation and often dismissed as a form of 'identity politics' to be consumed by the wider class struggle.

The decolonisation process of the post-war era and the revolutionary situation in the newly independent 'third world' is taken up by Ian Birchall. Birchall describes how many in Britain looked to the third world as a revolutionary force that would be an antidote to the pessimism of the working class in the industrialised West. Though such potential was deemed to have passed by the end of the 1970s, such a focus brought issues of race to the fore. Indeed, the final three chapters explore social movements wherein the far left has arguably had the most influence: the anti-racist and anti-fascist movements. Satnam Virdee's chapter shows that the long estrangement between the (primarily 'white') far left and Britain's ethnic minority workers started to be broached in the 1970s, as the economic crisis of the mid-1970s and the rise of the National Front created a threat to both groups. There was, Virdee argues, improved mutual understanding on both sides to combat these threats, with the Grunwick strike of 1976–78 and the creation of the ANL serving as exemplars of cooperation. The 'story' is then taken up by Mark Hayes, who explores what happened on the far left once the threat of the NF subsided after the 1979 general election. While the NF was no longer numerically strong, fascists belonging to various splinter groups were still involved in racist violence and harassment into the 1980s (and beyond). Hayes outlines the history of one of the groups that was at the forefront of countering this violence, Red Action. Through Anti-Fascist Action, Red Action spearheaded the militant anti-fascist movement of the 1980s and early 1990s but, as Hayes points out, it was also involved in other causes, primarily support for the Provisional Irish Republican Army. Hayes' chapter uncovers the history of this small but influential group, seeking to analyse why Red Action started to waver after the British National Party (BNP) changed from its focus on 'controlling the streets' in the mid-1990s. The last chapter, by David Renton, takes up this theme, examining how the far left and wider anti-fascist movement were wrong-footed by the BNP's electoral approach. Ultimately, however, Renton argues that the left once more mobilised effectively against the BNP and will continue to adapt to the right-wing threat as it changes over time. These last three chapters take events from the mid-1960s up to the present day and this is indicative of the far left's significant contribution to anti-racist and anti-fascist activism, particularly when its influence in other areas of politics had declined.

As noted above, this collection cannot serve as a comprehensive history of the far left in Britain since the 1950s. At the very least, it hopes to encourage further research and point towards new sources relevant to the subject. We would, too, like to think that the collection will spark a dialogue amongst activists in the present era about the history of the far left since the mid-twentieth century and how this impacts upon contemporary left-wing politics. As Karl Marx famously wrote, 'the tradition of all the dead generations weighs like a nightmare on the brain of the living.'[43]

Notes

1 T. Ali, *The Coming British Revolution* (London: Jonathan Cape, 1972) p. 10.
2 C. Harman, *The Fire Last Time: 1968 and After* (London: Bookmarks, 1988) p. 226.
3 E. Hobsbawm, 'The Forward March of Labour Halted?', in M. Jacques and F. Mulhearn (eds), *The Forward March of Labour Halted?* (London: Verso, 1981), pp. 1–19.
4 L. Gardner, 'The Fringe Left', in Gerald Kaufman (ed.), *The Left* (London: Anthony Blond, 1966) p. 116.
5 K. O. Morgan, *Ages of Reform: Dawns and Downfalls of the British Left* (London: IB Tauris, 2011), pp. xi–xii.
6 J. Callaghan, *The Far Left in British Politics* (Oxford: Basil Blackwell, 1987) p. viii.

7 P. Sedgwick, 'Introduction: Farewell, Grovesnor Square', in D. Widgery (ed.), *The Left in Britain: 1956–1968* (Harmondsworth: Penguin Books, 1976), p. 35.

8 B. Reid, *Ultra-Leftism in Britain* (London: CPGB, 1969), pp. 7–8.

9 E. Hobsbawm, *Interesting Times: A Twentieth-Century Life* (London: Abacus, 2003) p. 201.

10 J. Callaghan, *Cold War, Crisis and Conflict: The CPGB 1951–68* (London: Lawrence & Wishart, 2003), p. 185.

11 Sedgwick, 'Introduction', p. 19.

12 M. Jacques, 'Trends in Youth Culture: A Reply to the Discussion', *Marxism Today*, June (1973), pp. 273–4.

13 This leaflet was reproduced in Widgery (ed.), *The Left in Britain*, p. 349.

14 W. Thompson, *The Good Old Cause: British Communism, 1920–91* (London: Pluto Press, 1992), p. 218.

15 R. Seifert and T. Sibley, *Revolutionary Communist at Work: A Political Biography of Bert Ramelson* (London: Lawrence & Wishart, 2012), p. 21.

16 M. Shaw, 'The Making of a Party? The International Socialists 1965–76', *Socialist Register* (1978), pp. 100–45; J. Higgins, *More Years for the Locust: The Origins of the SWP* (London: IS Group, 1997).

17 See D. John, *Indian Workers' Associations in Britain* (London: Oxford University Press, 1969), pp. 66–81; S. Josephides, 'Organizational Splits and Political Ideology in the Indian Workers Associations', in P. Werbner and M. Anwar (eds), *Black and Ethnic Leaderships in Britain: The Cultural Dimension of Political Action* (London: Routledge, 1991), pp. 253–76; S. Richards, 'Second Wave Anti-Revisionism in the UK', *Marxists Internet Archive*, www.marxists.org/history/erol/uk.secondwave/2nd-wave/section13.htm, accessed 27 February 2013.

18 J. McIlroy, '"Always Outnumbered, Always Outgunned": The Trotskyists and the Trade Unions', in J. McIlroy, N. Fishman and A. Campbell (eds), *British Trade Unions and Industrial Politics*, vol. 2 (Aldershot: Ashgate, 1999), p. 285; P. Baberis, J. McHugh and M. Tyldesley (eds), *Encyclopaedia of British and Irish Political Organisations* (London: Continuum International Publishing Group, 2005), p. 167.

19 P. Allen, '*Socialist Worker:* Paper with a Purpose', *Media, Culture & Society*, 7 (1985), p. 231.

20 M. Smith, 'Where Is the SWP Going?', *International Socialism*, 2, 97 (2002), p. 43.

21 P. Taaffe, *The Rise of Militant: Militant's 30 Years* (London: Militant Publications, 1995), p. 279.

22 B. Franks, *Rebel Alliances: The Means and Ends of Contemporary British Anarchisms* (Edinburgh: AK Press, 2006), p. 77.

23 A. Gamble, 'New Labour and Old Debates', in G. Hassan (ed.), *After Blair: Politics after the New Labour Decade* (London: Lawrence & Wishart, 2007), p. 31.

24 See, for example, Notes from Nowhere, *We Are Everywhere* (London: Verso, 2003); D. McNally, *Another World in Possible: Globalization and*

Anti-Capitalism (Winnipeg: Arbeiter Ring, 2002); R. Kiely, *The Clash of Globalizations: Neo-Liberalism, the Third Way and Anti-Globalizaton* (Chicago: Haymarket, 2009).

25 A. Murray and L. German, *Stop the War: The Story of Britain's Biggest Mass Movement* (London: Bookmarks, 2005).

26 Thompson, *The Good Old Cause*; F. Beckett *Enemy Within: The Rise and Fall of the British Communist Party* (London: Merlin Press, 1995); A. Thorpe, *The British Communist Party and Moscow: 1920–43* (Manchester: Manchester University Press, 2000); M. Worley, *Class Against Class: The Communist Party in Britain Between the Wars* (London: I. B. Tauris, 2002); J. Eaden and D. Renton, *The Communist Party of Great Britain since 1920* (Basingstoke: Palgrave Macmillan 2002); K. Laybourn and D. Murphy, *Under the Red Flag: A History of Communism in Britain* (Stroud: Sutton Publishing, 1999); Callaghan, *Cold War, Crisis and Conflict*; G. Andrews, *Endgames and New Times: The Final Years of British Communism, 1964–91* (London: Lawrence & Wishart, 2004).

27 G. Andrews, N. Fishman and K. Morgan (eds), *Opening the Books: Essays on the Social and Cultural History of the British Communist Party* (London: Pluto Press, 1995); J. McIlroy, K. Morgan and A. Campbell (eds), *Party People, Communist Lives: Explorations in Biography* (London: Lawrence & Wishart, 2001); G. Cohen, A. Flinn and K. Morgan, *Communists and British Society 1920–91* (London: Rivers Oram, 2007); T. Linehan, *Communism in Britain, 1920–39: From the Cradle to the Grave* (Basingstoke: Palgrave Macmillan, 2008).

28 A. Croft, *After the Party: Reflections on Life since the CPGB* (London: Lawrence & Wishart, 2012); A. Pearmain, *The Politics of New Labour: A Gramscian Analysis* (London: Lawrence & Wishart, 2011).

29 J. Callaghan, *British Trotskyism: Theory and Practice* (Oxford; Blackwell, 1984); Callaghan, *The Far Left in British Politics*.

30 K. Coates, 'How Not to Reappraise the New Left', *Socialist Register* (1976), p. 111.

31 T. Grant, *The History of British Trotskyism* (London: Wellred, 2002).

32 P. Shipley, *Revolutionaries in Modern Britain* (London: Bodley Head, 1976); B. Baker, *The Far Left: An Expose of the Extreme Left in Britain* (London: Weidenfeld and Nicolson, 1981); J. Tomlinson, *Left, Right: The March of Political Extremism in Britain* (London: John Calder, 1981).

33 M. Crick, *Militant* (London: Faber and Faber, 1984); M. Crick, *The March of Militant* (London: Faber and Faber, 1986).

34 P. Taafe, *The Rise of Militant: Militant's 30 Years* (Guilford: Militant Publications, 1995).

35 T. Cliff, *A World to Win: Life of a Revolutionary* (London: Bookmarks, 2000).

36 I. Birchall, *Tony Cliff: A Marxist for His Time* (London: Bookmarks, 2011).

37 C. Lotz and P. Feldman, *Gerry Healy: A Revolutionary Life* (London: Lupus, 1994).

38 B. Pitt, *The Rise and Fall of Gerry Healy*, www.whatnextjournal.co.uk/pages/healy/Contents.html, accessed 4 March 2013.

39 T. Buchanan, *East-Wind: China and the British Left 1925–76* (Oxford: Oxford University Press, 2012).

40 L. Parker, *The Kick Inside: Revolutionary Opposition in the CPGB, 1945–1991* (London: November Publications, 2012); W. Podmore, *Reg Birch: Engineer, Trade Unionist, Communist* (London: Bellman Books, 2004).

41 Franks, *Rebel Alliances*; D. Goodway, *Anarchist Seeds Beneath the Snow: Left-Libertarian Thought and British Writers from William Morris to Colin Ward* (Oakland: PM Press, 2012).

42 I. Bone, *Bash the Rich* (London: Tangent, 2007); S. Christie, *Granny Made Me an Anarchist: General Franco, the Angry Brigade and Me* (London: Scribner, 2004).

43 K. Marx, *The Eighteenth Brumaire of Louis Bonaparte* (New York: International Publishers, 1969), p. 15.

Part I

Movements

1

Engaging with Trotsky

The influence of Trotskyism in Britain

John Callaghan

Trotsky became known in Britain after the Bolshevik Revolution in association with Lenin, as he did across the globe. But as early as 1920 Bertrand Russell, who noted the 'lightening intelligence', vanity and charisma of the man while visiting Moscow, warned that Trotsky was 'not by any means' regarded as Lenin's equal by his Bolshevik comrades.[1] By January 1925, the Communist Party of Great Britain (CPGB) was depicting Trotsky, who had 'resigned' his government posts, as a disruptive factionalist who had adopted an 'anti-Party, anti-Bolshevik' outlook all of a piece with his Menshevik and individualist past.[2] The continuing campaign against Trotsky caused barely a ripple among British Communists as, between November 1927 and February 1929, he was successively expelled from the party, sent into internal exile and then finally thrown out of the country. The architect of the Bolshevik seizure of power, the man who created the Red Army, had by 1936 become the central fascist conspirator in the plot to overthrow the Bolshevik state uncovered by the first of the Moscow Trials. In January 1937, as the second of these show trials began, in which he was once again the chief defendant *in absentia*, the exiled Trotsky entered Mexico. In doing so he placed himself under the protection and care of his American followers as well as the government of President Cárdenas. He thereby loomed larger in the English-speaking world than hitherto, chiefly in the world of ideas. His defence against the 'Stalin school of falsification' would be conducted before a commission headed by the distinguished American philosopher John Dewey. His writings would be published in English by the American Socialist Workers Party (SWP) which constituted the largest section of his nascent Fourth International, launched from the living room of Alfred Rosmer's house in September 1938 in the Paris suburbs.

Trotsky's persecution and the fantastic charges brought against him –
upheld in court by even his closest colleagues, such as Christian Rakovsky
– were not universally reviled even in liberal circles. Many testified to
the scrupulous fairness of the Moscow legal process. It was recalled that
renegades, police spies, closet conservatives and proto-fascists were not
unheard of in the history of socialism. Why would Stalin's government
risk international obloquy, at a time when it needed allies, by staging
an elaborate legal farce? Among the Communists – though not only
Communists – it was taken for granted that socialism was being built in
the Soviet Union, that fascism was its extreme enemy, and that anything
harming Stalin's government could only strengthen these forces of the
dark, led by men who openly stood for everything that was anathema
to the left. How much worse then for those few who took Trotsky's side
and who knew that the Stalin dictatorship was engaged in the wholesale
destruction of Lenin's Bolshevik Party, that the confessions of the accused
had been extracted by torture, that mountains of lies had been written
about them and that the regime was actively eliminating left oppositionists
abroad, placing Trotsky's own life in the gravest danger?

As one of the co-founders of the Bolshevik state, Trotsky was unable
to accept that the Stalin dictatorship was rooted in anything promoted
by either himself or Lenin. Trotsky and his followers claimed that they
were the real Leninists, the real revolutionaries, and that Stalin and his
supporters had betrayed the revolution of October 1917. The revolution
itself had been authentic and Leninism was universally applicable; the
social democrats were as useless and treacherous as Lenin said they were;
the opportunities for future revolutionary advance were as rich as the
first four congresses of the Communist International had maintained; the
problem was Stalinism which could not protect the Leninist legacy either
at home or abroad. This was the basis of Trotsky's appeal in these circles
and also the reason why so few people were drawn to him. For the left
was overwhelmingly composed of people who could not believe either
that Lenin–Trotsky had the answers or that Stalin was the main problem.
Trotsky himself, however, exercised a broader fascination beyond the
Trotskyist ranks. He was a man of enormous and multiple talents who had
achieved much and fallen far. He battled on against a brutal and sinister
opponent who was backed by the resources of a state and an international army of followers. There was tragedy here, political drama and
intellectual brilliance. There was also the public struggle to understand
and report on the doings of Moscow, headquarters of a vast experiment
in social engineering. After the Wall Street Crash of October 1929, the
coincidence of world capitalist economic crisis and the advent of the first
five-year plans would ensure that everyone on the left had a stake in what

was happening in the Soviet Union. Many people were interested in what Trotsky had to say about it.

Understanding Stalinism

Trotsky maintained that the Bolsheviks had created a workers' state in October 1917. After 1933 he stressed the need for a political revolution to remove the Stalin regime but held that the fundamentally progressive element in the situation survived, consisting of the state-owned, planned economy. In *The Revolution Betrayed* (1937), Trotsky depicted the Soviet Union as a transitional regime between capitalism and socialism and argued that the Stalin dictatorship represented a privileged caste, the bureaucracy, which defended the gains of October only with policies likely to undermine them. Problems of waste, inefficiency and corruption were, like the bureaucracy itself, manifestations of Russian backwardness and shortages in the field of consumption. While international capitalism was heading for a catastrophic collapse, the state-owned economy of the Soviet Union was the sure foundation of its future progress. Thus, vis-à-vis the fascist and capitalist powers Trotsky insisted that the Soviet Union deserved to be unconditionally defended by his followers.

Yet Trotsky had also compared Stalin's regime to Hitler's as 'totalitarian'. He publicised the extreme violence and methods of thought control with which Soviet society was kept under the regime's control. Trotskyists knew all about the scale and cruelty of the labour camps and the secret police. They knew of the wretchedly low standards of living of the workers and the appalling conditions in which they laboured and the fact that there was no one to defend them against the state – their state. Some wondered what kind of workers' state this could be. The debate in Trotskyist circles was most vivid in the 1930s because Trotsky himself was one of its main protagonists.[3] This ensured that the doubters would achieve maximum publicity for their views – critics within the American Socialist Workers Party (SWP) and those like Bruno Rizzi (who published *La Bureaucratisation du Monde* in Paris in 1939) who depicted the Soviet bureaucracy as a (historically necessary) new ruling class exploiting the workers.

The Moscow Trials and the Communist persecution of other leftists in the Spanish civil war formed the context in which these ideas germinated.[4] The controversy intensified when, after the announcement of the Hitler–Stalin Pact in August 1939, Nazi Germany and the Soviet Union proceeded to partition Poland. The totalitarian states were active allies it seemed. Yet Trotsky argued that Stalin had exported the revolution abroad by nationalising industry and expropriating landowners in the occupied eastern provinces of Poland, despite excluding Polish workers and peasants from the process.[5] Max Shachtman now joined James Burnham in disputing the workers' state theory (and would go on to develop his own theory of bureaucratic collectivism) within the SWP. The imperialism which they perceived in Soviet actions in Poland surfaced again when Moscow demanded military bases in the three Baltic states in October 1939. War with Finland was begun when the latter refused to make concessions similar to those extracted in Estonia, Lithuania and Latvia. But Trotsky insisted that the Red Army was the progressive force in the Winter War and that Finnish forces were only serving the interests of capital.[6] Shachtman, Burnham, C. L. R. James, Irving Howe and Saul Bellow were among those who begged to differ. The lasting ideological legacy of these events was Burnham's *The Managerial Revolution* (1941), published soon after his disavowal of Marxism. The book took up much of Rizzi's argument that bureaucratic class rule was the shape of the future. Marxism had overestimated the power of the working class to make the world anew in its own interests. The future belonged to the managers who would solve the inefficiencies of capitalism by centralised planning, bringing the masses into a lasting subordination. Germany, Japan and the United States would dominate international relations as managerial powers, while the Soviet Union would be partitioned by the first two.

George Orwell

George Orwell followed these arguments with interest. Throughout the 1930s he gravitated to dissident Marxist circles and was preoccupied by questions such as those posed above about the nature of the Communist parties and the Comintern, the nature of the Stalin regime, and the direction taken by the Soviet Union. He wondered what 'the truth about Stalin's regime' was and argued in 1938 that 'all the political controversies that have made life hideous for two years past really circle round this question, though ... it is seldom brought into the foreground'.[7] Contrary to the judgement of his best biographer,[8] Orwell was not interested in totalitarianism *per se*; he made mostly fleeting and superficial remarks about fascism. Nor was he much interested in the British Labour Party or the mainstream political system in Britain. He was often mistaken for a Trotskyist, knew Trotskyists like Reg Groves and, especially when he returned from Spain, sometimes held views that derived from Trotsky's end of the political spectrum.[9] He admitted in 1947 to have been 'vaguely associated with Trotskyists and Anarchists', but others were less equivocal about his views; the Tribunal for Espionage and High Treason filed in Valencia while Orwell and his wife were still in the country described them as 'confirmed Trotskyists'. On leaving Spain, Orwell reported that 'all our friends and acquaintances are in jail ... suspected of "Trotskyism"'.[10] He wrote pieces which, by his own admission, were 'subtly Trotskyist' and his admirers – like Philip Rahv and Gleb Struve – thought they could see Trotskyist biases in his most famous works of fiction.[11]

Trotsky was a rich source of ideas and imagery for Orwell but he never accepted Trotsky's explanation of Stalinism or his defence of Leninism.[12] It was the Soviet Union that exercised his mind and it was to the radical left that he addressed his political writings in the 1930s. During the Second World War he continued to harbour revolutionary ambitions and maintained a continuing dialogue with former Trotskyists in the United States. At the end of the war he published the two books which brought elements of the story of Trotsky and Stalin to millions of readers, film and television viewers – *Animal Farm* and *Nineteen Eighty-Four*. Orwell's best-sellers took the view that revolutions were both possible and necessary. But as Isaac Deutscher observed in 1954, the massive impact of *Nineteen Eighty-Four* was that of 'an ideological super-weapon in the cold war' and it counted heavily against the Soviet Union.[13] Several of the 'New York intellectuals' whom Orwell kept in touch with became active anti-Communists during the early Cold War and Orwell might have been taking the same direction in the years before he died, supplying the police with the names of prominent Soviet sympathisers.[14]

But this is only a possibility. What is certain is that Orwell had been a socialist throughout his career as a writer and had attracted the interest of the secret police since 1929.[15] They thought he was some sort of Communist. He certainly did not fit easily into the Labour mainstream. As Peter Sedgwick noted, writing in 1968 for the journal *International Socialism*, Orwell's beliefs had pronounced radical dimensions at odds with the Labour Party's theory and practice, particularly in respect of the need for mass participation in the making of socialism.[16] When Crick says that there is no doubt where Orwell stood at the end of his life – a *Tribune* socialist – he is more than a little misleading.[17] The *Tribune* socialists stood collectively for little more than an extension to public ownership – to such an extent that they could regard the Soviet economy as a success story and one they perceived as historically superior to capitalism. We will examine this argument in more detail below. But Orwell's socialism contained a much stronger faith in the possibility and desirability of working class self-emancipation than the Tribunite parliamentarians ever found room for in their own thinking. Readers of Orwell in the 1960s, when his *Collected Essays, Journalism and Letters* (1968) were published in four volumes, would discover that the author of *Animal Farm* and *Nineteen Eighty-Four* shunned both the Labour and the

Communist parties and searched for something better than both of them. When Orwell was most committed to socialism his socialism did not sit easily with the standard Labour and Communist positions and much of his published political writing before 1945 is Trotskyist in the broad sense of denying Moscow's socialist credentials and challenging its monopoly of Marxist revolutionary politics with an alternative.

Orwell adopted Trotsky's understanding of the role of Moscow in world politics while in Spain with the International Brigades. He was attached to the quasi-Trotskyist POUM party, led by a former collaborator of Trotsky's, Andreu Nin. He came to believe that the Communist parties were docile instruments of Soviet foreign policy, a policy that was largely conservative.[18] Orwell's left-wing inclinations predate the Spanish civil war, however. His first political publications appeared in journals associated with the French Communist Party and gave accounts, in 1928 and 1929 respectively, of unemployment in Britain and British imperialism.[19] By his own testimony he had become 'very hostile to the Communist Party since about 1935'.[20] The research he did for *The Road to Wigan Pier* involved staying with working-class Marxists and the discussion of socialism in the second half of the book is written as if the world of serious socialist theory consisted only of Communist and Independent Labour Party (ILP) Marxists. Orwell was already versed in Marxist theory sufficiently to impress by his interventions at a summer school in 1936 organised by *The Adelphi*, a journal of dissident Marxism.[21] But it was in Barcelona where he witnessed the working class 'in the saddle' and where he came to believe in the possibility and desirability of its self-emancipation. Later he argued that 'it is only by revolution that the native genius of the English people can be set free', recognising that for that to happen 'there will have to arise something that has never existed in England, a socialist movement that actually has the mass of the people behind it'.[22] During the Second World War, immediately after the fall of France, Orwell wanted to 'arm the people' as both the best defence against invasion and because he believed that a social revolution was required to produce a successful war effort.

If we want to understand why 'this very English figure could somehow transcend the insularity of so much English socialism',[23] I think we have to acknowledge his education in dissident Marxist circles, like those of *The Adelphi*, *The New English Weekly* and *Partisan Review*, as well his experiences in Burma, France and Catalonia. *The Road to Wigan Pier* concludes with a call for the formation of a new socialist party which would be 'genuinely revolutionary' and what this might mean is revealed by his account of 'one of the most desolating spectacles the world contains' – the working-class MP or trade union leader detached from his roots, upwardly mobile and increasingly conservative. Even among the radicals, Orwell thought that 'The truth is that to many people calling themselves socialist, revolution does not mean a movement of the masses, with which they hope to associate themselves; it means a set of reforms which "we" the clever ones are going to impose upon "them", the Lower Orders.'[24] While Orwell's initial attachment to the POUM had been fortuitous, giving him the chance to meet what he called 'genuine revolutionaries', upon his return from Spain he adopted Trotsky's critical view of the Communist Popular Front tactic as it operated in both Spain and Britain. He joined the ILP when that organisation was searching for a revolutionary position and flirting with Trotsky's call for a Fourth International, reproducing Trotsky's analysis of the international situation as it did so. Like Trotsky, Orwell argued that there could be no defence of democracy against fascism outside of the struggle for socialist revolution:

> all the Popular Front stuff that is now being pushed by the Communist press ... boils down to saying that they are in favour of British Fascism (prospective) as against German Fascism.[25]

Like Trotsky, too, Orwell saw a contradiction in the fact that British democracy rested on an Empire in which freedom was denied to its subjects. The defence of British democracy thus involved 'the unspoken clause ... "not counting niggers"'. Our rule in India, Orwell asserted, 'is just as bad as German Fascism'.[26] It was a conclusion at odds with some of the more insightful analyses of fascism penned by Trotsky himself before February 1933, when he was at pains to insist that everything should be done to stop Hitler from coming to power – precisely because a Nazi dictatorship would be worse than some of the alternatives. The emphasis changed as the world approached war after Hitler's accession to power. In a war between these imperialist powers, Trotsky argued in 1938, 'the victory of any one of the imperialist camps would spell slavery, wretchedness, misery, the decline of human culture'.[27] Orwell clung to this position until Britain entered the conflict in September 1939. When he did say something of interest about fascism in the interval it contained elements of Trotsky's penetrating pre-1933 analysis of National Socialism. Crick points out that 'somehow right from the beginning [Orwell] rejected the conventional Marxist view of fascism as either part of the death-throes of the capitalist system' or 'the vanguard of late bourgeois capitalism'.[28] But if, by this poor summary of Marxist analyses (which are varied and span the period after 1919), Crick means that Orwell recognised that fascism was typically based upon a mass movement with revolutionary aspirations, that it appealed to and made use of the irrational in human behaviour, then these are emphases of

Trotsky's whose best work on the subject treated fascism as a profound phenomenon of social psychology.[29] Orwell, who initially regarded fascism as 'only a development of capitalism' eventually came to argue that it had put modern technology 'in the service of ideas appropriate to the Stone Age', noting, like Trotsky, a coexistence of science and superstition in capitalist society that was fertile soil for the growth fascism within the lower middle class in particular.[30] Orwell the avid collector and reader of political pamphlets would have encountered Trotsky's works on this subject in the dissident Marxist milieu he was familiar with.

The Revolution Betrayed appeared in an English translation by Max Eastman in 1937. The title is more vivid than the content. Trotsky presented the idea of a degenerated workers' state, which by virtue of 'Stalin's faction', merged party and bureaucracy, thereby creating 'the present totalitarian regime'.[31] The 'relations among men' in this state, he confessed, lagged behind the more cultured variants of actually existing capitalism. Stalin had revived a 'genuine Russian barbarism' and in various ways the Soviet bureaucracy was 'similar to every other bureaucracy, especially the fascist'. [32] For Trotsky:

> Stalinism and fascism, in spite of a deep difference in social foundations, are symmetrical phenomena. In many of their features they show a deadly similarity.[33]

In view of this reasoning it is unnecessary to speculate that Orwell learned the concept of totalitarianism from the later writings of Franz Borkenau.[34] Trotsky had got there before him, as Orwell would have known. Like some of Trotsky's erstwhile disciples he occasionally argued that a new form of class privilege had emerged in the Soviet Union, perhaps state capitalism.[35] His final view on the matter was the bleak dystopia of *Nineteen Eighty-Four*. He believed that the willingness to criticise Russia and Stalin was '*the* test of intellectual honesty' for socialists. The long-run effect of not doing so would be 'a violent reaction when the truth finally leaks out and people feel a sudden revulsion in which they may reject the whole idea of socialism'.[36]

Orwell is rightly remembered for having possessed the honesty which he recommended to others. It was a very rare occasion when he had anything positive to say about the Soviet Union, as when, in 1944, he described it as 'the real dynamo of the Socialist movement in this country and everywhere else'.[37] But even on this occasion he devoted most of his words to exposing the left's silence over 'purges, liquidations, the dictatorship of a minority, suppression of criticism and so forth'. When the *Manchester Evening News* refused to publish his article, Orwell and his friends supposed that the rejection came because he failed to pander to the prevailing 'russomania'.[38]

Isaac Deutscher later remembered this pro-Soviet mood when he recalled that Orwell first made contact with him in response to some articles he had written for *The Economist* , the critical tenor of which in relation to Russia were 'somewhat unusual' for the time.[39] It was in this context that Orwell reported that '"Trotskyism", using the word in a wide sense, is even more effectively silenced [now] than in the 1935–9 period.'[40]

His politics remained radical until well after the end of the war. The essay that signalled his change of mind upon its outbreak – 'My Country Right or Left' – was no simple submission to patriotism. The war was identified in his mind with the long-awaited British revolution and he was confidently anticipating 'red militias billeted in the Ritz' before it was over. His correspondence with *Partisan Review* shows that he did not completely abandon hopes for a revolution until 1944. In the summer of 1947 his contribution to a debate on socialism – 'Towards European Unity' – showed his realism in confronting what he saw as the bleak immediate prospect. The only hope was longer-term – in the creation of 'a socialist United States of Europe' – though he recognised, like Bertrand Russell before him, the power of the United States to obstruct socialism in the countries within its economic orbit.[41]

Trotskyism in the Labour Party

Trotskyists in the narrow sense in Britain numbered at most several hundred as the war drew to a close. The Revolutionary Communist Party (RCP) was formed from the fusion of rival organisations in January–February 1944 claiming just 400 members. The Fourth International (FI), of which the RCP was the British section, expected the war to end with revolutions and was thrown into factional confusion when events took a different turn. It was divided over what had happened in Eastern Europe in the years 1945–50 and on what to make of the apparent strength of Stalinism inside and outside the Soviet Union – and it was disoriented to find itself still marginal to political events on both sides of the Cold War. Inevitably the RCP, like the FI, was split by warring groups. Three distinct strands emerged in Britain around three leaders who remained important in Trotskyist circles for the next thirty years.[42] Recognising their poor prospects they separately calculated that there was more to be gained operating within the Labour Party than by trying to create rival parties on the outside. They would engage in what the Trotskyists called 'entrism' – that is organised infiltration. Outside far left circles they attracted little attention until the 1960s.

Labour's own left-wing was itself divided over the role of Stalinism. As the war drew to a close, its main weekly newspaper *Tribune* depicted the

United States as the main problem in international affairs and looked upon Russian domination of Eastern Europe with real sympathy for Moscow's security problem.[43] This changed dramatically in the wake of the American decision to assist European economic recovery in the summer of 1947. *Tribune* turned completely against the Soviet Union when the events of 1947 polarised international politics in the forms taken by the Cold War. It denounced Stalinism without reservation. But this stance changed again when the Korean War began in the summer of 1950. American anti-Communism now seemed the bigger problem because it dragged Britain along with it, jeopardised its economic recovery and threatened the survival of Labour's domestic welfare reforms. Whereas Orwell's major posthumous influence was support for the most fervent anti-Communism because of his depiction of monstrous evil in *Nineteen Eighty-Four*, some *Tribune* socialists became adherents of a rival, more optimistic, analysis of Stalinism with roots in Trotskyism.

Isaac Deutscher – one of the names on the list which Orwell gave to the Information Research Department set up by the Labour government – supplied this perspective by building upon Trotsky's idea that the Union of Soviet Socialist Republics' (USSR) fundamentally progressive character derived from the centrally planned, state-owned economy. Like Trotsky in relation to Poland and Finland, Deutscher saw Stalin's dictatorship in post-war Eastern Europe exporting the revolution and he put this argument to the readers of *Tribune* as early as February 1945.[44] Deutscher had been present to oppose the establishment of the Fourth International at its foundation meeting in 1938 but belonged to none of the small Trotskyist groups in Britain, his adoptive home from April 1939. Yet he probably exercised a bigger influence than any of them in encouraging a critical but sympathetic Marxist analysis of the Communist bloc (Orwell had Deutscher down on his list as a 'sympathiser only' of the Soviet Union, rather than a crypto-Communist). He exercised his influence through the power of his writing, especially in his biographies of Stalin and Trotsky. With the publication of *Stalin* in 1949, Deutscher showed how a ruthlessly brutal dictatorship had forced through socio-economic changes that enabled the Soviet Union to survive the Nazi invasion and emerge triumphant with its sphere of influence greatly enlarged. This success, he had no doubt, derived from the power of the 'fundamentally new principle of social organisation' which the dictatorship brought into existence from 1928 – the planned, state-owned economy. This had made the USSR the world's second industrial power and was 'certain to survive'.[45] Deutscher never sought to hide the barbarity of the Stalin regime or the sufferings of the people of the Soviet Union. But his consistent argument, up to and including his last published work in 1967, stressed the modernising forces unleashed by this new principle of social organisation. He reasoned that massive industrialisation and dynamic economic growth created a growing, increasingly educated, urban population that would outgrow the authoritarian political institutions that had brought it into existence. Stalin had unwittingly begun a process that would destroy Stalinism by overcoming Russia's backwardness.[46]

It was an argument taken up in the pages of *Tribune*, notably by the leading figure of the Labour Party's left wing in the 1950s, Aneurin Bevan.[47] Shortly after the publication of *Stalin*, Bevan wrote about the demands for an educated population which industrialisation generated and how this led inexorably to pressure from this population for 'full political status'. Nowhere was this better understood, he asserted, than in the Kremlin.[48] Bevan's disciple, friend and biographer Michael Foot acknowledged Bevan's Marxism, and this is one of the forms that it took. Stalin's death in March 1953 only strengthened the case for those who adopted Deutscher's reasoning, as Bevan's journalism demonstrated. It was reasoning that also fitted the needs of the Labour left in its ideological dispute with 'revisionists' in the party who had grown cold over the prospects for more public ownership of industry in Britain. Bevan argued that in the long-run democracy and capitalism were incompatible – one or the other must prevail and it is clear that for him the triumph of democracy rested on community control and ownership of industry.[49] The Tribunites were the nationalisers in the 1950s. For them it was the distinguishing economic demand of the left. Public ownership might be only a step to socialism but for Bevan it was the 'all-important first step, for without it the conditions for further progress are not established' – since nationalised industry was the 'direct instrument of planning'.[50] After Labour's 1959 general election defeat, *Tribune* bemoaned the dilution of the socialist case at the hands of Labour's timid leadership which had obscured the truth from electors that 'with a properly planned effort, Britain could advance to the standard of living taken for granted in America and now confidently expected by Russia's young generation'.[51] But while the Soviet economy was racing forward, showing what could be achieved, America obstructed the progress of 'the mass of mankind'.[52] Two weeks after the British general election, *Tribune* celebrated the achievement of *Lunik 3*, the Soviet spacecraft that had photographed the far side of the moon. This, it said, was an achievement of an economy that was 'one hundred per cent nationalised' and it demonstrated who was right in the Labour Party's ideological quarrel.[53]

Trotskyism in the 1960s

The perception that the Soviet Union in 1960 as dynamic and growing on the basis of the centrally planned, state-owned economy was not confined to elements of the left in Britain. Governments, politicians, intelligence agencies, military planners and other experts could share this belief.[54] As the United States stepped up its long-standing involvement in the war in Indo-China in the early 1960s, the conviction that the United States was a malign reactionary influence in the world was another position that was not confined to Marxists. Bertrand Russell, who had never altered his 1920 view of the Bolshevik dictatorship as a cruel and violent tyranny (so was not easily depicted as a dupe of the Communists), led the way in such criticisms. Russell had become convinced since the McCarthy era that the United States was a greater threat to world peace than the Soviet Union. In the 1950s, Russell was best known for his attempts to mobilise scientists, neutral states and public opinion against the threat of nuclear war posed by the conflict between the United States and the Soviet Union. Frédéric Joliot-Curie and Einstein were among those he worked with. From its inauguration in July 1957, the Pugwash Movement became the focal point of such activities designed to publicise the dangers of nuclear energy and advance schemes for control of nuclear weapons, with Russell as its president. Russell also wrote to world leaders warning against the proliferation of nuclear weapons and, in February 1958, he became a founder member of the Campaign for Nuclear Disarmament (CND) and an advocate of Britain's unilateral renunciation of nuclear weapons. CND in Britain was to become a focal point of activity for the New Left that had emerged since 1956, in the wake of Khrushchev's 'secret speech', the Soviet invasion of Hungary and the Anglo-French invasion of Egypt. Russell was soon associated with some of its leading activists.

In 1960, CND turned to mass civil disobedience under the guidance of Russell and Ralph Schoenman, a postgraduate student at the London School of Economics. Schoenman and others associated with the Trotskysant New Left – Robin Blackburn, Perry Anderson, Pat Jordan and Ken Coates – now worked as members of Russell's personal secretariat. Advocacy of the civil disobedience tactic within CND led to the formation of the Committee of 100, with Russell as its president. In February 1961, it organised a mass sit-down outside the Ministry of Defence involving several thousand people. Russell became a hero for young left-wing activists when he was imprisoned for his participation in these events. By now he was calling for Britain to leave NATO and to declare itself neutral of the superpowers. His association with the New Left was only strengthened when he responded to a personal plea from the Cuban

Ambassador in September 1962 over fears of an impending US invasion of the island. Russell called for the United States to publicly deny any such intention and for the Soviet government to stop supplying Cuba with arms. Days later, Kennedy announced the presence of Soviet missiles in Cuba. Khrushchev replied publicly to Russell to the effect that Russia would do everything to prevent the crisis escalating to nuclear war. This letter made the front pages of newspapers all over the world.[55] Russell publicly praised Khrushchev's responsible response and called on Kennedy to give up missiles in Turkey in return for Soviet withdrawal from Cuba. The next day the Russians took up this same demand.[56]

After the Cuban missile crisis, Russell became more hostile to US foreign policy and increasingly polemical. Between 1963 and 1968 he publicly sided with national liberation movements in the Americas and South East Asia against US imperialism. According to his biographer, 'Russell launched ... an attack on the United States that was the literary equivalent of carpet bombing.'[57] Most of the active opponents of the American intervention in Vietnam only materialised after years of warfare against the Communist 'bandits' in that country; but not so Russell. As early as 22 March 1963 – well before the anti-war movement became a presence in either America or Western Europe – he claimed that the United States was waging a 'war of annihilation in Vietnam' in a letter to the *Washington Post*. In January 1964, he drew the attention of readers of the *New York Herald Tribune* to America's chemical warfare in Vietnam, 'the wholesale destruction of villages', the herding of peasants into concentration camps, and the rottenness of the regime in Saigon.[58] He blamed the United States for preventing free elections as stipulated at the Geneva Conference in 1954 and for systematic sabotage of neutrality in South East Asia. He showed the vast scale of the American involvement in the destruction of Vietnam in the years before its involvement was made official.[59] Fear of Communism was now a bigger menace than Communism itself in Russell's opinion and successive American governments had nurtured it. The American military authorities seemed to Russell a bigger threat to world peace than their Soviet counterparts, who openly stressed the need for disarmament proposals.[60]

He also emphasised the problems of American society that had generated the increasingly reactionary role of the United States in world politics and the extent to which liberals and even socialists in Europe accepted the desirability of US overseas interventions wherever it saw fit to do so.[61] American freedom had become a 'myth'. The reality of America was crude persecution of dissidents, intolerance of critics of capitalism, an excessive role for the political police and the paid informer, a supine press, and the political dominance of the corporate business community.[62] Russell denounced US society for its everyday conformity and its acceptance of high levels of violence. He analysed the military-industrial complex in America showing the vast scale of its activities.[63] He wrote in ways that reinforced New Left writers such as Herbert Marcuse. His polemical exaggerations accurately reflected the mood of the activist left in Western Europe by 1968.[64]

When the Bertrand Russell Peace Foundation was launched in September 1963 for the furtherance of international work against nuclear war, the emphasis remained on the danger represented by the United States. Russell was a defender of Cuba in these years as well as a critic of the American war in Vietnam. In every country where the United States was guarantor of reactionary regimes Russell supported resistance to US imperialism.[65] In 1965, at the London School of Economics, he denounced the Labour government in Britain for supporting the United States in its campaign against the movements for independence in the former colonial world. Similar messages were given to the World Congress for Peace in Helsinki in July 1965 and the Tricontinental Conference in Havana in January 1966. World peace depended on the defeat of US imperialism, Russell insisted. To that end, the Peace Foundation set up the Vietnamese Solidarity Campaign under the leadership of Tariq Ali to campaign in Britain against the American war. In November 1966, it announced the creation of an International War Crimes Tribunal, with sessions in Sweden and Denmark in 1967, to mobilise world opinion against the United States. Russell's last published word on the subject – he died on 2 February 1970 – argued that 'the entire American people' were on trial; it was not enough to merely lack the will to continue the slaughter in Vietnam, it was necessary to bring the leading political and military war criminals to trial.[66]

Russell's authority was thus added to intellectual currents from this time powering Cold War revisionism; opposition to US imperialism; support for national liberation movements, including armed struggle; the perception that Cuba deserved the left's enthusiastic support; and that neither Moscow nor Washington could be supported by those fighting for justice in the world. By 1968, revived by the spectacular wave of global demonstrations and protests of which the prolonged disorder in Paris was only the nearest example, Trotskyist groups in Britain were able to attract a new generation of activists. Deutscher had been a particular intellectual guide for the New Left in both Britain and the United States.[67] Many of the most important Marxist theorists of this time had some connection with him and one or other variant of the Trotskyist tradition – including Tariq Ali, Peter Sedgwick, Neville Alexander, Perry Anderson, Daniel Bensaid, Robin Blackburn, Robert Brenner, Pierre Broué, Tony Cliff, Hal Draper, Terry Eagleton, Norman Geras, Adolfo Gilly, Duncan Hallas,

Chris Harman, Nigel Harris, Michael Lowy and Ernest Mandel. These intellectual influences are all the more important because the small Trotskyist groups hidden in the Labour Party largely failed to exploit the crisis in official Communism occasioned by the events of 1956. Though the CPGB lost around 10,000 members the highest estimate of defections to the Trotskyist groups is only 200.[68] Most of the prominent figures who resigned from the CPGB in 1956–57 and remained left-wing activists were wary of all forms of Leninism. The Trotskyists in the late 1950s were thus almost as few in number as they had been at the start of the decade.

Within a few years of one another (1965–69), three of the Trotskyist entrist groups emerged from the Labour Party competing for attention as the Socialist Labour League, the International Socialists and the International Marxist Group. They were divided, as ever, by what to make of the Soviet Union and all the currents claiming some relationship to the Bolshevik revolution. The combined membership of the Trotskyist left was still less than one thousand by 1965, even including those who remained within the Labour Party – the Militant Tendency entrists organised around the weekly *Militant* journal. Yet there was clearly a perception by the mid-1960s that such radicalism as there was in Britain was not being catered for by either the Labour or the Communist parties. Official individual membership figures for the Labour Party suggest that the organisation lost around a quarter of a million members during the period of the Wilson governments, 1964–70. The life of a typical constituency Labour Party was often devoid of politics. Attendance at meetings was tiny. In certain districts these bodies were ripe for take-over, if a sufficiently motivated and organised unit could be bothered to make the effort. Most Trotskyists were not interested. Membership of these groups began to rise through participation in the Vietnamese Solidarity Campaign and by involvement in student politics, which grew more radical as the numbers of full-time students in British universities increased from just under 200,000 in 1960 to over 400,000 in 1970. The CPGB, by contrast, remained a significant player in the trade unions and still had a predominantly working-class composition. But the membership of the CPGB was falling and the leaders seemed old, ideologically conservative and out of touch.

In the decade from 1965 there was much to suggest a renewal of left-wing thinking in Britain, as elsewhere, and to encourage belief that a more radical left-wing politics would emerge with deeper popular support. There was the growth of Marxism in the universities, an explosion of left-wing publications and the growth of radical thinking outside the Marxist-Leninist and social democratic orthodoxies. Much of it was inspired by developments in American politics. New currents developed outside the old organisations of the left – second wave feminism, environmental politics, community politics, anti-racism, concern for North–South issues, opposition to Western imperialism and gay politics. At the same time there was evidence of corrosion in the post-war consensus. Violence became a permanent feature of politics in Northern Ireland and directly affected English cities. Racism became a more conspicuous problem which far-right organisations sought to exploit. The trade unions were more alienated from the Labour parliamentary leadership than at any time since the formation of the party in 1900. Industrial conflicts grew in number. Many had a distinct political dimension as stagflation took hold in the early 1970s and the Conservative government introduced new legal constraints on collective bargaining. In the years 1968–74, industrial disputes reached levels not seen since the General Strike of 1926 or the strike wave of 1910–14. Trade union leaders became less deferential to the Labour leadership and more critical of the revisionist Croslandite–Gaitsk-ellite policies that had dominated the 1950s and 1960s. Labour annual conferences and the party's ruling National Executive Committee began to adopt more radical policies. Dissident Marxist material even surfaced on television in the dramas of people such as Trevor Griffith, Ken Loach and Jim Allen.

This was the context in which the Trotskyist groups grew. They assumed that what was wanting so that all these fragments could be given coherence and brought into an effective unity was a Marxist analysis and a Leninist leadership – though the International Socialists were admittedly equivocal about the latter until the mid-1970s. But their growth in the late 1960s and early 1970s was very modest and none of the far left groups, including the CPGB, profited organisationally from the wave of industrial unrest. By the mid-1970s, moreover, it was also becoming clear that the new social movements were differentiating ideologically, becoming more fragmented rather than less. Marxism was of diminishing appeal in these quarters and certainly could not supply a unifying language or programme. Though two of the Trotskyist groups declared themselves parties – the Workers Revolutionary Party (WRP) (1973) and Socialist Workers Party (SWP) (1977) – neither justified the title. The Trotskyism that seemed to matter belonged to the Militant Tendency within the Labour Party which rose to prominence as the left around it grew and the internal politics of Labour polarised. By 1979, after the May general election which brought Margaret Thatcher's Conservative Party to government, the left seemed to be in the ascendant within the defeated Labour Party. And yet the next decade was characterised by comprehensive defeat.

Orwell's search for a mass socialist party came to nothing. Trotsky's expectations of a post-war capitalist crash, the military destruction of the Soviet Union and socialist revolutions in the West were all disappointed.

Deutscher's alternative vision of the relentless economic, technological and cultural progress of the Soviet Union leading to socialist democracy was confounded by the collapse in 1989–91 of the Communist regimes, popular rejection of both the political and economic systems that Stalin had created, and the apparent hegemony of liberal democracy. By then the British moment of Trotskyism had also passed, entangled to the last with the Labour Party as it retreated from social democracy. By the end of the twentieth century the era opened by the Bolshevik Revolution was over and the future of any sort of socialism in doubt.

Notes

1 B. Russell, 'Impressions of Bolshevik Russia', *Collected Papers of Bertrand Russell*, vol. 15 (London: Routledge, 2000), pp. 176–98 and 'Why Russia Endures Bolshevism', pp. 200–1.

2 C. M. Roebuck (Andrew Rothstein), ' The Resignation of Trotsky', *Workers' Weekly*, 25 January 1925; A. McManus, review of *Lenin* by Trotsky, *Workers' Weekly*, 24 April 1925; W. N. Ewer, 'Trotsky and His "Friends"', *Labour Monthly*, June (1925), p. 373.

3 For summaries of the many dissident Marxist accounts of the Soviet Union see Marcel van der Linden, *Western Marxism and the Soviet Union* (Chicago: Haymarket Books, 2009).

4 Bertrand M. Patenaude, *Stalin's Nemesis: The Exile and Murder of Leon Trotsky* (London: Faber and Faber 2009), p. 188.

5 L. Trotsky, 'The USSR in War', *In Defence of Marxism* (London: Pathfinder, 1966), pp. 3–26.

6 Ibid., pp. 212–22.

7 G. Orwell, *Collected Essays, Journalism and Letters*, vol. 1 (London: Penguin Books, 1970), pp. 368–9.

8 B. Crick, *George Orwell: A Life* (London: Secker and Warburg, 1980), pp. 192–3.

9 T. S. Eliot and H. G. Wells were among those who mistook him for a Trotskyist; Reg Groves – one of the Balham Communists who converted to Trotskyism in 1932 – was among his acquaintances from 1935. See Crick, *Orwell*, p. 175.

10 P. Davison (ed.), *George Orwell: A Life in Letters* (London: Harvill Secker, 2010), pp. xii, 31, 81, 189.

11 Ibid., pp. 135–6, 271. For Philip Rahv's view see J. Meyers (ed.), *George Orwell: The Critical Heritage* (London: Routledge and Kegan Paul, 1975), pp. 299, 369.

12 Orwell, *Collected Essays*, vol. 1, p. 419.

13 I. Deutscher, '"1984" – The Mysticism of Cruelty', in his *Heretics and Renegades* (London: Cape 1955 and 1969), pp. 35–50.

14 Timothy Garton Ash, 'Orwell's List', *New York Review of Books*, 25 September 2003.

15 L. McKinstry, 'Was George Orwell a Patriot or a Traitor?', MailOnline,

6 September 2007 www.dailymail.co.uk/news/article-480187/Was-George-Orwell-patriot-traitor.html, accessed 22 February 2013.

16 P. Sedgwick, 'George Orwell, International Socialist?' *International Socialism*, June–July (1969), pp. 28–34 and 'Orwell: Honesty, Courage and Faith in the "proles"', *Socialist Worker*, 9 November 1968.

17 B. Crick, 'Orwell's Socialism', *Labour Leader*, October (1983).

18 G. Orwell, 'Spilling the Spanish Beans', in which he says the Popular Front is as 'weird as a pig with two heads' and 'Communism Is Now a Counter-revolutionary Force'. *Collected Essays*, vol. 1, pp. 302–3.

19 'Censorship in England' appeared in the Communist literary front weekly *Monde* in Paris on 6 October 1928; four more articles appeared between December 1928 and May 1929 in *Progress Civique* under the collective title 'Wretched Poverty of the British Worker'. See P. Davison (ed.), *Complete Works*, vol. 10 (London: Secker and Warburg, 1986).

20 Orwell, *Collected Essays*, vol. 1, p. 347.

21 R. Rees, *George Orwell: Fugitive from the Camp of Victory* (London: Secker and Warburg, 1961), pp. 52–3, 146–7.

22 G. Orwell, *Collected Essays, Journalism and Letters*, vol. 2 (London: Secker and Warburg, 1968), pp. 86, 90.

23 Crick, *Orwell*, pp. 186–7.

24 G. Orwell, *The Road to Wigan Pier* (London: Penguin Books, 1962), pp. 155, 157.

25 Orwell, *Collected Essays*, vol. 1, p. 317.

26 Ibid., pp. 437, 318.

27 L. Trotsky, *The Writings of Leon Trotsky 1938–39* (New York: Pathfinder 1974), p. 32.

28 Crick, *Orwell*, p. 192.

29 L. Trotsky, 'What Is National Socialism?' (1933), in *The Struggle Against Fascism in Germany* (London: Penguin Books, 1971), pp 406–16, 413.

30 Orwell, *Collected Essays*, vol. 1, p. 318; vol. 2, pp. 139–45, 32.

31 L. Trotsky, *The Revolution Betrayed* (London: New Park, 1967), p. 279.

32 Ibid., pp. 104, 248

33 Ibid., p. 278.

34 Crick, *Orwell*, pp. 228, xx.

35 Orwell, *Collected Essays, Journalism and Letters*, vol. 3 (London: Penguin Books, 1970), p. 365.

36 Orwell, *Collected Essays, Journalism and Letters*, vol. 4 (London: Penguin Books, 1970), p. 36

37 G. Orwell, 'Rejected Review', piece 2435, in P. Davison (ed.), *Complete Works*, vol. 16 (London: Secker and Warburg, 1998), pp. 122–3; H. Laski, *Faith, Reason and Civilization* (London: Gollancz, 1943).

38 Dwight MacDonald, editorial, *Politics*, November 1944. See Davison, *Complete Works*, vol. 16, piece 2518 (London: Secker and Warburg, 1986).

39 Deutscher, '1984', fn p. 48.

40 Orwell, *Collected Essays*, vol. 3, p. 152.

41 J. Newsinger, 'The American Connection: George Orwell, "Literary

Trotskyism" and the New York Intellectuals', *Labour History Review*, 64, 1 (1999), pp. 23–43; for Russell's argument see his 'Hopes and Fears as Regards America', *New Republic*, 15 and 22 March 1922, in B. Feinberg and R. Kasrils (eds), *Bertrand Russell's America, 1896–1945* (Boston: South End Press, 1973), pp. 220–7.

42 These were Gerry Healy, who led the Club from 1949, forerunner of the Socialist Labour League and Workers' Revolutionary Party: Ted Grant who formed the Revolutionary Socialist League in 1955, forerunner of the Militant tendency; and Tony Cliff, who led the Socialist Review Group, forerunner of the International Socialists and Socialist Workers' Party.

43 See J. Callaghan, *Socialism in Britain since 1884* (Oxford: Blackwell, 1990), pp. 146–9, 164–7.

44 'Revolution from Above', *Tribune*, 23 February 1945. D. Singer identifies Deutscher as the author of this article in his 'Armed with a Pen', in D. Horowitz (ed.), *Isaac Deutscher: The Man and His Work* (London: MacDonald, 1971), pp. 40–2, 55, fn. 16.

45 I. Deutscher, *Stalin* (London: Pelican Books, 1949, 2nd edn 1966), pp. 550, 534–5.

46 See Deutscher's *Russia After Stalin* (London: Cape, 1953); 'A Reply to Critics' in *Heretics and Renegades: The Unfinished Revolution: Russia 1917–67* (Oxford: Oxford University Press, 1967), pp. 36–7.

47 See J. Callaghan, 'The Left and the "Unfinished Revolution": Bevanites and Soviet Russia in the 1950s', *Contemporary British History*, 15, 3 (2001), pp. 63–82.

48 Nye Bevan, 'The People's Coming of Age', *Tribune*, 3 February 1950, pp. 3–4.

49 A. Bevan, *In Place of Fear* (London: Quartet, 1978, first published 1952), p. 23.

50 Ibid., p. 31.

51 *Tribune*, 16 October 1959, pp. 1, 6.

52 *Tribune*, 16 and 30 January 1959.

53 *Tribune*, 23 October 1959.

54 P. Krugman points this out in 'The Myth of Asia's Miracle', *Foreign Affairs*, November–December (1994), pp. 62–3, 65 fn.

55 R. Monk, *Bertrand Russell: The Ghost of Madness, 1921–70* (London: Vintage, 2001), p. 443.

56 Ibid., p. 444.

57 Ibid., p. 458.

58 B. Feinberg and R. Kasrils (eds), *Bertrand Russell's America, 1945–70* (Boston: South End Press 1983), p. 242.

59 Russell, 'War and Atrocity in Vietnam', ibid., pp. 361–70.

60 Russell, 'Thermonuclear War: Battle of Experts', *New Republic*, 3 April 1961, ibid., pp. 346–9.

61 Russell, 'Free World Barbarism', ibid., pp. 371–81.

62 Russell, 'The Myth of American Freedom', *The Minority of One*, May 1963, ibid., pp. 356–60.

63 Russell, 'The Imminent Danger of Nuclear War', ibid., pp. 350–5.

64 Monk, *Bertrand Russell*, p. 461.

65 Russell, 'Peace Through Resistance to US Imperialism', in Feinberg and Kasrils (eds), *Bertrand Russell's America, 1945–70*, pp. 394–8.

66 Russell, 'The Entire American People are on Trial', *Ramparts*, March 1970, ibid., pp. 408–9.

67 P. Sedgwick, 'Tragedy of the Tragedian: An Appreciation of Isaac Deutscher', *International Socialism*, 31 (1967–68), pp. 10–17.

68 Callaghan, *Trotskyism in Britain* (Oxford: Blackwell, 1984), p. 71.

2

The New Left

Beyond Stalinism and social democracy?

Paul Blackledge

The British New Left emerged in 1956 as a response to a global ideological crisis that opened with Khrushchev's secret speech, but which came to fruition when the revolutionary workers' movement in Hungary was suppressed by Russian tanks on the same weekend that Anglo-French troops invaded Egypt.[1] Together these events created a space for a critique of the world system as a totality. In this context the New Left aimed, by contrast both with the Communist Party's loyalty to Moscow and the Labour Party's support for an Atlanticist foreign policy, at renewing socialism by mapping a third way beyond the polarities of the Cold War. Within eighteen months of this ideological break with Stalinism and social democracy, New Left activists began to test their ideas in a new mass movement: the Campaign for Nuclear Disarmament (CND). It is difficult to imagine a more propitious encounter, for from early 1958 CND organised a series of marches that brought thousands of disaffected youth into conflict not only with the government but also with the leaderships of the Labour and Communist parties.[2]

Though these developments opened a political space beyond the parameters of traditional politics, it wasn't long before leading figures within the New Left and CND began to orientate towards the Labour Party as the most feasible vehicle for the advancement of the unilateralist cause.[3] This perspective seemed close to realisation when, at the party's 1960 conference, Labour's right-wing leadership was defeated by the left in debates over motions on the party's constitution and unilateral nuclear disarmament. As we shall see, many New Left intellectuals concluded not only that Labour might deliver on its unilateralist policies but also that it might become a vehicle for socialist advance.[4]

At its heart, this perspective greatly underestimated the power of the right wing within the Labour Party machine. Indeed, once the right mobilised its forces at the 1961 party conference the left was easily defeated. While a more realistic left might have taken this defeat in its stride, because the New Left had put so much faith in their ability to win this vote it was dragged into the vortex of the Labour left's defeat.[5] Raymond Williams commented, 'the reversal of the vote on nuclear disarmament in 1961 came as an astounding blow. There was no idea of the strengths of the Labour machine, or of the political skill with which the right was able to organise for victory within it'.[6] Unfortunately, since this was as true for the leaders of CND as it was for the leaders of the New Left, defeat in the vote on unilateralism signalled the beginning of the end both for the former and the latter.[7]

Thus it was that by the winter of 1961–62 the New Left, which had promised so much in 1956–57, was all but dead.[8] This is not to say that the 'political projects' of the British New Left can be dismissed, in Eric Hobsbawm's words, as no more than 'a half-remembered footnote',[9] for the elements of the New Left milieu that best resisted the lure of Labourism did act as a bridge to the socialist movements of 1968. In this essay I argue that though the dominant voices within the New Left failed adequately to come to terms with the issues of Stalinism and reformism, this was not universally true. In particular, Alasdair MacIntyre's critical defence of E. P. Thompson's socialist humanism extended Thompson's strategic insights in a direction that pointed towards the possibility of realising the New Left's goal of renewing socialism beyond the parameters of Stalinism and social democracy. Unfortunately, MacIntyre's insights have been obscured by the tendency amongst academics to reduce the New Left to writings in *New Left Review*, its predecessor magazines *Universities and Left Review* and *The Reasoner/New Reasoner*, and by extension *Socialist Register*. By contrast, Dorothy Thompson's suggestion that the New Left should be conceived as a broad political milieu opens a space for grasping how it helped alter the subsequent 'terms of political discourse' in Britain.[10] Following her lead I note the faltering links between the British new lefts of 1956 and 1968. I argue that the earlier movement marked a fork in the road at which a plurality of leftist currents momentarily converged through an attempt to map a left that was independent both of Stalinism and social democracy. Though the dominant voices within this milieu failed to transcend the limitations of these traditions, some of the minor voices did succeed in pointing beyond them, and in so doing provided a bridge between the New Left's of 1956 and 1968.

Third way socialism?

Stuart Hall suggests that the New Left 'attempted to define a "third" political space' between the polarities of the Cold War politics as embodied in the 'depressing experiences of both "actual existing socialism" and "actual existing social democracy"'.[11] While this may have been the intention, Madeleine Davis points out that in practice the New Left had an 'ambivalent' relationship to the Labour Party.[12] This is evident, for instance, in Edward Thompson's introduction to the New Left collection *Out of Apathy* (1960). In this essay Thompson combines a powerful critique of the Labour Party's existing policies, with a rather naive suggestion that, despite these policies, the Labour Party could be won to socialism.

Thompson opened the essay with an analysis of what he believed was one of the key political issues of the day: mass apathy. Defining apathy as the search for 'private solutions to public evils', he explained its contemporary prevalence, principally, as a function of a lack of real political alternatives for the electorate.[13] Developing this theme, he suggested that a solution to the problem of apathy should begin by presenting the electorate with a real, viable political alternative to what the *Economist* labelled 'Butskellism': the consensus between the policies of the Labour and Tory chancellors Hugh Gaitskell and Rab Butler. Concretely, Thompson aimed to win over the Labour Party to the New Left's vision of socialism. Thus he suggested that the transformation of Labour into a socialist party was not only possible, but also that this potential was being realised as he wrote: 'Labour is ceasing to offer an alternative way of governing existing society, and is beginning to look for an alternative society'.[14] He argued that the New Left's role should be to encourage this process, while remaining aware that if his more optimistic perspective for the transformation of the Labour Party were frustrated 'then new organisations will have to be created'.[15]

In retrospect this argument seems almost wilfully naive.[16] If Thompson's left-reformism had been but an idiosyncratic aberration it might justifiably be left to the enormous condescension of posterity. However, not only did Thompson's politics show a marked continuity across his break with Stalinism, they also cohered with a wide swath of opinion amongst other New Left activists. And this perspective had roots in the dominant New Left critique of Stalinism.

Since the 1930s, the Stalinist Communist parties had embraced the 'popular front' line. This strategy, which was articulated in Russia with a view to winning an alliance with Britain and France against Germany, saw the Communist parties, which had already become subservient to Russia, transformed into what were in effect left-reformist organisations.[17]

Nevertheless, though the Communist parties generally, and the Communist Party of Great Britain (CPGB) more specifically, had long since ceased to be revolutionary organisations, they continued to deploy revolutionary rhetoric. This came to an end in Britain with the publication of the party's new programme, *The British Road to Socialism*, in 1951.[18] This document marked an important turning point in Communist thinking: for the first time the CPGB made its break with revolutionary politics explicit. In part, this shift to a reformist strategy was underpinned by an argument, originating in Moscow but expressed in Britain by the CPGB general secretary Harry Pollitt, that the transitions to 'Communism' in Eastern Europe after the war had shown that 'it is possible to see how the people will move towards socialism without further revolutions, without the dictatorship of the proletariat'.[19] In an extension of this strategic 'insight', the CPGB argued that the Labour Party, once rid of its right-wing leadership, could act as the agency for the socialist transformation of society through parliament.[20] In practice this meant, like the New Left, the CPGB became very excited at the prospects for a left advance in the Labour Party after the defeats of the right wing over the issues of clause four and unilateralism at the 1960 Labour Party conference. Indeed, John Gollan, who replaced Pollitt as CPGB general secretary in 1956, argued that the key political task in 1960 was to 'redouble the struggle in the trade unions in support of the Scarborough decisions; to carry the struggle into the right-wing camp and win the trade unions now pledged to the right-wing policy for the Scarborough line'.[21]

This perspective was somewhat contradictory for a supposedly Leninist organisation. For Lenin, the organisational forms taken by socialist groups derived from the nature of the political tasks they set themselves. Thus, a centralised party was a necessary prerequisite for a successful revolutionary challenge to state power, while parties that aimed only to reform the existing system could manage with a decentralised structure.[22] Paradoxically, in 1950s Britain, the CPGB maintained the facade of Leninism, in its bastardised Stalinist form, through the adherence to a strong centralised party structure, while rejecting the revolutionary political content of Lenin's thought.

But why should socialists remain wedded to a centralised organisation if its politics were reformist? The first New Leftist to point to the incoherence between the CPGB's structure and its politics was Ken Alexander. He argued that while it was true that a Leninist party was a necessary prerequisite for the execution of a successful revolutionary strategy, once in power Leninist parties had acted and would inevitably act as agencies of the degeneration of the revolution into some form of totalitarianism.[23] This argument implied that Marxism's traditional rejection of the reformist alternative to revolutionary strategy had, as its corollary, the argument that Stalinism or something like it was the only conceivable alternative to capitalism. However, if, as the CPGB insisted, peaceful transitions to socialism had occurred in Eastern Europe, then not only was a new reformist socialist strategy conceivable, but it could also be imagined that this strategy might be prosecuted without a Leninist party.

Thus Alexander took Pollitt's claim that the East European transitions had shown that revolutions were an unnecessary step on the road to socialism, and derived from it two conclusions. First, that history had moved on from Marx's day – reformism had become a realistic socialist political strategy; and, second, that Lenin too had become equally redundant: centralised organisations were no longer the necessary evil through which socialists must fight for the overthrow of capitalism. This second conclusion was drawn coherently from Alexander's old Stalinist frame of reference. If a revolutionary strategy had ceased to be the only realistic option open to socialist activists, revolutionary parties were becoming historically redundant. Indeed the only function of a Leninist party, according to Alexander, would be to act as the agency of the degeneration of socialist democracy in a post-capitalist regime.[24] Alexander was therefore one of the first ex-Communists of the 1956 generation to generalise from the reformist assumptions of the CPGB to a critique of its formal Leninism.

Within the New Left, criticisms of Leninist organisational forms quickly merged into more general arguments against any strategy that aimed to build an independent socialist organisation. Indeed, Edward Thompson famously wrote that:

> the New Left does not offer an alternative faction, party or leadership to those now holding the field ... once launched on the course of factionalism, it would contribute, not to the re-unification of the socialist movement, but to its further fragmentation; it would contribute further to the alienation of the post-war generation from the movement; and the established bureaucracies cannot be effectively challenged by their own methods ... The bureaucracy will hold the machine; but the New Left will hold the passes between it and the younger generation.

In fact, socialist intellectual work was not 'best accomplished by joining anything'.[25] Furthermore, Thompson argued that intellectuals 'should not ask which party should I join? But what else shall I do to stir up the dormant socialist traditions of this country'?[26]

Despite the stridency of his earlier opposition to building an independent party, by the end of the 1950s Thompson had moved to embrace some form of organisational politics. Thus, in his parting editorial for the last issue of *The New Reasoner*, published immediately prior to its merger with the *Universities and Left Review* (*ULR*) to become *New Left Review*, he argued that 'we think that the time has come for our readers, together with the readers of *ULR*, to pass over from diffuse discussion to political organisation ... We must now put this thinking to *use*, and carry it outward to the younger generation, and inward to the traditional labour movement. In particular we must establish far more contact between the New Left and the industrial working class'.[27] Specifically, Thompson insisted, new activists 'must learn from the steady attention to organisation, and from the true moral realism which has enabled men, year in and year out, to meet each situation as it has arisen'.[28] And although he thus opened a space within the New Left for a serious engagement with the question of political organisation, his broad acceptance of the reformist assumptions expressed by Alexander, and indeed by Pollitt, meant that of one thing he was sure: a revived Leninism was not the answer.

Once the New Left had moved from acting merely as a loosely organised propaganda body towards political intervention proper, the problem of its factional nature came to the fore. The peculiar manner in which this occurred followed from the New Left's structure: while it was only a very small milieu it boasted the affiliation of some very prominent activists. This was nowhere more pronounced than in Fife where Lawrence Daly, an important national figure both within the New Left and the National Union of Mineworkers, had a significant local following. Daly had left the CPGB in 1956 after years of activity, and in 1957 he set up the Fife Socialist League, through which he maintained both close links with the labour movement and 'a vigorous correspondence in the local press on questions of national or international significance'.[29] Combined with his local standing and his desire not to be labelled as a mere oppositionist, this assault quickly put him at the centre of local politics; a position from which, in 1958, he stood as a credible candidate for council. In the end Daly actually won the council seat; a victory which, in turn, set the stage for his ultimately unsuccessful stand against the sitting Labour MP in the 1959 general election. It was this act that put the issue of standing as a national alternative to Labour to the forefront of debates within the New Left.[30]

A number of important New Left leaders chose to support Daly's stand.[31] This was a momentous choice; for any decision to stand against the Labour Party in an election was tantamount to a declaration of political war. However, the New Left's support for Daly's candidature was not unequivocal. Rather, many of the leading intellectuals argued that Fife was a unique case, and while they would support Daly this did not imply a universal break with the Labour Party. John Saville suggested that as it was a key role of the New Left to 'recreate a vigorous movement for socialism amongst the ordinary people', it should develop a body of ideas that was capable of refuting the dominant Fabian consensus in a language that was open to easy translation into cultural and political activity.[32] Such a project could sometimes be best served by the New Left operating wholly within the Labour Party, sometimes wholly without and sometimes, probably mostly, 'partly within, partly without'. Fundamentally, there were to be no organisational 'sacred cows' to which the New Left would bow.[33] To counter the New Left's weakness Saville argued for a flexible approach to politics. In West Fife, local conditions favoured standing a socialist candidate against the incumbent Labour MP: the sitting MP was not only a right-winger, he was also distrusted by a large section of the local population; the Communist vote was declining; and finally, the weakness of the Tories in the area meant that even if the left's vote was split three ways between Communist, Labour and socialist this would not have disastrous consequences as one of these three would still triumph.[34]

However, Saville's approach was not quite as flexible as it at first appeared. For in the midst of his essay he reaffirmed the New Left's unwillingness to form a new party: 'We have set our face against the development of a new political party; both our past history and our present analysis reject this'.[35] So despite his support for Daly's *de facto* party, Saville was wary of constituting the New Left as an independent organisation. While this position was reinforced by the sense of demoralisation felt by many New Leftists after Daly's defeat in the parliamentary election, it was rooted in the reformist theoretical assumptions of the milieu from which the New Left sprang: assumptions that were inherited from the CPGB, and most powerfully articulated by Edward Thompson.

Thompson developed his analysis of the tasks of the contemporary left most eloquently in his essay 'Revolution'. The explicit aim of this article was to steer a political course between the twin rocks of Leninist apocalyptic insurrectionism and Fabian evolutionism. If the essay's title was meant as a challenge to Fabian gradualism, its substance was aimed at a series of Leninist political positions. Leninists, he argued, had seriously misconstrued the nature of the coming revolution, and consequentially they were incapable of adequately preparing for it. Thompson argued that the past century had been witness to a series of structural reforms that had been granted by capital to labour. These reforms were not the product of capital's philanthropic nature; rather they were a corollary of its instinct for self-preservation: capital retreated, inch-by-inch, before the pressure for reform that originated at the base of society. The weakness with Fabianism did not lie in its belief in the possibility of reform; these all too palpably existed, but rather in its misdiagnosis of their cause. Leninism, meanwhile, was incapable of reorienting to the changed situation. In particular,

Leninists could not comprehend the implications of the enormous reforms that had been brought about through the war: for it was in the period from 1942 to 1948 that the most significant reforms had been won. These changes allowed Thompson to look forward to a 'peaceful revolution in Britain'.[36] In fact, Thompson suggested, radical change could be instituted relatively easily:

> the Establishment appears to rest upon an equilibrium of forces so delicate that it is forced to respond to determined pressure ... if we nationalise ... if we tax ... if we contract out of NATO ... At each point the initiative might provoke repercussions which would necessitate a total transformation of relations of production, forms of power, alliances and trade agreements, and institutions: that is, a socialist revolution.[37]

If such a peaceful 'revolution' was possible, then what of the Labour Party; Britain's traditional vehicle of reformist socialist aspirations? Against Thompson's earlier rejection of the case for socialists joining any organisation, other prominent members of the New Left, such as Rodney Hilton and Mervyn Jones, argued that as the Labour Party was 'still a mass movement of the British working class', and 'a battleground in which opposing trends are free to contend for leadership', socialists should join it.[38] These arguments seemed to be confirmed when the left won victories in the votes over clause four and unilateralism at the 1960 conference. Thus it was that even Ralph Miliband, just prior to the publication of his own powerful critique of Labourism, argued at the time that 'it is not inevitable that the Labour Party should continue towards the political graveyard'. Moreover, he suggested that socialists might act to transform the party into a socialist organisation, 'before it was too late'.[39] Furthermore, in an argument first published in 1961, he argued that 'the leadership whose purpose it is to reduce the Party's commitment to socialist politics can no longer rely on the trade unions to help it in achieving its aims'.[40] As we have seen, by 1960 Thompson appeared to have gravitated to a similar position; believing not only that the Labour Party might be won for the left but also that it might thereafter be used to win the battle for socialism.

John Rex made a similar argument for joining Labour. He began his case by noting, somewhat counter-intuitively, the 'powerful system of bureaucratic control which operates within the party': indeed, 'the big unions or their officials do in fact control the Labour Party'. However, despite this structural limitation to the influence on policy by the ordinary members of the party, he argued that 'we must either educate a new generation of socialists to take over the local and national party machine, the trade unions and the parliamentary party, or we must be prepared to set about the building of a new socialist party'. As he did not believe that there was much hope for the formation of a new socialist party, he aimed to build a strong socialist presence within the Labour Party: New Left activists should be prepared 'to become collectors and ward secretaries as well as councillors and trade union officials'.[41] Indeed, in a letter to their readers, *New Left Review*'s editors wrote that 'the struggle for socialism is in a very important sense the struggle for the "soul of Labour"'.[42]

So the bulk of the New Left followed Hilton and Jones to fight for the transformation of the Labour Party. Indeed Thompson interpreted the alarm bells sounding in the national press at the time as an indication that bourgeois society was becoming anxious of the developments within the Labour Party, developments which should therefore excite and energise the New Left.[43] Moreover, victory over clause four and unilateralism at the 1960 conference seemed to confirm the general validity of the strategy for transforming Labour.[44]

A year later, the editors of *New Left Review* found themselves politically paralysed when the right reasserted its control over the party through the medium of the trade union block vote at the 1961 conference.[45] In these depressing circumstances the erstwhile activists of the New Left eagerly grasped at any sign, however meagre, of a revival in the fortunes of the left. It was thus with Gaitskell's early death, and Harold Wilson's election to the leadership of the Labour Party in 1963, that the reformist illusions that had previously opened the door to the New Left's disastrous strategic goal of transforming the Labour Party into the agency of socialist transformation, now led them to believe that even in defeat the left had been victorious: Wilson it seemed was going to lead the left to the promised land; and from then onwards 'all hopes were now focused on Labour'.[46] Indeed, Perry Anderson, the new editor of *New Left Review*, wrote that Wilson had stepped into the fray just as the objective circumstances favoured the left as they had never done before. Therefore, he argued, Wilson 'may in the end represent a certain moment in the auto emancipation of the working-class movement in England'.[47] So, by the early 1960s, the New Left's aim of creating a socialist voice independent of both social democracy and Stalinism had collapsed into the train of Harold Wilson's general election bandwagon.

Beyond the impasse

The New Left's trajectory from a critique of Leninism through left-reformism and on towards Wilson's Labour Party was not in any sense preordained. Indeed, voices within the New Left both criticised and pointed beyond this impasse. Thus, in 1963, Alasdair MacIntyre wrote that 'to accept Wilsonism is to have moved over to the right at least for the moment no matter what other professions of socialism are made'.[48] Like Thompson, MacIntyre had been a member of the CPGB, though he had left the party somewhat earlier. He subsequently joined with his erstwhile comrades after 1956 to become one of the most prominent voices on the far-left of the New Left milieu. It was from this perspective that he critically engaged with Thompson's thought in a way that pointed beyond the limitations both of his politics specifically and the tendency within New Left circles towards a reconciliation with Labourism more broadly.

MacIntyre first outlined his thoughts in this direction through a critical engagement with Thompson's 'Socialist Humanism: An Epistle to the Philistines' (1957). This essay was a brilliant and original contribution to both the analysis of Stalinism and to Marxist moral theory more generally. At its heart Thompson's essay involved, as Kate Soper has argued, a reaffirmation of 'moral autonomy and the powers of historical agency' within historical materialism.[49] According to Thompson, Stalinism was an ideology whose characteristic procedure was to start from abstract ideas rather than from facts. Moreover, this ideology represented the worldview of a 'revolutionary elite which, within a particular historical context, degenerated into a bureaucracy'. The Stalinist bureaucracy had acted as a block on the struggle for socialism, and thus the human revolt which underpinned the struggle for socialism had become a revolt against Stalinism. Negatively, this revolt was a revolt against ideology and inhumanity. Positively, it involved a 'return to man', in the social sense understood by Marx. It was thus a socialist humanism: human, because it 'places once again real men and women at the centre of socialist theory and aspiration'; socialist, because it 'reaffirms the revolutionary perspectives of Communism'.[50]

Whatever the obvious power of this argument, Thompson's essay embraced a fatal contradiction, which even his grand rhetorical flourishes were unable fully to conceal. He opened his essay with the claim that one quarter of the earth's surface was controlled by a new society, which, despite its many abhorrent features, represented a qualitative break with capitalism: 'The instruments of production in the Soviet Union are socialised. The bureaucracy is not a class, but is parasitic upon that society. Despite its parasitism, the wave of human energy unleashed by the first socialist revolution has multiplied the wealth of society, and vastly enlarged the cultural horizons of the people.'[51] However, in contrast to this characterisation of the Soviet system as at once socialist while yet morally unpalatable, he nevertheless insisted that 'the "end" of Communism is not a "political" end, but a human end'.[52] This formulation suggested a tremendous gap between the human ends of the Soviet experiment and the inhuman means through which these ends were, at least partially, being realised. Consequently, while Thompson implied that a plurality of means could be utilised to achieve the end of Communism, he was aware that these means were not morally equivalent. Concretely, in the Soviet case, he argued that the flaws of the Stalinist system could best be understood as a consequence of the inadequate model of Marxism that had guided the Bolsheviks. They, or so he claimed, had embraced a mechanical interpretation of Marx's base–superstructure metaphor such that agency, in the form of the conscious activity of the masses, was lost, only to find expression through the monolithic party which became the guardian of true socialist consciousness. Following from this, the 'immorality' of replacing the actions of real individuals with those of cardboard abstractions became 'embodied in institutional form in the rigid forms of "democratic centralism"'.[53] Thus, Thompson's moral critique of Stalinism involved a call both for a more flexible interpretation of Marx's theory of history, and a rejection of the Leninist form of political organisation.

In *Notes From the Moral Wilderness*, MacIntyre aimed to extend and make more coherent some of the themes opened by Thompson in light of criticisms made of the piece by Harry Hanson, Charles Taylor and others.[54] The substance of MacIntyre's argument was an attempt to provide a basis for a moral critique of Stalinism that overcame the limitations of the implied Kantianism of those 'ex-Communist turned moral critics of Communism', who 'repudiate Stalinist crimes in the name of moral principle; but the fragility of their appeal to moral principles lies in the apparently arbitrary nature of that appeal'.[55] Such an ethical socialism, he believed, required a reassessment of historical materialism. In place of the orthodox interpretation of historical materialism, MacIntyre insisted that if the moral core of Marxist political theory was to be retrieved and reconstructed from the fragments that Marx had written on the subject then it must be carried out alongside a similar reconstruction of Marx's theory of history.

MacIntyre suggested that the Stalinists had, through the medium of a teleological vision of historical progress, identified 'what is morally right with what is actually going to be the outcome of historical development', such that the '"ought" of principle is swallowed up in the "is" of history'.[56] It was not enough to add something like Kant's ethics to this existing Stalinist theory of historical development if one wished to reassert moral principle into Marxism, for this theory of history negated moral choice. However, neither was it right to reject, as immoral, any historical event from some supposed higher standpoint, as 'there is no set of common, public standards to which [one] can appeal'. Indeed, any such manoeuvre would tend to gravitate to an existing tradition of morality which, because these had generally evolved to serve some particular dominant class interests, would 'play into the hands of the defenders of the established order'.[57] Therefore, MacIntyre suggested, apologists for both the East and the West in the Cold War based their arguments upon inadequate theoretical frameworks. A 'third moral position' could thus be constructed by 'replacing a misconceived but prevalent view of what Marxism is by a more correct view'.[58]

The Stalinist insistence that history's general course was predictable rested, or so MacIntyre insisted, on a misconception of the role of the base–superstructure metaphor in Marxist theory. What Marx suggested when he deployed this metaphor was neither a mechanical nor a causal relationship. Rather, he utilised Hegelian concepts to denote the process through which society's economic base provides 'a framework within which superstructures arise, a set of relations around which the human relations can entwine themselves, a kernel of human relationships from which all else grows'. Indeed, MacIntyre wrote that in 'creating the basis, you create the superstructure. These are not two activities but one'. Thus, the Stalinist model of historical progress, according to which political developments were understood to follow automatically from economic causes, could not be further from Marx's model: in Marx's view, 'the crucial character of the transition to socialism is not that it is a change in the economic base but that it is a revolutionary change in the relation of base to superstructure'.[59] This approach to ethics was intended to point beyond the contemporary moral impasse where 'both the autonomy of ethics and utilitarianism are aspects of the consciousness of capitalism; both are forms of alienation rather than moral guides'.[60] So, once the political left has rid itself both of the myth of the inevitable triumph of socialism, and of the reification of socialism as some indefinite end which justifies any action taken in its name, then socialists will truly comprehend the interpenetration of means and ends through the history of class struggle, and will understand Marxist morality to be, as against the Stalinists, 'an assertion of moral absolutes', and 'as against the liberal critic of Stalinism it is an assertion of desire and history'.[61]

The political corollary of this theoretical argument was a restatement of Marx's view that socialism could only come through the self-emancipation of the working class. As MacIntyre wrote a few years later in a review of the final volume of Isaac Deutscher's biography of Trotsky, 'socialism can be made only by the workers and not for them'.[62] Consequently, in extending Thompson's humanist reinterpretation of Marx, MacIntyre suggested an absolute rupture with Stalinism that went beyond anything that Thompson had written on the subject. Whereas Thompson insisted that 'the October Revolution and its aftermath in East Europe and the Chinese Revolution have effected a fundamental revolution in property relations, and have vastly increased the real potential for intellectual, cultural and democratic advance within these societies', MacIntyre argued that Marx's model of socialism as proletarian self-emancipation 'marks a decisive opposition to Fabianism and all other doctrines of "socialism from above"'.[63] By thus rejecting the socialist credentials of the Stalinist states, MacIntyre could not accept the New Left assumption that peaceful transitions to socialism had been realised by Russian tanks in Eastern Europe.

This perspective laid the groundwork for his critique of Thompson's hopes for the Labour Party. For if the East European states were not socialist then the claim that their recent history could be mined for examples of a viable reformist strategy fell. This argument, in turn, informed MacIntyre's reassessment of Lenin's legacy; and, in particular, his attempt to unpick Lenin's model of democratic revolutionary leadership from the Stalinist ideology of Leninism. In his essay 'Freedom and Revolution' (1960), MacIntyre argued that because capitalism emasculates freedom, to be free means to involve oneself in some organisation that challenges capitalist relations of production: 'The topic of freedom is also the topic of revolution.' More concretely, he argued that though the working class, through its struggles against capital, might spontaneously generate emancipatory movements, it has proved incapable of spontaneously realising the potential of these struggles. Assuming, with Marx, that freedom cannot be handed to the working class from above, how then might it be realised from such unpromising material? MacIntyre answered that socialists must join revolutionary parties, whose goal is not freedom itself, but to act in such a way as to aid the proletariat to achieve freedom: 'the path to freedom must be by means of an organisation which is dedicated not to building freedom but to moving the working class to build it. The necessity for this is the necessity for a vanguard party'. Indeed, MacIntyre suggested that 'the road to socialism and democratic centralism are ... inseparable'.[64]

Conclusion

The dominant themes of the New Left critique of Leninism were rooted in the Stalinist assumption that peaceful a transition to 'socialism' in Eastern Europe entailed that reformism was viable strategy for socialism elsewhere in Europe and consequently that Lenin's revolutionary perspective was obsolete. It is hardly surprising that this standpoint opened the door initially to a rapprochement with social democracy and subsequently to a full scale collapse into the train of Wilson's Labour Party. One consequence of this process was that though the two journals most associated with the legacy of the New Left, *Socialist Register* and *New*

Left Review, flourished in the decades after its demise, they never again became the focus of a socialist *movement*.[65]

By contrast with this trajectory, MacIntyre's defence of Leninism was predicated upon root and branch criticisms both of the view that the Stalinist states were in any sense socialist and of Stalin's distortion of Lenin's theory and practice into the ideology of 'Leninism'. This argument informed his decision to join the International Socialism group in 1960.[66] As I have argued elsewhere, this group came closest to realising the New Left's hope of building a socialist movement independent both of social democracy and Stalinism. And though MacIntyre gave up on his wager on the working class in the mid-1960s, the upsurge in working-class militancy in the late 1960s and early 1970s marked the point at which the 'International Socialism group' began *mutatis mutandis* to realise its potential, as John Saville suggested it might do, of making 'the transition from a fairly open sect to something approaching a small party'.[67] In so doing it showed that the left was able to move beyond the impasse in which the New Left had found itself in the early 1960s without embracing the revisionism of those post-Marxists who saw this impasse as evidence of a 'fundamentally altered landscape' whose coordinates negated Marx's vision of 'socialism form below'.[68]

Notes

1 This essay draws on various of my earlier articles including 'Morality and Revolution: Ethical Debates in the British New Left', *Critique*, 35, 2 (2007), pp. 211–28; 'Alasdair MacIntyre: Marxism and Politics', *Studies in Marxism*, 11 (2007), pp. 95–116; 'The New Left's Renewal of Marxism', *International Socialism*, 2, 112 (2006), pp. 125–53; 'Freedom, Desire and Revolution: Alasdair MacIntyre's Early Marxist Ethics', *History of Political Thought*, 26, 4 (2005), pp. 696–720; 'Reform, Revolution and the Question of Organisation in the First New Left', *Contemporary Politics*, 10, 1 (2004), pp. 99–116.

2 Both Labour and Communist parties initially opposed CND's demand for unilateral nuclear disarmament. W. Thompson, *The Long Death of British Labourism* (London: Pluto Press, 1992), p. 116, and W. Thompson, *The Good Old Cause: British Communism, 1920–91* (London: Pluto Press, 1992), p. 64.

3 R. Hilton, 'Socialism and the Intellectuals – Four', *Universities and Left Review*, 2 (1957), p. 16; M. Jones, 'Socialism and the Intellectuals – One', *Universities and Left Review*, 2 (1957), p. 16.

4 Lin Chun has suggested that the Labour Party 'left too little room for the construction of an organisationally based New Left politics'. As we shall see, the truth is that the dominant voices within the New Left never had the theoretical resources to begin such a project. See L. Chun, *The British New Left* (Edinburgh: Edinburgh University Press, 1993), p. xvii. This also explains why, in Michael Kenny's words, 'much of its energy was expended as a

lobbying group, conscience and critic of Labour'. See M. Kenny, *The First New Left: British Intellectuals after Stalin* (London: Lawrence and Wishart, 1995), p. 198.

5 P. Anderson, *Arguments Within English Marxism* (London: Verso, 1980), p. 136.
6 R. Williams, *Politics and Letters* (London: Verso, 1979), p. 365.
7 J. Hinton, *Protests and Visions* (London, Hutchinson, 1989), p. 178.
8 P. Sedgwick, 'The Two New Lefts', in D. Widgery (ed.), *The Left in Britain* (Harmondsworth: Penguin, 1976), pp. 131–53.
9 E. Hobsbawm, *Interesting Times* (London: Abacus, 2002), p. 214.
10 D. Thompson, 'On the Trail of the New Left', *New Left Review*, 1, 215 (1996), p. 100.
11 S. Hall, 'The "First" New Left: Life and Times', in Oxford University Socialist Discussion Group (eds), *Out of Apathy* (London: Verso, 1989), pp. 13–23.
12 M. Davis, 'Labourism and the New Left', in J. Callaghan, S. Fielding and S. Ludlam (eds), *Interpreting the Labour Party* (Manchester: Manchester University Press, 2003), pp. 39–56.
13 E. P. Thompson, 'At the Point of Decay', in E. P. Thompson (ed.), *Out of Apathy* (London: Stevens and Sons, 1960), pp. 5–8.
14 Ibid., p. 19.
15 Ibid., p. 29.
16 Anderson, *Arguments within English Marxism*, p. 136.
17 F. Claudin, *The Communist Movement* (London: Penguin, 1975); D. Hallas, *The Comintern* (London: Bookmarks, 1985); C. L. R. James, *World Revolution* (New Jersey: Humanities Press, 1993).
18 CPGB, *The British Road to Socialism* (London: Communist Party, 1952). Both critics and supporters of the 'popular front' line embraced by the Comintern in the 1930s are agreed that it marked a qualitative break with the tradition of revolutionary socialism. See E. Hobsbawm, *Politics for a Rational Left* (London: Verso, 1989); L. Trotsky, *The Spanish Revolution* (New York: Pathfinder, 1973 edn). Others have argued that the right turn in Comintern strategy taken in 1924, and the 'third period' policy of 1928–34, both, in their own ways, marked the retreat of the Comintern from its earlier revolutionary politics. See James, *World Revolution*, p. 217; Hallas, *The Comintern*, p. 126. Nevertheless, Willie Thompson is right to stress the importance of the political shift that occurred in the late 1940s and early 1950s (Thompson, *The Good Old Cause*, p. 10). There were two new programmatic developments in the CPGB in this period: first, the concept of the dictatorship of the proletariat was explicitly dropped from the party's programme; and, second, within the *British Road to Socialism* there was a deployment of evidence based upon the supposed success of the 'people's front' policy in Eastern Europe.
19 Quoted in J. Callaghan, *The Far Left in British Politics* (Oxford: Blackwell, 1987), p. 163.
20 J. Gollan, *Which Way for Socialists?* (London: Communist Party, 1960).
21 J. Gollan, *Gaitskell or Socialism?* (London: Communist Party, 1960), p. 12.
22 P. Le Blanc, *Lenin and the Revolutionary Party* (New Jersey: Humanities Press,

1990), p. 44. See also T. Cliff, *Lenin: Building the Party* (London: Pluto Press, 1975), p. 84; N. Harding, *Lenin's Political Thought* (London: Macmillan, 1983), p. 137; M. Liebman, *Leninism under Lenin* (London: Jonathan Cape, 1975).

23 K. Alexander, 'Democratic Centralism', *The Reasoner*, 1 (1956), p. 9.
24 Ibid., p. 10.
25 E. P. Thompson, 'The New Left', *The New Reasoner*, 9 (1959), pp. 15–17; E. P. Thompson, 'Socialism and the Intellectuals', *Universities and Left Review*, 1 (1957), p. 34.
26 E. P. Thompson, 'Socialism and the Intellectuals: A Reply', *Universities and Left Review*, 2 (1957), p. 21.
27 E. P. Thompson, 'A Psessay in Ephology', *The New Reasoner*, 10 (1959), pp. 5–6.
28 E. P. Thompson, 'Commitment in Politics', *Universities and Left Review*, 6 (1959), p. 55.
29 Kenny, *The First New Left*, p. 40.
30 J. Saville, *Memoirs from the Left* (London: Merlin Press 2003), pp. 120–1.
31 Kenny, *The First New Left*, p. 40. Daly's call, in late 1958, to build 'a genuinely revolutionary socialist party' was dismissed even on the Trotskyist left (Callaghan, *British Trotskyism*, p. 74).
32 J. Saville, 'A Note on West Fife', *The New Reasoner*, 10 (1959), p. 11.
33 Ibid., p. 12; J. Saville, 'Apathy into Politics', *New Left Review*, 1, 4 (1960), pp. 8–9.
34 Saville, 'A Note on West Fife', p. 12.
35 Ibid., p. 11.
36 Thompson, 'Revolution', Thompson (ed.), *Out of Apathy*, p. 302.
37 Thompson, 'At the Point of Decay', in Thompson (ed.), *Out of Apathy*, pp. 8–10.
38 R. Hilton, 'Socialism and the Intellectuals – Four', *Universities and Left Review*, 2 (1957), p. 20; M. Jones, 'Socialism and the Intellectuals – One', *Universities and Left Review*, 2, (1957), p. 16.
39 R. Miliband, 'The Sickness of Labourism', *New Left Review*, 1, 1 (1960), p. 8; M. Newman, *Ralph Miliband and the Politics of the New Left* (London, Merlin Press, 2002), p. 76.
40 R. Miliband, *Parliamentary Socialism* (London, Merlin Press, 1972), p. 346.
41 J. Rex, 'The Labour Bureaucracy', *The New Reasoner*, 6 (1958) pp. 49–60.
42 *New Left Review*, 'Letter to Readers', *New Left Review*, 1, 2 (1960), p. 71.
43 E. P. Thompson, 'Revolution Again', *New Left Review*, 1, 6 (1960), p. 19.
44 *New Left Review* , 'The Consequences of a Conference', Editorial, *New Left Review*, 1, 6 (1960), pp. 3–7.
45 P. Anderson, 'The Left in the Fifties', *New Left Review*, 1, 29 (1965), p. 16.
46 R. Fraser, *1968: A Student Generation in Revolt* (Chatto & Windus: London, 1988), p. 61. Dorothy Thompson, speaking at the British Marxist Historians and the New Social Movements conference at Edge Hill College in June 2002, recounted the story of the night that she, Edward Thompson, Robin Blackburn and Perry Anderson euphorically celebrated Wilson's victory in the 1963 Labour Party leadership election.

47 P. Anderson, 'Critique of Wilsonism', *New Left Review*, 1, 27 (1964), p. 22.
48 A. MacIntyre [1963], 'Labour Policy and Capitalist Planning', in P. Blackledge and N. Davidson (eds), *Alasdair MacIntyre's Engagement with Marxism* (Leiden: Brill, 2008), p. 285; P. Foot, *The Politics of Harold Wilson* (Harmondsworth: Penguin, 1968), p. 317.
49 K. Soper, *Troubled Pleasures* (London: Verso, 1990), p. 89.
50 E. P. Thompson, 'Socialist Humanism', *The New Reasoner*, 1 (1957), pp. 107–9.
51 Ibid., p. 138.
52 Ibid., p. 125.
53 Ibid., p. 121.
54 H. Hanson, 'An Open Letter', *The New Reasoner*, 2 (1957), pp. 79–91; C. Taylor, 'Marxism and Humanism', *The New Reasoner*, 2 (1957); C. Taylor, 'Socialism and Intellectuals – Three', *Universities and Left Review*, 2 (1957), pp. 18–19.
55 A. MacIntyre [1959], 'Notes from the Moral Wilderness', in Blackledge and Davidson (eds), *Alasdair MacIntyre's Engagement with Marxism*, p. 46.
56 Ibid., p. 47.
57 Ibid., p. 50.
58 Ibid., p. 53.
59 Ibid., p. 55.
60 Ibid., p. 61.
61 Ibid., p. 66.
62 A. MacIntyre [1963], 'Trotsky in Exile', in Blackledge and Davidson (eds), *Alasdair MacIntyre's Engagement with Marxism*, p. 273.
63 E. P. Thompson, 'Agency and Choice', *The New Reasoner*, 5 (1958), p. 93; A. MacIntyre, Alasdair [1964], 'Marx', in Blackledge and Davidson (eds), *Alasdair MacIntyre's Engagement with Marxism*, p. 297.
64 A. MacIntyre [1960], 'Freedom and Revolution', in Blackledge and Davidson (eds), *Alasdair MacIntyre's Engagement with Marxism*, pp. 123–34.
65 P. Blackledge, 'On Moving On from "Moving On": Miliband, Marxism and Politics', in C. Barrow, P. Burnham and P. Wetherly (eds), *Class, Power and State in Capitalist Society: Essays on Ralph Miliband* (London: Palgrave, 2008); P. Blackledge, *Perry Anderson, Marxism and the New Left* (London: Merlin, 2004).
66 P. Blackledge 'Freedom, Desire and Revolution', pp. 696–720.
67 J. Saville, 'Britain: Prospects for the Seventies', *Socialist Register* (1970), p. 208; for a survey of the ideas of the International Socialism group (latterly the Socialist Workers Party) in this period, see N. Harris and J. Palmer (eds), *World Crisis* (London: Hutchinson, 1971).
68 Compare the conclusions of my 'The New Left's Renewal of Marxism' with those of Kenny's *The First New Left*, p. 210.

3

Narratives of radical lives

The roots of 1960s activism
and the making of the British left

Celia Hughes

In 1958, 14-year-old Di Parkin accompanied her mother, a housing worker, collecting rents from council tenants in London's Notting Hill. The middle-class teenager was shocked to see several households sharing a single outside toilet. At one address a female tenant did not know how to write her name, and had to be helped by Di's mother to sign the form. Upon rounding a corner the teenage girl was confronted with her most memorable image from the visit: 'I can't remember the exact wording, but it was something like "Niggers Out", and the outside of the houses had all been burned and were all black, and I said to my mother "What was that?"'[1] The charred brickwork testified to the physical violence of the race riots that had engulfed Notting Hill and the surrounding districts of North Kensington in the summer of that year. When her mother explained to her daughter that some people didn't want black people living in the community, Di thought this 'the most bizarre and incomprehensible notion ... There weren't that many [black] people in London so it just seemed bizarre and shocking, really shocking, and it really, really stuck with me'.[2] The memory signified a formative moment in the shaping of Di's early 1960s female self. The teenager's remembered shock of the poverty, illiteracy and racism that marked the lives of the Notting Hill people she met suggests a particular 'structure of feeling' or 'underlying feeling' that would underpin the socialism of her early adult years.[3]

In 1959, Di's membership into the West Surrey Federation of Young Socialists marked the start of twenty years of activity on the revolutionary left. A single mother in the 1970s, 'the business of being a revolutionary and a mother were woven together' through membership in the Trotskyist organisation, the International Socialists (IS).[4] But in the early 1960s Di's activism occurred in the context of the class conscious teenager negotiating new and older patterns of social and economic inequality. In the late 1960s she was one of a small cohort of young people whose political activity around Britain's anti-war movement, the Vietnam Solidarity Campaign (VSC), resulted from involvement with social and political subcultures encountered earlier in the decade when boundaries between left groups were fluid and in the process of transition.

In June 1966, individuals around the Bertrand Russell Peace Foundation and the International Marxist Group (IMG) founded the Vietnam Solidarity Campaign (VSC) as a national coordinating committee for Britain's anti-war movement. By the time of its demise three years later, the VSC had become the heart of an all-encompassing new left scene that incorporated Trotskyist, non-aligned and counter-cultural-inspired artistic, theatrical and community groups alike. As teenagers, apprentices and undergraduates, young working-, lower- and middle-class men and women immersed themselves into these groups, concentrated mainly in North and East London, though not excluding cities and towns in both northern and southern regions of Britain.

This chapter uses oral histories recorded with men and women who were politically active within this extra-parliamentary left network, in order to explore the political, social and emotional roots of their radical journeys. It seeks to understand the structures of feeling that underlay individuals' encounters within particular sites of post-war society, politics and culture. As agents shaping new left cultures in the late 1960s, it will begin to consider how young activists' desire for new ways of seeing and being on the left can be found rooted in their experiences in the family, local community, school and the expanding international arena of Cold War politics. The chapter will show how sensitivity to class dynamics, social injustice, racism and emotional and intellectual affinity for the left developed within these sites. It is concerned with the ways in which early subcultural experiences and engagement with the left occurred in the context of individual histories of feeling and being. To this end it is informed by the recent subjective turn in twentieth-century history that seeks to explore the relationship between 'the self and the social' as well as the emotional and the political.[5]

The post-war family

Stories of 1960s activism began in the family. Sally Alexander has shown how 'iconic moments in spoken and written [London] childhood memories reveal the (remembered) child's self-awareness in relation to the outside world and to the child's own place within it'.[6] These moments of self-awareness often arose through the child's feelings as they observed and communicated with family members. Childhood memories, mediated through the trope of the mother and the father, illuminate the emotional signals and unfulfilled, even unconscious dreams children picked up from parents and other relatives, all of which helped to foster an early relationship to the wider social world. Paul Thompson has shown how the family transmits 'social values and aspirations, fears, world views, domestic skills, and taken-for-granted ways of behaving'.[7] Fragments of childhood memory redolent with 'primitive' and 'visceral feeling' suggest possibilities for understanding the relationship between the childhood landscape and subjectivity.[8]

Post-war Britain remained a society indelibly imprinted by class and class consciousness. Recent historical writing about the 1950s and early 1960s emphasises the continuing dominance of class as a relational social identity.[9] Social surveys of the 1950s and especially the 1960s showed a preoccupation with class.[10] In a 1950–51 questionnaire printed in the *People*, 90 per cent of respondents assigned themselves to a social class without hesitation.[11] However, in a shift from the interwar years when unemployment, economic insecurity and real poverty had, for example, defined experiences of working-class life, in the 1950s and 1960s class differences increasingly interacted with affluence, consumption and teenage culture as well as with new tenets of gender and sexuality. New experiences of class created new subjectivities on the part of both the young and old, men and women.[12] Yet, as Pat Thane argues, the post-war economic boom and the welfare state did not herald a total transformation.[13] The testimonies of former activists show that material circumstances continued to shape youngsters' engagement with their social landscape. Consciousness of having or not having defined early life experiences and social relations, arousing in the child their first sense of awareness that they existed in relation to other people who had more or less than themselves. From such awareness often came the realisation that 'their lives were controlled by more powerful people' who acted seemingly without care for those below them.[14] Raphael Samuel noted how in the 1950s the 'vertical division between "us" and "them" was the dominant idiom in the perception of social life, informing not only politics and culture but also personal comportment'.[15] It was class as a social relationship rather than simply as a hierarchical social structure, and class as a determinant of identity, that registered in the child's consciousness and marked respondents' memories.

As children, interviewees developed an awareness of class from impressionistic, emotional responses to parents' interactions with the social community and the state. Working-class children often grasped early on the unfairness of the social system their parents negotiated every day. Sue Bruley grew up in Surrey in a newly built council estate close to Epsom Downs race course. The working-class estate was part of the extensive post-war urban redevelopment that included council housing programmes financed from government subsidies paid to local authorities. Sue's parents took part in the working-class migration from the inner cities to suburbs situated in the New Towns that came into existence after 1946.[16] Yet the leafy surroundings of the estate failed to disguise her parents' weekly struggle to make ends meet. The sight of the Friday money pile denoted the family's hand-to-mouth existence where 'every penny had to be justified'.[17] As in many working-class households, Sue's mother combined part-time work with the management of the family, including the finances.[18] The traditional domestic gender balance within the household gave Sue close insight into the strain responsibility for the weekly budget placed on her mother:

> My father would get paid on a Friday and there would be piles of money on the table to sort out the bills, and it was weekly pay, you know, and so they would have these conversations about what they could afford … then on Tuesday she would get the family allowance, which was I think seventeen or eighteen shillings … I had to go down the shops with her … because we didn't have a car or anything like that … she was waiting for that money on a Tuesday to feed us on Wednesday, Thursday, Friday, until my Dad got paid on a Friday. It was hand to mouth stuff, so if something happened.[19]

Working-class children learned about the social nuances of class from the uncomfortable feelings they could engender. Interviewees attest to the ways in which childhood sensitivity to the economic insecurities of working-class life framed an uncomfortable relationship to society. Childhood lived 'on the borderlands' could invoke an early sense of injustice towards the social authorities that intervened to bring hardship and humiliation to theirs and their parents' lives.[20] Alan Woodward remembered how his first-hand experiences of near 'abject poverty' in Broadstairs, Kent, fuelled his early antagonism towards society. Prior to leaving school at 16, he undertook four part-time jobs to supplement his parents' meagre wages. The endless round of paper deliveries and car washing induced weariness with a life barely begun, but like Sue it was the distress of witnessing his mother's daily suffering that made him angry. He expressed this anger towards the most visible source of social authority in his life: 'It was a religious society. There was a Catholic church you could see from my back garden and I went to a Church of England school, so it became a natural focus of my … resentment.'[21]

The political and cultural implications of class were often also learned inside the family. Family stories played a role in transmitting emotional and cultural attachment to the Labour left. Roger Cox's father was a lorry driver for the Cartage Department of the Eastern region of British Rail at London's Liverpool Street. As a child he heard repeated stories about his father's battles to defend members of the Bishopgate Branch of the National Union of Railwaymen. From these stories he felt that 'something was not quite right with the world'.[22] For the 1960s activists who went on to develop new cultural expressions of solidarity, the political patterns of post-war social life framed a particular relationship to the social and political landscape. Loyalty to the Labour Party was in this period often 'a hereditary affair'.[23] Working-class children developed an understanding of the longstanding political and cultural ties between the working class and the Labour left through familial relations shaping the social and emotional contours of their early years. In the early 1950s, the Labour Party was a mass organisation with extensive ties to the workingmen's and labour clubs, and to the Co-operative stores marking working-class communities. Raphael Samuel noted that '"Labour" homes and "Labour families" could be numbered in tens of thousands; there would be at least one in any working-class street'.[24]

The 'mental horizons' of class that shaped working-class youngsters' attachment to the Labour Party and the labour movement seemed to have altered little since Richard Hoggart noted the social divisions between 'us' and 'them' characterising his inter-war working-class Leeds.[25] Bob Light described the 'tribal class' in which he and his brothers grew up in the East End of London.[26] From within this tightly knit neighbourhood he assumed a passive acceptance that people like himself, his family and his neighbours voted for the Labour Party and identified with the politics of the Labour left. The social patterns of the household played an important role in transmitting to Bob his family's longstanding left identity. His paternal uncles visited on most Sundays throughout the year; all 'were socialists of one sort or another', though none as strongly left as his Communist father.[27] The brothers' 'violent' political arguments formed part of the 'verbal furniture' of Bob's childhood, interspersed with discussions about football.[28] The close emotional and cultural ties children absorbed between the Labour left and the working class were strengthened through games and childhood talk. At the 1955 general election, Bob was six years old. At his infant school he and his class mates were 'aware that we were Labour, and I don't mean just me, but everybody in the class was aware of that'.[29]

It was not only working-class families who transmitted to children loyalty to the Labour left. In middle-class families too, children inherited the left-wing values of Labour-supporting parents. Martin Shaw's mother was the daughter of a grey-hound stadium manager. Along with her siblings, she had broken from the family's Conservative Party roots to become a firm Labour Party supporter. His father had worked in a butcher's shop until a grammar school education had taken him into a teaching career in adult education. He and Martin's mother both adhered to the liberal Catholicism that identified them as Labour voters. Similarly to working-class children, Martin was sensitive to the left-wing politics shaping his parents' moral values and everyday conversation. In 1956, news of the Suez crisis and the Hungarian uprising so upset the nine-year old that he organised his first activity for the left. He remembered: 'We didn't have a television so it must have been in the newspapers, and I organised a jumble sale outside the gate of our house, which I think raised about two pounds in old money, so that was a formative influence.'[30]

The Communist Party family

In spite of the confident 'never had it so good' discourses of the 1950s and 1960s, post-war Britain was a social and political landscape riddled with uncertainties and contradictions. The Profumo affair of 1963 illuminated the Victorian social policies and value systems still shaping public and private life. But the affair also symbolised the uneasy coexistence of such policies and systems with liberal champions of opinion, who were striving to assemble more egalitarian just social scripts and to cultivate cultural openness.[31] Inside their families, interviewees became alive to the social and moral hypocrisies of their elders and they learned to challenge them. Their narratives testify to the ways in which they lived out the insecurities of the social landscape as subjectivities. Integral to the process of forming a left consciousness was learning to identify with the 'others' living on the margins of British society. In the late 1960s, young activists declared political solidarity with foreign and British agents struggling against oppression, from North Vietnamese guerrilla fighters in the National Liberation Front (NLF) to striking British seamen. The concept of solidarity came to assume powerful subjective meaning; young activists inhabited the imagined identity of radical 'other' to live out a sense of themselves as political and social agents fighting alongside foreign and British subversives.[32] This process too was first practised inside the family.

Children who were raised in Communist Party families often came from an early age to identify themselves and their family members as 'outsiders' or 'other'. Raised to be critical thinkers, many became critically conscious of established authority through direct encounters with its manifest unjustness. Raphael Samuel memorably described the British Communist world as 'a complete society' that was accompanied by a 'complete social identity transcending the limits of class, gender and nationality'.[33] Children born into this world followed the example set by their parents, understanding political activism and discourse as normal, everyday social behaviours. Only when they stepped outside beyond the party did they see the 'otherness' conferred upon them by a hostile establishment. In 1949,

Sarah Cox became entranced by the stories of fellow school pupils recently returned from a large youth rally in Eastern Europe. She was eager to join in their Communist activities, but was dissuaded by her father who had left the party in 1940 when he joined the civil service. He urged her, '"Please don't", because it would have put his job at risk. He got investigated by a really quite nasty guy ... he got put through the mill and it nearly drove him into a nervous breakdown, but he would still go on and talk about Marxism.'[34]

Although Britain escaped the worst excesses of America's McCarthyism, anti-Communist investigations conducted amidst the paranoia of the Cold War still wrought personal devastation upon their victims.[35] Steve Jeffery's first experience of being attacked as part of a dissident collective occurred in 1962. The British secret service made an application to his school's headmaster to find out about any Communist Party members at the school.[36] In the wake of the William Vassall spy case of that year, the threat came closer to home after Steve's uncle was blacklisted and thrown out of his job as civil service union officer. After questions were raised in the House of Commons about why the headmaster should be exposing the political affiliation of his pupils, Steve felt a sense of 'who' and 'we' being defined.[37]

Communist culture instilled in children distrust of established authority. Interviewees raised within this background learned to question the opinions and actions of authority where they contravened their own moral framework. This manner of thinking was vital to young activists' willingness to challenge the political and social values of late 1960s university, state and government authorities. Steve explained: 'This was a period in which you were not expected to question authority. You were expected just to sit down and do what you were told, and here, largely because of the political ideas we had, which were running counter to the system, we were most likely to be saying, well what about this, what about that?'[38] Within this framework of critical questioning, Communist Party children often gained their first experiences of political resistance alongside parents and neighbours. The act of demonstrating became normalised as an extension of family and community culture. Children learned to think of political protest as ordinary everyday acts of resistance. Steve remembered the clashes between his protesting parents and the police in 1949. His earliest memory of demonstrating with his family was 'being pushed in a wheel chair in a demonstration [against German rearmament] the Communist Party organised ... in Downing Street. We were charged by police horses'. Steve's memory signified the start of a seamless progression of political activity that began with participation in Youth Campaign for Nuclear Disarmament (CND), and moved on to membership in the

Committee of 100, the non-violent direct action group campaigning for nuclear disarmament, from 1961. By the time Steve went to the London School of Economics (LSE) in the autumn of 1965, he carried with him eight years of activist experience within a left milieu that included New Left intellectuals John Saville and Edward Thompson, Jewish Communist intellectuals, and white South African, Jewish émigrés living nearby in London's Highgate district. The latter brought stories of underground activities on behalf the African National Congress (ANC) party whose militant Defence Campaign was a world away from the good-natured, picnic atmosphere of CND marches. All of these discourses he 'put into a kind of melting pot of political ideas and interests', which he carried into the metropolitan activist scene following the LSE occupation in April 1966.[39]

Jews, immigrants and anti-racism

Sensitivity to the plight of 'outsiders' was deeply imprinted in children of immigrants or refugees, who carried with them the burden of their parents' displacement. In the 1950s, children of Jewish refugees struggled to live up to the task of belonging bestowed upon them from birth. They inhabited an imagined image of 'other' conjured from unspoken signals parents and older relatives transmitted. For this wartime generation, 'becoming English' offered the protection of belonging, and adopting the social and cultural tenets of their new homeland was a method of survival in a society in which to be a Jew was not an invitation to social acceptance. Tony Kushner has argued that in the immediate post-war years, austerity and the retreat from Empire resulted in a loss of esteem that contributed to a new inward-looking English national identity.[40] The immigration policies of the British government carried a clear message about which outsiders could or could not become British. As David Cesarani has stated, 'East Europeans were deemed worth this exertion [to integrate], but Jews, Blacks and Asians were not'.[41] The Jewish terrorism that arose over the 'British-Jewish' Palestine conflict, and the August 1947 riots targeting Jews in several British towns, made British Jews uneasily conscious about their marginality. This sense of insecurity was heightened by recent revelations about the nature and scale of the Holocaust in Western and Eastern Europe.[42] Surrounded by unexplained contradictions, children of refugees lived with an unspoken legacy of a profound trauma adults tried to conceal. Victor Seidler explained his understanding of the silences within the family home:

> I don't know what or how I knew it, but I knew something *bad* or dramatic or catastrophic had happened ... I knew there was no family ... but you couldn't ask about it, it was kind of unspeakable ... [this] meant that often

we were in rooms where people were talking and we did understand, but we
were told that we didn't. But we did.[43]

Insecurity could be expressed in different social, cultural and psychological
forms, but a common effect was to make children uneasily conscious of
their marginality.

Mica Nava discerned her parents' foreignness through observing their
deliberate, but awkward efforts to belong. The family lived in the middle-
class, Tory Home Counties, near Newbury, where assimilation meant a
particular kind of Englishness. Her mother impressed upon her daughter
the important relationship between social behaviour and belonging; she
dressed in the conservative fashions worn by women in the area, and
encouraged Mica to participate in the local pony club and gymkhanas.
Yet she also clung to the radical tenets that had marked her teenage years
in Vienna before the war. She broke the Home Counties political-gender
norms by standing for the parish council as a Labour Party candidate. In
later years, as a 1950s teenager, Mica expressed the radicalism her mother
had struggled to suppress, gravitating to radical corners of European cities
from London to Paris. Her self-expressed identity of rebel and outsider
seemed to be a specific response to her parents' half-hearted attempts
at assimilation. She echoed their 'boldly expressed political views and
emotions' that spoke of a 'need to protect others and correct injustice'.[44]
Instilled with an instinctive empathy for those on the social margins, in the
early 1960s she took on the injustices surrounding racial politics, and by
the end of the decade found a home within underground and cosmopolitan
enclaves around the London VSC.

As they began to be conscious of wider societies and international
politics, the insecurity children picked up from Jewish and refugee
parents coloured their engagement with the Cold War conflicts of the
late 1950s and early 1960s. Sabby Sagall was born in September 1937. His
parents were Russian Jews who had fled to Britain in the mid-1930s. He
explained how his childhood understanding of living in an unstable world
was compounded by the developing impetus of international events he
witnessed in the 1960s.

> You had a sense, in the mid-1960s, of a world that was falling apart, that
> had been reconstructed, you know, and on all sides you looked you had
> the Vietnam War and the anti-Vietnam War movement, the VSC, the civil
> rights movement in the United States, you had, you know, massive student
> movements developing in German, France, Italy, crucially in 1968, so all
> these factors, you know, gave one a sense of a world in turmoil.

Politically, Sabby first expressed his sense of otherness by supporting the
Labour Party. In the mid-1960s he was also one of a small number of male

LSE students for whom Zionism was integral to the socialist identity they invested inside the Socialist Society and the IS prior to the June War of 1967. The events surrounding 1956 had discounted the Communist Party as a serious political option for most critically thinking young people moving to the left. Even before they became aware of the significance of this year, the legacy of persecution that first generation migrants transferred to their children inculcated a stridently anti-Communist stance. Anna Paczuska's parents were Poles who had come to Britain during the 1940s to escape the worst excesses of Communist-controlled Poland. During the Second World War they had fought with the Polish Free Forces, and prior to that Anna's mother had been interned in prisoner camps in Russian and Poland. By 1964, Anna had begun to think of herself as a socialist, but she had heard enough stories about the brutal suppression of Soviet Communism and wanted to find an alternative Marxism. At Durham University, in 1967, she joined the IS, which espoused the slogan 'Neither Washington nor Moscow, but International Socialism'. She explained the group's appeal in the context of her family's history:

> About that time the International Socialists ... translated into English from a French translation of a Polish pamphlet, called an 'Open Letter to the Party', and it was a letter by two Polish socialists called Jacek Kuroń and Karol Mozelewski ... It was an open letter criticising the so-called socialism in Poland. It basically argued that without meat and without people having enough to eat, how could this be socialism, and it sort of struck a chord with me, because I suddenly realised that you could be left, but disagree with the regimes in Eastern Europe.[45]

Race and the left

As part of young activists' journeys towards the left, experiences of alterity came in different forms, and occurred in various public and private sites. Anti-racist tenets were often transmitted through liberal-minded parents. James Swinson remembered his mother being 'staunchly anti-apartheid'. She was a cook at the LSE and would often invite South African students to join them for Christmas.[46] Other interviewees learned to embrace the plight of the other as part of their stand against the hypocrisies of middle-class parents and neighbours. In her teenage diaries Prue Chamberlain expressed dislocation from a morality her parents equated with education and social status. She took it for granted that she would vote Labour because the party represented the antithesis of her father's rural middle-class values.[47] Respondents' narratives of anti-racist beliefs illuminate the complex relationship between selfhood, politics and culture in post-war Britain. Defining themselves against the middle-class norms of parents

and institutions, they negotiated themselves in relation to represen-
tations of otherness within the prevailing culture. This was especially
so for the lower middle-class boys who rejected the elite masculinity of
their public schools. Against the schools' pre-war imperial codes, the
image of the non-white male battling for self-determination provided
a sort of self-distancing from the boys' own immediate struggles. At
Liverpool College, in the late 1950s, Max Farrar was only half-aware of
Liverpool's black under-class population. However, consciousness of race,
otherness and the fight for civil rights came from tales of discomfort his
half-Trinidadian friend told about his father's experiences inside his white
middle-class medical circles. Surrounded by perverse, unjust authorities,
the American civil rights movement provided a point of identification, and
he and his friend began to read the novels of the civil rights activist James
Baldwin. Around the same time, Max became drawn into a bohemian
youth subculture that led him into CND and, in 1965, he joined Medical
Aid for Vietnam.[48]

The timing of these teenagers' anti-racist sensibilities was no coincidence.
In the late 1950s and early 1960s, discourses of race were to be heard
loudly in British politics, culture, and society following the acceleration
of immigration by non-white Commonwealth citizens. Di's memory of
racial discord in Notting Hill, mentioned at the beginning of the chapter,
indicates that as children and adolescents, interviewees were alert to some
of the tensions concerning the expanding non-white population. Novels
and films such as *Saturday Night and Sunday Morning* made reference
to incidents of racial abuse occurring at workplaces and on the streets
of Britain's urban landscape. News reports of America's burgeoning civil
rights struggle only added to youngsters' impressions of the profound
injustices contradicting post-war narratives of equality and freedom won
by the two wartime democracies, Britain and the United States of America.
These were intertwined with the 'uncritical and conservative narratives of
the war' colouring British life, and subscribed to by their parents.[49]

Overseas travel also brought some interviewees direct early experiences
of the racial inequalities that remained entrenched in the vestiges of
Britain's post-war Empire. In the mid-to-late 1960s, before and following
university, overseas travelling and volunteering brought a number of
young activists first-hand experiences of injustice, racism and foreign
national liberation struggles in countries including South Africa, North
and South America, Palestine and Vietnam. In these foreign landscapes,
individuals fostered international political perspectives and, through
friendships and love affairs, formed personal ties to countries that gave
issues an immediate urgency. Many returned home unable to settle back
into their old lives, compelled to invest themselves into campaigns for

social and political justice. In 1964, Prue undertook Voluntary Service Overseas (VSO) teaching in Zimbabwe. Exposed to daily racial prejudice, she began to reflect on the severe poverty and inequalities she observed in relation to her earlier European travels. During her first year in the copper belt she became uncomfortably conscious of her privilege as a white middle-class woman. Desperate to experience the 'real' Africa, she defied her school authorities, and joined a group of white Europeans, who were working in the all-black, rural area of Kasama. But away from the confines of the whites-only school, she was shocked by the intensity of the poverty she observed ('children with huge pot bellies'), and by the 'blank hatred' she heard black people express towards white people.[50] Her teenage diary reveals how her experiences in Zimbabwe prompted a crisis of faith in the conservative morality of her Anglican upbringing. They stimulated a social conscience that asked difficult questions about her social responsibilities as a human citizen. She questioned, 'Would I have had sufficient courage to denounce Nazi atrocities?'[51] Upon returning to Britain in December 1967, the class inequalities that greeted her in the local Hackney comprehensive framed her moral conscience within a socialist framework, but she struggled to find a left group that could accommodate her particular experiences. Before she finally joined the IS in 1970, Prue participated in various anti-racist projects in the capital through associations such as the Campaign Against Racial Discrimination (CARD) and the Action Campaign to Outlaw Racial Discrimination (ACORD).[52]

Radical youth subcultures

The new left cultures that emerged around the VSC in the mid-1960s grew from radical subcultures young activists shaped earlier in the decade. Encounters with these subcultures often occurred in late adolescence, when 'angry' literature and theatre, new wave films and the radical bomb culture surrounding CND reinforced 'ways of looking and being receptive to the fine nuances and meanings' embedded within social interactions, politics and cultures.[53] They spoke to youngsters' concern with the tangible and the present that the unfairness and instability of the surrounding world provoked. The accumulated experience of their early lives transformed the meaning of these radical youth cultures to provide new ways of seeing social norms, relationships and Cold War politics. Above all, in the company of like-minded young people within these subcultures, interviewees heard calls for autonomous action.

In 1959, John Charlton and his friends formed the core members of an unofficial socialist youth group founded in Gateshead,

Newcastle-upon-Tyne. The society existed amidst a fluid left culture that included links with the Labour Party, CND, the New Left and even the Young Communist League. At a time when socialist ideas existed 'in a very fluid state' and when activism in CND appealed to members' youthful desire for action, the milieu enabled young socialists to experiment with political ideas and forms, and to make sense of themselves in relation to a variety of individuals and experiences. The young men belonged to a milieu of working- and lower middle-class grammar school boys who shared each others' class conscious feelings. In 'Angry Young Men' literature such as Kingsley Amis's 1954 novel, *Lucky Jim*, and John Wain's *Hurry on Down*, the young men shared a collective cultural 'effervescence' around class.[54] John remembered 'lots of argument, lots of discussion going on all the time'.[55]

By 1962, the New Left was in decline; many of its activists had begun to drift away to more promising milieus such as the Labour Party and the CND. The Labour Party Young Socialists that John, Di and other working- and lower middle-class teenagers joined were situated on the edge of the old New Left, the Labour left and CND. A small cohort of the men and women who joined the two main Trotskyist groups in the VSC, IS and the IMG, first encountered these groups thorough Labour Party and Young Socialists (YS) circles. In February 1960, the decision of the Labour Party to launch a new national youth organisation prompted Trotskyist groups, the Socialist Review Group (the name of the IS prior to 1964) and the Socialist Labour League to use the opportunity for recruitment.[56] Through CND, YS meetings and the Socialist Review's youth paper, *Young Guard*, YS men and a few women were absorbed into a youthful revolutionary culture that combined beer drinking and folk-singing with activity in the labour movement.[57] As the main youth organisation on the left, the YS attracted a predominantly working-class base – from manual, though occasionally white-collar homes – and involved a specifically working-class political culture.

The appeal of early left cultures often derived from the release, friendship and fun their lively sociability offered adolescents. As with other sites of early 1960s subculture, the folk and jazz clubs, skiffle and beat cellars, coffee bars and pubs, the left youth spaces of this period could bring together young people from different social classes.[58] In 1958, aged thirteen, Victor discovered a local youth club across the road from the family's Hendon home in north-west London. Members were sons and daughters of Jewish families, many of them working class with a range of migration experiences. However, the fact that the youth club was a Jewish space gave Victor a sense of belonging that his middle-class male peer group at school was unable to. The group introduced him to intellectual writings such as Martin Booba, whose work provided a root back to the Jewish cultural tradition that Victor's father had introduced him to in the synagogue. It also introduced him to CND.[59]

In the late 1950s and early 1960s, CND prepared the political and cultural terrain for the New Left milieus at the end of the decade. As the largest extra-parliamentary organisation in post-war Britain, the Campaign provided the first 'brave cause' through which youngsters could hone a critical voice against the moral bankruptcy of state power.[60] James Hinton referred to the 'magnificent moral simplicity' of the Bomb that 'started me off [on the left]'.[61] What distinguished young CND activists from teenagers who wore the upturned 'Y' CND badge or who drifted to marches simply to annoy adults, was their 'propensity to identify themselves with certain remote events' most of their peers were 'less keenly sensitised to'.[62] To adolescents already engaged in the international politics fuelling the nuclear crisis, CND activism seemed to be self-evident. Bernard Reagan explained: 'It always struck me that, if this is what one thought, you should try and do something about it.'[63] The resounding sentiment, aside from the sense of community the marches fostered, was that the strength of the movement's appeal owed much to its capacity to engender spontaneous action and individual initiative. The experience of direct action young activists tasted in the Committee of 100 sit-downs ruined many for 'committee meetings and points of order' forever more.[64] CND established the foundations for grassroots canvassing that would be fundamental to the do-it-yourself-politics surrounding the VSC.

For many interviewees, CND provided a rite of passage into socialist politics inside the YS, the IS, the Socialist Labour League and the Week (from 1968 the IMG), or involvement in a variety of anarchist or libertarian groups that had sprung up in the vicinity. On CND's 1966 Easter march, Phil Hearse and his friends saw 'a group of people carrying red flags and banners stating the National Liberation Front'.[65] The marchers were an early contingent of VSC supporters whose declaration of solidarity with the Democratic Republic of Vietnam and the National Liberation Front (NLF) represented a radical departure from the left's moderate stance over the Vietnam War. As a sixth-former at Ealing boys' grammar school, Phil joined the Week group, and he began organising pupils from his school onto early VSC demonstrations.[66]

The social community fostered by CND marches and early left milieus only added to youngsters' feeling that they had become 'political in a different kind of way'.[67] Nineteen-sixties pop music, dancing, desire and the promise of sex were social and cultural practices that characterised many early 1960s left spaces where teenagers found a sense of belonging. This was a feeling young activists would carry on into the left groups and socialist societies many went on to join at metropolitan and provincial universities in the mid- to late 1960s. From 1967, activity against the Vietnam War, through the VSC, and the growth of the student movement, transformed the left subcultures of the early 1960s into the eclectic New Left cultures of the late 1960s. From 1966 onwards, IS and the IMG expanded steadily in alignment with the VSC. These two groups began increasingly to displace the Labour Party as the left organisations of choice for students disappointed by the moral and political betrayals of Harold Wilson's Labour government. Public spending cuts, wages restraint forced by the Prices and Incomes Board, immigration and race, the Industrial Relations Bill of 1969 and the overseas problems of Rhodesia, all added impetus to the increasing radicalisation of young activists. The early tenets of left consciousness often found active expression at university where exposure to longstanding labour politics occurred in ever greater dialogue with an international New Left politics. Henceforth, political subjectivity became invested with an internationalism that took working-, lower and middle-class students, geographically and imaginatively, further away from home. Young activists saw at first hand or through the visual mediums of television, film and photographs, the possibilities which the actions of foreign students and workers presented for external and subjective change. These new political possibilities would inform their own grassroots activism in the anti-war movement, in student strikes, in the factories, docks, tenants' campaigns and, by 1968-69, for women, in the Women's Liberation Movement.

Conclusion

This chapter has considered the stories activist men and women told about their entry into the New Left spaces that emerged around the VSC in the late 1960s. For this radical cohort, the activist network which spread from the capital and expanded to incorporate contact with international movements formed the site of adult lives where men and women sought to live out authentic and liberated forms of being as political, social and sexual subjects. The chapter has focused on their childhood and adolescent encounters with a post-war landscape that exuded confusing and often contradictory messages about the meanings of British modernity. To understand the new political, cultural and social patterns that defined Britain's New Left spaces, it is important to consider the makings of the early subjectivities that informed it. Interviewees' narratives show how, in the late 1950s and early 1960s, they projected childhood structures of feeling (related to loneliness, alterity and responsibility for the past and the present) onto local and foreign struggles for human justice in order to make sense of their individual histories and experiences. Radical left identity evolved through ongoing dialogue between the individual, their milieu, and the dominant culture and body politic. Consciousness of otherness created a search for belonging, which interviewees often found on the margins of the left where they were able to incorporate tastes for European existentialism and the cultural radicalism of the late 1950s and early 1960s. Not only did this provide an avenue of escape from childhood insecurities, but for some interviewees it also facilitated a cultural connection with their European heritage that placed emphasis on the quality of experience in the present. In a world where the past felt threatening and the Bomb made the future uncertain and potentially destructive, young activists found release in the agency early left spaces offered for improving the quality of current individual and collective experience.

Notes

1 Di Parkin, interview, Totnes, 27 April 2009.
2 Ibid.
3 P. Filmer, 'Structures of Feeling and Socio-cultural Formations: the Significance of Literature and Experience to Raymond Williams' Sociology of Culture', *British Journal of Sociology*, 54, 2 (2003), 202; S. Alexander, 'Memory Talk: London Childhoods', in S. Radstone, and B. Schwarz (eds), *Memory: Histories, Theories, Debates* (New York: Ford University Press, 2010), p. 236.
4 Letter from Di Parkin to Annie Howells, spring, 1973, in the Private Archive of Di Parkin (hereafter DPA).
5 C. Feely, 'From Dialectics to Dancing: Reading, Writing and the Experience of Everyday Life in the Diaries of Frank P. Forster', *History Workshop Journal*, 69 (2010), p. 92; M. Francis, 'Tears, Tantrums, and Bared Teeth: The Emotional Economy of Three Conservative Prime Ministers, 1951–63', *Journal of British Studies*, 41 (2002), pp. 354–87; J. Hinton, *Nine Wartime Lives: Mass Observation and the Making of a Modern Self* (Oxford: Oxford University Press, 2010); 'Sisterhood and After: the Women's Liberation Oral History Project', www.sussex.ac.uk/clhlwr/1-7-11-3.html, accessed 12 September 2012.
6 Alexander, 'Memory Talk', p. 236.
7 P. Thompson, 'Family Myths, Models and Desires in the Shaping of Individual Life Paths', in D. Bertaux and P. Thompson (eds), *International Year Book of Oral History and Life Stories: Between Generations: Family Myths, Models and Memories*, vol. 2 (Oxford: Oxford University Press, 1993), pp. 14–37.
8 Alexander, 'Memory Talk', p. 236.
9 S. Brooke, '"Slumming" in Swinging London? Class, Gender and the Post-war City in Nell Dunn's *Up the Junction* (1963)', *Cultural and Social History*, 9, 33 (2012), pp. 429–49; S. Brooke, 'Gender and Working Class Identity in Britain during the 1950s', *Journal of Social History*, 34, (2001), pp. 773–95;

C. Langhamer, 'The Meanings of Home in Postwar Britain', pp. 341–62; M. Savage, 'Affluence and Social Change in the Making of Technocratic Middle-Class Identities: Britain, 1939–55', *Contemporary British History*, 22, 4 (2008), pp. 457–76; S. Todd, 'Affluence, Class and Crown Street: Reinvesting the Post-war Working Class', *Contemporary British History*, 22, 4 (2008), p. 510.

10 Todd, 'Affluence, Class and Crown Street', p. 510.

11 Cited in D. Kynaston, *Family Britain, 1951–57* (London: Bloomsbury, 2009), p. 135.

12 Brooke, '"Slumming" in Swinging London?', pp. 429–49.

13 P. Thane, 'Introduction. Exploring Post-War Britain', *Cultural and Social History*, 9, 2 (2012), p. 273.

14 Ibid.

15 R. Samuel, *The Lost World of British Communism* (London: Verso, 2006), p. 10.

16 M. Clapson, 'Working-class Women's Experiences of Moving to New Housing Estates in England since 1919', *Twentieth Century British History*, 10, 3 (1999), p. 346.

17 Sue Bruley, interview, London, 14 May 2010.

18 Brooke, 'Gender and Working Class Identity', p. 780.

19 Sue Bruley, interview, London, 14 May 2010.

20 C. Steedman, *Landscape for a Good Woman: A Story of Two Lives* (London: Virago, 1986), p. 144.

21 Alan Woodward, interview, London, 2 January 2009.

22 Roger Cox, interview, London, 24 March 2009.

23 Ibid., p. 63.

24 Ibid.

25 R. Hoggart, *The Uses of Literacy* (Harmondsworth: Penguin, 1961), p. 72.

26 Bob Light, interview, London, 28 March, 2009.

27 Ibid.

28 Ibid.

29 Ibid.

30 Martin Shaw, interview, Brighton, 15 January 2009.

31 See M. Donnelly, *Sixties Britain* (Harlow: Pearson Longman, 2005) and F. Mort, *Capital Affairs: London and the Making of the Permissive Society* (London: Yale University Press, 2010).

32 C. Hughes, 'The Socio-cultural Milieu of the Left in Post-War Britain', (unpublished Ph.D. thesis, University of Warwick, 2012), pp. 173–6.

33 Samuel, *The Lost World of British Communism*, p. 13.

34 Sarah Cox, interview, London, 24 March 2009.

35 P. Hennessy and G. Brownfeld, 'Britain's Cold War Security Purge: The Origins of Positive Vetting', *Historical Journal*, 25, 4 (1982), pp. 965–74.

36 Steve Jefferys, interview, London, 13 November 2008.

37 Ibid.

38 Ibid.

39 Ibid.

40 T. Kushner, 'Anti-Semitism and Austerity: The August 1947 Riots', in P. Panayi (ed.), *Racial Violence in Britain, 1840–1950* (Leicester: Leicester University Press, 1993), p. 159.

41 D. Cesarani, *Justice Delayed: How Britain Became a Refuge for Nazi War Criminals* (London: Phoenix, 1992), p. 81.

42 Kushner, 'Anti-Semitism and Austerity', pp. 159–60.

43 Victor Seidler, interview, London, 13 December 2011.

44 M. Nava, *Visceral Cosmopolitanism: Gender, Culture and the Normalisation of Difference* (Oxford: Berg, 2007), pp. 138–9.

45 Anna Paczuska, interview, London, 4 January 2010.

46 James Hinton, interview, London, 2 February 2010.

47 Prue Chamberlayne, interview, London, 8 May 2009.

48 Max Farrar, interview, Leeds, 5 June 2009.

49 M. Francis, *The Flyer: British Culture and the Royal Air Force 1939–1945* (Oxford: Oxford University Press, 2008), p. 7.

50 Prue Chamberlayne, interview.

51 The diary of Prue Chamberlayne, 20 September 1964, p. 43.

52 Prue Chamberlayne, interview.

53 C. Lichtenstein and T. Schregenberger, *As Found: The Discovery of the Ordinary* (Baden: Lars Müller, 1993), p. 10.

54 J. Charlton, *Don't You Hear the H-Bomb's Thunder? Youth and Politics on Tyneside in the Late 'Fifties and Early 'Sixties* (Pontypool: Merlin Press, 2007), p. 66; John Charlton, interview, Newcastle-Upon-Tyne, 2 June 2009.

55 John Charlton, interview.

56 P. Shipley, *Revolutionaries in Modern Britain* (London: Bodley Head, 1976), pp. 92–5.

57 I. Birchall, 'Building "the Smallest, Mass Revolutionary Party in the World": Socialist Workers Party, 1951–79' www.marxists.org/history/etol/revhist/orthordox/smp/smp1.html, accessed 13 May 2009.

58 A. Marwick, *The Sixties: Cultural Revolution in Britain, France, Italy and the United States, c. 1958–c.1974* (Oxford: Oxford University Press, 1998), p. 55.

59 Victor Seidler, interview.

60 J. Osborne, *Look Back in Anger!* (London: Faber, 1957), pp. 84–5.

61 James Hinton, interview, Coventry, 20 November 2008.

62 F. Parkin, *Middle-Class Radicalism: The Social Bases of the Campaign for Nuclear Disarmament* (Manchester: Manchester University Press, 1968), pp. 160–1.

63 Bernard Reagan, interview, London, 20 August 2009.

64 S. Rowbotham, *Promise of a Dream: Remembering the Sixties* (London: Verso, 2000), p. 69.

65 Phil Hearse, interview, London, 24 December 2008.

66 Ibid.

67 Cited in R. Fraser (ed.), *1968: A Student Generation in Revolt: An International Oral History* (New York: Chatto and Windus, 1988), p. 35.

4

Marching separately, seldom together

The political history of two principal trends in British Trotskyism, 1945–2009

Phil Burton-Cartledge

The Socialist Party (SP) (formerly the Militant Tendency) and the Socialist Workers Party (SWP) traditions have proven to be the most durable and high profile of all of Britain's competing Trotskyist tendencies. Their opponents in the International Marxist Group and the Socialist Labour League/Workers' Revolutionary Party (SLL/WRP) each met limited success and influence in the labour movement and wider social movements, but by the end of the 1980s both had splintered into very small competing groups. The SWP and Militant/SP on the other hand outlived the 'official' Communist Party of Great Britain (CPGB) and from the collapse of the Soviet Union to the present day have continued to influence labour movement and wider politics, albeit episodically.

This chapter is concerned with providing an overview of their development, dating from the end of the Second World War to the onset of the 2009 economic crisis. More attention is paid here to the period between the fall of the USSR and the fall of Lehman Brothers for the simple reason there is next to no readily available reference material dating from 1992 onwards. The discussion aims to partially address that gap.

It will argue that their development must be located in the context of the extensive restructuring of British capital, the shift toward post-industrial and post-Fordist economics and work patterns, and with that the attendant recomposition of the working class and the sharp decline of labour movement strength.[1] I suggest their development can analytically be divided into two distinct post-1989 phases – an initial move away from a 'one true party' building project (which, in a number of ways, was sustained by the particular configuration of labour movement politics during the post-war settlement) to more cooperative political working with each other and smaller organisations on the far left. The second sees a subsequent renewal of emphasis on party building. Simultaneously, each of the two parties tried turning outward via a number of party-led initiatives that tried engaging with wider forces, but ultimately if these campaigns threatened party integrity they were quickly wound up.

This chapter omits discussion of the acrimonious 2006 split in the Scottish Socialist Party, despite each organisation playing an active role in it (and, in the case of the SP's Scottish co-thinkers, the prime movers in founding it). The discussion below therefore pertains to both organisations with respect to England and Wales.

The post-war period

Discussion of golden ages always run the risk of myth making, but the 1945–79 period saw the labour movement reach the peak of its strength in terms of absolute numbers of trade unionists, percentage of industry governed by collective bargaining and the closed shop, and ability to challenge capital through industrial action.[2] This was the age of truly 'classical' working-class organisation. Politically, the mass membership Labour Party contested power against an even more massive Conservative Party apparatus.[3] The political route for labour was unambiguously through Labour. As far as the space to its left was concerned, the CPGB possessed considerable – by far left standards – weight in the unions, but apart from the 1945 election it never again returned candidates to parliament. Politically and industrially, the room for smaller Trotskyist alternatives to Labour and 'official' communism were tightly circumscribed.

Militant and the Labour Party

All British Trotskyist organisations can trace their lineage back to the Revolutionary Communist Party (RCP), the 'official' section of Trotsky's Fourth International (FI). During its short life (1944–49) it formally united all active Trotskyists in Britain. However, from 1947 onwards a *de facto* split opened in the organisation. The debate over the expansion of official communism, the election of a reform-minded Labour government, the division between work inside and outside Labour, and factional moves internationally prised the party apart. By 1950 the RCP was no more.[4]

Ted Grant, the acknowledged founder and leader of what later became the Militant Tendency, rose to early prominence in Trotskyist politics with the Workers' International League, one of two small groups that fused to form the RCP in 1944. After a series of disputes with post-RCP successor groups, and with little room for an open party-building project, Grant and his supporters entered the Labour Party. By the mid- to late 1950s the group numbered around 20 members scattered across several constituency parties in London and Liverpool. Summer 1957 saw it adopt the name

Revolutionary Socialist League (RSL) and began publishing *Socialist Fight* in early 1958. The rationale for its 'entrism'[5] was established at the outset and remained Grant's view until his death in 2006:

> When the masses first begin to move, they always turn to the traditional mass organisations. They will turn to the Labour Party time and time again because there is no alternative – no mass revolutionary party.[6]

The RSL sought to maximise its impact on Labour's structures by capturing positions with maximum political leverage and a minimum of routine work. But the RSL initially found progress difficult, partly owing to the place occupied by the SLL, and similar-sized competition from the Socialist Review Group/International Socialists (SRG/IS) and forerunners of the 'official' Fourth International franchise, the International Marxist Group (IMG).[7] Nevertheless, in 1964, *Militant* was launched from an organisational base of around 40 members.[8]

Another fortuitous development came in 1969 with the setting up of Labour Party Young Socialists. Previously the Labour hierarchy had expelled the SLL over the control of its youth section.[9] Their retreat from entrism in late 1964 in conjunction with similar turns made by their IS rivals presented Militant (as the RSL became known) a clear field. By 1970 Militant secured a majority on the Labour Party Young Socialists (LPYS) National Committee and in 1972 obtained the seat on Labour's National Executive Committee (NEC) reserved for the youth representative. Militant had won control of a strategic section of the party apparatus that provided a conveyor of young activists, possessing 1,000 members by 1975, 1,800 in 1979, 4,700 in 1983 and 8,000 in 1986.[10]

It was during the 1980s that Militant's influence reached its peak. Labour Party rules demanded Militant maintain the facade of being 'just' a paper with a network of supporters. By 1983 the deception was no longer enough and five members of the paper's 'editorial board', including Grant and Militant/SP general secretary, Peter Taaffe, were expelled. The year 1983 also saw two supporters, Terry Fields and Dave Nellist, elected as Labour MPs, and Militant won the leadership of Liverpool City Council's ruling Labour group. The latter led to a bitter dispute with the government as the council battled for the resources to finance house building and job creation schemes, often mobilising mass demonstrations of support. At this point Militant claimed 1,000 adherents on Merseyside alone.[11] The struggle climaxed with the council group failing to set a legal rate (adopting a deficit budget) and the national Labour leadership moved to expel nine leading Liverpool activists for crossing the line into illegality. Simultaneously the government surcharged 47 Liverpool councillors who were subject to heavy fines and bans from office.

The second key struggle for Militant was the movement against the poll tax and its leadership of the Anti-Poll Tax Federation. Not only did this allow them to claim they contributed to the resignation of Margaret Thatcher, it also implanted them in a small number of working-class communities, particularly central Glasgow.

All this was made possible because Militant had grown up within the traditional party of the British working class. The discipline of entry work allowed Militant activists to capture party structures and use them as leverage to open up more of the 'host' to their influence. By adapting itself with some success to the political conditions of post-war working-class politics, it built itself up as a distinctive Trotskyist brand that became something of a household name. But this was to change as the character of class politics changed.

The rise of the SWP

The immediate origins of the SWP are located in the RCP and FI disputes over the class nature of the USSR and its client states. It escalated at the outbreak of the Korean War, where, in opposition to the rest of the Trotskyist movement and raising the slogan 'Neither Washington nor Moscow', Tony Cliff's group adopted a neutral position on the conflict. In 1950 Cliff's group of 33 activists began publishing *Socialist Review* and formalised itself as the Socialist Review Group a year later.[12] Like its opponents, SRG pursued an entry course throughout the 1950s, believing the political environment for independent work was too hostile. Therefore its efforts were directed toward recruiting from the Labour League of Youth and trade unions but remained 'a purely propaganda group; it was not able to make any meaningful intervention in the class struggle'.[13] Unlike Healy's deep entry 'Club', it failed to benefit from the 10,000-strong exodus of Communist Party members after its official defence of the 1956 Soviet invasion of Hungary.

Fortunes changed in the early 1960s. The moribund Labour League of Youth (LLY) was relaunched as Young Socialists in 1961, which gave the SRG's entry work a new lease of life. The vehicle for this was primarily *Young Guard*, a collaborative journal with other broad left tendencies not under the SRG's editorial control, but who informally provided its political line. In 1962 it became the International Socialists and through its YS work and paper, *Industrial Worker* (later *Labour Worker*, and today *Socialist Worker*) managed to expand to 200 members by 1964. Four years later it had 1,000 adherents.

A key difference between the SRG/IS and its orthodox rivals was on organisation. Unlike the SLL and RSL, up until 1968 the group was officially federalist, operating with looser party discipline and a more open culture of political dissent. Its Trotskyist opposition were committed to building monolithic democratic centralist parties. For Birchall it meant IS could advantageously work in the 'broader movement', but a comparative lack of discipline meant it lacked focus.[14] But in 1968 the group's independent work perspective changed. The radicalisation associated with the Vietnam anti-war movement, student militancy, French May events and the Prague Spring seemingly broke the political deadlock around independent party building. The IS decamped from Labour. It appealed for unity with other revolutionaries and was largely ignored, attracting only the small Workers' Fight (WF) group (today's Alliance for Workers' Liberty), which remained an internal faction for three years. The open turn coincided with Cliff's 'rediscovery' of Leninism[15] and emphasis on building rank and file groups within unions. This met most success in the Nation Union of Teachers and was later replicated in several sectors of heavy industry. The 'Bolshevisation' of the IS led to WF's expulsion in 1971, the 'Right Faction' (today's Revolutionary Communist Group) in 1973 and the 'Left Faction' (today's Workers' Power) in 1974. Opposition also formed around leading members like Roger Protz and Jim Higgins to Cliff's desire to dilute *Socialist Worker's* content in pursuit of rapid growth, which in turn led to their expulsions.[16] Cliff's move, however, was not entirely without foundation. The membership grew from 880 in 1970 to 2,351 in 1972, 2,667 in 1973 and 3,900 in 1974.[17] But Cliff had overestimated the opportunities. In 1977, in anticipation of further rapid growth and a quickening of the class struggle, IS renamed itself the SWP. Unfortunately for the newly revamped organisation, this was well past the decade's peak for newspaper circulation and membership. The rebranding came when the party was in relative decline and not on the cusp of wider influence.

The mid- to late 1970s saw the SWP initiate important campaigns. Key was the Anti-Nazi League (ANL), founded in 1977 to confront the growth of the National Front. It attracted widespread support, including from Labour MPs, unions and even the CPGB.[18] Also significant was the intervention in the feminist movement via its *Women's Voice* journal (founded in 1972), and the spread of sponsored groups from 1978–81 – until they were shut down when the SWP lost members to the feminist movement.[19] By 1980 membership had grown to 4,100 but its independent existence outside of Labour and opposition to Militant meant it barely benefited from the resurgence of Labour's left. Part of the problem was Cliff's forecasting of the 1980s as a period of class struggle 'downturn', combined with the prediction that union leaders would betray the rank and file in trade union-based struggles.[20] While the SWP took part in miners' support groups, local anti-poll tax groups and supporting other key disputes in the 1980s, it largely failed to attract significant numbers of activists, despite the implosion of its IMG, WRP and CPGB rivals. Up until the significant growth of the early 1990s recruitment remained at replacement levels.[21]

In both cases, Militant and the IS/SWP pursued their own narrow party-building projects. Incubating a solid core of activists in the period of 'high' Fordism, Militant stuck with entrism while IS attempted to relate simultaneously to the Labour–trade union nexus and the movements attending the radical upsurge of the late 1960s. As the restructuring of British capital got underway in the 1980s, the same strategies were pursued but these were time-limited by the crisis facing the labour movement, particularly after the decisive defeat of the 1984–85 miners' strike.

Building in the 'New Times'

By the turn of the decade, the mass workplaces, the 'traditional' communities of solidarity, the very bedrock of the labour movement, were dissolving. The globalisation of capital, communications technologies, risk and social relationships eroded the political and economic nationalism Keynesianism implicitly rested on. As two proponents of the theorisation of this shift put it:

> the world has changed, not just incrementally but qualitatively ... Britain and other advanced capitalist societies are increasingly characterised by diversity, differentiation and fragmentation, rather than homogeneity, standardisation and the economics and organisations of scale which characterised modern mass society.[22]

As organisations rooted in the labour movement, though to different extents, the severe weakening of their core constituency would present a new set of challenges.

Militant's open turn

At the turn of the decade Militant explored the possibility of abandoning 'entrism' in the Labour Party to organise openly. With the phased closure of LPYS in the late 1980s a new source of recruitment had to be found. In 1991 a refuse collection dispute in Liverpool saw Militant back six 'Broad Left' local authority candidates, five of whom were elected. The death of Walton's left-wing Labour MP, Eric Heffer, shortly afterwards saw the selection of Militant opponent Peter Kilfoyle to fight the by-election. Militant backed Lesley Mahmood as the 'Real Labour' candidate, who went on to poll 2,613 votes.[23] The intervention in the Walton by-election led to an immediate adoption of a 'twin-track' approach: open work as an independent party in Scotland and Liverpool and the maintenance of 'entrism' elsewhere.

An unexpected result of the Walton experience was a leadership split. Grant, Alan Woods and Rob Sewell argued that despite the changes in Labour, the working class would still turn to it again. While this line of reasoning was employed to justify Militant's forty years of entrism it cut little ice with the majority of the organisation. They believed an 'open turn' would enable them to intersect with class-conscious activists who were leaving Labour and appeal to those on the left who remained outside the party. At 1991's November conference the positions of the Grant group gained 7 per cent support and soon decamped from the organisation.[24]

Meanwhile Labour moved against Militant's two MPs, Terry Fields and Dave Nellist. Fields' refusal to pay the poll tax saw him serve a 60-day prison sentence, which enabled the leadership to expel him on the grounds that he broke the law. Nellist was put before Labour's NEC and told to repudiate Militant or be deselected. He refused and was suspended from the party, and went on to (unsuccessfully) defend his seat in the 1992 general election. In Scotland Scottish Militant Labour (as Militant was known) benefited from Tommy Sheridan's election campaign, which he fought from his prison cell for poll tax non-payment. Fields also fought his old seat as 'Broadgreen Socialist Labour'. In the end Nellist came third, polling 10,551 votes; Fields 5,952; and Sheridan second with 6,287 votes.[25] Sheridan was victorious in May's council elections, securing Glasgow Pollok's council seat.

Militant Labour was launched as an independent organisation in early 1993 (Scottish Militant Labour (SML) north of the border) and was initially buoyed by two campaigns: Youth against Racism in Europe and the Campaign against Domestic Violence. The former made interventions in anti-racist and anti-fascist mobilisations, particularly the march on the BNP headquarters in Welling in October that year.[26] However, despite the perspectives informing the open turn, 1993's council elections saw the loss of one councillor and the failure to pick up any new seats. The twin track strategy bore fruit in 1994 when Wally Kennedy, a Militant supporter, was elected as a Labour councillor in Hillingdon but for the rest of its candidates there were no breakthroughs, though SML polled 12,113 votes and secured third place in Glasgow in the year's European elections.[27]

The 1990s saw an overall downturn in Militant's fortunes, and measures to arrest it were not successful. Launched in 1991, Panther UK was an attempt to intersect with black and Asian youth. Though formally an independent organisation, the 'where we stand' column of its paper was virtually indistinguishable from the equivalent in *Militant*. Its primary concerns were anti-racism, anti-fascism and grassroots community work, but by 1993 the organisation drifted away from Militant's politics and later split.[28]

After a couple of years of slight but measured membership decline, in 1996 the leadership concluded a relaunch was necessary to boost the morale and profile of the group, and a debate began over a change of name. The proposal to change from Militant Labour to Socialist Party was 'on the questionable grounds of *Militant's* allegedly unfavourable association with terrorism and fundamentalism, and the unattractiveness of *Labour* to youth', according to a former longstanding cadre.[29] Eventually 'Socialist Party' won with around two-thirds support.[30] This measure did not extend to the Scottish organisation, which retained its SML name.

Ultimately the change did little to alter the SP's fortunes. The 1997 general election saw a significant decline in Nellist's vote, and September saw a small-scale split by the 'Socialist Democracy' faction.[31] Two more significant setbacks were to come the following year. Being virtually autonomous since foundation, the SML and SP leadership divided over the founding of a broad socialist organisation in Scotland. The SML executive favoured transferring their resources to a new party and proposed liquidating their group into an organised faction within it. The SP National Committee opposed.[32] Majority support in SML was secured and the Scottish Socialist Party (SSP) was founded in 1999. The final split between what became the International Socialist Movement and the SP occurred in 2001, leaving behind a small rump of loyalists active in the SSP.[33]

The second split was with the majority of its Merseyside organisation in October 1998. The National Committee suspended the regional committee of around fifty members. Those expelled claimed that disagreements over the leadership's handling of the group's (then) financial difficulties were the root cause. For the SP the issue was a matter of local 'misleadership' and a winding down of party activity.[34] The splinter went on to become the Merseyside Socialists but ultimately failed to develop independently.

Because of these difficulties, combined with its formal position of seeking to found a new workers' party to fill the role perceived to be vacated by Labour, by the turn of the century the SP's development began converging with that of its SWP rivals.

SWP growth

The chief casualty of the USSR's collapse on the British left was the CPGB, which voted to close its organisation and relaunch as the Democratic Left in 1991.[35] As official communism was embroiled in factional infighting prior to its demise, the SWP recruited activists who may have once turned to the CPGB. In addition, the 1990–91 anti-Gulf War movement and the party's decision to relaunch the ANL in 1993 presented opportunities for growth. In these movements the SWP believed it could attract activists not (initially at least) on the basis of its politics but by being the 'best builders'. The problem for the International Socialist Group (which split from the SWP in 1994) was that activists were being won to the party on a 'primitive' basis: there was no systematic attempt to develop recruits as Marxist cadre, and therefore whenever the SWP shifted emphasis from one campaign to another, a layer of membership was lost.[36]

Despite this turnover the SWP grew overall, to around 6,000 by 1994 and by 1996 was claiming 10,000 members. However, 'primitive' recruitment engendered further bureaucratisation of the organisation, even to the extent of the Central Committee issuing an edict banning members from participating on an internet discussion forum on pain of disciplinary action![37]

As the decade wore on membership growth gave way to replacement, leading the leadership to conclude that more outward-facing party building strategies were required. This convergence of perspectives with the SP and a host of smaller revolutionary groups saw the main trends of British Trotskyism briefly unite for the first time since 1949.

Revolutionary regroupment, 1992–2005

Throughout the 1990s there were a number of moves toward regrouping the far left. The earliest was the Coventry and Warwickshire Socialist Alliance, which emerged during Nellist's re-election campaign and became a model for similar groups. Over the next five years these informally brought together 'independents' and activists from rival groups, and very slowly linked up with one another.

With the breaking up of the labour movement and the subsequent rise of New Labour, there appeared a political space outside of Labour to its left. This and the apparent diminishing basis for competing revolutionary projects saw the beginnings of a generalisation of the Coventry experience. The turn to more cooperation between the various fragments of the far left also saw the SP focusing more on the labour movement and the SWP reaching beyond it.

The 'space' for the Socialist Alliance (SA) became wider as the Socialist Labour Party (SLP) imploded as an activist organisation. The SLP was founded in 1996 after the miners' leader Arthur Scargill left Labour and called for a new socialist party. Militant was involved in discussions around the project but Scargill made clear his party would not allow for open factions, and Militant quickly departed.[38] After its founding conference, a year long purging of smaller Trotskyist organisations and 'undesirables' convulsed the SLP. The December 1997 conference of the party was the significant turning point – every motion not meeting the leadership's approval was voted down by a 3,000-strong block vote wielded by a Scargill loyalist.[39] This sparked a walkout by some delegates and virtually the entire active membership resigned over the coming months – many of whom subsequently involved themselves with the SA in England and Wales.

Reflecting the slow development of the SA in England and Wales, and the relatively significant material advantages the shrunken SLP could deploy up until 2001, it was not until the 1999 European elections that the SA appeared on a ballot paper. The West Midlands SA with Nellist as its lead candidate polled 7,603 votes, while SAs elsewhere tended to support the SLP or other left-of-Labour tickets.

The SP did not play the same role in England and Wales as the SML had in Scotland. Whereas the SSA was central to its sister organisation's electoral and campaigning work, in the south 'SP work' was prioritised, and despite the efforts of some of the smaller groups (for example a fledgeling London-wide SA was launched on the initiative of the tiny CPGB) the lack of SP input meant development was much slower. This changed in 1999 when the SWP became involved in abortive talks around the European elections. Any intention to stand was abandoned when the SLP announced it would be standing regardless of what the rest of the left was doing – with the exception of the West Midlands.

Talks were resumed afterwards and it was agreed to stand a slate of candidates under the London SA (LSA) banner for the 2000 London Assembly elections. Almost immediately, the project was put under strain. At first the SP leadership prevaricated over supporting the LSA as one of its members was standing for the Campaign Against Tube Privatisation (CATP) ticket. Once the matter was settled in favour of the LSA the SP insisted its local councillor, Ian Page, contested Lewisham. Overall the campaign was judged a success by all component organisations, polling 2.9 per cent of the constituency and 1.6 per cent in the list vote in the face of other left challenges by CATP, SLP and OutRage! activist Peter Tatchell.

The SA assumed momentum as the SWP initiated new local groups and poured more activists into the project. Conferences in late 2000 and early 2001 saw the SA put on a firmer organisational footing and agreement reached on a manifesto. Again a dispute erupted between the SP and the rest of the SA as the former designated 12 constituencies for its supporters without discussing it with their partners, and demanded control of these campaigns. Furthermore, two candidates were run on a Socialist Alternative as opposed to an SA ticket. Despite this the SA managed to field 98 candidates in the June 2001 general election and polled approximately 57,000 votes. Thereafter the dispute between the SP and SA broke out anew. The SP argued that the SWP was attempting to enshrine its numerical majority constitutionally by moving from a federal structure guaranteeing component organisations an equal say to one-member-one-vote. The SP declared this intolerable and would walk out if the changes were voted through. They subsequently were and in November that year the SP withdrew.[40]

This marked the high point of the SA. Thereafter the SWP wound the organisation down, briefly reviving it at election time. The only success the SA had was the election of a single councillor in 2003.[41] However, while the SA was in abeyance, the SWP threw its energies into developing Stop the War Coalition (StWC). Founded following the 11 September 2001 attacks, StWC took off in the lead up to the Iraq War. Reflecting the mood, between 3 August 2002 and 18 April 2003, 28 out of 38 issues of *Socialist Worker* led with the build up to war, including the first 18 weeks of 2003.

The neglect of the SA did not draw a halt to the regroupment process. The expulsion of Glasgow MP George Galloway from Labour saw him ally with the SWP and Muslim activists radicalised by the wars in Afghanistan and Iraq. This became the Respect coalition at the start of 2004.[42] Initially the SWP attempted to transfer SA assets wholesale to the new organisation but was met with opposition from some remaining affiliates. Therefore, as Respect began to develop, the SWP neglected the SA: electoral work was now done under Respect's name, and the SA existed in name only until formal dissolution in 2005.

The SWP theorised Respect as a united front of a 'special type',[43] locating it as an attempt to give voice to the 'huge, vibrant movement against war and occupation. There is also widespread opposition to privatisation, coupled with anger over pensions and top-up fees'.[44] At Respect's founding conference, Lindsey German of the SWP declared a moderate platform was required 'because it is built on the anti-war movement, and because there are large Muslim communities, and we want to reach out to them as well as the traditional left'.[45]

Respect was heavily criticised by the SWP's rivals for this perspective. However, its concentration on Muslim communities saw it win significant support. In July 2004 Respect polled 3,724 votes (12.7 per cent) and 1,282 votes (6.3 per cent) in Leicester South and Birmingham Hodge Hill by-elections respectively, coming fourth in both. But its dependence on a so-called 'Muslim vote' was underlined by September's Hartlepool by-election, where the coalition secured fifth place with only 572 votes (1.8 per cent). This duality was replicated in the 2005 general election. Its 68,094 votes shared between 26 candidates (6.85 per cent average) hid stark disparities. For example Respect's top five candidates scored in excess of 6,000 votes apiece (with Galloway elected for Bethnal Green and Bow after polling 15,801 votes), while its bottom five scored between 0.45–0.95 per cent.[46]

The SWP leadership, writing in its members' bulletin, acknowledged the unevenness but offered upbeat advice:

> Galloway's election victory means that all bets are off. Even if your local result was disappointing the Bethnal Green and Bow result means that we can build a whole new Respect in your area in short order. Of course we have to learn many lessons from each local campaign. Of course we have to ask if we were able to tap into the networks that Respect keyed into in East London and Birmingham. But it would be crazy to generalise from a poor vote when we have just had an MP elected.[47]

The circular instructs branches to organise meetings around Respect's electoral results. Under the heading 'A historic opportunity for the SWP', *Party Notes* encourages members to recruit non-aligned Respect activists to the party, or at the very least ensure they regularly receive *Socialist Worker*: in effect an approach building on the SWP's earlier 'movementism' where they strived to appear to be the 'best builders' and attempt to attract activists by example.

Realignment and retrenchment

Since returning to work under its own banner, the worst years of the SP seem behind it. The period after 2001 could be described as one where the party gradually built up its position, while the SWP appeared to be making most headway with the anti-war movement and Respect. The SP generally eschewed realignment projects, despite being formally committed to building a broad new working-class party to the left of Labour. In the SP's opinion an alliance of small parties alone cannot provide the nucleus for a new party – this depends on the trade unions.[48]

This pragmatism can be seen in relation to post-SA regroupment projects before 2009. Despite the acrimonious split from the SA, both Galloway and the SWP approached the SP with an offer of executive places if it affiliated to the coalition. In a letter distributed to Respect's founding conference, the SP explained it would not be joining because the SWP had failed to draw the necessary lessons from the SLP and SA, particularly with regard to democratic organising. The SP argued Respect needed to reach out to wider forces prior to the conference (including themselves) but instead the project had just been announced. It voiced concern that Respect was not appealing to Muslims on a 'class basis' and was in danger of succumbing to populism.[49] That said the SP was willing to support Respect in the 2004 European and Greater London Assembly elections (once again it insisted on standing Ian Page in Lewisham, who appeared as a Respect candidate on the ballot paper).

For the 2005 general election the SP came to an agreement with a number of small left groups over seats. The Socialist Green Unity Coalition (SGUC) stood 28 candidates in total, 17 of whom were SP members. Unlike the SA at its height SGUC had no real dynamic independent of the groups involved, and each candidate stood under their party label, not that of the SGUC. Compared at least with the votes won by Respect the average percentage of Socialist Alternative candidates was low (1.57 per cent), securing a total of 9,398 votes between them. It marks a decline from its 2001 performance when the 14 candidates won 10,368 votes (an average of 2.11 per cent).[50] Nevertheless the SP argued, 'for Socialist Party members up and down the country this was the best election campaign we have ever been involved in'. They also said, 'our vote in no way reflected the support we found for our ideas', citing an anecdote from a mock school election as evidence.[51]

From the autumn of 2007 the far left in England and Wales entered a state of flux, and the dominant position held by the SWP came under a sustained challenge that primarily benefited the SP. There are five key developments to account for this. First of all, a dispute within Respect exploded into a faction fight that placed the SWP on one side and the bulk of non-SWP members on the other.[52] According to the SWP they were victims of a witch-hunt and were being driven out of Respect.[53] The position of their opponents, grouped around George Galloway MP and Birmingham councillor Salma Yaqoob, was that the SWP had too much power concentrated in its hands, and there was a fear Respect came second to the SWP's basic work around paper sales, promotion and recruitment. This led to an unseemly public split, culminating in the two factions standing against each other at the 2008 London Assembly elections.[54] The major consequence for the SWP was the damage inflicted on its reputation.

The second key development was the economic crisis and global recession. From autumn 2008 the neoliberal rhetoric and policy preferences of Western governments were thrown into chaos. States injected vast sums into the banking system to prevent the collapse of the world's financial system. The terms of political reference changed entirely. Keynesianism and nationalisation re-entered mainstream political discourse and finance is no longer held up as the hegemonic model of capital accumulation. A tentative but real revival of interest in Marx is also evident in political and media circles. None of this has led to a dramatic increase in the influence of British Trotskyism, but the shifting political gravity, on paper, should prove to be more fruitful for socialist politics. Both the SP and SWP certainly saw things this way.[55]

Third has been the attitudes the SP and SWP took to the Lindsey Oil Refinery and related disputes in January–February 2009. The dispute involved the employment of Portuguese workers at the expense of locals and was in contravention of existing collective agreements between refinery operators Total and the trade union. The slogan 'British Jobs for British Workers' was prominent on the picket line and in the media. The SP, having a member on the strike committee, intervened and was able to steer the strike away from nationalist demands. In so doing the party accumulated much political capital within the far left and the labour movement.[56] However the SWP's stance focused on the 'BJ4BW' slogan and was very critical of the strike.[57] While the party's position was more nuanced than outright opposition, its supporters on the far left's main internet debating forums were not and caused further injury to the SWP's damaged reputation.

This directly led to a major far left realignment. In March 2009 the No2EU platform, comprising the Rail, Maritime and Transport union (RMT), the Communist Party of Britain and the SP announced its intention to stand candidates in June's European elections. Senior RMT officials in alliance with the CP initiated this body – the SP was later invited to participate after the name and much of the platform had been decided. What was significant was their refusal to approach the SWP, which previously would have been unthinkable. The stated reason for not doing so was their position on Lindsey strikes.[58]

No2EU performed relatively poorly in the elections (153,236 votes, 1.01 per cent),[59] but it did prove a national campaign could be mounted by the far left independently of the SWP. It has also meant, thanks to the SP's alliance with the RMT, that when it comes to future negotiations around joint election platforms with trade union backing, the SP has the initiative.

The final development was associated with the European elections. The contest saw the return of two MEPs for the British National Party (BNP) in the North of England. This sparked a number of debates around anti-fascist strategy in the labour movement. Shortly afterwards the SWP released an open letter calling for the rest of the left to put aside past differences and work together to provide an anti-political establishment alternative to the BNP. All organisations of the left responded to the call with varying degrees of enthusiasm. For the first time since the foundation of Respect far left unity was again being advocated openly by one of its principal organisations, though, characteristically, the call received a guarded response from the SP and their allies.[60]

Despite this ongoing process of realignment, Trotskyist organisations have continued to play key mobilising roles in significant social movements and protests. The SWP still provides the key personnel for Unite Against

Fascism, which continues to mobilise against the BNP and the far right. The SP recruited a number of key workplace activists and expanded its influence at Lindsey Oil Refinery, which gives it a position of influence in future disputes. Its activists also played important parts in occupations that swept the factories belonging to Ford's car component manufacturing subsidiary, Visteon.[61] Also, the SWP, SP and smaller groups were crucial to the so-called red-green alliance that came together in defence of a factory occupation at wind turbine manufacturers Vestas[62] and both have gone on to become key organisers of anti-cuts protests at the local level.

Marching separately – again

As regroupment gave away to realignment, the SP's and SWP's disengagement from unity initiatives that put into question their continued legitimacy as discrete parties, both have, once again, become focused more on narrow party building. Early 2010 saw the launch of the Trade Unionist and Socialist Coalition, which possesses a similar structure to the earlier SGUC, but with the RMT on board. Both organisations are affiliates but as an electoral flag of convenience and with limited electoral impact, it is highly unlikely to develop a dynamic of its own. But apart from this, both organisations have more or less returned to the 'ourselves alone' practice of the post-war period, albeit this time without the Labour Party. And particularly where the SWP are concerned, who have undergone a series of important and damaging splits, it would appear they will be hard pressed to find outside forces willing to work with them on an organisational basis.

However, both of their returns to the old way of doing things are not sustainable in the long term. The political space for party-centred Leninist-Trotskyist politics has contracted and the continued commitment by the present government to even greater flexibility in the labour market will work against developing the constituency the far left needs. While it is likely the SP and SWP will persist for many years yet, their ability to episodically influence wider politics has diminished. The ongoing crisis of British capitalism – long forecast by their theoretical screeds – has not proven to be their saviour, and there is no sign that either can overcome their marginality in the near future.

Notes

1 E. Hobsbawm, 'The Forward March of Labour Halted', *Marxism Today*, September (1978), pp. 279–86; S. Hall and M. Jacques (eds), *New Times: The Changing Face of Politics in the 1990s* (London: Lawrence and Wishart, 1989).

2 A. Campbell, N. Fishman and J. McIlroy (eds), *British Trade Unions and Industrial Politics*, vols 1 and 2 (Farnham: Ashgate, 1999).
3 SN/SG/5125, F. McGuinness, *Membership of UK Political Parties*, House of Commons Library, Briefing Note, December 2012.
4 M. Upham, 'The History of British Trotskyism to 1949' (unpublished Ph.D. thesis, University of Hull, 1980), www.marxists.org/history/etol/revhist/upham/upmen.htm, accessed 21 December 2012.
5 T. Grant, *The Problems of Entryism* (London: publisher unknown, 1959), marxist.net/openturn/historic/script.htm?entrism.htm, accessed 21 December 2012.
6 T. Grant, 'Interview with Ted Grant on the *Militant*' (2004), www.marxist.com/interview-ted-grant-militant101004.htm, accessed 21 December 2012.
7 J. Callaghan, *British Trotskyism: Theory and Practice* (Oxford: Blackwell, 1984).
8 P. Taaffe, *The Rise of Militant* (London: Militant Publications, 1995).
9 M. Webb, 'The Rise and Fall of the Labour League of Youth', unpublished Ph.D. thesis, University of Huddersfield (2007).
10 J. Callaghan, *The Far Left in British Politics* (Oxford: Blackwell, 1987).
11 P. Taaffe and T. Mulhearn, *Liverpool: A City That Dared to Fight* (London: Fortress Books, 1988).
12 Callaghan, *The Far Left in British Politics*.
13 I. Birchall, 'History of the International Socialists – Part I: From Theory to Practice' (1976), *International Socialism*, 1, 76, pp. 16–24, www.marxists.de/intsoctend/birchall/theoprac.htm, accessed 21 December 2012.
14 Ibid.
15 T. Cliff, *Lenin Volume One: Building the Party* (London: Bookmarks, 1975).
16 J. Higgins, *More Years for the Locust* (London: International Socialist Group, 1997).
17 Callaghan, *The Far Left in British Politics*, pp. 98–9.
18 Birchall, 'Facing the Crisis'.
19 Workers' Power, *The Politics of the SWP* (pamphlet, London, publisher unknown, 1992).
20 T. Cliff, 'Building in the Downturn', *Socialist Review*, 53, 4 (1983) pp. 3–5, www.marxists.org/archive/cliff/works/1983/04/building.htm, accessed 21 December 2012.
21 Workers' Power, *Federalism vs Bureaucratism?* (London: publisher unknown, 1996), www.fifthinternational.org/content/swp-international-splits-federalism-vs-bureaucratism, accessed 21 December 2012.
22 Hall and Jacques, *New Times*, p. 11.
23 J. Callaghan, 'Spanish Lessons for Militant and the Labour Party?', *Journal of Communist Studies*, 8, 2 (1992), pp. 172–80.
24 R. Sewell, *How the Militant Was Built – And How It Was Destroyed* (online article, 2004), www.marxist.com/militant-built-destroyed101004.htm, accessed 21 December 2012.
25 P. Taaffe, *Fighting for Socialism* (London: publisher unknown, 1995), www.socialistparty.org.uk/militant/, accessed 21 December 2012.

26 YRE, *Stop the Nazi BNP!* (online article, undated), www.yre.org.uk/history. html, accessed 21 December 2012.
27 Taaffe, *The Rise of Militant*.
28 Workers' Power, 'Militant after Grant: The Unbroken Thread?', *Permanent Revolution*, 10 (1994).
29 R. Silverman, *Reflections on the History of the CWI* [Committee for a Workers International] (location and publisher unknown, 1997), www.movementsfor socialism.com/archive/reflections_cwi.html, accessed 28 August 2005.
30 Socialist Party of Great Britain, 'Militant Dishonesty', *Socialist Standard*, February 1997.
31 M. Fischer, 'Socialist Party Conference: Cracks Begin to Open Up', *Weekly Worker*, 23 October 1997.
32 Socialist Party, 'The Scottish Debate' (online article, 2002), www.marxist.net/ scotland/index.html, accessed 21 December 2012.
33 M. Fischer, 'SSP Split' (online article, 2000), www.cpgb.org.uk/worker/361/ sspsplit.html, accessed 28 August 2005; M. Fischer, 'ISM Leaves CWI' (2001), www.cpgb.org.uk/worker/367/ismleavescwi.htm, accessed 28 August 2005.
34 T. Aitman, 'Appendix', in *Militant's Real History* (online article, 2002), www. socialistparty.org.uk/militant/reply/reply2frame.htm?intro.htm, accessed 21 December 2012.
35 K. Hudson, 'Communist and Former Communist Organisations in Britain', *Journal of Communist Studies and Transition Politics*, 10, 4 (1994), pp. 97–103.
36 Workers' Power, *Federalism vs Bureaucratism?*
37 Socialist Workers Party, 'Statement on the IS List' (location and publisher unknown, 1995), www.uplandtrout.co.uk/isdoc03.html, accessed 28 August 2005.
38 G. R. McColl, 'The Shape of Things to Come' (location and publisher unknown, 1996), www.fifthinternational.org/content/socialist-labour-party-shape-things-come, accessed 21 December 2012.
39 S. Harvey, 'Where Now for SLP Democrats?', *Weekly Worker*, 8 January 1998.
40 H. Sell, 'The Socialist Party and the Socialist Alliance', *The Socialist*, 23 November 2001.
41 *Socialist Worker*, 10 May 2003.
42 *Socialist Worker*, 24 January 2004.
43 J. Rees, *Socialism in the 21st Century, International Socialism*, 2, 100 (2003), www.isj.org.uk/index.php4?id=3&issue=100, accessed 21 December 2012.
44 Anon, 'Every Respect Vote Will Make a Difference', *Socialist Worker,* 5 June 2004.
45 *Weekly Worker*, 5 February 2004.
46 *Socialist Worker Election Results Special*, May 2005.
47 SWP *Party Notes*, 9 May 2005.
48 Anon, 'The Case for a New Workers' Party', *The Socialist,* 16 March 2006.
49 Anon, 'Socialist Party and the Respect Convention', *The Socialist*, 31 January 2004.
50 Socialist Unity Network, 'Election 2005', online article, http://socialistunity network.co.uk/electiion2005/alternatives/lefties, accessed 28 August 2005.

51 Anon, 'Socialist Ideas Adopted by a New Generation', *The Socialist,* 6 May 2005.

52 A. Newman, 'SWP Purges Dissidents' (online article, 2007), www.socialistunity. com/?p=824 accessed, 21 December 2012.

53 Socialist Workers' Party, 'An Appeal to Respect Members' (online article, 2007), www.swp.org.uk/respect_appeal.php, accessed 19 September 2009.

54 P. Owen, 'London Assembly: Who Is Standing?', *Guardian*, 30 April 2008.

55 C. Bambery, 'No Bail Out for Banks: Seize Their Profits!', *Socialist Worker*, 30 September 2008; E. Brunskill, 'Their Failure, Their System: Make the Capitalists Pay', *The Socialist*, 23 September 2008.

56 A. Tice, 'Lindsey Refinery: Workers Show Their Strength', *The Socialist*, 4 February 2009.

57 Socialist Workers' Party, 'Why British Jobs for British Workers Is Not the Solution to the Crisis (online article, 2009), www.socialistworker.co.uk/art. php?id=17004, accessed 21 December 2012.

58 C. Heemskirk, 'European Elections: Why No2EU?', *The Socialist*, 15 April 2009.

59 H. Sell, 'No2EU: A Step Towards a Workers' Political Voice', *The Socialist*, 10 June 2009.

60 Socialist Party, 'Workers' Party Must Be Built', *The Socialist,* 24 June 2009.

61 Socialist Party, *Lindsey, Visteon, Linamar: Lessons from the Disputes of Spring 2009* (London, Socialist party pamphlet, 2009).

62 Alliance for Workers' Liberty, 'Vestas Factory Occupation' (online article, 2009), www.workersliberty.org/trade-unions/trade-union-issues/defending-jobs/ vestas, accessed 19 September 2009.

5

Opposition in slow motion

The CPGB's 'anti-revisionists' in the 1960s and 1970s

Lawrence Parker

In common with other national parties in the world 'official' communist movement, the Communist Party of Great Britain (CPGB) gave birth to pro-Chinese and pro-Soviet inner-party oppositional groupings in the 1960s and 1970s. While there were important structural impediments to the growth of such oppositions,[1] this article focuses particularly on the ideological problems associated with these trends and thus maps out a thesis as to why such groups proved to be a dead end. The first part of this chapter looks at the evolution of the pro-Soviet CPGB opposition of the 1960s and 1970s, and the debilitating effect of the inconsistent narrative of 'anti-revisionism'. The second part considers the disastrous impact that the Stalinised version of 'Leninism' had on the pro-Chinese CPGB oppositionists of the 1960s.

Roots of rebellion

The roots of the CPGB's pro-Soviet and pro-Chinese 'anti-revisionist' groupings of the 1960s and 1970s were in the reaction to the party's political line in the latter stages of the Second World War, and in an opposition that particularly manifested itself during debates at the CPGB's congress of November 1945.[2] The evidence shows that this was an utterly traumatic period for a section of the party's rank and file. There were, for example, complaints about the stifling of inner-party democracy during the war, the 'swamping' of older comrades with large amounts of uneducated 'paper' members and arguments around the party's inability to support or give a lead to the 1945 dock workers' strike. The decision to dissolve the CPGB's factory branches and distribute the members across residential branches had also been controversial. The opposition voiced disagreement with the party's passive, 'tailist' attitude towards the newly elected Labour government, particularly in regard to its imperialist and anti-Soviet foreign policy. In arguing, in March 1945, for a continuation of the national government, the Executive Committee (EC) was seen as being completely out of touch with working-class sentiment. A major controversy at the congress was that of 'Browderism', which related to Earl Browder's liquidation of the Communist Party of the United States in favour of the looser Communist Political Association in 1944.[3]

The idea of 'revisionism' and its attendant dangers was present in the debate on 'Browderism'. Jacques Duclos of the French Communist Party, entrusted by the leadership of the 'official' communist movement with the literary task of stamping on this trend, argued: 'Despite declarations regarding recognition of the principles of Marxism, one is witnessing a notorious revision of Marxism on the part of Browder and his supporters, a revision which is expressed in the concept of a long-term class peace in the United States, of the possibility of the suppression of the class struggle in the post-war period and of establishment of harmony between labour and capital.'[4] This was reflected in the rhetoric of militants such as Bob McIlhone: 'It can no longer be denied that Browder's dissolution of the American Communist Party [sic] has been reflected in Britain by these serious retreats from the basic positions of a Leninist party. Thus the tendencies for the party to lose its separate identity, to become little more than a ginger group in the labour movement.'[5]

However, this use of the narrative of 'revisionism' to criticise the CPGB's leadership was, in fact, a much more cautious enterprise than appears at first glance. Looking back on the arguments voiced against the CPGB leadership in 1945, no one had been directly critical of cross-class Popular Frontism, the international politics of the Soviet Union and the wartime alliance with British imperialism. All of the *consequences* of these factors were thoroughly debunked but the root source of the CPGB's opportunist errors in this period went unchallenged and apparently *unnoticed*. It is crystal clear that Browderism and its British version under Pollitt was essentially the politics of the Popular Front as practised in alliance with British and US imperialism during the Second World War, elaborated into a strategy for 'winning the peace'.

There were strong factors militating against this line of reasoning. Most oppositional figures of this period mistakenly believed in the revolutionary credentials of Stalin and the Soviet Union as against the practice of the CPGB. Eric Heffer, an inner-party oppositionist of the 1940s, said: 'Looking back on our challenge to the CP, we were completely blind to the realities of Stalin and the Soviet Union. We thought that if only Stalin knew what was going on in the British CP he would be on our side. It was seriously suggested at one point that we should send someone over to tell him about our situation.'⁶

Nevertheless, even presented in this crippled political fashion, this opposition was clearly grappling with the imposition of 'socialism in one country', albeit around twenty years too late and without coming remotely close to assessing the role of the Soviet Union. This is perhaps unsurprising given that the 'collaborationist' experience of the CPGB during the Second World War represents an extreme form of the distorted politics that would be expected of a diplomatic bargaining chip. As we shall see, this sense of an 'opposition in slow motion' was one that would infect the CPGB's oppositionists at a number of levels. Thus the 'anti-revisionist' opposition in the CPGB began its life with a huge ideological impediment. Unlike the British Trotskyist movement (which, ironically, ended up stumbling over the same issues as the CPGB in the post-war period), the various currents of this opposition didn't have a coherent theory to explain the degeneration of the Soviet Union and the Comintern; therefore they were ultimately stripped of weapons to deal with the opportunism of the CPGB itself.

Further evidence of the uncomfortable ideological bed that the subjective revolutionaries of the CPGB's left had made for themselves can be seen in the debate around the events of 1956 in the run-up to the 1957 congress. In that debate, party members identified what they called a 'left sectarian' wing of the organisation – essentially the remnants of the opposition of the 1940s.⁷ Thus, Geoff Loxton from Somerset said: 'Reference has already been made to a sectarian tendency, which in the past has been intensified by the cult of Stalin's personality. It is this which largely hinders us from close contacts with the masses, and in its "cult" aspect has inhibited the branch-initiative side of democratic centralism.'⁸ Although hostile and somewhat overblown, Loxton's quote identifies something we have already observed: those CPGB members who advocated a tighter, more selective (and thus more revolutionary) party, grouped this outlook with an advocacy of Stalin and the Communist Party of the Soviet Union (CPSU).

In order to defeat the 'right' opposition in 1957 (i.e. those grouped around a strong criticism of the actions of Stalin and the Soviet Union in Hungary, and calling for a root and branch change to the CPGB's structures – if they weren't questioning the party's continued existence), the leadership faction of the CPGB made an appeal to the aforementioned 'left sectarians' by branding the 'right' as 'revisionists', thus articulating the language of the party's militant wing, albeit in more circumscribed terms. John Gollan argued in 1957:

> We use the word 'revisionist' advisedly. Not as a bit of name-calling, but to describe objective tendencies, not subjective ones. These were

the contributions attacking the essential basis of the party, democratic centralism, and its leading role. They would relegate the position of the party to that of an auxiliary of the Labour Party, and forbid it to contest elections. There was in some contributions a retreat from Marxist-Leninist conceptions to social-democratic ideas and even capitalist ideas on essential issues of the state, democracy and class struggle.[9]

Rather than seeing through this tactic, there is some evidence to suggest that elements of the CPGB's left accepted the reasoning. In 1971, Eddie Jackson and others in Bexley branch CPGB were expelled from the party after distributing a factional document outside the national congress of that year. This document, *Congress: An Appeal to Delegates*, among other points, argued that the CPGB should move away from the strategy of the *British Road to Socialism* (*BRS*) toward a revolutionary road to socialism in Britain. Back in 1957, Jackson held similar views but articulated why, with some reservations, he had accepted the right of the leadership to lead a struggle against 'revisionism'. He talked of 'a healthy scepticism on the part of many comrades when they find leaders ardently, and somewhat patronisingly, correcting in others faults arising out of a petty bourgeois outlook, when they know that until recently these same leading comrades were party to serious errors which stemmed from the same weakness'.[10] However, Jackson concluded: 'We must not allow our scepticism to become destructive and lead to a panicky "sack the lot" policy at congress.'[11]

In 1971, Jackson explained that the CPGB's 'leadership [in 1956-57] remained, on balance, revisionist, but not strong enough so [sic] to prevent the staunchness of Pollitt, Dutt and Mahon carrying the party into supporting the Russian intervention in Hungary'.[12] Similarly, an oppositionist in 1977 talked of 'the working class integrity of the party of Dutt, Pollitt and Gallacher'[13] while the foundation document of the New Communist Party (see below) suggested that the crisis in the CPGB was rooted in the events of the 1960s and the 1970s, being careful to steer clear of a critical account of the 1940s and 1950s.[14] The problem here is that the various named leadership figures were precisely, as Jackson suggests above, the people that oppositionists in, say, 1945, would have seen as carriers of 'revisionism'. Indeed, the realisation that the CPSU approved of the CPGB's post-war strategy was a contributory factor in the eventual demise of the Appeal Group, set up by Jackson and others after being expelled from the CPGB.[15] The widening of the canon of 'anti-revisionism' to include Dutt, Pollitt, Gallacher and Mahon indicates the conservative cast of the CPGB's left. It was storing up immense ideological problems for itself through an inability to deepen its critique of the 'official' communist movement.

At the CPGB's 1965 congress, leaders of what was a growing pro-Soviet opposition trend – Sid French, Surrey district secretary, and Les Howey, Hants and Dorset district secretary – were critical of the leadership's handling of the Sino-Soviet conflict in relation to a March 1965 19-party meeting in Moscow. However, this tendency had no Maoist leanings whatsoever. It was more concerned that the British party had been seemingly reluctant to attend the aforementioned meeting and that the British and Italian parties had opposed a subsequent communiqué calling for the convening of an 81-party international conference.[16] What lay behind these rumblings was concern over the CPGB leadership's attempt to steer something of a neutral course in the Sino-Soviet split (in the midst of a broadly pro-Soviet line) and the party thus appearing to be out of step with Moscow.

Up until 1977 this opposition was centred on Surrey district with its full-time secretary Sid French, often with the assistance of Hants and Dorset, another of its strong areas. There were also networks of comrades – often led by a local operator who kept his or her own group in contact with more senior factional leaders – who did not have the luxury of controlling their own districts.[17] After French and the majority of the activists in the Surrey district had departed to form the New Communist Party (NCP) in 1977, ex-student organiser Fergus Nicholson and lecturer John Foster emerged as key spokesmen of this shadow 'party within a party'. For the most part, this opposition worked in what was subsequently classed as a 'disciplined manner',[18] which in practice meant a mixture of subterranean plotting, utilising the limited democratic forums that the leadership offered.

The broad outlines of this faction's politics emerged over the next decade with the Surrey district and Sid French taking a clear leadership role (unsurprisingly, since the energy and resources of a CPGB district were a useful bridgehead in the context of a vertically organised party). Key battles were over the name change of the *Daily Worker* (which became the *Morning Star* in April 1966), where the opposition challenged the appeasement of the bourgeois inclinations of non-manual workers (many of whom, ironically, were having their roles steadily proletarianised) and the undemocratic manner in which this was decided (i.e. without reference to a party congress).[19] The events of 1968 were also important for the pro-Soviet wing. The opposition of the majority of CPGB members to the Soviet invasion of Czechoslovakia in that year was a confirmation that sections of the party were moving away from the auto-Sovietism insisted upon by French and company. Despite being relatively easily defeated on the issue at the 1969 congress, 2 of 18 district committees (Surrey, and Hants and Dorset) had voted against an EC resolution that was critical of the Soviet action, while 3 of 18 district congresses (Surrey, Hants and Dorset, and the North East) had also rejected it. The actions of the Soviet Union and its allies were defined by this trend as 'working-class internationalism'. 'Anti-Sovietism' (and hence, in this rhetoric, 'anti-communism') was deemed to be a weapon of the capitalist class through its Trotskyist and anarchist agents: 'The newspapers, television and radio back up these ultra-leftist attacks on the Soviet Union and real socialism, using their lies to combat the growing influence of socialist ideas among young people, especially the working-class youth.'[20]

However, underlying this opposition's more conservative ideological predilections was a clear (and correct) recognition that the CPGB was in the throes of a very deep decline and was moving into crisis. For example, in April 1966, the Surrey District Committee prepared a document for an EC discussion on electoral work, calling for a 'fundamental re-examination of our electoral work and perspectives'. It argued: 'As we have concentrated more and more on elections the party has been able to give less and less attention to the planning and leadership of mass struggle.' The document, somewhat rhetorically, added: 'Has our electoral work really helped advance our congress line of unity [of the labour movement]? In fact many see the way we contest as a contradiction of our unity policy in the context of large Labour votes side by side with small and declining communist votes.'[21] In May 1967, French wrote to John Gollan, CPGB general secretary, to request some space in the party press to discuss the organisation's specific problems. He felt the wider party should be made aware of the negative features in the organisation, for example, declining sales for the *Morning Star* and *Comment*, and shrinking votes. French also wondered why on May Day in London a '"splinter group" ... had 85 per cent as many on the march as did the party'.[22]

1977 and all that

The year 1977, like 1945, was another year of rebellion for a significant section of the CPGB's left opposition. In that year, a new draft of the *BRS* was presented to the CPGB membership as a continuation of the organisation's programmatic development since the end of the Second World War. Indeed, an article was written by James Klugmann to emphasise this point.[23] Alongside this piece, Chris Myant introduced the 1977 draft to the party. He placed it in the context of 'class confrontations involving important sections of the "traditional" labour movement' occurring alongside 'the appearance of new forces outside of the movement's historic boundaries.'[24]

Even a Eurocommunist-influenced historian such as Thompson is forced to concede that the changes from the 1968 edition of the *BRS* 'were more of style and terminology than of real substance'.[25] Geoff Andrews, another Eurocommunist sympathiser, says compromise pervaded the content of the draft, which reflected the fact that it had been drawn up by a group split by Eurocommunist and more traditionalist influences (the actual writing fell to Martin Jacques and George Matthews).[26] Even the much-trumpeted shift to so-called 'new social forces' (such as the women's movement) in the shape of the 'broad democratic alliance' merely meant a perceived broader constituency to either adapt to and/or impregnate with the CPGB's post-war reformist strategy. Unfortunately, as we shall see, the instinct of many members to rebel against the draft foundered on the illusion that the 1977 draft was substantively new, thus investing it with a historical importance that it really did not deserve.

The most far-ranging critique of the 1977 draft from the left of the CPGB came from Charlie Doyle,[27] who independently published his own pamphlet: *A Critique of the Draft British Road to Socialism: Revolutionary Path – or Diversion?* Doyle contended that the 'concept of the *British Road* is a serious revisionist error' and that he did 'not think that this [draft] document can be amended, either to improve it or transform it into a viable Marxist-Leninist programme'.[28]

Doyle was somewhat ambiguous on the relationship of the 1977 draft to its *BRS* predecessors. He said of the 1951 version: 'Then the party was united and immersed in working-class struggle and it was felt a creative contribution was being made ... Whatever validity it may have had in 1951 has long since vanished.'[29] However, alongside such notions, which suggested the earlier *BRS* was defensible in a particular context, other passages suggest the whole basis of the *BRS* 'project' was fundamentally flawed. Doyle argued: 'To attempt, as we do, in this and previous editions of the *British road* to predetermine and predict the course of objective change to suit subjective wishes is to make a mockery of revolutionary theory and transform it into a lifeless pedantic exercise, or at best a pessimism which leads us to embrace bourgeois democratic forms as the only instruments for change and parliament as the executive institution for shaping the new socialist society.'[30]

The ambiguity over previous versions of the *BRS* and the draft's relationship to it was a common feature of the left's critique that year. Brian Davies, a Welsh Committee member from Swansea,[31] did try to isolate what was different in the 1977 draft that made it the decisive turning point toward 'reformism'. Davies argued unconvincingly that: 'A parallel reading of the draft and the previous editions of the *British road* shows that what we are now presented with is in many respects a new programme.'[32] He thought that the main shift was embedded in the premise that the 'government of the revolutionary transition is to be led by the Labour Party. Only in "subsequent left governments" would the Communist Party acquire "a more significant presence"'. Davies added: 'So the "major development" in the new *British road* ... turns out to be the relegation of the Communist Party to the second division of working-class politics. There have always been differences in the party over the *British road*. But these are now at a qualitatively different level.'[33] A similar point was made by the Surrey District Committee: 'If the draft is endorsed by congress the party remains communist in name only. In actuality it becomes a left social-democratic party with a left social-democratic programme.'[34] The irony behind this critique is that it was precisely this 'relegation' that had been a common argument from the CPGB's left oppositions since 1945. The *BRS* itself was, in part, a product of the party's tailist practice toward the post-war Labour government. This is what lies behind the 1951 programme's assertion that: 'The united action of all sections of the working-class movement – Labour, trade union, cooperative and communist – is the vital need. Only by united action between all sections of the labour movement can the working class rally all its forces and all its allies for decisive action to win a parliamentary majority and form a people's government.'[35]

Therefore, supporters of the 1977 draft, such as Victor Adereth, were correct when they argued 'it is not just the 1977 draft these people object to, but the essence of the strategy for revolution which the party has been elaborating since 1951'. He added: 'Though the 1951 programme was approved by comrade Stalin, what's good enough for the CPSU is clearly not good enough for Sid French. That's his problem.'[36] One suspects that Adereth was rather perceptive in isolating a major reason behind some of the CPGB left's inability to comprehensively dismiss the precursors of the draft.

We have seen previously that the 'anti-revisionist' canon had always generally included Stalin and the CPSU, and had been widened to include other figures who had overseen the early incarnations of the *BRS*, such as Pollitt and Dutt. However, John Gollan had in 1964 underlined the fact that Stalin had overseen the early incarnations of the *BRS*.[37] This posed a deep ideological problem for the pro-Soviet left opposition and meant that it had to make peace with earlier versions of the *BRS* and invest the 1977 draft with 'innovative' properties it didn't have. Essentially, the debate around the 1977 draft was in fact a confused proxy war for a debate that should have been conducted in the early 1950s as the phenomenon of 'opposition in slow motion' reared its head once more.

As a result of the debate in 1977 and because of the probable intention of the CPGB's leadership to 'reorganise' the Surrey district, around 700 members eventually left the CPGB to form the NCP. It had strong concentrations in Surrey and Sussex, as well as significant components in Hants and Dorset, Yorkshire and Lancashire. Sid French became the first general secretary of the NCP (and effectively its leader).[38] Unsurprisingly, the NCP proved unable to develop any kind of rounded revolutionary critique of the *BRS* or any such critique of the Soviet Union. Indeed, as CPGB critics such as Adereth quickly noted, while his organisation was still discussing the 1977 draft, the NCP seemed somewhat reticent to discuss issues of strategy: 'The manufacturers of the "New Communist Party" are not only opposed to the 1977 draft and the essence of the strategy we've been developing since 1951; they are opposed to having a strategy at all. If the draft is a load of rubbish, there must be a viable alternative. Why have they not been spelling it out at the meetings they have addressed?'[39] It is not surprising that the NCP was reticent to make a definitive programmatic statement, split as it was between those who wanted to defend earlier versions of the *BRS* and those who disavowed all versions and were in favour of a return to the revolutionary positions espoused in the CPGB's *For Soviet Britain* (1935).[40]

A pamphlet issued by the NCP after it had split from the CPGB in 1977 talked of the crisis in the CPGB being 'a result of growing opportunism in the party and a move towards reformism in its policies'.[41] The NCP leaders characterised the rewriting of the *BRS* by the CPGB's right-opportunist leadership in the run-up to the 1977 congress as completing 'the destruction of the CPGB as the revolutionary party of the working class of Britain'.[42] Beneath the leftist rhetoric, the implication of this analysis is that the *BRS* – the programmatic source of the CPGB's reformist ills – is not a problem *per se*; rather, it is rewriting it that shifts the 'official' party into non-revolutionary terrain; in other words, defeat today's reformist 'revisionism' with yesterday's reformist 'revisionism'. A later publication expanded this analysis. According to the NCP: 'The *BRS* was first revised in 1957 – the start of a process culminating in 1977 which deprived it of all revolutionary content.'[43]

The tolerance being shown towards the *BRS* was not limited to the NCP. Leading members of the rump opposition who remained in the CPGB after the 1977 defection subsequently founded the journal *Straight Left* (launched in 1979).[44] However, the reigning *modus operandi* of this publication – Brezhnevite 'internationalism' under a 'broad labour movement' cloak – was nothing but a 'traditionalist' distillation of the CPGB's post-war reformist drift. A similar standpoint infected the opposition that emerged around the *Morning Star* in the 1980s, which ended up forming the breakaway Communist Party of Britain in 1988 around a version of the *BRS*. Thus, the glacial-like pace of the pro-Soviet opposition's ideological development ended up with it making peace with the very 'revisionist' ideas and practices that had led to its emergence in 1945.[45]

Doing the splits

Although the CPGB's pro-Chinese factions did not generally run aground on the specific issue of the heritage of the *BRS* (although most of them hailed Stalin as a great revolutionary leader), the problem of an inherently 'Stalinised' form of party organisation was to prove their undoing as the 1960s progressed.

In 1968, one of a proliferation of British pro-Chinese factions looked back over the previous six to seven years of 'anti-revisionist' struggle in and around the CPGB: 'Split has followed split, often on the basis of personality issues. The way was laid open for the infiltration of highly dubious and bourgeois elements.'[46] This remark illustrates well the delusions of this trend. While the personalities and actions of certain leaders played a definite role it was the Maoist ideological inheritance that wreaked most havoc, an example of which was the constant (and often paranoid) attribution of error to alien, 'bourgeois' class elements.

While the pro-Chinese opposition shared similar roots to the pro-Soviet 'anti-revisionists' in the 1940s and 1950s, the Sino-Soviet split of the early 1960s offered a window of opportunity for such tendencies.[47] The Communist Party of China (CPC) denounced the CPSU (and thus parties such as the CPGB that followed a Soviet lead) from what seemed like an explicitly revolutionary standpoint. Soviet notions such as 'peaceful coexistence' with the capitalist West were forcibly attacked with revolutionary rhetoric and the CPSU itself was denounced as 'revisionist'. Unsurprisingly, many communists across the globe found explanatory threads (whatever the CPC's motives may have been) for the reformism that had infected their own 'national' organisations. By 1963, the CPGB had, for all intents and purposes, lined up on the Soviet side.[48]

A group of CPGB members, the majority based in London, led by Michael McCreery, secretary of Tufnell branch (Islington, London) and a member of the CPGB's economic subcommittee,[49] began to use the CPC's attack on the CPSU as a means to explain the reformism of its own party. The group emerged in 1961–62 and initial activities appear to have been based around interventions in internal CPGB meetings and schools, composing articles for the party press and visiting contacts around the country.[50]

There then followed an extremely fractious history of splits (both from the CPGB parent body and among the 'anti-revisionist' factions). The Committee to Defeat Revisionism for Communist Unity (CDRCU), led by

McCreery was founded in November 1963, leaving the CPGB and setting itself up as an open opponent. This foundation was, however, on the basis of a split with those who still wanted to retain membership of the CPGB and prosecute the inner-party struggle (who formed groups such as the *Forum* faction and the Committee for the Defence of Marxism-Leninism). The CDRCU began to fragment into a number of different splinters after the death of McCreery from cancer in April 1965, some of which chose to reorient themselves to the CPGB. Other pro-Chinese oppositional groups arose in the CPGB and the Young Communist League (YCL) over the next few years (some of them only organised on a regional basis), including those grouped around *The Marxist* discussion journal, which had leading CPGB trade unionist Reg Birch of the AEU on its editorial board. After his removal from the CPGB in 1967 Birch went on to found the Communist Party of Britain (Marxist-Leninist) (CPB (M-L)) in 1967-68 but he was also unable to unite the scattered forces of the pro-Chinese left, the CPB (M-L) being founded on a split with some of his former comrades around *The Marxist*, most of whom had also chosen to break with the CPGB.[51]

As we have seen, it was the issue of leaving or staying in the CPGB that was to constantly vex the pro-Chinese opposition; declaring the host organisation as 'finished' consistently pushed factions into departing to form themselves into open centres of competition with the CPGB. Even organisations such as the Action Centre for Marxist-Leninist Unity (ACMLU), which had seemingly worked out that McCreery's group had abandoned work inside the CPGB prematurely, then quickly went through its own cycle in late 1965/early 1966 of emptily declaring that: 'The Communist Party no longer exists in Britain!'[52] This followed an analysis of the CPGB's 1965 congress, which hadn't appeared to change anything fundamental in the party's post-war trajectory. Indeed most of the logic used to justify these splits was absurd. Therefore, when McCreery sought to explain why he had abandoned the CPGB he argued: 'In practice one *cannot separate* the [CPGB] from the leadership around which it has been built up over many decades.'[53] In fact, this is what had just happened: a small section of the rank and file had detached itself from the leadership and, as McCreery well knew, a number of them had been left behind in the CPGB after declining to join the CDRCU. Indeed, as we have seen above, after 1963 a number of pro-Chinese oppositions sprang up and, as the decade wore on, the rebellion had spread to the YCL as the 'second wind' of Maoism began to blow with the onset of the Cultural Revolution.[54] As late as 1968, the Glasgow Communist Movement reported: 'We had hoped that on the basis of our activity we could become a rallying point for those who dropped out of the YCL, especially after the 1967 congress. This has not yet taken place. It is apparent that many of the cadres who, disgusted with revisionism, have ceased to be active in the YCL [but] have remained members of the CP and some have adopted the position of economism.'[55]

This caution shown towards leaving the CPGB was lodged in reality given that the party, despite geographical unevenness, was embedded in the British labour movement in a way that small sects to its left were not and thus represented a formidable opponent. A sober appreciation of this and a serious commitment to working inside the CPGB while maintaining an independent journal (which the *Forum* group and the ACMLU had at least begun to perceive) could have begun to disinter the cycle of splits and demoralisation that had pervaded the pro-Chinese 'anti-revisionists' by the late 1960s. However, given the stance of the CPC, it was very unlikely that this conclusion would have been reached: 'Both internationally and in individual countries, wherever opportunism and revisionism are rampant, a split becomes inevitable in the proletarian ranks.'[56] The CPC taught its adherents in the international communist movement that it was the revisionist leaders of parties such as the CPGB departing from Marxism-Leninism and the 'proletarian revolutionary party' who were the real splitters, 'even when for a time they are in the majority or hold the leading posts'. Furthermore, the 'revisionists' were denounced as 'agents of the bourgeoisie'. [57] Messages such as these were unlikely to endear activists to a continued existence as a faction inside the CPGB, particularly when frustrations borne from the constrained nature of such struggles were brought into the mix.

This constant explanation of differences by reference to class positions (the so-called 'two-line theory') was even more disastrous when it spread across the various groups and factions, poisoning dialogue between and within them. Thus, in dealing with the emergence of *The Marxist*, the ACMLU outlandishly classed other anti-revisionist groups (such as *Forum*, the Irish Communists and the Finsbury Communist Association) as 'pursuing a consciously disruptive role'.[58] The ACMLU was also fairly sanguine about the splits that had taken place in the CDRCU:

> Comrades who envisage the development of a Marxist-Leninist movement as a smooth, gradual process of increasing understanding and numbers are flying in the face of all reality. This development occurs by means of contradictions and in the course of struggle. The 'splits' and 'polemics' were basically of a political character, and they were necessary and positive – the positive process of the 'anti-revisionist movement' into Marxist-Leninists on the one hand, and into pseudo-Marxists, liberals and neo-Trotskyists on the other. Or, in Mao's words, 'one divides into two'.[59]

Associated with this, the various factions adopted the essentially Stalinised version of 'Leninism' that was touted by the Chinese, with its stress on centralism and ideological unity. Organisations such as the CDRCU and the CPB (M-L) had already gone through a process of ideological purification, being set up on the basis of splits with people who didn't agree with them on secondary tactical issues. There was an essential bifurcation between more freewheeling groups that didn't advocate a single unitary line such as those around *The Marxist* and *Forum*; and pre-party formations (such as the CDRFCU and the ACMLU) through to the full-blown 'party' sect of the CPB (M-L), which did advocate a 'line', and thus polemic in their journals was mostly with 'outsiders' rather than between their own comrades. Even the presentations in *The Marxist* evolved into contributions between different factions and unattached individuals, rather than reflecting the internal debates *within* those groups. Ironically, this meant the 'anti-revisionists' had a more restricted political life than that of the CPGB, which did conduct *open* debates between party members, albeit on the leadership's terms and within limited time frames (such as around its national congresses). This meant that the internal life of, for example, the CDRCU was punctuated by a series of ugly internal squabbles and splits as its membership came to terms with the restrictions and centralism imposed upon it.[60] The article from the Joint Committee of Communists (JCC) quoted at the start of this section accused McCreery of 'overemphasising and ... distorting the role and possibilities of leadership' and an over-reliance on his own personal wealth.[61] However, this distortion of leadership was embedded in the Maoist inheritance of 'Leninism' as perhaps the authors of this piece partly perceived when they saw Reg Birch's CPB (M-L) showing 'striking political and organisational similarities' with the CDRCU.[62]

The ideology and practice of pro-Chinese 'anti-revisionism' was in fact perfectly constructed to secure split after debilitating split. The revolutionary rhetoric and, indeed, the relative profundity of various factional critiques of the CPGB, masked a toxic and ruinous ideological inheritance that the groups and individuals were simply unable to think their way out of. Given that this would have meant overthrowing the ideological authority of the Chinese communists (itself built on strong notions on centralised and top-down leadership alive in the general 'official' communist movement), it becomes clear that there was really very little room for manoeuvre.

Numerically, the pro-Chinese groups in Britain were unable to compete with the CPGB in the trade union movement and with the Trotskyists in the student and anti-war movements. Thus, apart from the partial exception of the CPB (M-L), most of the pro-Chinese groups did not prosper in the 1970s and 1980s, which coincided with changes in the political outlook of the CPC after the death of Mao.

Conclusion

Ultimately, both wings of the CPGB's 'anti-revisionist' trend stand as monuments to the failure of the 'official' communist movement. The pro-Soviet and pro-Chinese factions inherited ideas and practices from the history of Stalinism that crippled them, even as they were pulled toward revolutionary politics (and as they advanced some plausible ideas as to the nature of the CPGB's crisis). This reliance on what were perceived as 'authoritative' ideas from the commanding heights of the movement pulled the pro-Soviet trends back towards the practices that CPGB oppositionists had rejected in the 1940s and wrecked the pro-Chinese factions in a welter of frivolous splits and sectarianism.

Notes

1 See L. Parker, *The Kick Inside: Revolutionary Opposition in the CPGB, 1945–1991* (London: November Publications, 2012), pp. 39–40.

2 There are a couple of half-glimpses of inner-CPGB opposition on such matters in the 1930s. Palme Dutt told a CPGB Central Committee meeting in 1939: 'The [opening of the Second World War] has shown dangerous tendencies in the party ... We know anti-international tendencies, contemptuous attitudes to the International, anti-Soviet tendencies ... from the time of the [Moscow] Trials, talk of collapse of the International, talk of the Soviet Union following its interests and the like.' Cited in A. Murray, *The Communist Party of Great Britain: A Historical Analysis to 1941* (Liverpool: Communist Liaison, 1995), p. 93. In a similar vein, Edward Upward sketches a CPGB branch meeting where an oppositionist member, Mike Bainton, is expelled from the party for proselytising the idea that the Soviet leaders were in the process of abandoning international revolutionary communism. See E. Upward, *In the Thirties* (London: Quartet, 1978), pp. 165–84.

3 For more on the opposition at the November 1945 congress, see Parker *The Kick Inside*, pp. 15–31.

4 J. Duclos, *On the Dissolution of the Communist Party of the United States*, www.marxists.org/history/usa/parties/cpusa/1945/04/0400-duclos-ondissolution.pdf, accessed 14 November 2010.

5 *World News and Views*, 10 November 1945.

6 E. Heffer, *Never a Yes Man: The Life and Politics of an Adopted Liverpudlian* (London: Verso, 1991), p. 38.

7 For CPGB oppositionists in the late 1940s and early 1950s see Parker, *The Kick Inside*, pp. 32–6.

8 *World News*, 9 February 1957.

9 *Communist Party 25th Congress Report* (London: CPGB, 1957).

10 *World News*, 25 February 1957.

11 Ibid.

12 E. Jackson, *Congress: An Appeal to Delegates* (Bexley, 1971).

13 Gwyn Reed in *Comment*, 9 July 1977. Reed later joined the New Communist Party.

14 *The Case for the New Communist Party* (London: New Communist Party, no date but circa 1977).

15 For more on the Appeal Group, see Parker, *The Kick Inside*, pp. 77–80.

16 RFE/RL background report 'The British Communist Congress', 1 December 1965. See also pre-congress discussion contributions from the Surrey District Committee, *Comment*, 2 October 1965; and Sid French, *Comment*, 13 November 1965.

17 John Chamberlain played such a facilitating role in Hemel Hempstead in the 1970s, circulating oppositional documents through his contacts and organising meetings with key speakers. John Chamberlain, interview.

18 *The Case for the New Communist Party*, p. 8.

19 See, for example, a letter from Bexley Branch to the CPGB EC, 12 January 1966 in CP/CENT/EC/11/01.

20 *Unemployment and the Crisis of Capitalism* (Surrey: Surrey Young Communist League, 1976), pp. 14–15. French was criticised by Tony Chater at the CPGB's 1975 congress for claiming that the CPGB was fostering this anti-Sovietism. See 'The Crisis, Left Unity and the Communist Party: Tony Chater's Reply to the Discussion', *Comment*, 29 November–13 December 1975.

21 'Statement of Surrey DPC for the Executive Committee Discussion on 23.4.66 on Our Electoral Perspectives', CP/CENT/EC/12/01.

22 Letter from Sid French to John Gollan, 11 May 1967 in CP/CENT/EC/12/01.

23 J. Klugmann, 'A Brief History since 1945', *Comment*, 5 February 1977.

24 C. Myant, 'Up for Discussion', *Comment*, 5 February 1977.

25 W. Thompson, *The Good Old Cause: British Communism 1920–91* (London: Pluto Press, 1992) p. 171.

26 G. Andrews, *Endgames and New Times: The Final Years of British Communism, 1964–91* (London: Lawrence and Wishart, 2004), p. 165.

27 Charlie Doyle was a retired power worker who formerly worked at Battersea Power Station and had been active in the Electrical Trades Union. He was expelled from the union after leading unofficial strikes in the winter of 1962–63. Doyle, born in Scotland, had been a member of the Communist Party USA (CPUSA) and was deported back to Britain in 1953 in the era of McCarthyism. He had opposed the leadership line on Czechoslovakia. His wife, Mikki Doyle, was editor of the *Morning Star* women's page.

28 C. Doyle, *A Critique of the Draft British Road to Socialism: Revolutionary Path – or Diversion?* (London, 1977) pp. 2–3.

29 Ibid., pp. 12–13.

30 Ibid., p. 16.

31 Brian Davies was on the Welsh Committee of the CPGB from 1974–77, leaving the party to join the New Communist Party in 1977, an experience that Davies subsequently referred to as 'out of the frying pan into the fire': Brian Davies, interview, 1996. Davies was a founder member of the Niclas Society, a Welsh Marxist group.

32 *Comment*, 5 March 1977.
33 Ibid.
34 *Comment*, 30 April 1977.
35 *The British Road to Socialism* (London: CPGB, 1951).
36 *Comment*, 3 September 1977.
37 John Gollan, 'Which Road?', *Marxism Today*, July (1964). 'A number of communist parties at the time, including the CPSU, showed considerable interest in what we were thinking when we were drafting *The British Road*. The main ideas advanced in the programme, particularly that of the possibility of peaceful transition in Britain, were discussed in detail in conversations Harry Pollitt had with Stalin at the time, who approved fully of our approach. Following the adoption of the programme by our Executive Committee in January 1951, it was published in full in *Pravda*, again with Stalin's approval. The Soviet communists have always given it general support since then. If Khrushchev is a "revisionist" on this matter, then so, too, was Stalin.'
38 For more on the NCP split in 1977, see Parker, *The Kick Inside*, pp. 87–90.
39 *Comment*, 3 September 1977.
40 Jim Moody, interview. Further testimony to this point is that the NCP threw off a number of leftward-moving splits in the first few years after its foundation, namely *The Leninist*, *Proletarian* and the Vanguard Group.
41 *The Case for the New Communist Party*, p. 7.
42 Ibid., p. 9.
43 *The Revolutionary Party* (London: New Communist Party, 1982), p. 27.
44 Fergus Nicholson is the name most commonly associated with the journal, writing under the by-line of 'Harry Steel'.
45 *The Leninist* trend that emerged in the early 1980s was brave enough to reject many (although not all) of the 'official' communist dogmas that had marked its predecessors but only in the cause of making itself largely irrelevant to the CPGB's factional wars of the 1980s. See Parker, *The Kick Inside*, pp. 96–106.
46 Joint Committee of Communists, 'The Marxist-Leninist Movement in Britain: Origins and Perspectives', *The Marxist*, 12, autumn (1969).
47 See, for example, A. H. Evans, *Truth Will Out: Against Modern Revisionism* (London: CDRCU, 1964); and a 1946 paper criticising Harry Pollitt's *Looking Ahead*, CP/IND/MISC/22/08.
48 Thompson argues that although the CPGB lined up on the Soviet side of the dispute, 'it never accepted unreservedly the Soviet position'. Thompson, *The Good Old Cause*, p. 131.
49 Michael McCreery was the son of General Sir Richard McCreery, who commanded the British Eighth Army in northern Italy during 1944–45. Michael was educated at Eton and Christ Church Oxford, going on to serve with British Military Intelligence – see 'Michael McCreery' *Workers Broadsheet*, 1, 5, no date but circa mid-1969. McCreery had joined the CPGB in 1956 after a previous membership of the Labour Party.
50 See, for example, a report by Jack Cohen on the activities of comrades Muriel and Peter Seltman, McCreery and others at the Holiday School, Lyme Hall, 10–17 August 1963 (typed up by author 9 September 1963) in CP/CENT/

ORG/20/07. The Seltmans (of Barnet branch, London; Muriel was branch secretary), McCreery and another comrade were deemed to have worked as an 'organised group' throughout the duration of the school. They were reported to have been active during lectures and informally at mealtimes, and at the bar. They pretended not to know each other. They were 'open protagonists of the line of the CPC'.

51 For more on Reg Birch in the 1960s, see Parker, *The Kick Inside*, pp. 63–74.

52 'The Communist Party No Longer Exists in Britain!', *Hammer or Anvil*, 2, 1 (1966). For more on the ACMLU, Parker, *The Kick Inside*, pp. 51–2.

53 M. McCreery, *Destroy the Old to Build the New! A Comment on the State, Revolution and the CPGB* (London: CDRCU, 1963), p. 10.

54 Parker, *The Kick Inside*, p. 60.

55 'Report from the Glasgow Communist Movement', *The Marxist*, 1, 7 (1968).

56 Editorial Departments of *Renmin Ribao* (*People's Daily*) and *Hongqi* (*Red Flag*), 'The Leaders of the CPSU are the Greatest Splitters of Our Times – comment on the open letter of the Central Committee of the CPSU (VII)', February 4 1964, www.marxists.org/subject/china/documents/polemic/splitters.htm, accessed 16 February 2007.

57 Ibid. For a British version of this thesis, the *Forum* group explained opportunism by reference to middle-class elements infiltrating working-class organisations. See 'The Source of Opportunism in the Working-class Movement', *Forum*, 2 (1964).

58 'Review of Marxist-Leninist Press', *The Marxist' Hammer or Anvil*, 2, 3 (1966).

59 Ibid.

60 See Parker, *The Kick Inside*, p. 49.

61 Joint Committee of Communists, 'The Marxist-Leninist Movement in Britain: Origins and Perspectives'.

62 Ibid.

6

Dissent from dissent

The 'Smith/Party' Group in the 1970s CPGB

Andrew Pearmain

For Communist critics of the existing (party) leadership and policies ... random discontent, non-cumulative critical activity and inadequately elaborated alternatives are not enough.

Smith Group Bulletin, *No. Two* (1971/72)[1]

The 'Smith/Party Group' was an informal faction inside the Communist Party of Great Britain (CPGB) in the early 1970s. Its ideological orientation shifted over its few years of existence as its political economy took distinctive shape, but initially it defined itself by 'a rejection of the concept of a parliamentary transition to socialism, a lack of enthusiasm for the socialist countries, and a concern with the processes of Party democracy'.[2] It was called the Smith Group to begin with, later the Party Group. Deliberately obscure, in their operations if not their outlook, and relatively short-lived, just three or four years in the seventy-year existence of the CPGB, they left little recorded evidence and made little overt impact on the party's debates and activities.

The only written records are in small private collections owned by involved individuals, none of whom (as far as I'm aware) has written their own historical accounts. Many of these fragments are articles which had been rejected by the CPGB press on technical or political grounds – the Group complained that it was 'almost impossible to have critical articles in the Party press' – then circulated in *samizdat* form around Group members and contacts.[3] Up to now they have not been included in the 'official', generally comprehensive and well-ordered CPGB archive.[4] Smith Group members' own memories are fading with age, and with the demise of the organised political left in Britain. There is only the odd passing reference to the Group in published CPGB histories – a couple of cursory mentions in Geoff Andrews' semi-official *Endgames and New Times*, for example – and little considered appreciation of its political significance.[5]

And yet the Smith Group's discussions and interventions indirectly conditioned the CPGB's debates, activities and events in the 1970s and 1980s, not least by challenging this notoriously insular party's response (or lack of it) to the broader social and cultural changes going on around it throughout this turbulent period. Much of what became known as the '*Marxism Today* analysis' of ascendant hegemonic Thatcherism and the corresponding decline of the political left – announced in Eric Hobsbawm's 'The Forward March of Labour Halted?' (1978) and elaborated by Stuart Hall with a renewed emphasis on culture and ideology – echoes the Smith Group's critique of CPGB theory and practice and the shortcomings of the broader left in Britain, particularly the 'dead end' of Labourism.[6] The Group's work also has its own intrinsic interest, as a relatively creative, open-minded and cogently argued attempt to modernise the theory and practice of British communism and seek 'freedom from dogma'.[7] This was the last serious attempt from within that tradition at a new, objective, constructive, 'potentially hegemonic' political economy.

But its failure and dispersal (which it anticipated; see beginning quote) also helps to explain the grand historical failure of the British Communist Party. To this day, the Smith Group offers tantalising glimpses of a more effective but unrealised left-wing politics, a small but intriguing set of counter-factual 'if only-s' and 'what ifs', an invitation perhaps to a bout of 'wishful rethinking' or 'uchronia'.[8] Above all, what would a British Communist Party that was both rooted in the lives of ordinary people and open to the necessarily critical scrutiny of intellectuals – along the lines of the truly 'mass party' of Italian Communists – have achieved? This is one of the most important and intriguing 'roads not taken' in modern British politics.

A loose association of individuals[9]

Factions were outlawed in the CPGB under the terms of democratic centralism, the vertical model of inner-party discipline which allowed only for coordination through the party's official hierarchy of national and regional conferences and committees and local branches, up and down but never 'sideways'; hence the Smith/Party Group's innocuous name(s). According to founding Group member Mike Prior, they were careful not to be seen as an organised faction that would invite censure, with the ultimate threat of expulsion.[10] In retrospect he suspects they needn't have worried. The party was by now so focused on the 'industrial struggle' – the wage militancy that spread across much of British industry in the period 1971–74 and eventually contributed to the general election defeat of the

Heath government – that intellectuals were pretty much ignored anyway, even dissidents.

This was nothing like the period after the twin shocks of the Soviet invasion of Hungary and Khrushchev's 'revelations' of Stalin's crimes at the Communist Party of the Soviet Union (CPSU) Congress in 1956, when CPGB intellectuals were closely monitored for open dissent or deviant opinion. Many left in disgust at that point, and would provide the organisational and political basis for Campaign for Nuclear Disarmament (CND) and the first New Left (curiously this is disparaged in Smith Group materials as 'the exodus of the ultra-revisionists').[11] Other schisms followed, most substantially over the Sino-Soviet split in the early 1960s, which led to the formation of several Maoist breakaways from the CPGB, primarily the Communist Party of Britain (Marxist-Leninist) led by Reg Birch.

By the early 1970s radical left intellectuals were being drawn back towards the CPGB, partly in frustration at the failure of the leftist revolutionism of 1968 and its lack of roots in British society (exemplified by *New Left Review* at its most neo-Trotskyist), but also in disillusionment with right-wing Labour. But the party itself was not especially receptive – based as it always was amongst skilled manual workers, typically engineers, 'the more thoughtful kind of bloke' – or even much bothered with what these post-1968 intellectuals might have to contribute.[12] A certain indifference amongst officials and 'leading comrades', with an undertone of condescension and a semi-conscious marginalisation or 'quarantine' of the Communist University of London and even of the party's successful magazine *Marxism Today*, would later contribute to a further round of intellectuals' disaffection and departure, including most of those involved in the Smith Group.

The Smith Group was set up in 1971. Its undisputed leading figure was Bill Warren, a development economist who studied at Glasgow and Cambridge universities. From 1964 he worked at the School of Oriental and African Studies in London, with some time also spent at the University of Sudan. Warren – 'a wiry, determined character' (according to Mike Prior) – had previously worked as an apprentice in the Clydeside shipyards. The Group's founding core was very small: Warren, Prior, Derek Boothman, Chris Gilmore and Antonio Bronda (the London correspondent of *L'Unita*, the Italian Communist Party's daily newspaper), with other contacts in Warren's university party branch. There was never a fixed or even recorded membership, but rather 'a loose association of individuals', around 35 to 40 in London (according to Boothman) and a few others in contact elsewhere, mainly Manchester and Glasgow.[13] All of them were in or close to the Communist Party, though they came to the CPGB from a variety of sources, with no single intellectual thread.[14] When the Group dispersed in 1974/75, the few non-communists had either joined the party or left the Group, so by then it was (according to Mike Prior) entirely communist.[15]

The Group grew to include Prior's partner Buzz Goodbody (a theatre director at the Royal Shakespeare Company, whose Gestetner printing machine produced much of the Group's documentation), Marshall Harris, Bridget Harris, Adah Kay, Tom Kay, Bea Campbell and Bobby Campbell (both at that point journalists at the *Morning Star*), Alec Gordon, Julie Gordon, Klim McPherson (a statistician and later prominent epidemiologist), Colin Chambers, Steve Bodington (managing director of the CPGB publishing house Lawrence and Wishart), and Steven (later QC, then Lord) Sedley. According to Derek Boothman, 'there were others who in some ways were sympathetic to some aspects of the group but maybe didn't take part because they thought it was factional, or for geographical reasons, or because they weren't totally convinced politically of where we stood'.[16] Amongst people in contact outside London were the Manchester University economists Pat Devine, a lifelong communist, and David Purdy, soon to join the CPGB but at that point a member of the International Socialists, the 'libertarian' forerunner to the Socialist Workers Party.[17]

In its informality the Smith Group was as much a friendship group as an old-fashioned political faction. They met in front rooms rather than public meeting places and held open discussions rather than structured debates, albeit with agendas and records and written introductory papers. Given the number of academics involved, it also inevitably had something of the seminar about it; this would prove something of a handicap. Most of the group considered each other friends (and for all the vicissitudes of the intervening years, those still alive continue to do so) as well as comrades. A number were or became couples; several were housemates. They were very much based in inner-north London, in the boroughs of Camden, Islington and Haringey; south and east of Hampstead, with all the cultural distinctiveness that would imply (with the notable exception of Warren himself, who lived in suburban Barnet with his wife and son). They were also very young, in their twenties or early thirties (Warren, born in 1932, was a little older), at a time when the average age of CPGB members was around fifty.[18] In demographic terms, they were joining – and attempting to rejuvenate – a party of late middle age.

The Group's politics were 'revolutionary democratic' and firmly Marxist, heavily influenced by the post-1968 politics of liberation and personal identity, but tempered by awareness of the communist tradition and considerable sincere respect for its working-class base. According to Mike Prior (like others, the child of a 'party family'), they appreciated that unlike the *groupuscules* of the far left 'the CP [Communist Party] seemed capable of breaking up the traditional structures; it was respected and still had a working-class membership'.[19] The Group's political project was to fuse the social solidarity and industrial power of the British proletariat with the strategic vision and value base of the radical intelligentsia; labour 'muscle' with the 'spirit of 1968'. This was a distinctively British example of that much misunderstood Gramscian category, 'organic intellectuals'; or, to convey more precisely what Gramsci meant, critical activists or 'permanent persuaders'.[20]

Most Smith Group members were university lecturers or postgraduates, journalists or other non-affiliated professionals, what Gramsci would have characterised as 'traditional intellectuals', but radicalised (made 'organic') by the times (or 'conjuncture'). Several worked in what would now be called 'the creative industries', primarily the theatre and publishing. They brought with them a measure of transgressive bohemianism and engagement with 'alternative' values and lifestyles, in marked contrast to the social conservatism and cultural conformism of the CPGB's mostly 'respectable' working-class membership. They noted, with a mix of admiration and amusement, just how 'ordinary' most communists were.

This led, amongst other things, to a close association with women's liberation and (up to a point) the forms of educative discussion Sheila Rowbotham would later call the 'shared deep change of consciousness raising'.[21] They were disdainful of then orthodox CPGB animosity towards feminism, represented by 'ubiquitous Trot-hunter Betty Reid', in particular the party's tendency 'to reduce everything to equal pay and jobs, while ignoring the vital function of the family as an economic institution and a source of women's exploitation'.[22] They noted the CPGB's residual sexism, in Tower Hamlets for instance, where Group member 'Be [sic] Campbell's biography for a council election leaflet was altered from "24 years old; journalist" to "24 years old, married, journalist".'[23] Six of the Group's core members were women – a full third, a very high proportion for left-wing political groups of the time, if not actually for CP membership (also around one-third female) – and would all have described themselves as feminists as well as communists.[24] These women were all involved to some extent in the concerted struggle to import feminism into the CPGB, as well as the conferences and activities of the burgeoning Women's Liberation Movement, which held its first national gathering at Ruskin College in the same year the Smith Group began meeting.[25]

Several Smith Group women were later involved in the semi-official CPGB feminist magazine *Red Rag*. But the Smith Group was not itself feminist, and women's liberation was not one of its formal central concerns. According to Mike Prior, Bill Warren 'did not have much feel for feminism', with his Scottish working-class background and his own suburban nuclear family.[26] The feminist critique of left-wing politics was clearly a factor in the eventual dissolution of the Smith Group, with what one member would charge was the Group's 'contentious mode of expressing ourselves' and reluctance 'to consider the problems of sexism'.[27] The centrality (or otherwise) of feminism also became a major issue in the break-up of one of the Smith Group's successor initiatives, the journal *Politics and Power*, when all but one of its six female board members resigned (as well as a sympathetic Mike Prior).[28]

The Smith Group was not straightforwardly 'Euro-communist' either, which was a later label for the 'democratic' communism associated with the Italian Communist Party (PCI) at its mid-1970s electoral zenith (the PCI itself was always wary of the term) and later still for the 'reform' faction around *Marxism Today* during the CPGB's 1980s death throes. They were vaguely aware of the writings of Antonio Gramsci, whose seminal *Selections from Prison Notebooks* was published under the editorial direction of Group member Steve Bodington in the same year the Smith Group began, but not of their profoundly unsettling detail, which helps to explain the relatively orthodox Leninism of much of the Group's analyses. In fact, sporadic references to Gramsci were more likely to be about his pre-prison record as a party activist and leader. A 1973 critique of *The British Road to Socialism* (BRS) written by Bill Warren (rejected by *Marxism Today* then published in *New Left Review*) equated Gramsci's conception of the Factory Councils with Lenin's Soviets as a way to 'transcend the bureaucratic rigidities and economistic limitations of trade unionism', just as *NLR*'s Perry Anderson had in 1968, with no sense of Gramsci's highly sophisticated and decidedly 'post-Leninist' key-concept of hegemony.[29]

The Smith Group would never have referred to themselves as 'Gramscian' either, which was again a latter-day label used retrospectively by people around *Marxism Today* after the CPGB disbanded in 1991. In their own discussions and writings, they continued to adhere at least rhetorically to the central tenets of Leninism which had long directed most forms of official and less official communism, especially its contempt for parliamentary electoralism. On occasions, their critique of the party line was that, to use a classic communist formulation, it 'deviated from Leninist norms'. On others, it was a matter of disputed interpretation or application; the party bore 'the tradition if not the practice of Leninism'.[30] In broader terms its critique of the CPGB leadership and programme was that it was 'reformist' or 'revisionist', or even 'liberal Right', and over-reliant on collaboration with the 'left social democrats' in the Labour Party.[31]

As the Group developed, it became more clearly and stridently 'anti-Stalinist', while keeping a close eye on the CPGB's treatment of its internal 'Stalinist' opposition concentrated in (of all places) the party's

Surrey district. There were trans-factional common interests and attitudes in their shared animosity towards the party's central (and centrist) 'reformist' leadership. But unlike the Stalinists, the Smith Group's opposition was also based on a certain stylistic unease with the way the party conducted its business: stiff and superficial, hastily procedural and impatient with conceptual complexity, characteristic (for Mike Prior) of 'the hidebound structures of the established left'.[32] Within this were elements of the wider inter-generational conflict of the 1960s and 1970s, politically articulated as distaste for the 'old men's party' of Labour (to which the similarly aged CPGB leadership continued vainly to seek affiliation) and for the crumbling broader 'consensus' of social democracy and one-nation Conservatism; what Smith Group documents tended to call 'managed capitalism'.

The shibboleth of the welfare state, the crowning achievement of 'Butskellism' (after Tory Chancellor Butler and Labour leader Gaitskell), was regarded in these circles as more oppressive than enabling, more state than welfare, and a key component of patriarchy and 'the family'. This 'anti-statism' was a strong theme within liberation politics, especially in its anarchist or libertarian currents, and it helped to revive interest in the critique of the state in Lenin's early writings. The Smith Group had several formally introduced discussions of Lenin's work.[33] In keeping with the ideological volatility of the time, the Smith Group's politics also drew on other strands of leftism. There was some overlap in personnel and outlook with elements of the 'second' New Left, most notably the International Socialists with what Sheila Rowbotham called their 'theoretical openness and flexibility with an orientation towards a grass roots working-class politics' before they changed in the mid-1970s into the more traditionally workerist (if still recognisably Trotskyist) Socialist Workers Party. [34]

That same 'openness and flexibility' within a firmly class perspective characterised the Smith Group's politics – principled Marxism tempered by careful research, hard evidence and close argumentation; the basic method of historical materialism, 'revolutionary realism' or Gramsci's 'absolute historicism' – which not surprisingly bore fruit in the activities and writings of involved individuals and sub-groups long after the Group dissolved. Some of these later positions might be considered right wing in terms of the traditional alignments of the British political left and labour movement, and may reflect the general rightward drift of modern British politics. For example, the political potential of incomes policy as a tool of 'counter-hegemony' (revealing the growing influence of Gramsci's prison writings and Togliatti's post-war application of them), with the corollary that the 'social contract' between Labour and the Trades Union Congress might not actually be the 'con-trick' derided by the CPGB and the Labour left; or the constructive role of capitalism in post-colonial economies as a necessary prelude to socialism (usually considered the 'classical' or 'orthodox' Marxist view, associated with the Kautskyan revisionism of the Second International, and fiercely attacked by Lenin in his later 'anti-imperialist' phase); or perhaps most strikingly of all, an attempt to engage (at least intellectually) with the 'subaltern' Protestant working class within the Unionist 'historical bloc' in Ulster/Northern Ireland.

But in the Smith Group's own available records and writings there is little hint of where some of its members would go after it disbanded in 1974/75. To begin with, at its formation in 1971, the Smith Group's discussions focused closely on analyses of and interventions in CPGB congresses, which a small number of Group members would attend as branch delegates. Mike Prior recalls sitting alongside Klim McPherson in 1971, and suddenly realising that they were the only delegates out of several hundred to vote against a particular resolution. They found CPGB congress debates curiously perfunctory, disordered and muddled. This suited the party leadership, because the effect of all the confusion was to reserve overview and control to the centre, defuse dissent and avert any concerted challenge. Contributors were vetted by the Congress Arrangements Committee before debates began, and even if they were approved, were called in no particular order, so that 'no coherent argument emerges and it is very easy for the final (Executive Committee) speaker in summing up to destroy any half developed and half-forgotten criticism made some hours beforehand'.[35]

There were at this stage (1971) just a few hints of the broader dissident political stance the Group would develop: on the need for the *Morning Star* to become 'a more political paper' (a view shared with the Surrey Stalinists), for example, or criticism of the party leadership's deference towards the Labour Party and naivety in suggesting electoral deals. But for the moment the Group's dissent was largely procedural; its substantive politics were not yet clearly formed. And there was a basic acceptance of the 'Leninist conception of a Congress ... to receive a policy statement and analysis of the current situation from the leadership, discuss this, amend it on the basis of this discussion and then take this perspective back into the struggle.' But this was offset by an appeal to pre-Stalinist Bolshevik diversity in discussion and representation: 'The early Communist Parties accepted that leaders of particular tendencies should be included in leading positions, and that their viewpoints would be fully represented in debate.' For now, the Group was not openly dissenting from the CPGB's stated 'policies and perspectives' but arguing for the right to. Likewise, there were 'vague rumbles of discontent from certain people who see that things are not quite as they should be', but for now there was some hope that the CPGB could be genuinely revitalised.[36]

It was always going to be an uphill struggle. British Communists might be surprisingly ordinary – at the 1971 CPGB Congress, Caroline Ascherson noted in the *New Statesman*, 'people chatted over Thermoses and cheese sandwiches during the very brief lunch breaks at Camden Town Hall, or went out with their relations for fish and chips' – but that did not make them typical.[37] In the very earliest Smith Group documents, Mike Prior was warning: 'The fundamental problem of the British Communist Party has been that whilst its everyday actions have usually coincided with the everyday actions of the working class, its basic ideology has always been outside it. In a very real sense it has always been "foreign".' Prior observed that: 'An exaggerated national identity has never overcome this, nor could it, despite the pained feelings of many sincere members who have never understood why the working class was so ungrateful.' If the CPGB's 'mass influence is now and always has been negligible', at the same time it had never been an especially effective 'cadre' or 'vanguard' organisation, mainly because of the low size and calibre of its membership:

> The CPGB has a paper membership of just over 28,000 [in 1971]. The largest group within it however are what might be called the non-members, that is those members whose presence within the Party is purely nominal. The reason why such members remain are varied. Some stay because they are unable to resist the branch secretary anxious to reach his membership target, others because the Party card is the prop to memories of a socialist past. The largest single group of non-members may well be the Party wife, whose card is taken out with her husband's and whose sole political activity is working out which evenings she has to keep a late supper for a husband out at a meeting. There are also members totally disillusioned with the Party who nevertheless keep a card out of genuine political conviction. The numbers of such 'non-members' can never be known, but to judge from dues payments they may be as many as 50 per cent of the entire membership.[38]

The focus of the Smith Group's critique of the CPGB programme *The British Road to Socialism* was the party's attitude and demeanour towards the supposedly 'mass party of the British working class', the Labour Party; in particular the CPGB's 'would-be bedfellows on the Labour left',[39] with their 'promises of socialism to come ... and to come ... and to come ...'[40] The official Labour leadership would never reciprocate the CPGB's overtures, not least because they always carried the implicit threat of 'infiltration' and takeover, the tactic of 'entryism' frequently attempted by Trotskyists. British communists never really understood that the Labour Party was neither a conventionally broad-based British political party, with its origins as a parliamentary lobby on behalf of the trade unions, nor a typically European social democratic party, with its small, largely inactive and marginal individual membership and its exclusive practical focus on elections, not to mention its contempt for transformative strategy, theory and ideology. The CPGB always risked falling between two stools – 'the dominant reformist attitude of the *BRS* makes the party unattractive to the more revolutionary left, while its "reserved" attitude towards the Labour Party makes it unattractive to the left social democrats'.[41]

In reality, 'the policy of a closer alliance with the Labour Party could result in the virtual disappearance of the Communist Party and the continuance of a Labour Party inherently incapable of getting anywhere near socialism'. Prior summarised the options available: 'In the long run the Social Democratic group [in CP leadership] must get the Party into the Labour Party by affiliation, by alliance or by dissolution'. The first was intermittently attempted throughout the CPGB's history, the second provided the core of its post-war political strategy, *The British Road to Socialism*, and the third is *de facto* what happened: a kind of scattered entryism by those ex-communists still politically engaged – twenty more fruitless years after this extraordinarily incisive assessment.[42]

Towards dissolution

By 1973 the dominant view within the Smith Group – essentially Bill Warren's, with notable contributions from Mike Prior – was very much clearer, wider and bolder. Warren's mid-1973 'Notes on Characterising the Present Conservative Government and Political Situation' attempted to see things from the Heath government's perspective and to analyse the realistic options available to it (a form of 'objective' analysis which would come under challenge from within the Group, for consciously eschewing 'the perspective of the working people and oppressed sections of society').[43] According to Warren, British capitalism was in deep trouble, in both historical and international terms, with declining productivity and competitiveness.[44] The state, with Heath pursuing an economic strategy essentially the same as Labour's in government and opposition under Wilson, was seeking a workable technical response to the growing crisis. This would include flexible wage restraint, investment in training and technology, and increased 'participation' for workers and trade unions in managing the economy. This meant abandoning the initial 'laissez faire' stance of the 1970–72 period and adopting 'more state intervention', the model across the 'social democratic' Common Market to which Heath was negotiating entry, and where Britain's nearest 'competitors' were to be found (the Smith Group had been an early, and highly unusual on the left, supporter of British entry: 'We cannot consider opposition to the Common Market as being socialist').[45] The Tories were simply following 'the general trend of all sibling parties in advanced capitalist countries nowadays ...

aimed not at income redistribution through large profits but at competitive survival'.

These 'concessions' had in part been won by militant class struggle: 'the working class have smashed the Industrial Relations Act and Tory [state imposed] wages policy'. Heath's chastened Tories had recognised that 'British capitalism cannot now recover competitively without the active cooperation at national level of the working class'. This meant that 'Britain, more than any other capitalist country, is economically ripe for socialism', but the 'traditional left perspective of rising industrial struggle for higher wages' and its 'policies of opposition and withdrawal' offered no political strategy for achieving it. Instead, the struggle would have to be primarily democratic:

> Working class strategy must centre around struggle over control of the economy for whose interests, for what objectives, by what methods ... Such a strategy carries clear risk of integration of the working class into the state machine ... Consequently the struggle for the control of the economy must be a) conscious, with clear non-propagandist understanding and explanation of the workings of the economy and b) strengthening of the democratic character and independence of existing working class organisations.[46]

This was a notably optimistic assessment of the economic prospects for socialism in Britain arising from the latest round of capitalist crisis. At the same time, Warren's political analysis was becoming ever more pessimistic over the prospects for an effective response from the Communist Party and its 'broad left' allies in and around the trades unions and the Labour left. With good reason; the politics of 'opposition and withdrawal' would characterise the strategies of 'militant labourism' for the next twenty years, and provide a large part of the explanation for the deep hegemony of Thatcherism. Warren also recognised that much of his analysis would be anathema to the CPGB, especially his appreciation of Tory respect for liberal democracy and of recent 'extensions of democracy (and) participation', his acceptance of the technical rationale behind incomes policy, the notion that 'Tory economic and social policy (is) virtually indistinguishable from Labour's', the assertion that traditional industrial militancy was not inherently socialist, and the strategic promise of the 'working class developing parallel organs of power under capitalism' which bore little relation to the essentially 'parliamentary road' of the *BRS*.[47]

For the first time, in discussion of Warren's 'Notes', there is evidence of serious challenge from within the Group. A critique written by Marshall Harris provides a relatively orthodox, largely dismissive left-wing view of the Conservative government – based on the 'autarchic, aristocratic and anti-popular tradition present in Toryism' – as well as hints of later tensions over feminism, intellectualism and the relative weight of subjective experience and objective analysis.[48] Harris detects in Warren's account 'a serious misreading of the situation to suppose that the Tories have learnt that the class struggle must not become too bitter ... They have simply burnt their fingers in several confrontations, but this will not stop them from engaging in confrontations; it may make them a little more cautious or cunning in the way they go about them, but go about them they will because they can't do anything else!' Likewise, Harris challenges Warren's description of Tory policy as 'social democratic. Social democracy always had (emphasis on past tense!) a concept of Socialism; was the political nursery in which Leninism grew up; and differed largely from Leninism in its conception of the means of achieving socialism ... Nevertheless social democracy is in the same tradition as Marxism-Leninism, but this tradition has been abandoned by Labour and its European counterparts.'[49]

Towards the end of the following year, in October 1974, Harris circulated around what remained of the Group a very much more personal statement of disaffection, which both takes his critique of Warren's perspective further but also provides clear evidence of the Group's imminent dissolution.[50] 'The group has not been satisfactory for some time', Harris feels; 'for the last 2 years I have been extremely bored by a considerable part of the group's activity ... Almost every presentation has taken an economic analysis as its basis ... Such analyses deal in abstractions ... Academics and intellectuals write, talk and act as if the abstractions were the reality ... displaying a kind of idealism inherent in bourgeois ideology and academic methodology ... The Group's analysis has been Economist/Reductionist ... For me Economics is not important in the way it is for Bill, and possibly Mike, and others'. Interestingly, the 'arch sins' of 'economism' and 'reductionism' would become the centrepiece of later Euro-communist critiques of CPGB strategy. [51] Harris' impatience with abstraction – the way people 'talk about "the working class" ... and at the same time are incapable of relating to an actual worker' – goes further, to highlight the importance of 'feeling' and 'its effect upon the way each individual contributes to and interrelates with the group'. For him, 'anyone who is not interested in those feelings is not showing serious concern with the group'.[52]

It is partly a matter of the style of discussion, not actually listening to others but preparing one's own response. 'Tackling the personal, the internal, the individual's mode of thought and behaviour and perception is of prime importance for the future of the group'. Harris' critique imports the theory as well as practice of Women's Liberation, to compensate for 'the inadequacies of the Marxist conception of exploitation (which) does not address the situation of a woman doing housework for "her" family, in which she is exploited not just by the mechanism of the capitalist system but also by the nuclear family or men'. Citing the 'Women's Liberation Movement, Men Against Sexism, Gay Liberation', Harris contends that 'one way of humanising or concretizing our abstractions is to consider the problems of sexism, of our total historical heritage which is patriarchal, and how we can break through into a unitary human culture'.[53]

There is within this heartfelt critique of intellectualism a certain tetchy impatience, which would do much to undermine and demoralise the political left in the decades to come, and more than a hint of separatist self-righteousness (albeit expressed by a man; Mike Prior remembers a certain kind of 'reverse sexism' in operation). Harris declares 'If someone in the group is uncompromisingly wedded to a particular historic narrow view of exploitation, I feel it is impossible for me to conduct any useful exploration or dialogue with that person.' And in the very much longer term, there is an overestimation of the historical impact and longevity of organised sexual politics which recalls an assertion in one of the very first Smith Group documents: 'The effects of (feminism) will be around for much longer than the Scottish and Welsh Nationalism which passed its peak of activity some time ago.'[54] As we now know, in Britain at least, the 'identity politics' of regionalism and nationality would prove just as potent as gender and sexuality, especially in formally political spheres. The supposedly outdated politics of place and community would outlive what Stuart Hall in the late 1980s appreciatively called 'the revolution of the subject' and Tony Judt more recently and dismissively called 'the politics of self-examination'.[55]

What Smith Group members did next

In broad historical terms, the Smith Group's challenge to the hidebound structures and muddled politics of the CPGB failed completely. As Mike Prior puts it, the Group showed as clearly and competently as anyone what could be done: 'you organise things, publish things, meet as groups ... and nothing would happen'.[56] The CPGB leadership, generally so uninspired, insular and strangely naive in its dealings with the outside world, was highly adept at marginalising, absorbing and manipulating the party's own internal groupings. Much of the 'communist tradition', with what Samuel describes as its blend of 'extreme efficiency and political isolation', had after all developed towards this end.[57] The Smith Group was wound down in 1974/75, more from its own members' disillusionment and fatigue than any formal CPGB disciplinary measures. Most withdrew from active left-wing politics. Some were involved in the Communist University of London, but if they remained politically active, it was more likely to be in other movements – women, black liberation, community newspapers

– unrelated to the core concerns of the Smith Group. As Mike Prior, who was also involved in the *Haringey Free Press,* puts it, 'the CP was no longer our central activity'.[58]

The Smith Group's leading light Bill Warren left the CPGB in 1974 to join the Communist Organisation of Britain and Ireland, later renamed the British and Irish Communist Organisation, another shadowy band of displaced left-wing, mostly ex-CP, intellectuals. The British and Irish Communist Organisation numbered amongst its few dozen participants the historian Nina Fishman and the journalist John Lloyd. It continued to meet and publish its own 'bulletins' well into the 1980s, including a journal *Problems of Communism* which Warren co-edited. Warren's parting shots at the CPGB, and in many ways the last hurrah of the Smith Group, were an article accepted by *New Left Review* (*NLR*) (clearly intrigued by these signs of Leninist dissidence from within the CPGB) on the inherent reformism of the *British Road to Socialism,* and a pamphlet co-authored with Mike Prior and published by Spokesman in 1974 (after rejection by *NLR*), *Advanced Capitalism and Backward Socialism.*[59] The pamphlet was most notable for its espousal of the 'conflict theory of inflation', which had emerged from the CPGB Economics Committee (involving a number of Smith Group members and contacts) but was later suppressed by its chair, the venerable CPGB Industrial Organiser Bert Ramelson, because it explicitly questioned the value of wage militancy. For Warren and Prior, such struggle was 'inevitably divisive'; more promising prospects for progressive change lay in 'breaking out of the ghetto of merciless economism', and in the struggle for 'democratic control' of every level and sphere of society and the economy as a 'transitional tool' towards socialism.[60]

Warren subsequently published other articles in *New Left Review* and elsewhere, and a couple of well-received books, most notably the posthumous collection *Imperialism: Pioneer of Capitalism* (1980).[61] They were mainly about international development, his sphere of professional concern, with the characteristically iconoclastic (but historically astute) view that the 'anti-imperialism' of the Soviet Union was largely a smokescreen for Russian diplomacy, with its origins in Lenin's post-revolutionary revisions of Marx and the Soviets' desperation for international support against the encircling capitalist West. On this view, the 'national liberation movements' were at best representing the interests of their countries' nascent indigenous bourgeoisies and largely neglecting their small urban proletariats. The interests of the post-colonial working class would be better served by the development of Western-style capitalism than some form of 'third world' peasant-based socialism.[62]

Warren died from kidney failure aged 42 in 1978, 'suddenly and before his contribution to British Marxism could be fully recognised', according to a posthumous tribute by Mike Prior. Prior introduced the 1981 collection *The Popular and the Political* (which included contributions from other ex-Smith Group members and contacts David Purdy, Bea Campbell, Adah Kaye and Steve Bodington) with a dedication to Warren, who 'was among the first British Marxists to analyse the role of planning and conscious state control on the functioning of advanced capitalist economies. He recognised the importance of inflation as an endemic symptom of class struggle (promoting inequality and relative poverty, and thereby undermining working class political unity)... and the practical need for advanced forms of workers control and a socialist incomes policy'. [63]

Mike Prior became increasingly disaffected and by his own account ineffectual inside the party. He published *Out of the Ghetto* with Smith Group contact David Purdy, initially as a 'dissident' contribution to the 1977 CPGB congress debate on the *British Road to Socialism*. When it was rejected by the party press on the grounds of length, Prior and Purdy distributed it as a pamphlet; I remember purchasing my own copy at that year's Communist University of London. As if to demonstrate Prior's earlier point about the CPGB no longer taking its intellectuals seriously, he and Purdy were very lightly admonished by their party district secretaries for infringements that in previous eras would have seen them summarily expelled. In 1979 *Out of the Ghetto* was finally published as a book by Spokesman, the publisher supported by the Bertrand Russell Foundation and politically aligned to the neo-syndicalist Institute for Workers' Control, intrigued (like *NLR*) by signs of dissent within the CPGB. [64]

By that time *Out of the Ghetto*'s critique of left Labourism and of the CPGB's subservience to it, the central thread of the Smith Group's earlier 1970s analysis, had been largely superseded by the counter-revolution of Thatcherism and the 'hard left' response to it, though it would never disappear entirely from left-wing discourse. Prior was also on the editorial board of the short-lived journal *Politics and Power,* which ceased in 1981 amid another rancorous argument about sexism. He has since made a career as a consultant on energy policies, but continues to write and publish analyses of current affairs and political history. Prior had left the CPGB in 1979. At that year's congress, the centrist leadership allied with the 'neo-Stalinists' to halt the reform drive on internal party democracy; realising a fear first expressed by the Smith Group in 1971 that 'the EC and the neo-Stalinist opposition will recognise the basic identity of their positions and unite to crush the left'. [65]

Bea and Bobby Campbell had been amongst the first to leave the Smith Group, because they feared for their jobs as journalists on the *Morning Star.* Bea Campbell has made a living and a reputation as a journalist and broadcaster, with a certain brand of sharp-eyed popular feminism. Bobby Campbell became a senior sub-editor and columnist for the *Sunday Times* and later *The Scotsman*. Derek Boothman moved to Italy, worked as an academic, and translated and edited the writings of a number of Italian communist leaders and intellectuals, most notably Gramsci's *Further Selections from Prison Notebooks* (1995). He also contributed a number of commentaries on British politics to the Italian left-wing press, mainly *Il Manifesto*, whose 'democratic revolutionary' politics closely resembled the Smith Group's, and likewise criticised the 'reformist' or 'social democratic' stances of the Italian Communist Party leadership, especially its 'confusion of state intervention with socialism'.[66]

David Purdy resigned from the CPGB in early 1980. His parting shot was a hugely prescient outline of the prospects for British political economy: 'either the workers' movement fights for, and when possible agrees to, a radical social contract or, if one rules out naked coercion against the trade union movement, inflation must be contained by orthodox deflationary economic measures which impose indirect market discipline on the size and distribution of pay increases'.[67] Thatcherism would alternate between these latter approaches of political coercion and economic management to reshaping, reviving and adapting the capitalist economy. One measure of its ultimate success would be the almost complete disappearance of the 'revolutionary democratic' left-wing politics of the Smith Group and eventual disbandment of the CPGB.

Notes

1 'The State of the Party and the State of the Nation', article non-attributed but written by Mike Prior, *No. Two*, Smith Group Bulletin (1971–72). The CPGB archive is held at the People's History Museum, Manchester, where I have deposited the materials consulted here.

2 'Congress, Its Resolutions and the Party' (1971), non-attributed but most probably Mike Prior (Circular/1972/2/Congress and General/71).

3 Ibid.

4 Introduction, *No. Two,* Smith Group Bulletin (1971-72).

5 G. Andrews, *Endgames and New Times: The Final Years of British Communism 1964–91* (London: Lawence & Wishart, 2004), pp. 63, 128, 198; Andrews (p. 63) promises a discussion of 'the wider significance of the group in later chapters', but does not deliver. His chapter 'Intellectuals and the CP Leadership in the 1970s', in G. Andrews, N. Fishman and K. Morgan *Opening the Books: Essays on the Social and Cultural History of the British Communist Party* (London: Pluto Press, 1995) provides rather more detail (pp. 228–30), but mostly in terms of Smith Group members' contribution to CP feminism.

6 *No. Two*, Smith Group Bulletin (1971–72).

7 M. Prior, 'Congress, Its Resolutions and the Party' (1971).

8 For application of the concept of 'uchronia' to British left-wing political history, see A. Pearmain, 'Remembering the Left', *Soundings* (2005).

9 Mike Prior's description of how the Smith Group operated; personal interview, 12 October 2011.

10 M. Prior, interview.

11 M. Kenny, *The First New Left: British Intellectuals After Stalin* (London: Lawrence & Wishart, 1995); Prior, 'Congress, Its Resolutions and the Party'.

12 R. Samuel, *The Lost World of British Communism* (London: Pluto Books, 2006).

13 D. Boothman, email correspondence, 16 October 2011.

14 M. Prior, interview.

15 M. Prior, email, 15 February 2012.

16 D. Boothman, email correspondence, 16 October 2011.

17 Just as interesting is the list of CPGB members *not* involved, especially those later most publicly associated with 'Euro-communism' like Eric Hobsbawm, Martin Jacques and Monty Johnstone, who may have been aware of the Smith Group but chose not to join in.

18 *No. Two,* Smith Group Bulletin (1971-72).

19 M. Prior, interview.

20 A. Gramsci, *Selections from Prison Notebooks* (London: Lawrence & Wishart, 1971), p. 10.

21 S. Rowbotham et al., *Beyond the Fragments: Feminism and the Making of Socialism* (London: Merlin Press, 1979), p. 134

22 'All Women Are Oppressed', document in Smith Group Archive, undated and unattributed.

23 Prior, 'Congress, Its Resolutions and the Party' (1971).

24 'Women in Society: An Alternative', in *No. Two,* Smith Group Bulletin (1971–72).

25 'MsUnderstood', exhibition at the Women's Library, October 2009.

26 M. Prior, interview.

27 M. Harris, 'Problems of the Group', 25 October 1974.

28 M. Prior, 'Letter of Resignation', *Politics and Power*, 4 (1981).

29 B. Warren, 'The British Road to Socialism and the Strategy of Revolution', *New Left Review*, 63 (1970).

30 'The Crisis in Capitalism and the Crisis in the CP', article (unattributed but by Mike Prior – confirmed by email, 16 February 2012), in Prior, 'Congress, Its Resolutions and the Party'.

31 M. Prior, 'Congress, Its Resolutions and the Party' and 'The Labour Party'.

32 M. Prior, interview.

33 Lenin's *State and Revolution* (1902) is cited several times in Smith Group materials.

34 Rowbotham, *Beyond the Fragments*, p. 26.

35 Prior, 'Congress, Its Resolutions and the Party'.

36 Ibid.

37 C. Ascherson obituary, *The Times*, 29 March 2012.

38 Prior, 'The Crisis in Capitalism and the Crisis in the CP'.
39 Prior, 'Congress, Its Resolutions and the Party'.
40 *No. Two,* Smith Group Bulletin (1971–72).
41 Ibid.
42 Prior, 'Congress, Its Resolutions and the Party'.
43 M. Harris, 'Critique of Notes on Characterising the Present Conservative Govt. (by BW)'.
44 B. Warren, 'Notes on Characterising the Present Conservative Government and Political Situation – 28/6/73', Article 9/73.
45 *No. Two,* Smith Group Bulletin (1971–72).
46 B. Warren, 'Notes on Characterising the Present Conservative Government and Political Situation – 28/6/73'.
47 Ibid.
48 M. Harris, 'Critique of Notes on Characterising the Present Conservative Govt. (by BW)'.
49 Ibid.
50 M. Harris, 'Problems of the Group', October 1974.
51 R. Samuel, *The Lost World of British Communism.*
52 M. Harris, 'Problems of the Group', October 1974.
53 Ibid.
54 Prior, 'Congress, Its Resolutions and the Party'.
55 S. Hall and M. Jacques (eds), *New Times* (London: Lawrence & Wishart, 1989); T. Judt, *Ill Fares the Land: A Treatise on our Present Discontents* (London: Allen Lane, 2010).
56 M. Prior, interview.
57 Samuel, *The Lost World of British Communism,* p. 119.
58 M. Prior, interview.
59 B. Warren and M. Prior, *Advanced Capitalism and Backward Socialism* (Nottingham: Spokesman, 1974).
60 Ibid.
61 B. Warren, *Imperialism: Pioneer of Capitalism* (London: Verso, 1980).
62 Ibid.
63 M. Prior (ed.), *The Popular and the Political: Essays on Socialism in the 1980s* (London: Routledge, 1981), pp. v–xii; B. Warren and M. Prior, *Advanced Capitalism and Backward Socialism.*
64 M. Prior and D. Purdy, *Out of the Ghetto* (Nottingham: Spokesman, 1979).
65 Prior, 'Congress, Its Resolutions and the Party'.
66 D. Boothman, 'Britain, the Coming Election and the Parties', *Il Manifesto,* undated.
67 D. Purdy, Letter of resignation from the CPGB (1981), personal collection.

7

British anarchism
in the era of Thatcherism

Rich Cross

The late 1970s and early 1980s were a period of unexpected resurgence for the British anarchist movement, and for wider libertarian political initiatives circling in the orbit of an expanding anarchist core. The renaissance of anarchism in the UK was not something which many contemporary commentators on the British political fringe had anticipated. But British anarchism's recovery and renewed confidence was not only unexpected, it took on political hues, adopted practices and rallied around political priorities which were themselves novel and innovative (if often controversial). That British anarchism should encounter a period of revival in the unprepossessing context of the arrival of a new neoliberal, free-market, strong-state government appeared surprising, but for a significant number of political activists that combative context served to increase the attractiveness of the 'anarchist alternative', especially as the assault of Thatcherism seemed to place so many of the long-standing assumptions of the British extra-parliamentary left in doubt.

What is notable about this period in the history of post-war British anarchism is how far the political centre of gravity within the movement would shift over the course of a decade – as the pre-eminence of perspectives based on militant anti-militarism, individualism and counter-culturalism were challenged first by internal political developments and then by a largely external reassertion of anarchism based on class politics and the celebration of nascent oppositional instincts within existing, mainstream working-class culture.

That these breakthrough political initiatives could ignite such interest, and inspire the engagement of significant numbers of radical militants, is evidence of the continually innovative nature of the British anarchist impulse, of its continuing resilience and of the movement's capacity to reinvent and recover itself. That these new anarchist agents were to discover within so short a timespan that they appeared to have reached the limits of their own restorative agenda (far short of their stated ambitions) seemed to confirm once again the cyclical nature of the advance and retreat of British anarchism.

British anarchism into the 1970s

For libertarian, autonomist, left-communist and anarchist movements across post-war Europe, the political, social and cultural upheavals of 1968 provided both a contemporary touchstone and a turning point in their modern histories. In the UK, at only a few points in the twentieth century had anarchism intruded into the mainstream of extra-parliamentary opposition; and in the post-war environment the current's varied traditions had struggled to find purchase outside of the radical political fringe. In the UK, the 1950s 'had been a period of hibernation for anarchist ideas',[1] which only entered a nascent period of recovery in the 1960s, pushed forward by the emergence of hippy counter-culture and anti-authoritarian currents around the Campaign for Nuclear Disarmament (CND), notably the Committee of 100,[2] and within that subversive anti-militarist initiatives such as the 'Spies for Peace' affair.[3] The tumult which engulfed Paris, Prague and other cities in 1968 left a great deal of volatile political ferment in its wake across Europe, and although the repercussions in the UK were far more muted those ripples were conducive to the advance of libertarian forms of organisation and practice.

Prior to the 1970s, the history of post-war British anarchism had been a story of patchy, partial and inconsistent advance, intertwined with often prolonged periods of retrenchment.[4] The Anarchist Federation of Britain (AFB), an unstable alliance of anarchists of widely different hues ('from syndicalists and libertarian communists through hippies and liberals to individualists')[5] which had been re-established several times (most recently in 1963), had once again unravelled, suffering defections to the International Socialists (IS) and the International Marxist Group (IMG). The Organisation of Revolutionary Anarchists (ORA), originally set up as 'a reaction to the powerlessness and lack of formal structure' of the AFB, as a small ginger group within the federation (around the paper *Libertarian Struggle*), had first become independent, and then in 1975 evolved into the new Anarchist Workers' Association (AWA); an organisation defined by an explicit orientation to industrial and workplace struggles and determined to move beyond the frustrations of 'synthesis' politics.[6] The AWA declared that: 'class struggle has been the primary factor in the determination of the form and structure of society', adamant that capitalism would be overthrown 'through the development of working-class organisations and by means of a violent social revolution'.[7] Despite its attempts at political redefinition, the AWA endured a volatile existence, suffering further splits and losses, whilst struggling to rally the organisation to the struggles of the day. The main current to emerge from the last major schism in the AWA (which came to a head at the May 1977 conference), became the LCG (Libertarian Communist Group), which was launched in 1978.[8] The LCG announced the group's departure from the British anarchist tradition which it insisted had rendered itself 'unable to intervene actively in the struggles of the working class'.[9]

The 1979 general election, which brought to power the first Thatcher government, became the political nadir for the fractious 'post'-anarchist group, who opted to commit the organisation to the Trotskyist-led electoral Socialist Unity initiative. After dismal poll results, the LCG majority opted for fusion with the libertarian leftist group Big Flame.[10]

Elsewhere within the anarchist movement there were signs of greater political resilience. From within the British anarcho-syndicalist tradition, the Direct Action Movement (DAM) was formed in March 1979, from remnants of the earlier Syndicalist Workers Federation (SWF),[11] later acknowledging that 'syndicalism in this country has not really existed since the early 1920s'.[12] Early editions of the *Direct Action* newspaper had an irreverent style and the cut-and-paste design motif of a punk fanzine, only later adopting a more sober tenor for its industrial reportage. The more high-profile *Black Flag* newspaper which had been founded by Albert Meltzer and Stuart Christie in 1970 (initially entitled *Bulletin of the Anarchist Black Cross*, to emphasise its focus on anarchist prisoner support), stood firmly within the 'revolutionary class struggle' traditions of anarchism.[13] *Freedom*, the longest running of British anarchist newspapers, reflected the interests of a wider libertarian readership, and had stronger roots in the more liberal, artistic, cultural and intellectual traditions of the movement. The long-standing and bitter animosity between the latter two publications was partly refracted through the loyalty of a divided partisan readership, which (particularly in the uniquely intense political hot-house of the radical London milieu) often identified exclusively with one title or the other.

Yet when taken together, despite the politically receptive environment, the formal organisations and publications of British anarchism had failed to benefit from the seemingly more conducive post-1968 context and had again slid into the fringes at the close of the 1970s. Almost a decade earlier, Meltzer and Christie had written a landmark text on contemporary British anarchist theory which (anticipating the forward surge of the movement) concluded that the 'floodgates holding back anarchy are cracking'.[14] Ten years on and the official anarchist movement appeared to be stuck in the political backwaters, with the prospect of gains in either influence or organisation fast receding.

The impetus for the political revival of British anarchism in the late 1970s and early 1980s came from something of an unexpected quarter. Punk band the Sex Pistols, who burst into mainstream cultural notoriety in 1976–77, may have declared themselves as advocates for 'Anarchy in the UK', but the band's ideological ambitions (where they existed at all) were chaotic, and for all the band's nihilistic protestations, their political manifesto was threadbare at best. It was the emergence of a consciously anarchist current within the 'second wave' of British punk (1978–79) which became the catalyst for the revival in the energy, initiative and momentum of the forces of British anarchism.

The rise of anarcho-punk

Two unusual and highly distinctive punk bands share a pre-eminent role in the emergence of the new genre of 'anarcho-punk'. Based in a farmhouse on the outskirts of north London, the band Crass formed in 1977, but did not come fully to wider prominence in the UK punk scene until the closing months of 1978. Crass embraced a new fusion of punk and anarchism, concocting a mixture of individualism (infused with elements of bohemian culture and the ethos of hippy) and insurrectionism to inform a politics infused with anti-militarism, atheism, feminism, anti-authoritarianism and implacable anti-statism.[15] The band's sound was as distinctive as its orientation to the punk idea: a harsh, guitar layered aural assault, backed by militaristic drum patterns, and atonal soundscapes. The band's uncompromising, didactic approach (if not their musical motif) was shared by Poison Girls, a political punk band formed in Brighton, with strong anarcha-feminist credentials and a background more rooted in nightclub cabaret and theatre than in rock and pop.[16] The band's libertarianism was no less anti-state than Crass's, although Poison Girls' early lyrical focus concentrated on the themes of gender identities and the alienated experiences of women; particularly in the context of the family. Though their approaches had their differences, both bands shared a common recuperative aim: to rekindle the subversive, revolutionary original ambitions of punk. Founder member of Crass, Penny Rimbaud, later recalled: 'When in 1977 the Sex Pistols harped on about anarchy in the UK, it became pretty obvious to me that their interest was not in revolution but in their bank balance [...] We saw Johnny Rotten's "no future" rantings as a challenge. We believed that there was a future if we were prepared to fight for it, and fight for it we did.'[17] Following Poison Girls' relocation to London, both bands began a period of intense and close cooperation; collaborating on shared record releases, live gigs and tours; and a broadly similar approach to the practice of design, presentation and political publishing.

Anarcho-punk provided the momentum to re-energise the movement, but its impact changed its profile and the centre of political gravity within it. The political priorities of anarcho-punk were very different from what had gone before. Clear political foci were provided by the anti-nuclear and anti-war movements, but the attentions of anarcho-punk extended to include a matrix of other issues – including militant vegetarianism and animal liberation; civil liberties and opposition to police powers; struggles against wage slavery; feminism and struggles over gender equality; opposition to organised religion; and opposition to cuts and the reductions in the wider 'social wage'.[18]

Key to anarcho-punk identity was a focus on the practice of Do-It-Yourself (DIY); an approach to production and distribution based on the assumptions of not-for-profit, independence and autonomy, anti-commercialism, and driven by strong anti-hierarchical and collaborative considerations.[19] Over the next four to five years, with next to no formal organisation to support it, an independent network of radical punk practitioners identifying with the ethos of anarcho-punk came together through the shared production of recordings (on vinyl and cassette tape), fanzines and magazines, gigs (usually outside the circuit of commercial venues), and a diverse array of punk propaganda in a variety of different formats, all designed to make the anarchist case.[20]

As anarcho-punk was not much interested in the traditional prescriptions of the movement, conflict and disagreement accompanied this resurgence.[21] For many traditionalists, the insurgency of young punks was confusing, unwelcome or irrelevant to the 'real business' of the movement.[22] Many of the papers and organisations of the existing movement were unsure of how to respond to a revival that they could claim little responsibility or credit for.

In the early 1980s it was from within anarcho-punk that so many of the profile events and developments which bore the imprint of the anarchist movement drew momentum – including the celebrated 1982 Zig-Zag squat gig (a large one-day anarchist-punk festival held in a mothballed London nightclub); the series of Stop the City demonstrations held in the financial district of London in 1983 and 1984; the rise of a newly militant animal liberation lobby; the surge of punk activity at 'peace camps' outside nuclear air bases – and from its ranks that so large a percentage of the anarchist contingent of innumerable political demonstrations was rallied. At the same time, principally through the agency of the political punk fanzine, a plethora of new anarchist publications (of a wider variety of punk vernaculars, politics and styles) were produced and distributed through makeshift independent networks. The different communities of anarcho-punk produced a large array of tapes, singles and albums, and self-organised thousands of gigs at venues across the country. But political engagement was as central to the anarcho-punk idea as DIY cultural production. Rimbaud judged that: 'most anarchist punks were just as happy tearing down the barbed wire fences of military bases as they might be going to a gig'.[23]

Anarchism in the early years of Thatcherism

In the early 1980s, a shared agenda of opposition to the prescriptions of the Thatcher government proved sufficient to maintain the (albeit fragile and largely untested) unity of the reviving anarchist movement; or at least prevent a reoccurrence of the fractures of the 1970s. Anarchists of most hues could find common cause in the battles raging over cuts in the social wage, in opposition to increased powers for the police and court systems, and through joint struggles on other fronts. Despite the major differences in analysis as to the causes of the renewed nuclear arms race most anarchists could support the anti-militarist logic of the 'peace movement' (through the shared conviction that peace required not just the decommissioning of the nuclear arsenals but the dismantling of the 'war state' itself).

Although the nature of the underlying critiques again differed, anarchists from the syndicalist to the peace-punk wings of the movement shared a hostility to the politics and practice of the contemporary Bolshevik left in Britain. By virtue of on-the-ground political proximity, much critical attention was directed towards what were seen as the manipulative, self-serving 'front organisations' of the Trotskyite left in general, and of the Socialist Workers Party in particular: including the Right to Work campaign, Rock Against Racism and the Anti-Nazi League. Anarchists together opposed the party-building pre-occupations which were seen to drive them.

The short-lived London Anarchist Centre (August 1981–March 1982) based in the Docklands area of the capital provided another example of political cross-over between different wings of the movement, but put into sharp relief many of the tensions and conflicts which hampered efforts at collaboration. Start-up funds for the centre had been provided through a joint Crass and Poison Girls benefit single, but relations between the anarchist punks, the London Autonomists group and others remained fraught and, although the venue hosted many gigs and a number of political events, the centre closed within a year.[24]

Division and disunity still afflicted sections of the anarchist movement, but the upturn in the current's fortunes and the volatile political context of early Thatcherism continued to keep centrifugal pressures in check. At the large CND rallies in London in the early 1980s (such as the 250,000-strong march in October 1981) activists from around the country would gravitate together to form impromptu 'anarchist blocks', identifiable from afar by the black and black-and-red flags waving above them. To the frustration of march organisers (and many of the other marchers nearby) this anarchist contingent showed itself determined to barrack and heckle platform speakers from political parties and other organisations judged as antithetical to the anti-militarist struggle. By the time of the June 1982 rally, this assemblage of anarchists was subject to additional marshalling by a combination of police and CND stewards. Frustrated by the lockdown, a breakaway group of around 300 anarchists marched towards London's Oxford Street where their demonstration was swamped by police and 48 arrests were made.[25] A defence campaign rallied cross-movement support.

Joint efforts in shared arenas of struggle notwithstanding, key lines of political fracture still stressed the British anarchist milieu. The politics of contemporary anti-fascism were one such sharp dividing line. In the context of the resurgence of the National Front and other formations of the British far-right, large sections of the anarchist movement rallied around the long-standing 'no platform' policy, which sought to deny fascists the ability to organise in public. While some questioned whether the threat posed by the far-right merited the level of opposition many in the movement were prepared to commit to the anti-fascist struggle, others went further, arguing that the 'the politics of anti-fascism' were a disabling political cul-de-sac for the movement. Perhaps unexpectedly, anarcho-punk's rejection of the prescriptions of the anti-fascists drew them into close alignment with that current on the class politics wing of the anarchist and left-communist movements which saw the 'fascist threat' as a chimera. What did distinguish the anarcho-punk approach was the willingness to accept the attendance at gigs of those who held far-right ideas with the aim of engaging with and challenging their worldview. This was allied with a philosophical rejection of the authoritarianism seen as inherent in the effort to silence (by law or by force) the opinions of others, however objectionable.

The riots which erupted in a number of British inner-cities in the summer of 1981 exposed again many long-standing disagreements amongst anarchists in the UK over the questions as diverse as: the interplay between class politics and questions of race and racism; the utility and legitimacy of recourse to political violence; and the issue of revolutionary strategy itself. Differences in the perception of the centrality of 'the class struggle' were also manifest, in the early 1980s, in the extent to which anarchist militants identified with those strikes in the public and private sector that were called to oppose the early efforts at the neoliberal restructuring of the economy attempted by the first Thatcher administration.

The Falklands War was a defining moment in the modern history of both Thatcherism and the British state, and for the anti-Thatcherite opposition. The iconography and rhetoric of CND and that of the 'peace movement' had, in the context of the early 1980s, appeared interchangeable. The Campaign for Nuclear Disarmament had made little effort to distinguish its narrower unilateralist nuclear remit. In the context of a 'conventional war' to reclaim British 'sovereign territory' in the South Atlantic, CND shed this duality and reasserted its anti-nuclear mission statement. It was a logical move, but one which hobbled independent opposition to the war and deprived a small but vociferous anti-Falklands War movement of any campaign structure or organisation. In the vacuum, anarcho-punk played an important contributory role in articulating anti-war and anti-militarist sentiment, outraging Tory politicians with blunt and 'obscene' anti-Falklands War singles (such as Crass's excoriating *How Does It Feel to Be the Mother of a Thousand Dead?*) and public statements which led to 'questions in the House', and putative legal moves against the band.

New anarchist forces in the 1980s

Military victory in the South Atlantic transformed the electoral prospects of a Thatcher administration which had been beset with the problems of soaring unemployment, economic decline and domestic unrest. The resilience of Thatcherism after her second general election victory in 1983 accelerated the mood of pessimism and self-doubt across all 'progressive' forces in the UK. As the 1980s progressed, and in response to that deepening mood of despondency, the anarcho-punk movement became a more diverse and disaggregated force.

Poison Girls began concerted efforts to position the band as an artistic force within the independent sector of the music business, eschewing much of the didactic 'baggage' (as they now saw it) of their earlier practice, and restyling the band as 'cultural saboteurs', making forays into the territory of the commercial enemy. By contrast Crass, increasingly frustrated by what the band saw as their inability to respond effectively to the political challenges of the hour, came to see their rock'n'roll medium as increasingly unfit for purpose. Their musical releases and live performances became more intense, atonal and politically direct and shorn of the usual punk musical trappings.[26] Anarcho-punk band Conflict were attracting attention from the music press for adopting a more consciously 'street level', confrontational anarchist punk method; one which set aside any associations with a hippy pre-history and which felt in no way bound by pacifist precepts. (Conflict would later collaborate with *Class War* on the 1986 anti-royal wedding single *Better Dead than Wed*).

While Poison Girls continued working until 1989, Crass ceased operations in 1984 (as the band had always pledged). In their first full statement on their dissolution Crass explained: 'We felt no compulsion to continue gigging. We were no longer convinced that by simply providing what had broadly become entertainment we were having any real effect. We'd made our point and if after seven years people hadn't taken it, it surely wasn't because we hadn't tried hard enough.'[27]

Their disbandment signalled a key turning point in the history of the original anarcho-punk wave. Political differences within Crass over the band's future political orientation had been growing for some time, and the winding up of the band meant that hard-fought debates over future strategy were left unresolved. Rimbaud suggested that the logic of the Crass's later work was the advocacy of an increasingly clandestine campaign of unattributed actions by punk militants. The pronouncements of the 1984 *You're Already Dead* single were not cast in orthodox class terms, but spoke clearly of the need to confront the entrenched power and military might of capitalism and state directly and (it was increasingly implied) through whichever uncompromising political actions were required. Speaking to *Maximumrocknroll* magazine in the autumn of 1983, Crass suggested that: 'the class thing is gonna become central over the next five years. The struggle between the people as one class and the elite as another class'.[28] It was though as anarcho-punk's first wave began to peak that new agencies promoting revolutionary class-based anarchism again began to make the political running within the movement, exemplified by the group which coalesced around a new provocative tabloid.

Class War was a militant anarchist newspaper (and later organisation) originally set up by Ian Bone and other activists in 1983.[29] The initiative had its origins in Swansea, Wales, developing out of the work of a group of activists who produced local paper *The Alarm*, which focused on strong 'community newspaper' issues such as corruption within local government and invidious police practices. Bone suggests that the paper was distinguished by its willingness to 'name names' and print detailed evidence of its allegations (with little concern for the legal risks), and by its mischievous humourist style; approaches which would later find echoes in the pages of *Class War*.[30]

After abortive experiments with standing *Alarm* candidates for the local council, and a short-lived involvement with the Welsh Socialist Republican Movement, Bone relocated to London. Bone approached the London Autonomists group and a decision was reached to produce a tabloid-style anarchist newspaper which would reach a wider audience, and be particularly aimed at young anarchists, including anarcho-punks.[31]

From its first issue, the *Class War* newspaper displayed a strong affinity with punk sensibilities, but expressed these in the context of a tabloid style newspaper which revelled in the celebration of working-class violence against authority; combined humour, self-consciously outrageous text and imagery to celebrate assaults on the police; picket line violence; inner-city revolts; and to pour scorn on what it derided as the timidity of 'middle-class left'.[32]

As anarcho-punk had been able to do five years earlier, *Class War* seized the initiative and the notoriety of the movement. *Class War* 'the paper' only later became Class War 'the organisation', and throughout its lifespan, its numerical strength (initially, editors and networks of paper sellers; later, signed-up members) remained extremely small. Even at its height, the Class War Federation 'never had more than 150 members', with paper sales peaking at between 15–20,000 copies.[33]

Class War organised a short series of 'Bash the Rich' marches (first in Kensington, then in Henley-on-Thames, and then finally in 1985 in Hampstead and then Bristol). These highly theatrical demonstrations of 'class hatred' (which saw the march led by a banner proclaiming 'Behold your future executioners!') met an increasingly uncompromising response from the authorities, with the final Hampstead event being completely swamped by a large police mobilisation. Although the pages of *Class War* lauded the success of the marches, others in the anarchist scene judged the marches as absurd and politically inept. Speaking the following year, Bone conceded: 'I think most people in *Class War* would acknowledge that the 'Bash the Rich' marches were unsuccessful.'[34] Years later, Bone suggested that the Hampstead event: 'was to prove a disastrous farce for *Class War*', reinforced by the abortive last-gasp re-enactment in Bristol.[35]

Just as the insurgency of anarcho-punk had not been universally welcomed by the existing anarchist movement, *Class War*'s arrival was also met by wary scepticism from some and outright opposition by others. *Black Flag*'s Meltzer suggested in his autobiography that the new paper: 'came as a cultural shock ... to many older revolutionaries', who were initially unsure 'whether it was a one-off parody of anarchists' or 'a modern version of the caricature-sheet', though he acknowledged that the group 'quickly became the most popular anti-establishment youth grouping for years'.[36] In contrast, one correspondent to *Freedom* reported the emergence of the group's 'crudely nihilist broadsheet' with some alarm, concluding that the paper's amoral advocacy of crude class violence meant its ideas had 'more in common with Marxist dictatorship than with anarchy'.[37]

Anarcho-punk had (collectively) resisted attempts to germinate formal organisation out of the subculture's networks. Within three years of the paper's launch, the majority view within *Class War* was to support the shift toward a new anarchist support structure. In 1986, supporters of the paper agreed to form the national Class War Federation in an attempt to place the production of *Class War* on a sounder footing; a move which heralded a minor split: 'Some people could not accept the idea of such a degree of organisation and left', the group later acknowledged.[38]

At a conference in Manchester in 1990, a majority of the federation voted to become 'a membership organisation, with membership fees, and a straightforward constitution',[39] effectively completing the evolution of *Class War* from an informal editorial collective to a more orthodox anarchist organisation. The March 1990 anti-poll tax riot in Trafalgar Square once again thrust all of the UK's anarchist organisations into the limelight, as the British press began the obligatory post-riot hunt for the 'outside agitators' responsible for the violence. Amongst their peers *Class War* exploited the publicity opportunities this provided to greatest effect, with member Andy Murphy's appearance on national television news to defend the 'working-class heroes' who battled with the police being reported internationally.[40]

Despite such notoriety, the poll tax struggle would in retrospect prove to be a high water mark in the organisation's influence – and its self-confidence. By the mid-1990s, the Class War Federation was finding the challenges of operating as a more traditional anarchist formation (and the longer-term limitations of the group's simple political lexicon) increasingly problematic.

Self-critical voices inside the organisation gathered momentum, and at the organisation's annual conference in Nottingham in 1997, Class War again split: the majority agreeing to dissolve the organisation, while a far smaller minority (based around the London group) determined to continue without the 'quitters'. The Leeds editorial group announced that issue 73 of *Class War* would be the last ever, and focused on 'an open letter to the revolutionary movement' which would raise the question of potential political regroupment of class struggle anarchist forces. Announcing that 'Class War is dead ... long live the class war', the final issue's editorial offered a political balance sheet of the organisation's history concluding: 'The Federation remains a tiny group with a big image that has outlived its usefulness. The appeal of our paper has become too narrow and limited', and insisting that the time had come 'to try something new.'[41] The London Class War minority fitfully produced editions of *Class War* for several years (announcing in its first issue that: 'Just as the Labour Party had to get rid of its 'militant' tendency, we have got rid of our non-militant tendency')[42] before winding-up operations in the mid-2000s.

Other class struggle anarchist forces judged that although *Class War* had served a useful disruptive role, it no longer served a productive purpose. The Anarchist Federation praised the group for 'helping the breakaway of serious class struggle anarchism from lifestylism and do-gooding liberalism, typified by the anti-nuclear movement of the time', but criticised the Class War Federation for its flimsy political rubric and its organisational self-obsession.[43] The short-lived Anarchist Workers Group (1988–92) declared more damningly: '*Class War* has ended up a mirror image of the pacifist ghetto it so despises: chaotic, disorganised and lacking politics and strategy, [*and*] firmly stuck in the ghetto of its own making.'[44]

Conflict and continuity: *Class War* and anarcho-punk

Historian of anarchism Peter Marshall suggests that *Class War*'s style and method shared 'some of the shock tactics and "fuck-off" graphics of punk', but judges that 'the similarity stops there.'[45] Yet although the two approaches (the anarchist punk and the class warrior) appear on first glance to be sharply defined dichotomies in the modern British anarchist tradition, the distinctions between the two are less pronounced, and the overlaps far greater, than many have acknowledged.

Although they wrestled with the dilemmas differently, both these anarchist currents celebrated the 'otherness' of oppositional culture in their different settings – Crass idealised the hippy experience of rejecting the existing social order, seeing its subversive potential reinvented in the punk counter-culture; *Class War* championed a very specific (and in its own way no less romanticised) reading of the incendiary elements of British working-class culture. Both of these readings of anarchism celebrated radical 'moments' as having values in themselves – in anarcho-punk, the thrill and excitement of gigs and other aspects of punk culture; for *Class War*, street ruckuses and clashes with the forces of law and order. Those actions were seen as having genuine (if temporary) liberating value in themselves, and also hinting at and anticipating the more seismic possibilities to come. In doing so both manifestations of the anarchist politic appealed and made their strongest pitch to a similar core audience – primarily the disaffected, urban young.

Both movements revelled in the idea of 'saying the unsayable', seeing great value in the deployment of shock and of being provocative and intentionally seeking to offend and outrage (and at the same time attract those intrigued by such provocations). The anarchism of both approaches shared a strong (and, at times, unconvincingly overstated) anti-intellec-tualism, which was refracted through the neglect of the established canon of nineteenth- and twentieth-century anarchist thought. Although both were keen to position their political efforts within a longer-term historical context (Crass and anarcho-punk, through a sense of affinity with the tradition of the counter-culture's rejection of the power of the state; *Class War*, by association with the history of uncontrolled working-class resistance to authority, police and state) neither saw particular value in explicit identification with the anarchist heritage, in Britain or internationally.

Both currents shared a strong opposition to mediated forms of political representation – trade unions, political parties, and in particular a deep hostility to the organised far-left and to the interference of front organi-sations in the arena of political activism (although initially Crass, at least, were more supportive of those campaigning bodies and single-issue pressure groups which were not seen as driven by organisational fetishism). Genuine, empowering political action was, for both currents by definition, direct, autonomous and self-directed. But the particular culture and form of the anarchist punk milieu and that surrounding *Class War* made the brokering of alliances with other activist forces extremely difficult, reinforcing an isolating 'otherness'.

The lack of clarity over strategy (and the absence of any clearly articulated sense of how this anarchist activity might, over time, be generalised into a combative revolutionary catalyst) had a number of repercussions; not least that it made it difficult to assess how political progress might be quantified, and increased the sense of frustration when these sketchily defined political advances were not forthcoming. Such uncertainties were reinforced by a reluctance within both currents to disentangle the degree of *informed support* for the substance of their political ideas from the (relative) popularity of the *form* and *presentation* of their political-cultural output.

Both *Class War* and the anarcho-punks shared a sense of uncertainty about questions of organisation and strategy – sharing a deep suspicion of formal organisation and fixed structures; and both inspired by an innate belief in the power of spontaneous initiatives that would thrive without alienating hierarchies. As both *Class War* and the militants of anarchist punk responded to the realities of the peaking of their own political experiments, they each struggled with the recognition that their circles of influence did not correlate directly with the popularity of their current's cultural output. Crass had long been frustrated at how many punk enthusiasts who identified with the anarcho-punk canon appeared reluctant to put their ideas into practice and to move beyond the position of music fandom to political engagement. There was a sense that, amongst the movement's ranks, there often appeared to be too many passive record collectors and too few engaged, self-directing militants. The editors of *Class War* appeared to lack similar self-reflective skills (and were far less self-critical of their publishing practice), appearing reluctant to accept that a significant proportion of the paper's readership treated the paper as an 'anarchist *Viz*' rather than as an irreverent, hard-hitting political tabloid. The renovating majority of Class War reflected the difficulty that the organisation had faced in mobilising committed supporters, noting that while many believed the group had 'thousands of people about to go on the streets and fight', the reality was 'that we are a group of super-active individuals who do it for them, an essentially passive readership'.[46] Such problems seemed to typify the dangers set-out in Jo Freeman's celebrated critique of anarchist disorganisation, *The Tyranny of Structurelessness*.[47] The group belatedly suggested: 'In many respects it's true to say that *Class War* failed to become much more than a "punk" organisation.'[48]

Despite these, often unacknowledged, instances of convergence, significant and irreconcilable differences between the two forms of anarchist practice persisted. Most fundamental was the disagreement on the question of revolutionary agency and the conduct of revolutionary action. *Class War* identified collective class conflict as the axis of the struggle against capitalism and the state. Anarcho-punk began with a belief that the individual is the agent of resistance to the compound tyrannies of the state, and that the maximisation of personal liberty is the cumulative guarantor of social freedom.

Class War's account of privation and exploitation was grounded in a (fairly crude) material interpretation of class and class relations; Crass's understanding of oppression and alienation extended beyond the narrowly material to propose philosophical, existential explorations of the idea of individual freedom. *Class War* embraced (and made definitional) the idea of the use of direct physical force (even in pre-insurrectionary conditions) while Crass's message was (in the early years of the group's work at least) one of militant pacifism. Although acts of material sabotage and the destruction of the property of the 'war state' were exempted, Crass expressed philosophical concerns about the impact on the individual psyche of a recourse to violence, and on the social level of the corrupting authoritarianism of Blanquism.

There were sharp differences too over the question of the agency of the revolutionary 'organisation' itself. Although acutely aware of their prominence within the scene Crass, Poison Girls and other anarchist punk bands were reluctant to have their message 'branded', and actively resistant to the efforts of others to profit from the commercial exploitation of their work and popularity. In contrast, the organisers of *Class War* seized every opportunity to promote the paper and the organisation's brand, producing and selling the type of self-promoting merchandise that was anathema within anarcho-punk.

Class War's public position was that its paper and organisation represented the single legitimate expression of contemporary British anarchism, and the paper rarely acknowledged the existence of other anarchist currents. Crass and other anarcho-punk artists tended to have a much more open and expansive (not to say generous and inclusive) sense of the wider anarchist movement, and to groups and campaigns beyond it (many of which Class War would have dismissed as irrelevant or even counter-revolutionary).

Impacts and legacies

By the time of the 1984–85 miners' strike, the British anarchist movement was in a more vital and dynamic condition than it had been a decade before. Its numerical strength had been much improved; its press was stronger and more visible; its ability to mobilise its forces again proven; and its orientation to contemporary political concerns reinforced.

Although the bands that were together the catalysts for anarcho-punk did not set out to re-energise the British anarchist *movement* (their interest was in the vitality of British *anarchism*), anarcho-punk brought in a renewed sense of dynamism and (in relative terms) a major influx of enthused young militants, raising the formal anarchist movement from its doldrums, and proposed radical new counter-cultural practices. Crass founder-member Rimbaud has claimed that the intervention of anarcho-punk 'changed the minds of a generation'. That claim is hyperbole, but within the radical milieu the impacts of anarchist punk culture, politics and practice were significant and far reaching.

Class War reasserted the primacy of uncompromising class politics in the making of the anarchist case, and again reinvigorated the anarchist movement with a brash new sense of confidence. As Class War faltered, new anarchist organisations advanced – notable amongst them the Anarchist Communist Federation (ACF), which offered a more considered and theoretically grounded articulation of the anarchist class war impulse; based on a specific 'anarchist-communist' identity: 'the term anarchist has often been misused: 'anarchist' can range from the hedonistic individual to the naïve pacifist. We felt the need to define ourselves in stricter terms'.[49] In terms of existing class-based anarchist alternatives, the ACF later explained: 'The objections to anarcho-syndicalism which would become more defined in the following years, precluded us joining DAM. Whilst we welcomed the imaginative approach of *Class War*, we saw that they lacked a strategy for the construction of a coherent national organisation and for the development of theory.'[50] The group, which retitled itself the Anarchist Federation in the late 1990s, later suggested its efforts were largely discontinuous with earlier anarchist initiatives in the UK: 'Although there is some historic continuity with earlier anarchist groups in Britain, the federation was mainly a new phenomenon, drawing on people new to anarchism in the 1980s.'[51] This was yet another 'restorative' claim by an emergent British anarchist agency.

By the close of the decade, the cyclical nature of British anarchism's advance and retreat appeared to be reconfirmed. Neither the anarcho-punk experiment nor the *Class War* dalliance with unreconstructed 'class politics of the mob' had settled the key questions facing the movement. The issues of organisation, practice, alliance formation, the relationship between reform and revolutionary ambition, resilience, flexibility and more – none of these had been decisively resolved.

The mid-1980s to the mid-1990s were a period in which class politics remained resurgent within British anarchism, even as the recuperative perspectives of *Class War* unravelled. New forms of mobilisation which came to the fore after the anti-globalisation protests in Seattle in 1999 (such as Reclaim the Streets, anti-roads protests, Earth First! and more recently the world-wide Occupy! initiative) have evoked more echoes of the activist-centred anarchist punk practice than the orthodox class perspectives of 1970s. These new radical libertarian initiatives and forms of organisations have posed new answers to the questions of agency, strategy and to the challenges of combining political autonomy with the ability to mobilise credible coalitions.

In many of these struggles the 'revolutionary subject' has been the voluntary collation of self-motivated, self-directed militants rather than an insurgent proletariat. Class struggle anarchist organisations in Britain have not responded to the emergence of such new radical forces with the hubris of dismissal which would have been commonplace in the 1980s. Indeed, these struggles have often been supported as authentic expressions of resistance to capital being waged in arenas beyond the community and workplace, by legitimate anti-capitalist forces. Although it was not the intention of either, perhaps the contemporary outcome of the 'restorative' political efforts of the agents of *Class War* and of anarcho-punk has been to contribute to the convergence of an anarchist politic able to see value in the battles being fought in both the counter-cultural and the class wars.

Notes

1 G. Woodcock. 'Anarchism: A historical introduction', in G. Woodcock (ed.), *The Anarchist Reader* (Glasgow: Fontana, 1977), pp. 11–56 at p. 49.

2 See, for example, V. Richards, *Protest without Illusions* (London: Freedom Press, 1981); R. Bradshaw, D Gould and C. Jones (eds), *From Protest to Resistance: The Direct Action Movement against Nuclear Weapons* (Nottingham: Mushroom, 1981); G. Woodcock, 'Anarchism', pp. 50–1.

3 Anon, 'The Spies for Peace and after', *The Raven: Anarchist Quarterly*, 2, 1 (1988), pp. 61–96.

4 B. Franks, *Rebel Alliances: The Means and Ends of Contemporary British Anarchisms* (Edinburgh: AK Press, 2006), pp. 49–70; P. Shipley, 'The Libertarian Alternative', in *Revolutionaries in Modern Britain* (London: Bodley Head, 1976), pp. 172–206.

5 M. Curtis and H. Stone, 'A Short History of the Libertarian Communist Group', available online at *Big Flame, 1970–1984*, http://bigflameuk.files. wordpress.com/2009/12/lcghist.pdf, accessed 17 December 2013.

6 G. Foote, 'Building the Revolutionary Party?', *Libertarian Communist Review*, 1, winter (1974), http://flag.blackened.net/revolt/ora/rev_party.html, accessed 17 December 2013; M. Curtis and H. Stone, 'A Short History of the Libertarian Communist Group'.

7 AWA, 'Aims and Principles', *Anarchist Worker*, July (1977), p. 7.

8 Editorial Collective, 'What's in a Name? Why We're Changing', *Anarchist Worker*, October (1977), p. 2; M. Curtis and H. Stone, 'A Short History of the Libertarian Communist Group'.

9 'Build This New Paper', *Libertarian Communist*, January–February (1978), p. 4.

10 'Libertarian Communist Group [LCG] (Groups Who joined Big Flame No. 2)', *Big Flame, 1970–1984*, 3 December (2010), http://bigflameuk.wordpress. com/2009/12/03/libertarian-communist-group/, accessed 17 December 2013; B. Franks, *Rebel Alliances*, p. 74.

11 Direct Action Movement and International Workers' Association, *Anarcho-Syndicalism: History and Action* (Manchester: DAM, n.d., but circa 1980), pp. 20–1.

12 Direct Action Movement, 'Introduction to Syndicalism', *Direct Action*, 4 (n.d.), pp. 6–7.

13 See, A. Meltzer, *I Couldn't Paint Golden Angels: Sixty Years of Commonplace Life and Anarchist Organisation* (Edinburgh: AK Press, 1996); S. Christie, *Granny Made Me an Anarchist: General Franco, the Angry Brigade and Me* (London: Scribner, 2004).

14 S. Christie and A. Meltzer, *The Floodgates of Anarchy* (London: Stanmore Press, 1970), back cover; *passim*.

15 For histories of the band's work, see: Crass, *A Series of Shock Slogans and Mindless Token Tantrums* (London: Exitstencil Press, 1982); G. McKay, 'Crass 621984 ANOK4U2', in G. McKay, *Senseless Acts of Beauty: Cultures of Resistance since the Sixties* (London: Verso, 1996), pp. 73–101; P. Rimbaud, *Shibboleth* (Edinburgh: AK Press, 1998); G. Vaucher, *Crass Art and Other Pre Post-modern Monsters* (San Francisco: AK Press, 1999); R. Cross, '"The Hippies Now Wear Black": Crass and the Anarcho-punk Movement, 1977–1984', *Socialist History*, 26 (2004), pp. 25–44; B. Cogan, '"Do they Owe

Us a Living? Of Course They Do!": Crass, Throbbing Gristle, and Anarchy and Radicalism in Early English Punk Rock', *Journal for the Study of Radicalism*, 1, 2 (2007), pp. 77–90; G. Berger, *The Story of Crass* (Oakland: PM Press, 2009); S. Ignorant and S. Pottinger, *The Rest Is Propaganda* (London: Southern Records, 2010); A. Bandez, *You Can't Sing the Blues While Drinking Milk* (Coventry: Tin Angel, 2012).

16 The history of Poison Girls has been only sparsely written to date. Key articles from the contemporary music press include: P. Du Noyer, 'Passion and Poison', *New Musical Express*, 17 October 1981, p. 17.

17 P. Rimbaud, 'Introduction', in P. Rimbaud, *The Last of the Hippies: An Hysterical Romance* (London: Active Distribution, 2009), pp. vii–xxi at vii–viii.

18 See, for example, the approaches outlined in: Crass, *A Series of Shock Slogans and Mindless Token Tantrums*.

19 For an appraisal of the practice of contemporary 'DIY culture', see A. Spencer, *DIY: The Rise of Lo-fi Culture* (London: Marion Boyars, 2005); for a discussion of the struggle for independence by independent punk record labels, see: A. O'Connor. *Punk Record Labels and the Struggle for Autonomy: The Emergence of DIY* (Lanham: Lexington Books, 2008).

20 For a collection of participant accounts of their involvement in anarcho-punk culture in the UK, see I. Glasper (ed.), *The Day the Country Died: A History of Anarcho-punk, 1980–1984* (London: Cherry Red Books, 2006); R. Wallace (dir.), *The Day the Country Died – the DVD* (London: Cherry Red Films, 2006).

21 B. Franks, *Rebel Alliances*, pp. 71–4.

22 See the discussion in R. Cross, '"There Is No Authority But Yourself": The Individual and the Collective in British Anarcho-punk', *Music & Politics*, 4, 2 (2010), pp. 1–20; K. Dunn, 'Anarcho-punk and Resistance in Everyday Life', *Punk & Post-Punk*, 1, 2 (2012), pp. 201–18.

23 P. Rimbaud, 'Introduction', p. ix.

24 A. Martin. 'Autonomy Centres, Riots and the Big Rammy', *Smile* 12, (1994); G. Berger, *The Story of Crass*, pp. 191–3; P. Rimbaud, *Shibboleth*, pp. 121–4.

25 'Anarchists Attacked', *Freedom*, 12 June 1982, pp. 1–2.

26 R. Cross, '"There Is No Authority But Yourself"', pp. 1, 14–15.

27 Crass, 'In Which Crass Voluntarily Blow Their Own', republished in *Black Flag*, 28 April 1986, pp. 4–5.

28 R. Schwartz (interviewer), 'Crass', *Maximumrocknroll*, 9, October–November (1983).

29 B. Franks, *Rebel Alliances*, p. 75; Class War, *This Is Class War: An Introduction to the Class War Federation* (Stirling: AK Press, 1989); for I. Bone's own account of *Class War*'s history, see I. Bone, *Bash the Rich: True-life Confessions of an Anarchist in the UK* (Bath: Tangent Books, 2006).

30 A. Brown (interviewer), 'Sound and Fury', *Solidarity*, 13 (1986), pp. 10–13.

31 A. Murphy. 'Class War: A Serious Business', *The Heavy Stuff*, 1, December (1987), pp. 4–10.

32 See I. Bone, A. Pullen and T. Scargill (eds), *Class War: A Decade of Disorder*

(London: Verso, 1991); Class War Federation, *Unfinished Business: The Politics of Class War* (Stirling: AK Press, 1992); and I. Bone, *Bash the Rich*.

33 B. Franks, *Rebel Alliances*, p. 78; Bone, *Bash the Rich*, p. 177.

34 A. Brown (interviewer), 'Solidarity and Class War Meet Uptown', p. 4.

35 I. Bone, *Bash the Rich*, p. 262.

36 A. Meltzer, *I Couldn't Paint Golden Angels*, pp. 338–40.

37 D. Isiorho, 'Class War', *Freedom*, 30 July 1983, p. 5.

38 Class War, *This Is Class War*, p. 8; A. Brown (interviewer), 'Solidarity and Class War meet uptown', p. 6.

39 Class War, *This Is Class War*, p. 8.

40 An off-air recording of the interview with Murphy is included in the anonymously produced documentary *The Poll Tax Revolt* which was widely circulated amongst protest groups (in VHS format) in the early 1990s.

41 Class War, 'Class War Is Dead … Long Live the Class War', *Class War*, 73 (1997), p. 2.

42 Class War (London), 'Editorial', *Class War*, 74 (1997), p. 2.

43 Anarchist Communist Federation, 'Revolution: An Unfinished Business', *Organise!*, 47 (1997), pp. 7–8 at p. 8.

44 Anarchist Workers Group, 'Anarchism in the Thatcher Years', *Socialism from Below*, 1, August (1989), pp. 6–11 at p. 8. With its origins in the Direct Action Movement, the founders of the AWG 'broke' with anarcho-syndicalism and positioned the group in the tradition of the anarchist *Platform* (based on the 1926 *Organisational Platform of the General Union of Anarchists (Draft)* written by Russian anarchists determined to counter the 'swamp of disorganisation' and the 'interminable vacillations on the most important questions of theory and tactics' within the international movement, and establish a more tightly defined degree of political and organisational rigour). The AWG's 'recuperative' efforts found little echo within the British anarchist movement (where its reading of the *Platform* proved contentious even amongst those in the milieu sympathetic to its perspectives) and it soon disintegrated in disagreement. A number of founding members joined Trotskyist organisations; echoing in many ways the trajectory seen in the history of the Anarchist Workers Association and Libertarian Communist Group a decade earlier.

45 P. Marshall, *Demanding the Impossible: A History of Anarchism* (London: Harper Perennial, 2008), p. 494.

46 Class War, 'The Second Coming: An Open Letter to Revolutionaries', *Class War*, 73 (1997), pp. 3–9 at p. 8.

47 First published as Jo Freeman, 'The Tyranny of Structurelessness', *The Second Wave*, 2, 1 (1972), available (in revised form), www.jofreeman.com/joreen/tyranny.htm, accessed 17 December 2013.

48 Class War, 'The Second Coming: An Open Letter to Revolutionaries', *Class War*, 73, p. 8.

49 Anarchist Communist Federation, *Anarchism as We See it* (London: ACF, n.d., but circa 1987), p. 21.

50 Anarchist Communist Federation, 'ACF: The First Ten Years', *Organise!* , 42, Spring (1996), pp. 19–20 at p. 19.

51 Anarchist Federation, 'The Anarchist Federation: In Thought and Struggle', *Organise!*, 78 (2012), pp. 7–11. 'In the late 90s we changed our name to the Anarchist Federation, not because we had changed our politics, but for pragmatic reasons.'

Part II

Issues

8

Jam tomorrow?

Socialist women and Women's Liberation, 1968–82: an oral history approach

Sue Bruley

This chapter aims to explore the connections between the far left in Britain and women's liberation from the heady days of '1968' to the bleak impact of Thatcherism. It assesses the experiences of women in left groups in this period and examines the possibilities for the engagement of revolutionary socialism and women's liberation. Using illustrative case studies it follows the experiences of eight women in the far left.[1] In documenting these women's lives it is primarily a social rather than a political history. To explore the subjectivity of women's accounts, the most appropriate methodology is oral history, which gives voice to people whose accounts might not otherwise be known.[2] I am especially interested in women from working-class backgrounds. Although there are numerous autobiographical accounts of socialist-feminists from these years,[3] I have aimed to minimise use of these sources to give room for my oral history respondents. At the same time, as I do not expect that a few life histories can depict the full complexity of this story, where necessary, I have supplemented my oral narratives with other published accounts, media and archive sources. Oral history is necessarily a process of public self-reflection and performance.[4] This involves a conversation with one's earlier self, which is not always comfortable. As an oral historian I have to accept the terms on which people offer their stories. Three of my respondents requested that their accounts be anonymous. Consequently the names 'Helen', 'Barbara' and 'Karla' are pseudonyms.

The women depicted here were all born between 1940 and 1952 and were involved in at least one far left group between 1968 and 1982. Together with seven oral history narratives I have added (briefly) my own autobiographical experiences as I fit the criteria for this study. All eight women have a London connection, the city being a key focus for socialist-feminist activity. There is a strong working-class element to this sample; only two women came from professional families, four were manual working class, the other two being a trade union official and a low-grade clerical worker. They grew up within the advent of the welfare state and rising living standards, but for some this was slow to make an impact. Barbara, Karla and Helen all lived in Hackney, East London, in very poor rented accommodation. All three spoke of living a fairly basic, hand to mouth existence. When Karla went to grammar school she was made aware of her poverty: 'I was definitely the poorest girl there, no question about it.'[5] Karla and Barbara were both Jewish, but non-observing. Likewise Annabelle was brought up in South London to immigrant Irish parents who sent her to Catholic schools. Practising religion, however, does not appear to have played a big role in her life, whereas for both Helen (non-conformist sect) and Celia (Unitarian) religion did figure significantly in their upbringing. All became aware of class differences early on. Celia, who grew up in a mining town in the Midlands where her father was an industrial chemist, recalled: 'I went to the local primary school. It's a mainly working-class town. Class issues were very, very, very much to the fore … I was aware of class from a very early age.'[6] The respondents are mainly grammar school women, except for Annabelle, who attended a Catholic secondary, and myself, who went to a secondary modern. All took advantage of the new opportunities for higher education and went on to university, facilitated by maintenance grants and free tuition. A sideline here is that of social mobility. All the women had access to professional careers except for Karla, who dropped out, became a bilingual secretary and later moved into the print industry in a traditional masculine occupation.

Although aware of gender differences these narratives of childhood speak more of class than sexism. Two of the sample, Karla and Jane, came from Communist Party families. In addition, Sue C's parents were both deeply embedded in local Labour politics and her father was a trade union official. Celia's parents were left-leaning reforming Liberals. Only two women had family backgrounds unsympathetic to left wing politics; Helen and Annabelle. The influence of positive female role models is also evident. Sue C's mother was a shorthand typist at a time when most mothers were in the home; 'I was actually quite proud that my mum went to work, it didn't do me any harm whatsoever.'[7] Karla's mother was active in the National Assembly of Women. Celia's grandmother was a suffragette and her mother, who had been an actress before marriage, joined the Campaign for Nuclear Disarmament (CND). Sue C's grandmother was a very vocal, campaigning Labour councillor. Annabelle's mother gave up her job as a nurse to become a full-time housewife but was no docile, passive figure; 'my mum was quite sparky, [a] feisty person … she was always very assertive'.[8]

The theoretical background to this issue is the Marxist text, Engels's *Origins of the Family, Private Property and the State,* which situated women's oppression historically within the rise of class society and private property. Under this analysis, women could not achieve full equality under capitalism. Subsequently both Lenin and Clara Zetkin addressed issues of women's emancipation. Both argued that the feminist movement was a blind alley for working-class women as it could only lead to formal, legal rights rather than real equality and, for this, women needed to join the struggle for a proletarian revolution. [9] For orthodox Marxism therefore there was no room for an autonomous women's movement. It was also held that revolutionaries must lead 'respectable' lives and not indulge in sexual promiscuity. This analysis stood firm in all far-left groups until the late 1960s and beyond for many Marxists and still has some support today. Fundamentalist Marxist groups such as the Socialist Labour League (later Workers' Revolutionary Party), Militant and Maoists (often known as Marxist-Leninists) continued to denounce 'bourgeois feminism' throughout this period and some women Marxists were happy to be involved on these terms, often doing mundane tasks under the political leadership of high status male activists. Women in such groups rarely constituted more than 20 per cent of the membership and were often the wives of party cadres.[10] Political and strategic emphasis on the industrial male working class involved acceptance of 'family wage' ideology which downgraded the status of women's work and undermined equal pay campaigns.

For many, however, the reassuring certainties of orthodox Marxism were blown apart by the tumultuous events of 1968–69 and the advent of the 'new politics'. The Vietnam Solidarity Campaign (VSC) and the outburst of student occupations produced a new and powerful dynamism on the left – as well as models of masculinity and gender relations which emphasised elitist revolutionary male cadres and marginalised female subordinates. At the same time women in the labour movement were asserting themselves, the Ford dispute of June 1968 over grading being just one of many disputes involving low paid women factory workers. This resulted in a real groundswell campaign for equal pay. As women began to analyse their oppression and male behaviour they did not have very far to look. Out of these thoughts the Women's Liberation Movement (WLM) erupted. Although the movement has always eschewed leaders and hierarchies, Sheila Rowbotham's pamphlet *Women's Liberation and the New Politics* was a key text for the new movement which was also influenced by feminist writings from abroad.[11] Theoretically, women tried to move beyond the strait-jacket of the Engels/Lenin/Zetkin analysis of women's oppression and ask why these thinkers did not challenge the sexual division of labour.[12] The WLM also challenged the fundamental division between public and private lives and argued that 'the personal is political' and that women must start changing their lives *now* rather than wait until 'after the revolution'. Women struggled to reinvent themselves with new feminist identities and eagerly sought models from history, such as Sylvia Pankhurst and Alexandra Kollontai. Economistic and reductionist thinking which revered the male industrial working class and marginalised women's struggles was condemned. The first women's liberation conferences in Oxford in February 1970 outlined a series of demands for women: equal pay, equal education and opportunity, free contraception and abortion on demand and 24-hour nurseries.[13] Women's liberation groups sprung up all over the country so that by 1972 nearly all the large towns in Britain had such a group. However, how did these two movements interact? How did left-leaning activist-inclined women, such as those in our sample, react to the rise of the WLM? Did they negotiate a path which enabled them to express both socialism and feminism? How did these choices affect their personal lives? In analysing the life histories of these eight women we also learn something about the changing political culture on the left in this period and the possibilities for a genuinely socialist-feminist movement.

In our sample group of women, Jane, the oldest, was born in 1940 in Cambridge. The family moved to Ipswich in 1949 when Jane's father took up a teaching position in a state boarding school. Although a Communist he did not always live out his egalitarian principles in his own life, deciding to partly educate his two daughters in private schools: 'he gradually went back to his, what I would call his class attitudes actually'.[14] Jane remembers attending Aldermaston peace marches whilst doing her 'A' levels. She trained as a social worker at Newcastle University but soon switched to teaching. Whilst at Newcastle she was drawn to the Communist Party of Great Britain (CPGB) students group. The CPGB by this time had moved from a strict interpretation of the Leninist Party and was advancing the 'The British Road to Socialism' which promoted a broadly based democratic transition involving both parliamentary and extra-parliamentary forces. Although in decline, the CPGB still had significant presence in industry and was also popular in some student circles, providing a left-wing alternative to the Labour Party. Jane met her husband through the CPGB students group. She was also active in Newcastle University CND, of which she became chair. After graduation, the couple moved to Hackney, where Jane taught. In the mid-1960s Jane had two children in quick succession and four years later they adopted another child. In 1968 the family moved to Hemel Hempstead where Jane and her husband found it easy to meet other left wingers and soon started up a monthly socialist discussion group. By this time, 1969, word was spreading about the Women's Liberation Movement, so an evening was set aside for the group to discuss women. From this a women's liberation group emerged in Hemel Hempstead. Jane pointed out that the group was mainly middle class and that few of them joined the CPGB, but she was not concerned about this as the women's group had an important impact on her:

> it was a new way of looking at the whole thing about women's equal rights really, because you know the Communist Party had prided itself on thinking that it had it all sewn up but it didn't really, it, you know this was a new way of looking, you're looking more at personal lives, you know, division of labour within the family and all that sort of thing, which had never been discussed by ... within the CP to my knowledge ... And at one time ... I used to go around to other groups giving talks about women's lib and what it meant and ... these demands.[15]

Jane helped to produce leaflets and travelled outside Hemel to talk about various women's campaigns, such as defending family allowances and abortion rights, and thoroughly enjoyed it. Engulfed in domesticity, with small children and a husband rarely around to help, Jane felt the group raised her morale. The Hemel WLM group proclaimed itself to be practical rather than theoretical and 'dismissed the idea of consciousness-raising as a bit sort of navel gazing'.[16] Jane admitted though that, although it was not acknowledged, the group did in fact engage in consciousness-raising activity. Jane felt a conflict between theoretical critiques of the nuclear family and her need to bring up her children in the best way she could. Sticking to very practical campaigns, the group declined to talk about sex and were scornful about the influential pamphlet *The Myth of the Vaginal Orgasm*: 'it seemed ... kind of irrelevant to women's lives, but actually with hindsight again you know I think there was probably a lot of sense in it.'[17] The group were almost entirely married women with children. The only woman who came out as a lesbian declared that she did not fit in. Jane defended women's right to determine their own sexuality but was worried about feminists being so anti-men that they put off women from joining women's liberation.

'Barbara' was also in the CPGB but in many ways her experiences were different. She was born in 1949 and raised in Hackney, the only child of second-generation Jewish migrants from Eastern Europe. Both her parents worked in the clothing industry. Although her parents were not members of the CPGB they were steeped in traditions of class consciousness, anti-racism and anti-fascism. Barbara feels that her involvement in the CPGB, women's liberation and anti-racism 'gave an expression to something that was obviously there all the way through my childhood'.[18]

Barbara went to a local grammar school, where she led a deputation of girls to the head teacher asking to be taught Economics, only to be told 'that's not a subject for girls'.[19] In 1966 she joined the local Labour Party Young Socialists (LPYS) whose members were heavily influenced by the growing Trotskyist movement, particularly the International Socialists. Other members of the LPYS included the young Sheila Rowbotham.[20] From school Barbara progressed to a London polytechnic where she read Sociology and Economics. She was soon swept up in the student movement and was involved in a sit-in at the college. Barbara was also active in the Anti-Vietnam war protests. By the third year at college, 1969–70 she was analysing the position of women in society and began to feel annoyed by the left-wing men around her. She remembers being 'very irritated about the way that women were expected to be pretty little things ... and I was aware that there was a sort of bombast around the men ... I was irritated by the way the men dominated'.[21]

After graduating in 1970 Barbara became a member of the CPGB and soon after joined a group of CP women attending a women's liberation march. The effect was profound:

> I was completely amazed ... I expected it to be just silly middle-class girls and it was mums with kids and older women and all sorts ... I was really very impressed and when I saw what the slogans were, I thought 'this is bloody good' ... it was just thrilling ... it was terribly exhilarating and it was fun as well ... they were wearing masks and they were dressed up and there were clowns and everybody was looking at us ... whereas I'd been in plenty of marches in Oxford Street which were quite aggressive ... I remember feeling bowled over by it.[22]

Between 1971 and 1973 Barbara was a post-graduate student in Birmingham. She was gradually immersed into internal CPGB politics, eventually becoming a member of the central executive. By this time the CPGB was actively accommodating itself to 'the new politics' by offering support to broadly based radical causes such as the women's movement rather than seeking to merely use these movements for recruitment to the party. Barbara was very much associated with the modernising 'Eurocommunist' wing of the party rather than the more traditional pro-Soviet line.[23] Whilst in Birmingham she became a strong supporter of the feminist publication *Red Rag*, whose editorial collective included Communist feminists such as Beatrix Campbell, Angela Mason and Elizabeth Wilson.[24] Returning to London in 1973 Barbara was very active in the London socialist-feminist scene and also worked with the editorial group around the CPGB women's paper *Link*, a more populist and less theoretical publication than *Red Rag*.

During the rest of the 1970s Barbara worked as a labour movement researcher and was a very active trade unionist, promoting women's rights within the labour movement. She became an effective public speaker and was very much aware that socialist-feminists like her were changing the political culture by challenging the previous male domination of left-wing activism. Barbara was involved in a huge range of organisations as well as party work, including anti-racist work as well as in the women's movement. She was also a member of her local CPGB women's group in south London. Although not officially a consciousness-raising group Barbara recalled that 'we increasingly had discussions which would be called consciousness raising'.[25] She felt that this experience raised her self-confidence and her self-esteem. As with all of these women, personal life and political life overlapped and Barbara took advantage of the prevailing libertarian attitudes to sex and increasing availability of effective contraception: 'Looking back on it I'm amazed, I used to do a full thirty-seven hour week ... you know all these things and have a couple of lovers going on the side as well.'[26]

The International Socialists (IS) date back to the Socialist Review Group, a small group of broadly based Trotskyist intellectuals around Tony Cliff in the 1950s which became the IS in 1962. During the 1960s IS gathered momentum and became known for its slogan of 'Neither Washington nor Moscow but International Socialism' and its libertarian form of Trotskysim. Sue C joined IS in 1966, the year after It had given up Labour Party entryism. Born in South West London in 1947 her oral narrative speaks of a very happy and secure childhood. Her parents who were stalwarts of the local Labour Party had a very strong influence on her. Unhappy at her grammar school she left at 16 and became a clerk in the civil service. She was soon active in the LPYS and life revolved around political meetings and related events. She moved quickly from what she described as the right-wing Labour of her father, who was a Labour councillor as a well as a trade union official, towards the local IS group which was active inside the LPYS. She met her husband through her political activities and was married within six months in 1968. By this time she had entered teacher training college as a mature student and was aghast that the college principal expected her to quit the course and leave college on account of her marriage. She insisted on continuing and whilst at college she challenged the sex role stereotyping then common in children's literature. Sue went on to work as a teacher in a local primary school. She had another child in 1975 and was at home most of the 1970s before returning to work part time.

The excitement and exhilaration of the women's movement seemed to have passed Sue C by. She was supportive of it but in rather a distant way: 'there was some really valid points to the whole feminist fight and ... it was being trivialised by the press with all this "burn your bras" and all that sort of nonsense'.[27] Whilst prepared to resist overtly sexist practices in her own life she did not relate this to a wider feminist movement. Sue had a very strong relationship with her husband, and did not feel that her situation at home with small children was oppressive. She was at pains to point out that her husband was very happy and willing to take a turn with childcare when he could, although this was very limited as he worked full time, was politically active and began studying for a part-time degree between the births of the children. Basically Sue did not have much time for an autonomous women's movement because she felt that the demands of the WLM should be taken up by men as well as women:

> Wasn't there a lot of interesting talk going on about people trying to live different lifestyles ... the whole commune thing was being talked about and stuff like that? So I was listening to all of that and ... I just had a very uneasy sort of, various uneasy thoughts that in a way it was letting men off the hook, if it was women who do all the thinking and the concern and the sorting out policies etc. on childcare ... these are their kids as well ... they should together be resolving these problems.[28]

However, one feminist campaign did spark off a big reaction in Sue, the right of women to have access to abortion. In 1975–79 there were several (ultimately unsuccessful) attempts to reduce the upper-time limit for women to obtain legal abortions: 'I was just absolutely horrified at that because ... my total belief was always that the best thing was that for every child to be a wanted child ... and that women should always ... easily get the contraceptive help they needed and ... feel prepared for having the responsibility of a child.'[29] Parliamentary attempts to limit access to abortion were assisted by the rise of a powerful 'pro-life' Lobby. In response to this the labour movement moved in support of 'a woman's right to choose'. The 80,000-strong march against the restrictive bill proposed by John Corrie in October 1979 was the first time the Trades Union Congress (TUC) had come out in force for a feminist demand.[30] Sue was very much part of this campaign, which she saw as a wider labour movement rather than feminist issue:

> there must have been ... various people from various left-wing groups, maybe the Labour Party as well. We got together to form an oppositional group. I remember we had quite a big public meeting in Surbiton Assembly rooms which got very nasty ... because the right produced these photos ... emotional blackmail and stuff like that ... I felt very, very strongly about that and fought that battle.[31]

The radicalisation of youth in the VSC and student movements led to an upsurge in IS recruitment from 1968 into the early 1970s with 3,310 members in 1974.[32] Less rigid in their Trotskyism than other left groups and possessing some young very charismatic leaders, such as Chris Harman, Paul Foot and John Palmer, IS developed branches in many universities and colleges. Myself, Karla and Annabelle all joined IS around this time. In many ways our stories are parallel. We can only summarise them here. I joined IS whilst attending a further education college in 1969. Already very conscious of both class and sex divisions I readily linked up with the few radical students at the college who then drew me into IS. Karla grew up with Communist parents but she felt CPGB politics were 'too narrow'. Living as a closet lesbian in 1971, both Karla and her lover became disgusted by the actions of the then Tory government: 'So, we thought it was time to get involved with something, checked out various left-wing groups, found IS very sympathetic and interesting and the others not.'[33] Annabelle told me that 'she was always kind of on the left'.[34] She attended Swansea University and during the 1972 miners' strike began leafleting and doing other work for the miners and was recruited to IS during this period. All three of us were integrated into local IS branches and Annabelle, after graduating, became a full-time studio assistant working on *Socialist Worker*. None of us became really established members of IS. I left in 1972, Karla in 1974 and Annabelle in 1975. After going to LSE [London School of Economics] in 1970 I became involved in the LSE women's liberation group. I was also volunteering for a few hours a week at the IS headquarters in Shoreditch, East London, collating leaflets and doing mundane office work. I found the overt sexism of some of the leading male IS comrades truly shocking and this was hard to reconcile with IS's commitment to women's liberation. Karla also had similar experiences: 'There was nothing specifically happening around women and yet that was part of our new left politics.'[35] Moreover she felt that, 'for those of us who were genuinely committed to both socialist politics and the women's movement our involvement in each place seemed to take part in two separate boxes … on a personal level that felt really alienating'.[36] IS increasingly behaved as if it was 'the' revolutionary party rather than part of the far left as a whole and none of us felt comfortable with this, particularly as the focus in IS had shifted almost exclusively towards industrial workers. We were all reading feminist literature and eager to become more involved in the WLM. There was by this time several IS women's groups trying to raise women's issues within IS and make the leadership take the WLM seriously. North London IS women's group organised a conference on women in June 1971 which was attended by over 200 IS women and men.[37] From 1971 there was an IS women's newsletter which became *Women's Voice* (*WV*) in 1972, but there seemed to be little going on for IS women in south London where all three of us were based. As previously mentioned we left IS at different times and subsequently all became involved in consciousness-raising (CR) and joined the same group in Clapham, a move which Annabelle described as 'life changing'.[38] Karla and I knew each other and joined together, but Annabelle joined in 1975 soon after I had left the group. Besides CR the group threw itself into many other WLM activities and was associated with the London Women's Liberation Workshop. It was a very exciting time and a welcome relief from the heavy demands of IS.[39]

Celia's story of her involvement with IS differed from that of Karla, Annabelle and myself described above. She stayed in IS for longer and was more involved in the organisation. Celia was born in 1945 and came from Warwickshire to study English at Bedford College, London in 1963. Whilst there, she joined the Humanist Society and through that became involved in abortion law reform, supporting the reform act of 1967 – which was at that time seen as a humanist or moral issue rather than a feminist one. After graduating, Celia studied for a postgraduate diploma in social science at LSE, where she encountered Marxism through the Socialist Society. She had by this time met her future husband and they joined IS together after taking part in the student occupation of 1967.

After leaving LSE Celia went to work for Lambeth social services and became involved in radical social work. The marriage did not last. Her husband pressed for an 'open' marriage which was quite common in radical circles; 'I felt he'd ... been running the show and it was really all about his needs not mine.'[40] After a few years of social work Celia retrained as a teacher, ultimately becoming an advisory teacher. These were years of intense political activity; IS, union work and women's liberation, 'I was out every night at something'.[41] She was a long-standing member of a socialist-feminist study group whose other members included Sheila Rowbotham and Juliette Mitchell, and which was heavily theoretical, particularly on a Marxist approach to sexuality. She also joined a consciousness-raising group in Islington which was revelatory; 'I suddenly started thinking "my god! ... this is what I've been missing!".'[42] CR enabled Celia to work through many issues: 'you have to deal with the psychology ... of self-hate ... that consciousness-raising group was absolutely crucial for me, it really, really helped me ... that's what brought me out of my marriage actually'.[43]

One of Celia's many commitments in IS was to assist in the production of *Women's Voice*. In 1976 IS became the Socialist Workers Party (SWP) and by this time WV had gained a considerable base of support. The paper also had a more professional look, not unlike the mainstream feminist magazine *Spare Rib* except it had more emphasis on issues related to working-class women. It gave comprehensive coverage of women's struggles at work, such as the successful strike of 200 women at the GEC engineering plant in Coventry over job timing in 1977 and, in addition,

WV profiled rank and file women trade unionists. It gave voice also to black women in Southall taking action against sweatshop labour and supported other black women's struggles. It was not just concerned with pay issues but also supported equal opportunities, for instance giving publicity to the first woman to become a train driver. It supported women's rights to financial independence, covered international struggles involving women, women's history and women's health issues. *WV* supported all the demands of the women's liberation movement including the right of women to determine their own sexuality and an end to violence against women (which were added to the original four demands) offering support for 'reclaim the night demonstrations' which are often associated with revolutionary feminists.

The success of *WV* led the SWP in 1978 to set up Women's Voice groups which contained SWP members and other women sympathisers.[44] Under the slogan of 'Fight with Women's Voice for Women's Liberation and Socialism' the edition for April 1979 lists 51 Women's Voice groups across the country, 13 of them in London. Just how solid these groups were is a matter of conjecture but on paper at least it looked impressive. In Hackney Celia recalled her local *WV* group as being a small but solid group of local women, who drew in support from outside SWP circles, including black women. The decision to form *WV* groups as a 'sister' organisation to the SWP was controversial from the start and led to fierce debate over the next three years.[45] The context here is significant. The early and mid-1970s had been times of offensive action for the labour movement and many socialist-feminists had campaigned for women's issues, such as equal pay and abortion, within the trade unions. By the late 1970s the economy was in recession and the labour movement had been put firmly on the defensive. Equally important, the initial euphoria of the WLM had subsided and the last ever national conference in 1978 was dominated by acrimonious feuding between socialist-feminist and radical/revolutionary feminists. Internal SWP bulletins show there was deep unease about *WV* groups, particularly fears that they were draining the organisation of resources and leading women out of SWP into the WLM rather than the reverse.[46] In addition, groups such as Hackney *WV* were resistant to democratic-centralist control, raising concerns about the SWP supporting autonomous women's liberation groups which was seen to be non-Leninist. It is clear that in 1980 the leadership had resolved to disband *WV* groups and by 1982 the paper itself ceased publication.[47] The SWP gave up all separate work on women, including the post of women's organiser. Theoretically, the leadership insisted that class was the root of all oppression and that working-class men do not oppress women.[48]

All this was devastating for Celia. Her political work was closely

intertwined with her personal and social life. After being expelled from the
SWP for 'persistent opposition' to democratic centralism she felt ostracised
from her community:

> Chanie Rosenberg [Tony Cliff's wife] has never spoken to me since …. But
> lots of people never spoke to us after that. It was a horrible experience, it
> was really horrible … it was quite damaging actually … I never anticipated
> that people who I'd been so close to would stigmatise me in such a way. And
> call me names, basically say I was anti-revolutionary, bourgeois, bourgeois
> feminist.[49]

The International Marxist Group (IMG) was also very active 1969–78. The
IMG was formed in 1968 but its origins reach back into the labyrinthine
depths of post-war Trotskyist politics. It rapidly gathered momentum in the
wake of the student movement, gaining about 800 members at its height in
1978.[50] Generally regarded as less sectarian and 'workerist' than IS, it was
also more demanding of its membership.[51] It is not surprising, therefore,
that male students comprised the great majority of the membership.
'Helen', who had recently entered teaching, joined the IMG in 1973
in West London after a brief period in IS. She was rapidly drawn into
political work within the Socialist Teachers Alliance and also rose up to
the higher ranks of the IMG internal organisation, becoming a leading
cadre and a particularly effective speaker. It was whilst doing postgraduate
work at a northern university that Helen had first encountered women's
liberation, whose demands she supported. The main activity of the group
was consciousness raising: 'it was, I thought, a lot of women sitting
round moaning … so I didn't stick with that'.[52] As an IMG activist Helen
subsequently did engage with the WLM over campaigns such as equal
pay and employment rights, but not as a feminist as such; 'it was more a
milieu to intervene in rather than as it were something to be in'.[53] Helen
did not want to have children and preferred to work on union issues such
as salaries rather than childcare. Within the IMG Helen was interested in
a wide range of political issues and did not want to be 'pigeon holed' into
women's issues. She was therefore the least engaged organisationally with
the WLM of the eight women whose stories are outlined here, preferring
to talk to me about what she regarded as 'equality' issues rather than
'women's oppression'.[54]

Looking more broadly at the IMG there is evidence of serious engagement
with the WLM. It was certainly less tolerant of sexist behaviour amongst
its male members than IS/SWP. Within the post-1968 student milieu the
IMG recruited a number of women who were keen to build a socialist-
feminist current as an integral part of the WLM, rather than crudely
trying to use the WLM as a recruiting ground for the 'revolutionary

party'. *Socialist Woman* was an important aspect of this work, starting in 1969 and produced until at least 1978. The paper covered a broad range of women's issues, including equal pay, international work and women's history. Unlike *Women's Voice*, it appears to have had few if any working-class women supporters. In April 1971 an open letter to the Chancellor, Anthony Barber, from a working-class woman outlining her weekly budget and struggle to make ends meet was reprinted from the York WLM paper *Scarlet Woman* – apparently the IMG had no one from within its own ranks who could write such a letter. The tendency towards lengthy, theoretical debate steadily increased so by the late 1970s the paper was more like an internal discussion forum on socialist-feminist theory. The IMG also supported *Socialist Woman* groups which were listed at the back of the paper. At its height these groups appeared to have numbered about twenty, mostly in large cities.

Finally, libertarian and non-aligned women also have a role to play in this story. Libertarian ideas have long traditions which reach back into the nineteenth century with thinkers such as Proudhon and Bakunin opposed to the hierarchical power and the oppressive rule of the state, emphasising direct action by local communities rather than rule imposed from above. Libertarian Marxists rejected Leninism and the idea of a vanguard party led by professional revolutionaries. Events of '1968' led to a revival of libertarian politics in Britain with small local groups springing up in many cities. Libertarian ideas have much in common with the WLM, particularly the opposition to leaders and hierarchies and the emphasis on local action and direct democracy. Some WLM activists were also attracted to the tendency within libertarian thought towards radicalism in personal life, particularly ideas of 'free love' as propounded by anarchist-feminist Emma Goldman in the United States. Regrettably, finding libertarian feminist oral history respondents to interview for this project in the time available proved impossible. There are, however, published autobiographical accounts which can fill the gap. In particular, there is that of socialist-feminist Lynne Segal who was active in Islington, North London from 1972, joining Big Flame in the late 1970s.[55] Big Flame was a libertarian Marxist group, influenced by the Italian group *Lotta Continua*, which did not propose to be 'the' revolutionary party but part of a wider movement for socialism.[56] It gave unqualified support for an autonomous movement for women's liberation and the idea of 'personal politics'. [57] The group supported local struggles such as those involving nurseries and tenants as well as industrial disputes. Islington had a thriving socialist community in the 1970s and the Islington Socialist Centre, founded in 1977, was one manifestation of this, emphasising non-sectarian joint work amongst the different left groups.[58]

The activities described by Lynne were part of an upsurge of autonomous socialist-feminist activity in the late 1970s. By then it was clear that the women's liberation movement as a unified national force could not be sustained and a clear socialist-feminist current was discernible. The movement was rapidly devolving into many different campaigns and tendencies and within this milieu socialist-feminists were organising conferences, newsletters, study groups and local campaigns. Disillusioned with vanguard politics, particularly the heavy emphasis on the industrial working class of Leninist sects and the persistent marginalisation of women, many left women were seeking a home outside of organised left groups. This movement came to a head with the publication of *Beyond the Fragments* in 1979. Authors Sheila Rowbotham, Lynne Segal and Hilary Wainwright contributed three separate accounts arguing for non-aligned, non-sectarian socialist-feminism. Rowbotham's long, meandering piece dominates. The booklet, rapidly acclaimed by the socialist-feminist community, was soon expanded and reissued and a conference on it in Leeds in 1980 attracted 3,000 people.[59] The tone of the conference was left unity and the search for new ways of organising 'to confront the ominous prospect of a new ideological conservative offensive, which arose after Margaret Thatcher's election of May 1979'.[60] All this enthusiasm, however, proved too little and the movement fizzled out fairly quickly. Lynne Segal attributes this to the inability of the left to move beyond narrow sectarianism. This was indeed the case. Left groups did not see beyond their own interests. Equally, Rowbotham was heavy on her critique of the left but extremely vague and tentative about alternatives and, in the face of the onslaught of economic neo-conservatism under Thatcher, the energy and optimism of the 1970s disintegrated.

Conclusion

This chapter aimed to analyse the connections between the revolutionary left and the women's liberation movement between the late 1960s and the early 1980s and to examine the possibilities of a genuinely socialist-feminist movement. Using the medium of oral history this account has mainly been written through the prism of eight different women's stories, illustrating a range of perspectives and choices available to socialist women in these years. As we have seen, women such as Helen and Sue C. intervened in a number of women's issues but did not make any personal commitment to the WLM and were steadfast in their belief in the central role of the revolutionary party to bring about sexual equality. The difficulty with this approach is that before the rise of the WLM in the late 1960s women in far-left groups who tried to work on feminist issues were marginalised and excluded, indicating that without a forceful autonomous women's movement the left did not take women seriously. The other left women were all drawn, in varying degrees, to the WLM and tried to blend in WLM work with their party work. As has been indicated, most left groups did support the idea of an autonomous WLM and provide space for their women members to be active within the women's movement. It proved impossible, however, to transform the political culture on the left so that sexist practices remained and the emphasis on the industrial male working class meant that issues of personal life and oppression within the family were downplayed for the sake of 'building the party'. IS/SWP in particular was so keen to recruit male industrial militants that it was prepared to overlook the reproduction of traditional gender roles within the organisation and in members' private lives, thus perpetuating patriarchal ideology and women's oppression. Eventually the SWP gave up all pretence of working with the WLM, forcing women members to choose between an increasingly centrally controlled, economistic, Leninist-style organisation – or total banishment.

The SWP was reacting to the dramatic change in political and economic climate in the early 1980s, in which support for socialist-feminist activity was rapidly declining. The time of mass WLM activity was over, although many feminists continued to work on different campaigns and there was increasing recognition of not one but many feminisms, allowing black feminists to challenge the domination of white feminists within the movement.[61] The early 1980s also witnessed a turn to local Labour Party activism among socialist-feminists and the growth of what has been termed 'municipal feminism', particularly in London. Three of our eight women were in the Labour Party in the early 1980s and in the case of Helen she played a significant role in local politics in the 1980s. It is also clear that by the early 1980s the 'generation of 1968' were having children, withdrawing from political activity and pursuing careers and there is recognition of this here. The women in this study all went on to have successful careers, except for Karla who was forced to retire early due to ill health. Jane, Celia, Sue C and myself had children. All are now in their sixties except for Jane who is in her seventies. Five are now retired and one semi-retired. None of the eight women is actively involved in a far-left group, although all still consider themselves to be left wing and most are still attending demonstrations, doing trade union work and, keeping up with the digital age, internet lobbying. Ultimately, the 'lived experience ' of these women has shown that for a brief period there was the potential for the twin forces of revolutionary socialism and women's liberation to combine, but this potential was never realised for the reasons we have outlined above. Moreover, by the early 1980s this historical opportunity had passed.

Notes

Acknowledgements: I would like to take this opportunity to thank 'Karla', Annabelle, Jane, Sue, 'Barbara', 'Helen' and Celia for welcoming me into their homes and allowing me to record their stories.

1 The respondents were selected from research data collected for a larger study of 'women's liberation and personal life', forthcoming, contact author: sue. bruley@port.ac.uk.

2 R. Perks and A. Thompson (eds), *The Oral History Reader* (London: Routledge, 1998), p. ix.

3 For example: M. Roberts, *Paper Houses: A Memoir of the 70s and Beyond* (London: Virago, 2007); L. Segal, *Making Trouble: Life and Politics* (London: Serpent's Tail, 2007); S. Rowbotham, *Promise of a Dream: Remembering the Sixties* (London: Verso, 2001).

4 L. Abrams, *Oral History Theory* (London: Routledge, 2010), chapter 7.

5 'Karla', interview with Sue Bruley, 6 July 2011, South East London.

6 Celia Burgess-Macey, interview with Sue Bruley, 19 April 2012, Hackney, East London.

7 Susanne Coysh, interview with Sue Bruley, 20 October 2011, Surbiton, Surrey.

8 Annabelle McLaren, interview with Sue Bruley, 27 July 2011, Sydenham, South East London.

9 See, for example *Lenin and the Emancipation of Women* (Moscow, 1965); *Decisions of the Third Congress of the Communist International* (Moscow 1921). The section on 'Methods of Work among Women of the Communist Party' was written by Clara Zetkin.

10 For example, Hertha Sturm produced a survey of women Communists in 1922 in *Bulletin of the Fourth Congress of the Communist International*, Moscow, 4 December 1922, with the percentage of women in the various national sections ranging from barely any to 20 per cent (Marx Memorial Library, London).

11 Spokesman Pamphlet, 17 (1971). An earlier version was published in 1969. S. de Beauvoir, *The Second Sex* (Harmondsworth: Penguin, 1972, originally 1949).

12 R. Delmar, 'Looking Again at Engels's *Origin of the Family, Private Property and the State*', in J. Mitchell and A. Oakley (eds), *The Rights and Wrongs of Women* (Harmondsworth: Penguin, 1976).

13 M. Wandor (ed.), *Once a Feminist: Stories of a Generation* (London: Virago, 1990), pp. 242–3.

14 Jane Bell, interview with Sue Bruley, 5 June 2012, North London.

15 Ibid.

16 Ibid.

17 Ibid.

18 'Barbara', interview with Sue Bruley, 16 July 2001 London.

19 Ibid.

20 S. Rowbotham, *Promise of a Dream*; C. Hughes, 'Young Socialist Men in 1960s Britain: Subjectivity and Sociability', *History Workshop Journal*, 73, 1 (2012), pp. 170–92.

21 Barbara, interview.
22 Ibid.
23 See J. Callaghan, *The Far Left in British Politics* (Oxford: Blackwell, 1987), chapter on the Communist Party.
24 See Val Charlton in Wandor, *Once a Feminist*, pp. 163–5.
25 Barbara, interview.
26 Ibid.
27 S. Coysh, interview.
28 Ibid.
29 Ibid.
30 A. Coote and B. Campbell, *Sweet Freedom: The Struggle for Women's Liberation* (London: Wiley-Blackwell, 1982), pp. 147–8.
31 S. Coysh, interview.
32 I. Birchall, *Tony Cliff: A Marxist for His Time* (London: Bookmarks, 2011), p. 372.
33 Karla, interview.
34 A. McLaren, interview.
35 Karla, interview.
36 Karla, email correspondence, 17 October 2012.
37 IS internal bulletins, July 1971, Will Fancy Collection, University of London Library, MS1171/box23/3.
38 A. McLaren, interview.
39 For a full account, see S. Bruley, 'Consciousness-raising in Clapham; Women's Liberation as "Lived Experience" in South London in the 1970s', *Women's History Review*, 20, 5 (2013), pp. 717–38.
40 C. Burgess-Macey, interview.
41 Ibid.
42 Ibid.
43 Ibid.
44 Birchall, *Tony Cliff*, p. 465.
45 For further details see the SWP internal bulletins 1978–81, see above.
46 Birchall, *Tony Cliff*, p. 466.
47 Celia Burgess-Macey had much to tell on this but due to restrictions on space this part of her story could not be included.
48 J. Molyneux, 'Do Working-class Men Benefit from Women's Oppression?', *International Socialism*, 25 (1984), pp. 117–23, argued against this line, but was defeated.
49 C. Burgess-Macey, interview. Anna Paczuska tells a similar story of disillusion with SWP in Wandor, *Once a Feminist*, pp. 138–84.
50 Callaghan, *The Far Left*, p. 154.
51 Ibid., p. 152.
52 'Helen', interview with Sue Bruley, 19 April 12, London.
53 Helen, interview.
54 Helen represents a strain of women in left politics who I regard as 'cadres': for details see S. Bruley, *Leninism, Stalinism and the Women's Movement in Britain 1920–39* (London: Routledge, 2012, originally 1987).

55 Segal, *Making Trouble*.
56 D. Widgery (ed.), *The Left in Britain, 1956–68* (Harmondsworth: Penguin, 1976), p. 479.
57 L. Segal, 'A Local Experience', in S. Rowbotham, L. Segal and H. Wainwright (eds), *Beyond the Fragments: Feminism and the Making of Socialism* (London: Merlin Press, 1979), p. 100.
58 Ibid., p. 97.
59 Segal, *Making Trouble,* pp. 104–5.
60 Ibid., p. 105.
61 H. Carby, 'White Woman Listen! Black Feminism and the Boundaries of Sisterhood', in Centre of Contemporary Cultural Studies, *The Empire Strikes Back: Race and Racism in '70s Britain* (London: Routledge, 1982), pp. 211–34.

9

Something new under the sun

The revolutionary left and gay politics

Graham Willett

When gay politics exploded onto the political scene in the West in the late 1960s, it came, seemingly, out of the blue, without warning or history or antecedents. And although four decades of research have revealed a long history of struggle – which in Europe dates back to the 1860s – in many ways homosexual politics actually was, in the 1960s, something new. The 'homosexual' that was referred to in polite, scholarly and professional circles now noisily renamed himself 'gay', and herself 'lesbian'. Gays and lesbians proclaimed a political programme of pride, equality, liberation. Self and society were to be utterly transformed and in a completely public way. There was no corner of society that was not challenged to reform itself; and friends, no less than enemies, found themselves facing demands that they change.

For the revolutionary left, already facing the challenge of new times, new demands and new constituencies, this presented one more pressure. What was it to make of these gays and lesbians? What was it to make of their demands, their new ways of living and loving and even dressing? Did these people represent the decay of society; were they one more piece of evidence that the choice facing the world was between socialism and barbarism? Or were they, perhaps, the eruption of a too-long repressed section of the population for whom socialism was the road to freedom?

In this chapter I want to explore the responses of the revolutionary left to the emergence of gay people and gay politics, focusing on the crucial first decade from about 1970 to 1980. In these years we see the revolutionary left at its best *and* its worst, at its most open-minded and creative and at its most narrow-minded and ossified. In particular, I want to examine the efforts of the three most important British revolutionary groups of the time – Militant/Socialist Labour League (SLL), the Communist Party of Great Britain (CPGB) and the Socialist Workers Group/International Socialists/

Socialist Workers Party (SWG/IS/SWP) – which between them account for
the largest portion of the far left in Britain during these years. Focusing in
this way has the advantage of allowing a detailed and close-grained study,
and limiting the time period does little damage to the story because, by
the end of the 1970s, the various political positions were largely set. The
subsequent decades exhibit not much more than the repeated application
of the various theories of gay equality/gay liberation developed early on.[1]

Prehistory

Homosexuality erupted onto the public agenda in the mid-1950s, as a
series of sex scandals drove the government of Winston Churchill to
establish a Home Office inquiry into prostitution and homosexuality. The
committee, named for its chairman, John Wolfenden, reported in 1957,
recommending, among other things, the decriminalisation of homosexual
acts. While the government and parliament declined to adopt such a
policy, the issue was now well and truly a public political issue.[2]

Among those who welcomed the recommendation were some of the most
influential Labour Party thinkers. In 1959 Roy Jenkins listed homosexual
law reform as one of the important outstanding issues that needed to be
addressed if Britain was to become truly 'civilised'.[3] Anthony Crosland
went further. In the *Future of Socialism* he included 'obsolete penalties
for sexual abnormality' in a lyrical discussion of the 'intolerable' laws
that reflected the influence of the 'prig and the prude' in public life.[4] They
were not alone in these views – progressive middle-class reformers had,
over the course of the twentieth century, come more and more to believe
that in matters of sex, as in any other social question, 'rational principles'
were the only basis for policy and that, in relation to homosexuality,
'homosexual acts between consenting adults carried out in private should
cease to be criminal', to quote from the Progressive League's submission to
the Wolfenden Committee.[5]

The revolutionary left was not unaware of the issues raised by Wolfenden.
In an article in *Socialist Review*, 'The Meaning of Wolfenden', C. Dallas (a
pseudonym for Chanie Rosenberg, one of the leaders of the International
Socialists), offered what was referred to as 'a socialist critique' of the report
and the government's response.[6] Dallas was unambiguous in her support
for the decriminalisation of homosexual acts and, unlike Wolfenden, was
opposed to the maintenance of any residual laws for the imprisonment
of homosexuals as a means of deterrence or for the protection of the
community. She was opposed, too, to entrapment activities by police.
The only form of incarceration that she was prepared to countenance
was where there were 'cases which might harm weaker members of the

community (those who are attracted to young boys, in particular)' – here she accepted the need for hospitalisation, with minimal restriction on freedom, while undergoing treatment.

Dallas shared with Wolfenden the view that homosexuality was a 'problem'; but her solution was radically different. The creation of a society in which men and women were genuinely equal, where no one was driven to sell their bodies for money, where psychological health was nearly universal – in short, a socialist society – would see homosexuality 'disappear naturally', she said, adding: 'If nature then produced an abnormality, which it might do in a small number of cases, medical treatment would take good care of it.' Since the rise of gay liberation Dallas has been criticised for these formulations;[7] her defenders argue that she was simply expressing what everyone thought at the time. Deciding between these positions depends on whether one assumes that socialists can be expected to transcend the limitations of their own times; whether they should be expected to hold to or, alternatively, to move beyond the most advanced politics available. In fact, Dallas' position is probably the best that could be hoped for in 1957; it is hard to think of anyone in public life – homosexual or heterosexual – who expressed the argument that homosexuality was, in fact, not a problem, that – as we came to think after 1970 – gay is good, that it is not the homosexual who is perverse, but the society in which he or she lives. Even homosexual rights organisations in the United States, where some members were groping their way towards these radically new ideas, rarely expressed them in any very public way.

The problem of homosexuality

Critics of the revolutionary left's response to the appearance of gay and lesbian activism usually write as if it ought to have been obvious how important this new movement was, and how it articulated with the struggle for socialism. In fact there are a number of reasons why this is an unreasonable and ahistorical position.

In the first place, this attitude fails to see what a remarkable new thing gay and lesbian politics was. The far left, as it existed in the post-war period, had no tradition to draw upon: there had never been a 'homosexual question' to exercise the minds of socialist thinkers, nor any homosexual struggle to capture the attention of activists. The Russian Revolution had decriminalised homosexual acts (as the French revolution had done more than a century earlier) but this was reversed by Stalin in 1934 – without, as far as can be seen, any protest from anywhere on the left at the time. In Germany, it is true, the Oscar Wilde trials in 1895, coupled with a push for decriminalisation spearheaded by sex reformers, had prompted Social

Democratic Party leaders – Eduard Bernstein in particular – to speak out
on the scientific and legal aspects of homosexuality,[8] but in the post-war
West this had long since been forgotten. And anyway, Bernstein was the
great 'revisionist' of social democratic orthodoxy, whose championing of
a cause was unlikely to recommend it to revolutionaries in the 1950s and
1960s, even if it had been known about. Beyond these articles there was
very little. Trotsky for all his interest in the problems of everyday life,
even Alexandra Kollontai who wrote prolifically on sex and sexuality, had
nothing to say on same-sex desire. If revolutionaries were going to make
sense of the gay liberation/gay rights movement that was emerging around
them in the early 1970s, beyond supporting the pretty obvious position in
favour of decriminalisation, they were going to have to make their own
way without any help from the tradition or the masters.

The difficulty was exacerbated by the fact that Gay Liberation was
unlike anything ever seen before. It was, it is true, a social movement,
and there had been a number of these even in the post-war period that the
revolutionary left had worked with, struggling to build them, fighting to
win leadership of them and to guide them onto the anti-capitalist road. In
the 1950s the Campaign for Nuclear Disarmament (CND), in the 1960s the
student movement and the opposition to the Vietnam War, had presented
opportunities to make the case that those who were serious about these
issues needed to be socialists and that the campaigns themselves needed
to orient to that class that alone could lead and win the struggle for a
better world. But *liberation* – of women or gays – was something very
different. The decriminalisation of homosexuality that was endorsed by
socialists on democratic grounds was, in fact, a matter of almost complete
indifference to the new militants. Gay Liberation was a project dedicated
to the root and branch transformation of society and culture, a rejection
of capitalism, to be sure, but also of patriarchy, heterosexual power, the
nuclear family, hierarchies of all kinds. It worked to confront power and
demand change, not just with petitions and protests and demonstrations
but via self-transformation – of sexual practices, of living arrangements,
of self-presentation. And more and more, activists came to believe that the
liberation of gay people was the task of gay people themselves; that, while
heterosexuals were, rhetorically at least, welcomed as allies, they had no
real role in the movement, and certainly no role leading it.[9] Revolutionary
socialism, with its traditions and policies rooted so firmly in the years
before and immediately after the First World War, was always going to
have a hard time adapting to this striking new phenomenon.

And, it could not have been, to many socialists, at all obvious that
they needed to take this phenomenon seriously. The startling rise of Gay
Liberation was followed by its equally startling demise. The organisation

was founded in October 1970; three years later it had disintegrated.[10] In retrospect, it is clear that the movement was bigger than any one organisation and its work of social transformation was to be carried on in rather surprising ways – but no one could have known that at the time.

The other important factor in the failure of the left to see gay liberation for the revolutionary force that it was has its roots in the nature of the period – and specifically in the upsurge in class struggle centred on the industrial working class, which convulsed British society in the decade from the mid-1960s to the mid-1970s; precisely the period, that is, when the gay liberation movement was rising and falling. Mostly overshadowed now in public memory, the Heath government of 1970–74 was blazing the path that Margaret Thatcher would later make her own, cutting spending, increasing government charges, deregulating parts of the economy and launching a major attack on trade unionism and trade union rights. In response to these attacks key sections of the working class took up the cudgels and by a fusion of industrial power and political goals had seen off the threat.[11] For the revolutionary left, for whom the working class was *the* instrument of socialist struggle, these were heady days. Their analysis of the world seemed confirmed and the future looked bright indeed.

It was really only the persistence of lesbian and gay activism after the demise of Gay Liberation in 1973 and the apparent impasse reached by working-class struggles after the mid-1970s that brought homosexuality to the attention of the revolutionary organisations in any significant way. And then the hard work started: What was homosexuality? What was its relationship to capitalism? To socialism?

Militant

The simplest way to respond to the challenge of the new social movements was to ignore them. This was the line adopted by Militant, the Trotskyist organisation headed up by Ted Grant which had entered the Labour Party in the mid-1950s and devoted itself to waiting for the crisis of capitalism that would shake the old Conservative Party and trade union leaders out of power. In order to avoid expulsion from the Labour Party, it was necessary for Militant's members to keep their heads down, to devote themselves as enthusiastically as they could to advancing the party's agenda, while maintaining their criticisms of the leaders' betrayals and vacillations.[12]

This strategy had certain consequences, the most important of which was a narrowing of the organisation's focus: 'zealous pursuit of the [Labour] party's objectives rather than campaigns for an alternative set of priorities ... Generally it has been loathe to upset the applecart by taking on issues which have been uncongenial to the Labour mind', as

Callaghan puts it.[13] Militant had steadfastly stood aside from the great political campaigns of the 1950s and after, from the Campaign for Nuclear Disarmament (1957–63) through to the Anti-Nazi League (1977–82).[14] And as for the political movements, they were understood by the Militant mindset as petit-bourgeois in nature and symptoms of the decay of capitalism; diversions from the important struggles of the working class rather than as responses to oppression.[15] When it did discuss women's oppression it was strictly within the confines of working-class – indeed almost entirely within workplace – frameworks. Militant addressed only those particular needs of women – 'low pay, prices, rents, nursery facilities and the like' – that could be addressed by Labour Party and trade union struggles. There was no space for, and no attention given to, sexism or other non-economic aspects of women's disadvantage.[16]

Gay people were given even less attention. The style adopted by Militant's members was, as Robinson puts it, working class, puritanical, cleancut, and it is not surprising that in the years before gay activism started to transform social attitudes (including those of working-class people), views that we would describe as homophobic went unchallenged within the organisation and its milieu.[17] Crick describes Militant as often 'hostile' to gays, believing as it did that homosexuality would disappear under socialism[18] – a point of view still being voiced as late as 1984[19] – and notes that 'If there are any gay members of Militant, they keep quiet about it'.[20]

Eventually, Militant adapted itself to the new realities of the British left environment. Its 1981 programme, updated in 1986, committed itself, under the heading 'Fight Sex Discrimination', to: 'Opposition to the harassment of lesbians and gay men and to all forms of discrimination on grounds of homosexuality.'[21]

The Communist Party of Great Britain

The CPGB, the oldest and largest of the British revolutionary organisations, adopted a very different attitude towards homosexual rights and gay liberation – an attitude that reflected both the impact of the movement and the party's own internal debates regarding the road to socialism. Like the rest of the left, it had been taken by surprise by the emergence of gay and lesbian politics and, in the early years of the 1970s, had shown little interest. With the industrial working class so active, it did not see the significance of this new phenomenon. But the CPGB was a less homogeneous organisation than the smaller, more tightly controlled and less socially embedded far-left groups and, as a consequence, it was more subject to the influence of new social forces. This had been true at least as far back as 1957, when the party hierarchy's suspicion of CND had been swamped by the enthusiasm of its younger members, especially the members of its youth wing, the Young Communist League.[22] Through the course of the 1960s a new generation of party activists emerged, less ground down by the grim Cold War years of the 1950s and more open to new issues, new attitudes, and new ways of thinking about and doing politics.[23] It was this generation, shaped by the 'the increasing significance of identity, culture and lifestyles as sites for political activity and commitment' that was open to the rise of women's liberation and gay liberation – and determined to bring these issues within the party's purview.[24] The role of young Communists within the National Union of Students gave them a forum in which to test and apply their new politics with relative freedom. And while the party's hierarchical structure limited the 'backflow' of ideas, it did not prevent it entirely.[25] In 1973, the *Morning Star* (the party newspaper) reported on the NUS motion supporting homosexual rights and, over the next year or so, activists in local branches started to agitate for the party to take a formal position on the substantive issues.[26]

In autumn 1975, the party congress received motions from a number of branches addressing homosexuality. These were not put to a vote; rather, there was what Bea Campbell (a party member and increasingly prominent agitator for gay and lesbian rights) called a 'very formal' and 'completely unsatisfactory' reference to homosexuality and a referral of the matter to the Executive.[27] Over the following months the national organiser worked with gay and lesbian comrades and, in September 1976, the Executive issued a lengthy statement which opened with the unambiguous statement that 'The Communist Party opposes discrimination and victimisation against homosexuals.'[28] The statement endorsed the principle that the 'criminal law should not distinguish homosexual activities from heterosexual activities' and went on to spell out what this meant: decriminalisation in Scotland and Northern Ireland and in the armed forces and the merchant marine (areas which had not been covered by the law of 1967), an equal age of consent, the same definition of privacy as applied to heterosexual acts, legalisation of homosexual personal contact advertisements and so on.

But the statement went further than decriminalisation. It called for anti-discrimination legislation to be passed covering employment, education and the provision of goods and services. Recognising that much of the discrimination experienced by homosexuals had deep social roots, the statement further demanded that homosexuality no longer be considered a mental illness; that gay parents should have full custody rights; that sex education in schools should include the issue; that police harassment cease. These fundamental changes in attitude would require 'political struggle and work to change the general climate of opinion' in society, in the left, in the trade unions and in the party itself. The Executive announced that it was setting up a committee to 'promote discussion and analysis on gay rights, and assist the party in activity on these questions'. The statement was remarkably thorough but to a certain extent this was due to the fact that it had come from the Executive rather than congress. Party members Sarah Benton and Bea Campbell acknowledged that the statement was 'very controversial' for some members, who found it almost impossible to question the naturalness of heterosexuality.[29] But it is clear that the members who had been inspired by gay liberation and had embraced its politics were in the ascendency at this time.

In part, however, this reflected developments within the party as much as the power of the ideas that were being advanced. What we can now characterise, with the benefit of hindsight, as the disintegration of the CPGB (which formally dissolved itself in 1991), seemed at the time to be a struggle within the party over its future direction. Broadly speaking, this was a struggle between those who wanted to continue on the existing and well-worn path, and those who sought a radically new direction. Over the course of the 1960s and 1970s, new social movements addressing new or hitherto under-noticed issues (student life, the American War in Vietnam, women's liberation, gay liberation, workers' power, the failures of Labour in government, the environment, reform communism in Eastern Europe, revisionism in southern European communist parties) began to reshape the political landscape. By the mid-1970s, these issues were being bundled together by Communists into a package labelled Eurocommunism. Class struggle started to be subsumed within a broader conception of a 'democratic alliance' of classes and social movements against economic exploitation and social oppression; the counter-hegemonic struggle replaced class war as the instrument of social transformation. In the CPGB all this thinking was embraced by a substantial section of the membership and found an outlet in *Marxism Today*, the party's theoretical journal. The ideas were, as Willie Thompson put it in his history of the CPGB, starting to 'percolate' up into the leadership[30] and the party programme, *The British Road to Socialism*, approved at the congress in 1977, embodied this new approach.[31] In relation to homosexuality, the reformers embraced an ever-broadening conception of gay rights. We have seen already how sweeping the Executive statement of 1976 was; but even that was criticised by Benton and Campbell for its limitations, reflecting, they charged, concessions to the less enlightened views of some of the membership.

What policy on gay rights the party might have come to cannot be known with any certainty of course. In 1987–88, party activists were deeply involved in the campaign to oppose Clause 28 of the *Local*

Government Act, which made it illegal for local government authorities to 'promote' homosexuality. In 1984–85, they were very visible in Lesbians and Gays Support the Miners, one of the most remarkable examples of solidarity the gay movement ever produced.[32] But this hardly reflected a particularly Communist take on the issue – most gay and lesbian leftists, party and non-party members alike, were involved in these campaigns. Perhaps the clearest picture of how the CPGB might have come to relate to the social movements that were increasingly the focus of its members' strategic thinking is captured in *Beyond the Fragments*, first published in 1979. In three essays, Sheila Rowbotham, Lynne Segal and Hilary Wainwright explored how the traditional organisations of the working class (trade unions, for the most part) and the new movements of the oppressed (women, gays and lesbians, blacks, young people) could be brought together, overcoming their fragmentary state with a common programme and perhaps even a form of organisation, that would allow them to realise their revolutionary potential.[33]

The International Socialists

If the CPGB had a challenger for the largest of the revolutionary left organisations in Britain (and it didn't, really), it would have been the International Socialists, an organisation that had its roots in the Trotskyism of the immediate post-war period and which had started to grow significantly in the 1960s.[34]

What makes the IS experience of value to the history of the far left and homosexuality is that so much of its debate has been published, or is otherwise readily available. As a significant force on the left by 1970, its political positions were of wide interest and many gay and lesbian people found themselves attracted to the organisation's programme and broad approach. One of these was Bob Cant, who explained his attraction to the IS as someone involved in union work, anti-imperialism and sexual politics: he was 'eager to join an organisation with a world view'.[35] He was, of course, aware that the organisation 'had no position on the gay question [but] was prepared to struggle for its integration into the wider programme of the IS'.[36] He lasted three years before, deciding that the Gay Group within the IS had been 'routed', he resigned. In retrospect he saw the IS as going through a particularly 'economistic' stage.[37]

Although Don Milligan had published on 'Gay Liberation' in the December 1972 *Bulletin*,[38] the issue first arose in a major way at the IS National Conference in April 1973, when motions from the Lancaster branch (where an IS Gay Group had been set up by gay and lesbian members)[39] proposed to amend the Draft Program with a section to be called 'Gay People'.[40] This section related homosexual oppression to class society and to the inferior status of women: by failing to play their appointed roles in the sexual division of society, gay men and women exposed themselves to intense oppression and repression – 'ridicule and violence; discrimination in jobs and housing; by police harassment and by the Sexual Offences Act'. The section identified a number of elements underlying gay oppression – the 'lies and distortions of the ruling class', 'reactionary ideas and laws', 'tyranically [sic] imposed sexual stereotypes and norms', 'the male dominated family'. And it proposed a seven-point programme of demands – an end to discrimination in jobs and housing, and to the treatment of homosexuality as a disease or sickness (including the use of aversion therapy), the right to free sex change and associated medical treatment, an end to exclusively heterosexual sex education in schools, the right to display affection in public places, an age of consent of 16 rather than 21, the abolition of legal discrimination including police harassment. Duncan Hallas, the National Secretary, replied on behalf of the National Committee and opposed the amendment on three grounds: it was too long relative to the programme as a whole; some of the demands could not be supported; and some of it was 'theoretically incorrect'. Of these, the first objection was probably right; the thinking behind the other two however was not spelled out in the minutes as published.[41]

Hallas stated clearly that the programme should include reference to 'homosexual repression' and successfully recommended that the matter be taken up by the National Committee. And then ... nothing. In June a dozen or so comrades gathered for a weekend conference which began the slow democratic process of drafting a document of their own for the internal *Bulletin*. Although Bob Cant said in 1976 that the document was never published,[42] Don Milligan published 'Homosexuality and the Oppression of Women' in the *Bulletin* in May/June 1973.[43] In this paper, Milligan advanced an analysis of homosexual oppression which located it in the needs of the capitalist family, thus beginning the process of generating a Marxist analysis of gay oppression and liberation – a task that was starting to be taken up by many socialists within the gay liberation movement.[44]

The National Committee finally responded. In October 1973, it produced a document which, while declaring the organisation to be 'utterly and vehemently opposed to attacks on homosexuals', instructed all members to withdraw from work in the gay movement and to dissolve the Gay Group itself. An attempt in 1974 to organise a conference on sexism (which was presumably an attempt to smuggle in a discussion of homosexuality via the then-established idea that homosexual oppression was inextricably linked to women's oppression was quashed.[45] A few members of the now-disbanded Gay Group met with the National Committee which, apart from confirming the levels of ignorance and homophobia in that body, achieved little.[46]

Organising continued. A number of branches protested the decisions.[47] The members carried on their struggle – Bob Cant refers to a 'subterranean' gay group[48] – and in 1974 and 1975 branch motions in support of taking up gay work were forwarded to the National Committee and conference (where they were defeated without discussion).[49] Cant speaks of years of struggle, of interest and support from many comrades, gay and straight, but also about the demoralising impact of the 'campaign of vilification, misrepresentation and silence' to which he and others were subjected. He finally resigned in 1976. Ironically, six months later the National Conference reversed the ban on gay work, reinstated the Gay Group and marked its reversal by including a statement in the 'Where We Stand' column in the paper declaring 'We are for an end to all forms of discrimination against homosexuals.'[50]

This reversal was generated in part by members and branches. Tower Hamlets and Edinburgh had both sent motions to conference calling for the statement of support and for better coverage of the issues in *Socialist Worker* (Tower Hamlets suggested that any failure to improve the coverage should be regarded a 'pandering to popular prejudice').[51] But Ian Birchall notes that a change of mind by IS leader Tony Cliff was also important. In the 1960s, it seems Cliff had been opposed to homosexuals being members on the grounds that they would be subject to blackmail; by the 1970s he was less concerned by this, but inclined to dismiss the issue as simply one of many forms of suffering in the world.[52] In 1973, during the controversy generated by the NC decision to withdraw from gay work, Cliff is said to have opined that he had no objection to members engaging in gay work as long as they did not think of it as political activity.[53] But an eight-hour session in which John Lindsey explained patiently and in great detail how a Marxist ought to look at this issue served to shift the leader's thinking.[54]

The political climate also had its effect. The rise of a new fascism in British society from the mid-1970s onwards, shot through with racism and homophobia, made it important to take up the struggle against anti-gay discrimination and violence, and to understand its roots in a more sophisticated manner.[55] But the successes of the gay and lesbian movement were also important. After the collapse of Gay Liberation in 1973, gay people had continued their fight for equality throughout the 1970s in a myriad of action groups – in trade unions, newspapers, radio programmes, election campaigns and so on. And in a number of areas they were making modest but real gains. This did not go unnoticed. A year after the IS took up gay work again, the National Conference motion on 'Gay Work' began: 'This Conference recognises that there are now significant opportunities for recruitment from the Gay Movement.'[56] Work to be undertaken included: participating in gay issues when they arise; selling papers at alternative gay discos and meetings; and drawing local gay groups into branch discussions and public meetings. Trade union rank and file groups (in which the SWP played a prominent role) were to educate and actively challenge discrimination; the party was to produce a Socialist Worker pamphlet. Which was all very well, but this raised the question of what the content of such interventions would be. The motion had called for a debate on the 'areas of sexual and personal politics' in the journal and at a specially convened national conference as a precondition for the production of the pamphlet. And the internal bulletin contains some discussion (though there no evidence that the conference happened).[57]

At the 1978 conference a motion on 'Gay Work' recognised that the 'growing interest in the political significance of personal relationships, sexual behaviour and sex roles' was of such 'excitement and interest' that it was 'essential' that the party take it seriously. But to avoid the danger that such a response might become 'abstract or "soggy"', it would be necessary to adopt a 'clear orientation to the workplace' with a focus on 'employment rights for homosexuals, trade union support for gay rights demonstrations' and an emphasis on getting the gay movement to recognise the 'necessity' of such work.[58] Although the conference regretted the non-appearance of the proposed pamphlet, it was, in fact, this motion that made the pamphlet possible. Here was the line that could guide the IS/SWP – by focusing on the centrality of the workplace to gay oppression and gay rights the SWP had a position that both reflected its interest in class and distinguished it from other organisations on the left. The issues of 'sexual and personal politics' previously raised by the 1977 conference; the complexities of sexism, patriarchy, the family, working-class homophobia that the Gay Group had opened up; the molecular processes of change that were already visibly undermining the oppression of gay people – all of these could be set aside in favour of a single-minded attention to the workplace discrimination.

The pamphlet that appeared in June 1979, *The Word Is Gay: Socialists and the Fight against Gay Oppression*, reflected this approach. It came with the imprimatur of the party leader – an introduction by Tony Cliff which opened with the quite remarkable claim that: 'In class-infested society there is oppressor and oppressed in all walks of life. Employer oppresses employee; man oppresses women; white oppresses black; old oppresses young; heterosexual oppresses homosexual.'[59] (This was, in fact, not at all what Marxist theory argued about oppression, which emphasised the structural and systemic rather than individualised oppression.) His suggestion 'that we should look forward now to the first leader of the London workers' council being a 19 year old black gay woman',[60] while well-meaning, must have struck many readers as rather patronising.

By and large, the pamphlet set aside the question of why gay people were oppressed, though the psychological threat that gay men presented to straight men and the threat that gay women represented by their independence were touched upon; for the most part *The Word is Gay* was 'intended as a brief guide to fighting gay oppression in our day-to-day lives, and particularly in our workplaces'.[61] Examples of workplace discrimination were presented, as were some of the deeper challenges that lesbians and gay men faced at work – treated as security risks in the civil service, as child-molesters in schools, as undesirables in the retail sector; subject to arbitrary transfer between workplaces because they do not have family ties; concentration in the poorly organised service sector; unwillingness to stand up for themselves for fear that their homosexuality might be revealed and used against them. The point of the pamphlet was to highlight the ways in which workplace struggles against discrimination could be won. Gay workers were urged to come out, to actively resist discrimination, to seek the support of their workmates, to resist all efforts to refer their grievance to an industrial tribunal or to leave it to the union officials. The emphasis was on the *rank and file* and on *struggle,* putting the issue of anti-gay discrimination firmly within the strategic orientation of the party.

This outlook was restated and explored further (with examples of particular unions which had adopted pro-gay policies or defended victimised members) in *Socialist Review* in January 1981, emphasising the special importance of the workplace and the unions: 'Gay rights organisations, while making genuflections towards the trade unions in the same breath as the churches have never recognised the workplace as a point of major influence'. Specifically, workplaces offered the opportunity for:

- winning the bulk of working people to an acceptance of the rights of gay people, and the understanding of how bosses use anti-gay fears to undermine workplace solidarity

- winning the bulk of gay people to the realisation that their interests are inextricably linked with the interests of the class as a whole, and that gay liberation, as with any other liberation, has to be achieved at the point of production.[62]

By the late 1970s, then, ten years after the rise of the gay liberation movement, the SWP had found a way to mesh the particular problem of gay oppression to the party's general political orientation – the workplace was identified as the site for building of the struggle for both socialism and

gay rights. The role of the party was to concentrate and generalise from
these struggles, to support them, to spread them, to learn from them and
teach from them – to build 'the size and self-confidence' of the socialist
minority, to recruit this minority to the organisation that would one day
lead the struggle for socialism.[63]

Conclusion

The 1970s had been a difficult decade for the revolutionary left. It opened
with levels of class struggle that seemed to confirm all that it had been
working for for so long. It ended with the Conservatives in government
under Margaret Thatcher who, if she was not yet the all-conquering force
that she would become, nonetheless provided evidence that things were
not going well for the left. Within a decade the Stalinist road to socialism
had been swept into the dustbin of history by the people of eastern Europe,
and the Leninist model of revolutionary organisation was fatally wounded
(though not all its adherents were aware of just how bad things had got
on that front). By a kind of toxic backwash, the wellsprings of Marxism
were themselves poisoned by these developments. The CPGB was no more,
dissolved after seventy years into a politically amorphous and short-lived
Democratic Left. Some of the Trotskyist organisations (notably the SWP)
lived on, but as shadows of their earlier selves.

Meanwhile, the Labour Party, which had seemed to be in terminal crisis
over the 1980s, had thrown off its old left-wing shell and emerged with the
toothily grinning human face of New Labour. Whatever its sins (and these
were many), New Labour provided a space in which gay and lesbian (and
later bisexual and transgender) activists could find a home and a vehicle
for social and political reform. If the revolutionary left had found a way to
link the struggles for socialism and gay rights, the barely reformist centre
had moved in on that territory, replacing liberation with equality, and
utopia with everyday achievements.

Notes

1 Perhaps the most obvious omission here is the other side of the story – efforts
  by gay and lesbian activists to develop a theory of the relationship between
  gay oppression, gay liberation and the broader revolutionary project. Such
  efforts are not entirely absent from the narrative, but they are subordinated to
  the particular story that I am dealing with here. A proper study of the gay left
  would require a piece at least as long again as this chapter.
2 On the Wolfenden Report and the subsequent debate see in particular S. Jeffery-
  Poulter, *Peers, Queers and Commons: The Struggle for Gay Law Reform from
  1950 to the Present* (London: Routledge, 1991) and P. Higgins, *Heterosexual*

Dictatorship: Male Homosexuality in Post-war Britain (London: Fourth Estate, 1996).

3   R. Jenkins, *The Labour Case* (Harmondsworth: Penguin, 1959), pp. 135–6.

4   C. A. R. Crosland, *The Future of Socialism* (London: Jonathan Cape, 1956), pp. 521–2.

5   Departmental Committee on Homosexual Offences and Prostitution, Evidence Submitted by the Progressive League, March 1955, HO345/8, CHP/43; and the transcript of evidence at HO 345/13, CHP/TRANS/22.

6   C. Dallas, 'The Meaning of Wolfenden: A Socialist Critique', *Socialist Review*, December (1957), pp. 6–7.

7   S. Edge, *With Friends Like These: Marxism and Gay Politics* (London: Cassell, 1995), pp. 27–8.

8   *Bernstein on Homosexuality: Articles from Die Neue Zeit, 1895 and 1898* (Belfast: Athol Books, 1977). Ironically, the British and Irish Communist Organisation, which published this useful pamphlet, were very clear that they supported decriminalisation, but added that 'we do not follow the "anti-sexist" movement in their demand that the law should oppose the social bias towards heterosexuality' (p. 5).

9   The liveliest history of gay liberation in England is L. Power, *No Bath but Plenty of Bubbles: An Oral History of the Gay Liberation Front, 1970–73* (London: Cassell, 1995).

10   Ibid.

11   P. Dorey, *British Politics since 1945* (Oxford: Blackwell, 1995), pp. 111–20; A. Marr, *A History of Modern Britain* (London: Macmillan, 2007), pp. 308–15, 337–48, 354–77.

12   J. Callaghan, *The Far Left in British Politics* (Oxford: Basil Blackwell, 1987), p. 198; M. Crick, *The March of Militant* (London: Faber and Faber, 1986), p. 90.

13   Callaghan, *The Far Left*, p. 200.

14   Ibid., p. 201.

15   L. Robinson, *Gay Men and the Left in Post-war Britain: How the Personal Got Political* (Manchester: Manchester University Press, 2007), pp. 99–101.

16   Callaghan, *The Far Left*, pp. 203–4.

17   Robinson, *Gay Men and the Left*, pp. 99–101.

18   Crick, *The March of Militant*, p. 90

19   Edge, *With Friends Like These*, p. 26.

20   Crick, *The March of Militant*, p. 90.

21   Ibid., p. 72. It is a striking fact that none of those who discuss Militant's stance on gay people and the lesbian and gay movement offer anything by way of sources for their assertions. I have reported their claims here, and in the case of Crick, I am relying on an author with a great familiarity with, and a balanced approach to, the organisation that he is writing about.

22   M. Waite, 'Sex 'n' Drugs 'n' Rock 'n' Roll (and Communism) in the 1960s', in G. Andrews, N. Fishman and K. Morgan (eds), *Opening the Books: Essays on the Social and Cultural History of British Communism* (London: Pluto Press, 1995), p. 211; Callaghan, *The Far Left*, p. 170.

188 *Part II Issues*

23 Waite, 'Sex 'n' Drugs 'n' Rock 'n' Roll', p. 223.

24 Ibid., pp. 221–2.

25 G. Andrews, 'Young Turks and Old Guard: Intellectuals and the Communist Party Leadership in the 1970s', in Andrews, Fishman and Morgan (eds), *Opening the Books*, p. 235.

26 Robinson, *Gay Men and the Left*, p. 97.

27 'Communist Comment', *Gay Left*, 4, pp. 9–11.

28 'Communist Comment', pp. 9-11; 'Statement Adopted on September 11–12', *Comment*, 16 October 1976, pp. 328–9.

29 'Communist Comment', p. 10.

30 W. Thompson, *The Good Old Cause: British Communism 1920–1991* (London: Pluto Press, 1992), pp. 164–5.

31 Ibid., pp. 172–83. This transformation was not uncontested, to say the least. Having fought against the shift for as long as they could, many of those most opposed to it sheared off in 1977 to found the New Communist Party.

32 Robinson, *Gay Men and the Left*, pp. 164–74. See also Colin Clews, 'Lesbians and Gays Support the Miners. Part One', www.gayinthe80s.com/2012/09/10/1984-lesbians-and-gays-support-the-miners-part-one/, accessed 17 December 2013.

33 S. Rowbotham, L. Segal and H. Wainwright (eds), *Beyond the Fragments: Feminism and the Making of Socialism* (London: Merlin Press, 1979), esp. pp. 5–7.

34 J. Higgins, *More Years for the Locust: The Origins of the SWP* (1997), www.marxists.org/archive/higgins/1997/locust/index.htm, accessed 17 December 2013.

35 B. Cant and N. Young, 'New Politics, Old Struggles', in Gay Left Collective (ed.), *Homosexuality: Power and Politics* (London: Allison and Busby, 1980), p. 117.

36 Ibid., p. 117.

37 Ibid., p. 117.

38 D. Milligan, 'Gay Liberation', *IS Bulletin*, December (1972), n.p. (An excellent collection of documents of the Socialist Review Group/International Socialists/Socialist Workers Party is located in the Will Fancy Papers, Senate House Library, University of London, MS1171.)

39 B. Cant, 'Normal Channels', in B. Cant and S. Hemmings (eds), *Radical Records: Thirty Years of Lesbian and Gay History* (London and New York: Routledge, 1988), p. 209.

40 'Amendment 2', *International Socialists Conference Bulletin*, April (1973), pp. 18–19.

41 Milligan responded in the May–June 1973 *Bulletin* to at least one of Hallas' points – namely that 'homosexuals had not been oppressed in classical Greece – by setting out the ways in which homosexuality had been, as we would say, regulated in ancient Greece around axes of class and sex in such a way as to make it reasonable to say that homosexuality was, in fact, oppressed: Don Milligan, 'Homosexuality and the Oppression of Women', *IS Bulletin*, May–June (1973).

42 B. Cant, 'A Grim Tale: The IS Gay Group 1972–75', *Gay Left*, 3, autumn (1976), pp. 7–10.

43 D. Milligan, 'Homosexuality and the Oppression of Women'.

44 In journals such as *Gay Marxist* and *Gay Left*, and in important early contributions such as D. Fernbach, 'Towards a Marxist Theory of Gay Liberation', *Gay Marxist*, July (1973) and D. Milligan *The Politics of Homosexuality* (London: Pluto Press, 1973).

45 Cant, 'Normal Channels', p. 209.

46 B. Cant, 'A Grim Tale', pp. 7–10.

47 'Resolutions to the December NC', resolutions 8, 9, 10. Will Fancy Papers, MS1171, Box 24/2.

48 Cant, 'A Grim Tale', p. 8.

49 Cant, 'Normal Channels', p. 210.

50 I. Birchall, *The Smallest Mass Party in the World*, www.marxists.de/intsoctend/birchall/crisis.htm, accessed 17 December 2013; I. Birchall, *Tony Cliff: A Marxist for His Time* (London: Bookmarks, 2011), p. 242. For a discussion of the state of the debate within the IS at the time, see the report by the 'self-styled convenor' of the 'very embryonic group of gays, bisexuals and fellow travellers', Sylvia Cook, 'The Gay Issue and the IS', *IS Bulletin*, April (1976), pp. 24–5.

51 *IS Bulletin*, May (1976), p. 10.

52 Birchall, *Tony Cliff*, pp. 423–4.

53 Cant, 'A Grim Tale', p. 8; Birchall, *Tony Cliff*, p. 425. This approach became notorious in a word-of-mouth version of the story that has Cliff being quoted (usually in a very bad imitation of his accent and with much waving of hands) announcing that they could form a model train society for all he cared, but that it wasn't politics. There may be some documentary evidence for this general approach in Will Fancy's papers where, on the document 'Resolutions to the December NC', someone (presumably Fancy himself) has jotted 'Cliff vs homo, Jew, OAP groups – Gay group not operational outwards' (Will Fancy Papers, MS1171, Box 24/2).

54 Birchall, *Tony Cliff*, p. 425.

55 Ibid., p. 423.

56 'Resolution on Gay Work', *National Conference Report* (1977).

57 See, for example, articles such as A. Bateman, 'Sexual Politics at Last', *IS Bulletin*, May (1976), p. 21; M. Carlton, 'Personal Politics', *SWP Internal Bulletin*, 5, June (1977); L. Starling, 'Politics and Sex', *SWP Internal Bulletin*, 7, October (1977); K. Ridges, 'Sexism on the Left', *SWP Internal Bulletin*, 7, October (1977).

58 'Gay Work', National Conference Resolutions, *SWP Internal Bulletin*, 1978.

59 Socialist Workers Party Gay Group, *The Word is Gay* (London: Socialist Workers Party, 1979).

60 Ibid., p. 4.

61 Ibid., p. 12.

62 J. Lindsay, 'Glad to be Gay – at Work', *Socialist Review*, January (1981), p. 30.

63 'The Alternative to Defeat', *Socialist Worker*, 5 March 1983, p. 3.

10

'Vicarious pleasure'?

The British far left and the third world, 1956–79

Ian Birchall

And my attitude to the other groups – I believe the majority of them, because of many, many years of frustration and isolation, in the end turn to the game of sour grapes. They accept their impotence, accept their weakness, and therefore they get vicarious pleasure from people struggling elsewhere ... They are experts about Bolivia, they are experts about Vietnam, ... But they know very little about British working-class history, they know very little about the British working class, they care very little about the struggle in this country.[1]

Tony Cliff

When Communist Party general secretary Harry Pollitt heard of his party's bad results in the 1949 St Pancras North by-election, he commented: 'We may not have won St Pancras, but we've got China.'[2] It summed up an attitude that would become widespread on the left over the following decades: a belief that the locus of revolutionary change had shifted from those countries in which capitalism was most highly developed to the territories of what came to be known as the 'third world'.

The 'third world' was short-lived, rising and falling within a single human lifespan. The term ('*tiers monde*') was coined by Alfred Sauvy in 1952; by 2007 it was described by the *Guardian* style guide as 'outdated' and 'objectionable'.[3] But for a couple of decades the 'third world' was a major source of inspiration to the British far left.

For the British left in the 1950s, the working class was something of a disappointment. Full employment and rising living standards resulting from the long post-war boom meant that while workers were often militant, there was little need for generalisation and hence for a political worldview. The result was 'apathy' – in E. P. Thompson's definition, the fact that 'people have, increasingly, looked to *private* solutions to *public* evils'.[4] The right wing of Gaitskell and Crosland dominated the Labour

Party as Tories won three successive general elections in 1951, 1955 and 1959. Not surprisingly some on the left began to seek an alternative agency for revolutionary struggle.

The picture in the rest of the world was very different. In 1949 the Chinese Communists had taken power. In 1954 defeat at Dien Bien Phu in Indochina had provided a massive humiliation for French imperialism and had ignited an even more dangerous revolt in Algeria. The 1955 Bandung non-aligned conference brought together delegates from 29 countries, representing half the world's population, including Nasser from Egypt, Chou En-Lai from China, Tito from Yugoslavia and Nehru from India.[5] In 1959 the Cuban revolution established an anti-imperialist beacon in the United States' sphere of influence; the second Vietnam war pushed the United States onto the defensive.

Until 1956 the British far left was dominated by the Communist Party (CPGB), which based its view of the world on Moscow's foreign policy. The CPGB's 1951 programme, *The British Road to Socialism*, stated:

> The enemies of Communism declare that the Communist Party, by underhand and subversive means, is aiming at the destruction of Britain and the British Empire. This is a lie ... [our aim should be] a new, close, fraternal association of the British people and the liberated peoples of the Empire. Only on this basis can true friendship be established between the peoples of the present Empire to promote mutually beneficial economic exchange and cooperation, and to defend in common their freedom against American imperialist aggression.[6]

American – not British – imperialism was the main enemy.

The New Left

The year 1956 was the turning-point. The Suez debacle was a death-blow for the British Empire, leading to rapid decolonisation in Africa. The Hungarian rising led to a wave of resignations from the CPGB, and the emergence of a 'new left'. This contained many tendencies and had no fixed political doctrine; but one important theme was the search for a political force independent of both Washington and Moscow. To some the newly non-aligned nations and the liberation struggles in the third world seemed to provide such a force.

The original *New Left Review* (NLR) was an eclectic journal reflecting various tendencies in the emerging new left. But an awareness of the third world was present throughout the milieu. Even Edward Thompson, whose roots were in the traditions of the British working-class movement, wrote in the introduction to *The Making of the English Working Class* that study of the Industrial Revolution was relevant because of parallels in the developing world: 'Causes which were lost in England might, in Asia or Africa, yet be won.'[7]

One element in the mix was a moralising third worldism represented by an article by Keith Buchannan, which praised Cambodian 'royal socialism', and wrote off the working class in developed countries:

> Having tasted the delights of affluence, European workers have tended to become 'embourgeoisé' and ever more Euro-centric in their attitudes. A Fanon may cry that the well-being and progress of Europe have been built with the sweat and corpses of black man and yellow man, Indian and Arab – but the cry is unheard amid the distractions of a new and delightful opulence.[8]

The rise of the New Left was closely linked to the growth of the Campaign for Nuclear Disarmament (CND). The *NLR* strategy was developed in John Rex's pamphlet for the 1960 Aldermaston March, which argued that Britain should align itself, through the United Nations, with third world countries independent of East and West:

> There must, however, be many people in Britain who take their stand with the colonial revolution which has brought about the new balance of power in the world. The fact that many of those who march with the Campaign, also take part in the fight for colonial freedom and in organisations like War on Want or the [South African] Boycott Movement bears witness to this. As much as any, they represent the new left in British politics ... But if Britain does accept that authority now resides with the underdeveloped countries, it follows that a major aim of her foreign policy should be to win friends and influence people in these countries.[9]

In 1962 a new, younger team took over *NLR*. Peter Sedgwick, who knew the milieu well, was scornful of their intellectual pretensions, describing them as 'Olympian' and as a bunch of 'roving postgraduates that descends at will from its own space onto the target terrains of Angola, Persia, Cuba, Algeria, Britain'.[10] Though this had some truth to it, it was a little unfair. According to Editorial Committee member Tom Wengraf, between 1962 and 1964 *NLR* concerned itself with 'comparative country studies', giving 'a definite primacy to the study of the empirical, the concrete, the historical' as distinct from *NLR*'s later concern with 'theory'.[11] Examples of such work were Anderson's study of the Portuguese colonialism[12] and the unfortunately uncompleted study of the Algerian Revolution by Tom Wengraf and Roger Murray.[13] Some of this work was of considerable descriptive and analytic value.

Maoism

A further impetus to third worldism came with the open and public break between Russia and China in 1963. British Maoism originated with Michael McCreery's Committee to Defeat Revisionism and for Communist Unity (CDRCU). This perceived the Chinese as siding with the third world, denouncing Khrushchev's policy of 'peaceful coexistence' as 'an outright betrayal of colonial and semi-colonial peoples now moving into action in Asia, Africa and Latin America'.[14] The CPGB was accused of supporting third world leaders like Nkrumah and Nasser, who used 'socialist' language but attacked their own working classes.[15] Attempts to impose the model of the Chinese Revolution on British society led to some strange debates among the various Maoist groups, for example the question of whether or not there was a British 'semi-proletariat' (possibly 'the family units of seaside landladies whose husbands work in a factory').[16]

Soon more serious elements began to align themselves with Maoism, notably when Reg Birch and other experienced trade union militants formed the Communist Party of Britain (Marxist-Leninist) (CPBML). The CPBML's 1971 programme rejected the idea that the working class had become 'a partner in imperialist plunder',[17] and a 1977 CPBML pamphlet totally rejected the notion of a third world:

> The definition of a third world is based on the theory that the greater the under-development the greater the potential for revolution, that the man with the ox is more militant, a greater force for change than the one who has passed that stage. Dialectically, if he did not have the ox he would be even more revolutionary ... It is a false premise that the undeveloped, less privileged, 'more' exploited are more prone to progress, to revolution.[18]

The CPBML broke with China in 1977 (briefly becoming pro-Albanian), accusing it of a 'bid to attain the status of a world imperialist power'.[19] It had been Maoist essentially in its attempt to transplant the third world strategy of guerrilla warfare into the British industrial context:

> Guerrilla struggle is an essential to the winning of a struggle, to prevent demoralisation and setback and is, in effect, the only course, the only strategy open to us. There is no other way at this time because of all the forces arrayed against us ... Guerrilla struggle enables those directly involved to control and conduct the struggle. Ultra-left calls for positional struggle, e.g. a general strike now, are a counsel of despair.[20]

A wider layer of intellectuals identified with China and the third world, often invoking a romanticised opposition to Western consumerism. Sheila Rowbotham recalled hearing the economist Joan Robinson 'grumbling about the materialism of the West, which she contrasted with China. "I bet you don't do all your own washing by hand," I thought, silent and resentful as she dismissed the need for washing machines'.[21] Raymond Williams, while expressing reservations, sympathised with the aims of the Cultural Revolution: 'When I heard pathetic stories about professors being taken from their libraries and laboratories and sent to help bring in the harvest I felt totally on the side of the revolutionaries ... I do not see why an ordinary healthy man or woman should not participate in manual labour.'[22]

The writings of many other third world leaders and militants were also becoming available. Frantz Fanon's *The Wretched of the Earth* argued that 'in the colonial territories, the proletariat is the nucleus of the colonised population which has been most pampered by the colonial regime'.[23] He concluded: 'the European game has finally ended; we must find something different. We today can do everything, so long as we do not imitate Europe, so long as we are not obsessed by the desire to catch up with Europe'.[24]

Régis Debray's influential book *Revolution in the Revolution* set out to theorise the achievements of the Cuban revolution and to challenge traditional Marxist scenarios. As Debray put it, he aimed to 'free the present from the past'. He cited with approval Castro's claim that 'the city is a cemetery of revolutionaries and resources', and put forward the provocative paradox that 'the mountain proletarianises the bourgeois and peasant elements, and the city can bourgeoisify the proletarians'.[25] Debray's writings received editorial commendation from *New Left Review* for 'their relentlessly Leninist focus on *making the revolution*'.[26]

Above all, the Cuban slogan 'the duty of the revolutionary is to make the revolution' encouraged a frenetic voluntarism which cheerfully disregarded such minor constraints as objective circumstances and, indeed, the consciousness of the mass of the working class. Anthony Barnett, a member of the *New Left Review* Editorial Committee, described the atmosphere in the late 1960s: 'Everybody was terribly young and didn't know what was going on. One had a sort of megalomaniac attitude that by sheer protest and revolt things would be changed ... The desire to do something became tremendously intense.'[27]

Trotskyism

British Trotskyism underwent a substantial revival in the early 1960s as a result of activity in the Labour Party's Young Socialists. The main Trotskyist currents all benefited from involvement in CND and then the movement against the war in Vietnam. As against the CPGB and the Maoists they had the advantage of not being aligned on any state's foreign policy.

The Socialist Labour League (SLL) was the strongest current up to the mid-1960s. The SLL advocated unity between national liberation movements and the working class in the imperialist countries. As its leading figure Gerry Healy wrote in 1956: 'The Arab people must place no trust whatsoever in the role of US imperialism – it must rather turn itself four square towards the working class and Labour Movement in the Imperialist countries ... We must halt this war on the Colonial people or it will eventually engulf the world. Only British Labour armed with a socialist policy can do it.'[28] Peter Fryer of the SLL argued that 'workers in Britain and workers in the colonies oppressed by British imperialism have a fundamental identity of interests'.[29] But this 'identity' seemed to be an assertion rather than the product of any serious analysis.

The SLL argued that Castro's Cuba was 'a bonapartist regime resting on state capitalist foundations'.[30] Yet Healy was not immune from his own brand of third worldism, as was shown by his later enthusiasm for Gaddafi's Libya – during the 1970s and 1980s he had several 'lengthy discussions with Gaddafi in his Bedouin tent'.[31] In 1965, the SLL launched – and then rapidly dropped – the slogan 'Arm the Vietcong!'[32] This was presumably intended to be a more radical alternative to the slogan 'Victory to the Vietcong' used elsewhere on the left. But its precise meaning in practice and the reasons for its rapid disappearance (perhaps due to divisions with the leadership) remain unclear.

In January 1961 the other main Trotskyist current, the International Secretariat of the Fourth International, adopted at its Sixth World Congress a document on 'The Colonial Revolution'. This noted 'the gap between the powerful and constantly renewed revolutionary activity of the masses in the dependent countries, and the decline of the revolutionary workers' movement in the advanced capitalist countries'. From this it went on to draw some highly optimistic conclusions which implied a complete reorientation of the International's activity:

> For valid historical reasons the development of the Fourth International was during a whole period centred on the advanced capitalist countries, considered, until the eve of the last war, as the No. 1 epicentre of the world revolution. Now it is necessary for the Fourth International to reorganize its activity as an International in terms of the principal sector of the world revolution, which is the colonial revolution, and carry on in this field, for a whole period, the essential part of its efforts.[33]

The Trotskyist left was involved in solidarity work with the Algerian revolution. The Labour MP John Baird, probably a clandestine member of the Fourth International, worked tirelessly for solidarity with the National Liberation Front (FLN). He collaborated with the FLN representatives in Britain, produced the newsletter *Free Algeria* and tried to win support for the Algerian cause among his colleagues in the Parliamentary Labour Party. He was also engaged in smuggling currency for the FLN.[34]

Michel Pablo of the Fourth International organised the construction of a secret arms factory for the FLN in Morocco.[35] Ken Tarbuck describes in his autobiography how workers were recruited from Britain:

> From Nottingham we were able to recruit several tool-makers and other skilled workers who were willing to go abroad and assist in this project. This had to be done in a clandestine manner since it was strictly speaking illegal to render such aid to 'rebels' operating against a 'friendly' power, that is, France.[36]

One of those who went was Jimmy Deane, a leading member of what was to become the Militant tendency, who 'as an electrical engineer ... volunteered to go to Morocco. This was in response to a request from the Algerian FLN ... to help them break through the electrified, Moroccan/ Algerian border fences'.[37]

The chief theoretician of what became the Militant tendency, Ted Grant, developed a distinctive position in a 1964 document entitled 'The Colonial Revolution and the Sino-Soviet Split'. Grant, like many of his contemporaries, observed that since 1945 'unprecedented upheavals in the colonial areas' had been parallel to 'a lag and delay of the revolution in the West'. He attempted to explain this in terms of Trotsky's theory of permanent revolution:

> Thus the lag of the revolution in Europe and other metropolitan countries has pushed the revolution to the extremities of the capitalist world, to the weakest links in the chain of capitalism. However, the development of Stalinism in Russia and its extension to China and Eastern Europe, the frustration of the revolution in the industrially decisive areas of the capitalist world, has meant that *the development of the permanent revolution in these underdeveloped countries has taken a distorted pattern.*

Hence while the revolutionary process in the third world could go beyond bourgeois limits, there were severe constraints on what the new regimes could achieve. In Burma the officer caste:

> *have begun the expropriation of the indigenous bourgeoisie.* They even threatened the nationalisation of the small shops. *They based themselves on the peasants and the working class. But they do not have a model of scientific socialism,* on the contrary, their programme is one of 'Burmese-Buddhist socialism'.

So, in the absence of Marxist leadership the only possibility was 'aberrations' such as Buddhist socialism, African socialism or Muslim socialism. While other Trotskyists were hailing the achievements of 'workers' control' in independent Algeria, Grant insisted that:

> Revolutionary victory in backward countries such as Algeria, under present conditions, whilst constituting a tremendous victory for the world revolution and the world proletariat, to be enthusiastically supported and aided by the vanguard as well as by the world proletariat, cannot but be on the lines of a totalitarian state.[38]

Whatever theoretical problems were posed by this analysis of 'deformed workers' states', Grant's followers were at least warned of the dangers of the adulation of third world revolutions. However, in 1966, *Militant* readers were assured that developments in Syria meant that the Syrian working class 'will never now have to alter the property relations of society'.[39]

The International Group, based mainly in Nottingham, which was to develop into the International Marxist Group (IMG), launched in January 1964 the news analysis magazine *The Week*, sponsored by left-wing union officials and Labour MPs. This had the perspective that the election of a Labour government (as happened in October 1964) would lead to the emergence of a mass Labour left. From the outset it had two parallel sets of preoccupations: on the one hand, industrial struggle, incomes policy and workers' control; on the other, solidarity with Algeria (till Ben Bella's fall in 1965) and Vietnam. The group played a central role in launching the Vietnam Solidarity Campaign (VSC) in 1966.

In effect this meant addressing two audiences. While there was some concern about Vietnam within the trade union movement, the demand for militant action came largely from the student milieu. As John Callaghan notes: 'The strains between these two wings of IMG activity – its engagement with the traditional mass organisations versus its success in mass mobilisation of a seemingly new vanguard – soon caused splinters within the group.'[40] *The Week* was wound up in 1968 when it was recognised that its hope of a growing Labour left had not been realised. The year 1968 accentuated the trend to third worldism in the IMG.

International Socialists

Some of the most interesting theoretical developments took place in the Socialist Review Group, which in 1962 became the International Socialists (IS). All the other tendencies of the far left – Communists, Maoists and orthodox Trotskyists – were united in accepting the Leninist theory of imperialism. The Socialist Review/International Socialists (SR/IS) group had originally defined itself by its description of Russia as 'state capitalist', but by the late 1950s its main theoreticians, Tony Cliff and Mike Kidron, were engaged in a revision of Leninist orthodoxy.

Tony Cliff set out to revise Trotsky's theory of 'permanent revolution', which was central to the orthodox Trotskyist understanding of revolution in the third world. In his book *Mao's China*,[41] and then more explicitly in an article, Cliff developed the theory of 'deflected permanent revolution'. He argued that while the theory of permanent revolution had been shown to be valid in Russia in 1917, the revolutionary role of the working class was 'neither absolute nor inevitable'. In Mao's China, Nasser's Egypt and Castro's Cuba, the Permanent Revolution was 'deflected' – the role that might have been played by the working class was instead taken over by the revolutionary intelligentsia. Cliff characterised this social group, so widely admired elsewhere on the left, in the following terms:

> They are great believers in efficiency, including efficiency in social engineering. They hope for reform from above and would dearly love to hand the new world over to a grateful people, rather than see the liberating struggle of a self-conscious and freely-associated people result in a new world for themselves. They care a lot for measures to drag their nation out of stagnation, but very little for democracy. They embody the drive for industrialisation, for capital accumulation, for national resurgence. Their power is in direct relation to the feebleness of other classes, and their political nullity.[42]

Kidron developed a more comprehensive critique of Lenin's theory of imperialism, showing that it failed to describe 1960s capitalism. 'Capital does not flow overwhelmingly from mature to developing capitalist countries. On the contrary, foreign investments are increasingly made as between developed countries themselves.' And he concluded:

> Lenin's *Imperialism* was supremely good theory in its day. It picked out the enemy, determined the crucial alliance, and explained what the battle was about. But the lines of battle have been redrawn and Lenin, however superb an example of the right approach to theory, is no more the complete manual.[43]

At the core of his critique was a concern to maintain the revolutionary role of the working class in the advanced capitalist countries, and to argue against those who claimed that the revolution would come through the oppressed countries of the third world. In a subsequent article Kidron concluded that:

> to believe nowadays that the short route to revolution in London, New York or Paris lies through Calcutta, Havana or Algiers, is to pass the buck to where it has no currency. To act on this belief is to rob the revolutionary socialist movement of the few dollars it still possesses.[44]

This position laid IS open to criticisms from its rivals. Tariq Ali, who opted for the IMG against the IS, found IS members 'refreshingly undogmatic', but considered the IS analysis to be 'bizarre and far too Eurocentric'.[45]

Vietnam

The Vietnam Solidarity Campaign (VSC) was central to the reshaping of the British far left.[46] Originally, opposition to the Vietnam War was mainly organised by the British Council for Peace in Vietnam, led by the CPGB and the Labour left, which ran a drab campaign in favour of negotiations. The VSC organised three major demonstrations in 1967 and 1968, drawing in a new generation who saw the Vietnamese National Liberation Front (NLF) as the vanguard of the anti-imperialist struggle. This view was reinforced by the successful Tet offensive in early 1968.

Enthusiasm for the NLF cause was widespread on the far left. The IS took a solidarity position and was involved in building the VSC, but kept its distance from the more adulatory aspects, giving its main attention to the industrial struggle in Britain. It was Chris Harman, in touch with the mood among students at the London School of Economics, rather than Cliff or Kidron, who helped to orient IS towards a greater involvement with the Vietnam question. In July 1967, IS members in the VSC argued for the building of a large demonstration; Harman in particular argued that the demonstration should 'aim to immobilise the American embassy for a token period'.[47] However, IS did not take an uncritical attitude to the Vietnamese struggle. The IS paper *Labour Worker* was one of the first publications to discuss the suppression of the Vietnamese Trotskyists in 1945.[48]

The most thoroughgoing left (indeed ultra-left) critique of the principle of support for the Vietnamese struggle came from the Solidarity grouping, strongly influenced by the French group *Socialisme ou Barbarie*, which had broken with Trotskyism. This published a number of articles and pamphlets about Vietnam and generalised its position – which by its own account had led to the group's 'isolation'[49] – in a statement 'third worldism or Socialism'. This repudiated the whole logic that had led most of the far left to back the Vietnamese struggle, and rejected the classic Marxist distinction between the nationalism of the oppressors and that of the oppressed:

> Nationalism and class struggle are irreconcilably opposed ... *All* nationalisms are reactionary because they inevitably clash with class consciousness and poison it with chauvinism and racialism ... The Trotskyist myth that a successful national liberation will later unleash 'the real class struggle' is false ... It is a rationalisation for the defence of new ruling classes in the

process of formation ... To this degree Trotskyism is a variety of vicarious
social patriotism ... For us, the main enemy will always be at home, and the
only way we can help ourselves and the workers and peasants of the third
world is to help to make a socialist revolution here. [50]

1968

The events of 1968, above all the Tet offensive, the French general strike
and the Russian invasion of Czechoslovakia, formed a new political
generation and greatly strengthened the forces of the far left. In terms
of attitudes to the third world the effects were contradictory. On the one
hand the Tet offensive showed the vulnerability of the world's strongest
imperialist power to guerrilla struggle. Tet played a role in inspiring
the French strike and the international student movement by extending
what Sartre called the 'field of the possible'.[51] Dave Widgery recorded an
exchange at a South London tenants' meeting. 'Member of the committee,
a veteran Communist, advocates caution. Tenant at the back disagrees:
"We've got to fight them with everything we've got, like them bloody Viet
Congs do"'; he recounted the story of building workers who, turned away
when lobbying the town hall about health regulations, linked arms and
marched into the building, chanting 'Ho, Ho, Ho Chi Minh'.[52]

But the French strike showed that the working class in the advanced
countries had a revolutionary potential. Czechoslovakia strengthened the
need for a revolutionary force independent of Washington and Moscow. The
fact that Castro backed the Russians made things a bit more complicated.[53]

The contradictions of 1968 were summed up in the journal *Black Dwarf*,
produced by a team of Trotskyists and Maoists. Initially it reflected the
new mood of 1968, in which traditional divisions seemed less important.
Black Dwarf could be simultaneously third worldist, student vanguardist
and oriented to the working class. But unity did not last very long. Within
two years there was a split, largely along Trotskyist/Maoist lines, leading
to the formation of the Fourth Internationalist *Red Mole*; *Black Dwarf*
disappeared in 1970.

A more sober perspective, recognising the way in which 1968 had
transformed the political scene, yet still rejecting Guevarist voluntarism
and vicarious identification with distant struggles, and stressing the
practical goals of the struggle in Britain, came in an editorial in the journal
International Socialism:

> What must be emphasised and re-emphasised is the immense gulf that
> separates the working class's revolutionary potential and our revolutionary
> ideas. There are no short cuts for overcoming this. No amount of verbal
> euphoria or frenetic activism will do this – especially if confined to the

university ghetto. What is required is not the heroic gesture or the symbolic confrontation (any more than the perfect resolution); nor is it vicarious participation in the self-activity of others (whether they be in Hanoi or Paris); rather we have to be where the various sections of the working class are as they begin to work out new ways of dealing with the new problems, in the factories, in the unions, in the estates and the localities, criticising existing ideas and the conceptions of action that flow from them, suggesting alternatives and linking these to a coherent revolutionary socialist world view. The task is not easy or glamorous; but without it the fire next time can still sputter out.[54]

The VSC demonstration of 27 October 1968 showed the potential that third world struggles had for mobilising significant numbers. Around a hundred thousand people marched; a *New Society* poll showed that 45 per cent of the demonstrators were non-student and that as many as 68 per cent considered they had come to protest at capitalism in general.[55] It was not necessarily the most militantly third worldist who benefited from the VSC; as Tariq Ali noted, it was the International Socialists – with their balanced position of critical support for the NLF – who recruited most successfully from the VSC.[56]

Yet even this, the peak of the Vietnam agitation, showed the left was deeply divided. The *Militant* remained aloof from the VSC;[57] some Maoists organised a breakaway demonstration. The most direct opposition to the VSC came from the SLL, which distributed a leaflet to demonstrators telling them they were wasting their time:

> The Socialist Labour League refuses … to participate in the demonstration. Our task is to direct all young workers and students towards serious consideration for the theory and role of Trotskyism and the Fourth International towards the building of the revolutionary party.[58]

The tensions and divisions within the left were made clear at the memorial meeting held for Vietnamese leader Ho Chi Minh in the autumn of 1969. One of the speakers was Chris Harman of the International Socialists, who began by stressing the significance of Vietnam:

> The struggle of the Vietnamese came to be the focal point for the hopes of millions throughout the third world who would no longer tolerate the poverty, exploitation and misery resulting from imperialism.

But he went on to make certain sharp criticisms of the Vietnamese leadership, recalling that in 1945 their policy:

> not only meant accepting continued French dominance over the southern province of Cochin China and allowing French troops to peacefully reoccupy key strategic points in Hanoi, it also meant the Vietminh itself murdering those, particularly the still influential Trotskyists around Ta Thu Thau

in the south, who agitated for the continuation of both the class and the
national struggle.

He concluded: 'North Vietnam is a one-party regime of the Stalinist
sort … It has nothing in common with socialism.'[59] Given the various
political tendencies assembled in the hall, it was not surprising that this
produced uproar.[60]

Contradictions of third worldism

Even deeper tensions were revealed by 1970. Many on the far left were
sympathetic to China and the ideology of the Cultural Revolution. But
there was a dividing line between those for whom support for China was
based on an alignment with the forces of third world liberation and those
whose support for China was essentially Stalinist, that is, followed the
same logic as support for Moscow foreign policy a generation earlier.

One striking example of the conflicts caused by the evolution of Chinese
foreign policy was the confusion within *New Left Review*. In 1968–69
the *NLR* editorial board had produced an internal discussion document
stating that 'Maoism was and is the systematic theory of the largest mass
revolutionary practice history has ever seen' and that 'in certain respects it
surpasses Lenin'. It prophesied that Maoism 'has a long future in front of
it' and that it had 'avoided the fate of the October revolution'.[61]

So, despite the journal's claims to be bringing theory to a benighted
British labour movement, there was consternation in 1971 when China
backed the military government in Pakistan against the demand for
independence in Bangladesh and supported the Sri Lanka regime against
the JVP (People's Liberation Front) rising. There was now a clear contradiction between Maoism and third worldism.

In an editorial statement the majority of the editorial board denounced
a 'Holy Alliance for the victory of counter-revolution in Ceylon', involving
'an unprecedented and infamous coalition of powers: USA, USSR, Britain,
China, India, Pakistan and Yugoslavia'. This was defined as 'a grim
warning' and an 'ominous precedent'.[62] Editorial Committee member Ben
Brewster responded angrily, announcing his resignation:

> To argue in this way is to reject the principles of what was originally called
> the theory of 'socialism in one country', but which I take today to imply the
> following: that the proletarian revolution will not spread rapidly and evenly
> over the world from one or two centres, but on the contrary will make
> geographically localised advances followed by temporary stabilisation and
> even retreat, over a long period; that socialist states will therefore have to
> survive for considerable periods in co-existence with an imperialist world
> itself riven by shifting internal contradictions.[63]

Many of the key issues about international perspectives were brought out in a debate in London in 1969 between Nigel Harris of the International Socialists, and Malcolm Caldwell, a non-affiliated activist with Maoist sympathies, on 'The Revolutionary Role of the Peasants'. Harris, arguing on the basis of classic Marxist formulations, stated that:

> The peasant is a figure of the utmost tragedy. He is grotesquely exploited, forced into self-subjection, forced into preserving all that is most backward and reactionary. And yet he makes his own strait jacket. He cannot, by his way of life, conceive of a real alternative. He cannot emancipate himself, and self-emancipation is one of the pre-conditions for socialism.

He concluded:

> In Vietnam, the American forces may be defeated, but this will not end the existence of Washington. The existence of the advanced capitalist powers, private and State, makes the prospects for any sustained economic development in the backward countries grim. Thus, the future of the backward countries, like the future of the peasantry, depends, not upon one defeat of one element of imperialism, but its global destruction. And it cannot be destroyed globally in Vietnam, nor can it be destroyed by the world's peasantry. It can only be destroyed in the advanced countries themselves, and only by the proletariat.

Caldwell rejected 'those who would deny to the peasantry the key role in social revolution in today's world, harking back to a mechanical interpretation of Marx's theories' and concluded:

> We may be sure that the peoples of Africa, Asia and Latin America themselves alone can transform their own lives. Since the vast majority of these peoples are peasants, the future must lie in their hands, whether it accords with one's preconceived theories or not. It is not the monopoly of revolutionary theory to assert that ultimately people are responsible for their own destiny. In the world of today the poor, the dissatisfied and the unprivileged are peasants: therefore [in Fanon's words] 'the peasants alone are revolutionary, for they have nothing to lose and everything to gain'.[64]

The end of third worldism

The spring of 1975 saw the final exit of the United States from Indochina. It was a significant defeat, which put American imperialism on the defensive for a number of years with the so-called 'Vietnam syndrome'. But it was also the end of third worldism. Within a few years came the military conflict between Vietnam and Cambodia and the appalling revelations about the atrocities enacted by Pol Pot. This caused considerable anguish and debate among the exponents of third worldism, with only the most hard-line aficionados still able to claim that revolution in the third world was pointing towards world socialism.

Russia's invasion of Afghanistan in the last days of 1979 revived the Cold War, which seemed to have ended in the mid-1960s. Now it was Russia that was fighting a destructive and doomed colonial war in a third world country. Russia was backed by Cuba, but opposed by many Muslim nations in Africa and Asia. The world of the 1950s to 1970s was gone for ever. Globalisation made the notion of a 'third world' less and less relevant.

There was much that was positive about third worldism. The movement against the Vietnam war contributed to making America's rulers realise that the war was both immoral and futile, and helped to deter future US governments from similar aggressions for nearly two decades. In Britain the mass demonstrations radicalised a new generation and introduced them to left politics.

More generally, it promoted a notion of international solidarity and recognition that social problems could not be resolved within national boundaries. Such attitudes were developed to their highest level within the relatively small far left, but had a much wider impact with such phenomena as the South African boycott. Eurocentric attitudes to the underdeveloped world had been widespread in the labour movement, ranging from paternalism to straightforward racism; while these were not eliminated they were certainly pushed back. As Harold Wilson had noted in 1958, the world 'no longer revolves around white races'.[65]

Yet the critics of third worldism also had some very valid points. Third worldism encouraged many illusions on the left, some of which evaporated quite quickly, often leaving their advocates demoralised. Give or take a few 'tigers', the countries of the erstwhile third world remain trapped in appalling poverty. The much-vaunted 'workers' control' in Algeria vanished with the 1965 *coup*, without any indication that the workers thus robbed of control had any interest in holding on to it. Events in Vietnam and above all Cambodia after independence rapidly belied any claim that they were moving towards socialism. Today, of the erstwhile array of so-called workers' states and regimes supposedly moving beyond capitalism, only Cuba retains any significant body of supporters. If China is praised nowadays, it is not for egalitarianism and spreading world revolution, but for its 'proactive and interventionist role in international financial affairs'.[66]

As Nigel Harris argued in 1987, the world has now moved into a new phase:

> The third world is disappearing. Not the countries themselves, nor the inhabitants, much less the poor who so powerfully coloured the original definition of the concept, but the argument. Third worldism began as a

critique of an unequal world, a programme for economic development and justice, a type of national reformism dedicated to the creation of new societies and a new world. It ends with its leading protagonists either dead, defeated or satisfied to settle simply for national power rather than international equality; the rhetoric remains, now toothless, the decoration for squabbles over the pricing of commodities or flows of capital.[67]

Today we have 'a sadder and a wiser' left. Of the two million people (twenty times more than the largest Vietnam demonstration) who marched against the Iraq war in 2003, there can have been few who adulated Saddam Hussein as a previous generation had adulated Ho and Mao, Castro and Ben Bella. Third worldism inspired many individuals and helped renew the far left. But it proved a political dead end. When an Italian Communist delegation asked Ho Chi Minh how they could help the Vietnamese fight against American imperialism, Ho responded 'make the revolution in your own country'. It was not bad advice.[68]

Notes

Acknowledgments: Thanks to John Charlton, Edward Crawford and Nigel Harris for comments on a first draft, and to Alun Morgan and Mick Brooks for helping me to locate documents.

1 Tony Cliff, interview with *Idiot International* (June 1970), in D. Widgery, *The Left in Britain, 1956–68* (Harmondsworth: Penguin, 1976), p. 446.
2 A. Macleod, *The Death of Uncle Joe* (Woodbridge: Merlin, 1997), p. 16.
3 D. Marsh and A. Hodsdon (eds), *The Guardian Book of English Language* (London: Guardian, 2008), p. 104.
4 E. P. Thompson (ed.), *Out of Apathy* (London: Stevens and Sons, 1960), p. 5.
5 M. Evans, 'Whatever Happened to the Non-aligned Movement?', *History Today*, 57, 12 (2007), pp. 49–50.
6 *The British Road to Socialism* (London: Communist Party of Great Britain, 1951), section IV, www.marxists.org/history/international/comintern/sections/britain/brs/1951/51.htm#4, accessed 27 November 2012.
7 E. P. Thompson, *The Making of the English Working Class* (London: Victor Gollancz, 1963), p. 13.
8 K. Buchanan, 'The Third World', *New Left Review*, 1, 18 (1963), p. 22.
9 J. Rex, *Britain Without the Bomb* (London: New Left Review pamphlet, 1960), p. 19.
10 P. Sedgwick, 'The Two New Lefts', *International Socialism*, 1, 17 (1964), reproduced in Widgery, *The Left in Britain*, p. 148.
11 T. Wengraf, 'An Essay on the Early New Left Review' (MA thesis, Birmingham, 1979).
12 P. Anderson, 'Portugal and the End of Ultra-Colonialism', *New Left Review*, 1, 15 (1962), pp. 83–102; 1, 16 (1962), pp. 88–123; 1, 17 (1962), pp. 85–114.

13 R. Murray and T. Wengraf: 'The Algerian Revolution – 1', *New Left Review*, 1, 22 (1963), pp. 14–65.

14 A. H. Evans, *Against the Enemy!*, cited in G. Thayer, *The British Political Fringe* (London: Anthony Blond, 1965), p. 121.

15 M. McCreery, *The Patriots* (London: CDRCU, 1963), pp. 15–16.

16 See P. E. J. Seltman, *Classes in Modern Imperialist Britain* (East Barnet: M. Seltman, n.d.), p. 86.

17 Cited in W. Podmore, *Reg Birch* (London: Bellman Books, 2004), p. 83.

18 *Britain in the World 1977*, cited in ibid., pp. 244–5.

19 Podmore, *Reg Birch*, pp. 142, 255.

20 R. Birch, *Guerrilla Struggle and the Working Class* (1973), cited in ibid., pp. 228–9.

21 S. Rowbotham, *Promise of a Dream* (Harmondsworth: Allen Lane, 2000), p. 97.

22 R. Williams, *Politics and Letters* (London: Verso, 1981), p. 404.

23 F. Fanon, *The Wretched of the Earth* (Harmondsworth: Pelican, 1983), p. 86.

24 Ibid., pp. 251–2.

25 R. Debray, *Revolution in the Revolution?* (Harmondsworth: Penguin, 1968), pp. 17, 67, 75.

26 'The Marxism of Régis Debray', *New Left Review*, 1, 45 (1967), pp. 8–12.

27 Cited in D. Thompson, *Pessimism of the Intellect?* (Monmouth: Merlin Press, 2007), p. 53.

28 G. Healy, *Hands off the Arab People!* (London: New Park, n.d. [1956]), p. 6.

29 P. Fryer, *The Battle for Socialism* (London: SLL, 1959), p. 59.

30 Cited in J. Callaghan, *The Far Left in British Politics* (Oxford: Basil Blackwell, 1987), p. 117.

31 C. Lutz and P. Feldman, *Gerry Healy: A Revolutionary Life* (London: Lupus Books, 1994), p. 47.

32 This appeared prominently as a banner above the title on the 8 May 1965 issue of the *Newsletter*, but was not to be found in any subsequent issue.

33 *Fourth International*, 12, winter (1960–61), pp. 33–47.

34 J. Plant, 'John Baird: A British MP Who Supported the Algerian Revolution', *Revolutionary History*, 10, 4 (2012), pp. 192–205.

35 S. Pattieu, *Les Camarades des frères* (Paris: Syllepse, 2002), pp. 174–9.

36 Cited in Plant, 'John Baird', 197.

37 http://web.archive.org/web/20091028050012/http:/www.geocities.com/socialistparty/LabHist/deaneobit.htm, accessed 27 November 2012.

38 T. Grant, *The Unbroken Thread* (London: Fortress Books, 1989), pp. 312–13, 318, 321–2.

39 R. Silverman, 'Class Struggles in Syria', *Militant*, October (1966).

40 Callaghan, *The Far Left in British Politics*, p. 121.

41 Published under the name Ygael Gluckstein (London: Allen and Unwin, 1957).

42 T. Cliff, 'Permanent Revolution', *International Socialism*, 1, 12 (1963), www.marxists.org/archive/cliff/works/1963/xx/permrev.htm, accessed 27 November 2012.

43 M. Kidron, 'Imperialism – Highest Stage But One', *International Socialism*,

1, 9 (1962), www.marxists.org/archive/kidron/works/1962/xx/imperial.htm, accessed 27 November 2012.

44 M. Kidron, 'International Capitalism', *International Socialism*, I, 20 (1965), www.marxists.org/archive/kidron/works/1965/xx/intercap.htm, accessed 27 November 2012.

45 T. Ali, *Street Fighting Years* (London: Verso, 2005), p. 188.

46 The best account is Celia Hughes, 'The History of the Vietnam Solidarity Campaign: The Substructure of Far Left Activism in Britain, 1966–69' (MA thesis, University of Warwick, 2008). See also Hughes' chapter (3) in this volume.

47 Author's interview with Chris Harman, April 2009; minutes of VSC National Executive, 11 July 1967.

48 J. Scott, 'Ta Thu Thau: A Great Vietnamese Socialist', *Labour Worker*, 7 September 1966.

49 Bob Potter, *Vietnam: Whose Victory?* (London: Solidarity pamphlet no. 43, 1973).

50 First published as an Appendix to *Ceylon: The JVP Uprising of April 1971* (London: Solidarity pamphlet no. 42, 1972).

51 J.-P. Sartre, *Situations VIII* (Paris: Gallimard, 1972), p. 273.

52 Widgery, *The Left in Britain*, pp. 398–9.

53 See Castro's August 1968 speech http://lanic.utexas.edu/project/castro/db/1968/19680824.html, accessed 27 November 2012.

54 '1968: The Ice Cracks', *International Socialism*, 1, 35, winter (1968/69), pp. 1–2.

55 Paul Barker, 'Portrait of a Protest', *New Society*, 31 October 1968.

56 T. Ali, *The Coming British Revolution* (London: Jonathan Cape, 1972), p. 138.

57 *Militant* (October and November 1968) made no reference to the demonstration.

58 'Why the Socialist Labour League Is Not Marching', in Widgery, *The Left in Britain*, p. 349.

59 I assume that Harman's speech was more or less the same as the article he wrote at the same time: C. Harman, 'Ho: He gave the "third world" Heart', *Socialist Worker*, 11 September 1969.

60 See the account in Widgery, *The Left in Britain*, pp. 412–15.

61 Cited in D. Thompson, *Pessimism of the Intellect?*, p. 61.

62 'Themes', *New Left Review*, 1, 69 (1971), pp. 1–2.

63 B. Brewster, 'Communication on Ceylon and China', *New Left Review*, 1, 70 (1971), pp. 110–11.

64 N. Harris and M. Caldwell, 'The Revolutionary Role of the Peasants', *International Socialism*, I, 41 (December 1969/January 1970), http://www.marxists.org/history/etol/writers/harris/1969/12/peasants.htm and http://www.marxists.org/history/etol/newspape/isj/1969/no041/caldwell.htm, accessed 27 November 2012.

65 Cited T. Buchanan, *East Wind: China and the British Left, 1925–76* (Oxford: Oxford University Press, 2012), p. 223.

66 See the book by former Eurocommunist Martin Jacques, *When China Rules the World* (London: Allen Lane, 2009), p. 434.

67 N. Harris, *The End of the Third World* (Harmondsworth: Penguin, 1987), p. 200.
68 Roberto Vitale, 'The Italian Left: A Report', *International Socialism*, 1, 31 (1967–68), www.marxists.org/history/etol/newspape/isj/1967/no031/vitale.htm, accessed 27 November 2012.

11

Anti-racism and the socialist left, 1968–79

Satnam Virdee

A western European Left which does not seek to understand and then to tackle racism head-on is cutting its own throat. The loss of support from proletarian socialists who are sympathetic to racialist explanations ... is better than endless equivocation, denial and ineffective compromise on this issue.

Dave Widgery[1]

In most histories of the New Left, 1968 is quite correctly identified as an important watershed, a turning point in the history of political struggles for social justice and equality. The formation of a militant anti-war movement against Western imperialist intervention abroad was accompanied by anti-racist struggles in the West. Alongside the ongoing process of decolonisation in the Global South, there was the awakening in Eastern Europe, marked first by the Prague Spring, but also protests in Yugoslavia, Poland and elsewhere. Significantly, 1968 marked the consolidation of second-wave feminism and the return of working-class power as a million workers gathered on the streets of Paris in May, in what was perhaps the apotheosis of that year's tumultuous events. And of course there were the students; at least in terms of popular memory, 1968 was the year when student campuses in Europe and the United States became battlegrounds for social change around war, racism and sexism. There can be little doubt, then, that 1968 was a transformative moment; a 'world revolution'.[2]

At the same time, however, there is a tendency within the left to write the history of this period as one absent of contradictions. It is sometimes forgotten that 1968 was also the year of racist reaction in parts of the West. Martin Luther King was assassinated, just one month before the May uprising in Paris; the Labour Party in Britain introduced legislation which denied entry to the Kenyan Asians who had been expelled by Kenyatta in his attempts to Africanise that society. And perhaps most importantly of all, 1968 marked the birth not just of the New Left but also the New Right. Whilst American cities burned in anger at the murder of King, Enoch Powell, the British Conservative MP for Wolverhampton South West, made his infamous 'rivers of blood speech'. Days later organised workers, including the traditionally militant dockers, struck and marched in defence of Powell proclaiming 'Back Britain, not Black Britain'.[3]

If 1968 marked the nadir of working-class resentment towards racialised minorities, a historic moment where questions of class came to be refracted through the prism of race, 1977 marks the symbolic moment where the struggles against racism and class exploitation in Britain partially entwined. In this essay, I develop an explanation for how such a transformation came about, particularly in the working class. I begin by focusing on the economic, political and ideological factors that transformed the political consciousness of key elements of the working class. As the hegemony constructed in the post-war era around the welfare settlement and the twin principles of active citizenship and full employment began to unravel, the collective action against the state and employers that followed transformed the class consciousness of significant sections of the working class. Out of this process of industrial and political struggle emerged a broader conception of class consciousness that could not easily be accommodated within existing notions of the common national interest. The chapter then moves onto consider the influential role played by socialist activists, especially those aligned to the left within the Labour Party, the Communist Party of Great Britain (CPGB) and the International Socialists/Socialist Workers Party (IS/SWP) – not only in the formation of such class solidarity, but particularly in politically realigning such class struggles to the ongoing struggles against racism by the black and Asian population. Through a focus on particular events and episodes, including the formation of Rock Against Racism (RAR), the solidarity extended to Asian women workers involved in the Grunwick dispute between 1976 and 1978, and the emergence of the Anti-Nazi League (ANL), it will be demonstrated how the working class bifurcated on the question of racism in the late 1970s. The resultant formation of a militant anti-racist, anti-fascist social movement in Britain saw levels of working-class participation that remain unseen anywhere on the European mainland or the United States to this day.

White racism, black resistance in the 1960s

Whilst those of Caribbean and Asian descent were subjected to racism and systemic discrimination in all spheres of social life from the moment such migration began to Britain in the 1940s and 1950s,[4] the 1960s witnessed a rising arc of racist reaction directed against their presence. Partly as a consequence of the 1958 racist riots in Nottingham and London's Notting Hill, previously localised manifestations of racist expression mutated onto the national political scene contributing to its racialisation. By 1962, the Conservative government had taken the step of introducing a racist immigration policy; racist in the sense that its intention was to restrict migration to Britain on the basis of a colour-coded selection process.[5] At the 1964 general election, British National Party candidate John Bean secured 9.1 per cent of the vote in Southall – an area of Indian Sikh settlement – the largest share of the vote for a minority party in the post-war era. During the same general election campaign, but this time in Smethwick – a small industrial town near Birmingham – the Conservative Party candidate, Peter Griffiths, publicly endorsed one of the racist slogans circulating in the town: 'If you want a nigger neighbour, vote Labour'.[6] And such racist strategising worked as he successfully went onto oust the sitting Labour incumbent, Patrick Gordon-Walker.

Lest there be any impression that associates Labour governments as being more progressive on matters of race and immigration than Conservative governments, one need note only that it was a Labour government, under pressure from the adverse public reaction generated at the arrival of a small number of Ugandan Asians, that enacted the 1968 Immigration Act, which further restricted migration from what was then called the 'New Commonwealth' countries. And then came Enoch Powell's 'rivers of blood speech'. Its significance lay not only in the fact that it represented a partial unravelling of conservative opinion from the bi-partisanship that had held sway since the Battle of Britain in 1940, but that its solution was to make racism a core aspect of its ideological project to establish a new hegemony. Powellism in this sense can be seen as one of the early threads of the broader New Right project to re-structure society that came to dominate British politics under Thatcher.[7] Labour and the patrician Tories, having already conceded much of the ideological terrain to racism through their continued support for immigration controls designed to exclude only those persons of a darker shade of skin tone, could do little to arrest such racist reaction apart from claim that those migrants already here were entitled as British citizens to some sort of social justice. This was neatly encapsulated by Roy Hattersley (a former Home Office minister) in his pithy formulation 'Integration without control is impossible, but control without integration is indefensible.'[8]

With the CPGB continuing its pre-war policy of securing support for a socialist project though the manufacture of a national-popular discourse, a vocabulary of internationalism and class solidarity between racialised minority and racialised majority workers was almost wholly absent from the social and cultural life of 1950s and 1960s Britain. The tragic consequences of such an approach were highlighted in the aftermath of the Powell speech when normally militant dockworkers marched in support. Whilst communist dockers like Jack Dash and Michael Fenn did attempt to distribute a leaflet at the West India Docks the morning after the strike 'attacking those who marched in violent language',[9] in the main 'most militants, including CP members, simply took the line of least resistance ... and kept their heads down'.[10] One concrete episode that encapsulated the ideological and political bankruptcy of the CPGB on the question of racism occurred at the Royal Docks on the morning of the strike on Friday 26 April when in an attempt to dissuade dockworkers from marching in support of Powell, a CPGB member of the liaison committee invited a Catholic priest and a Protestant minister to attend a dock gate meeting. 'The irony of a communist appealing to the Roman Catholic Church for help was not lost on many dockers.'[11]

Against this backdrop of overwhelming state and working-class racism and socialist inaction, black and Asian workers were forced to struggle on alone, relying heavily on the cultural and material resources of the racialised minority communities themselves.[12] They had been struggling alone for at least three years previous to the Powell speech. The first evidence of organised opposition to racism and exclusionary practices in the workplace had emerged in May 1965, when Asian and Caribbean workers went on strike at Courtauld's Red Scar Mill in Preston, Lancashire, a large rayon mill which produced industrial textiles.[13] This, as well as numerous other strikes by black workers, came increasingly to be informed by the ideology of 'political blackness',[14] where black and Asian activists appropriated the ascribed racial identity of 'black' previously used to disparage people of African descent and infused it with new ideological meaning out of which were forged new 'communities of resistance'.[15] By the close of the 1960s, Britain was two nations, stratified by race – one black, the other white – historically, politically and economically constituted in opposition to one another by the events of the two decades since the docking of the *Empire Windrush* at Tilbury.

Socialist activism and the return of working-class agency

If rising racism was one manifestation of the breakdown of the welfare settlement, another was the growing rift between sections of the organised working class and employers and the state. This crack in the tripartite consensus had first emerged during the late 1960s when the Labour government identified informal trade union activity as the primary cause of the poor productivity of British industry, especially the increasing ability of shop stewards to carry out bargaining in an informal manner at plant level.[16] The then Labour government contended that such a development encouraged disorder, especially 'wildcat' strikes. Thus, the 'shop steward came to be constructed as a symbol of trade union irresponsibility, and workplace conflict came to be seen as *the* major problem underlying poor productivity performance and Britain's economic problems'.[17] Although the *Donovan Report* (1968) actually identified poor management and not shop stewards as the problem, the Labour government pressed on regardless, releasing a white paper called *In Place of Strife* (1969) that outlined a series of legal measures to curb the 'problem' of wildcat strikes. Although the bill was defeated due to the pressure brought to bear on the government by the trade union movement, the incoming Conservative government of 1970 was determined to succeed where Labour had failed.[18]

Under Heath's leadership, they developed an Industrial Relations Bill which proposed replacing the collectivist laissez-faire system of industrial relations with a comprehensive legal framework intended to restrict conflict.[19] Such increased intervention by the state in employer–labour relations induced a major change in trade union strategy and resulted in a dramatic re-configuration of the class struggle. Many trade union activists and rank and file workers began to recognise that their material interests could no longer be maintained solely through the operation of free collective bargaining and so began the biggest class confrontations for half a century. The number of strike days lost increased dramatically from an average of less than 4 million days a year during the 1950s and 1960s to 24 million days in 1972 alone.[20] A significant proportion of these strikes were qualitatively different from those of the 1950s and 1960s because 'a wide range of traditionally moderate and peaceful workers, many of them women, had embarked on strike action, many for the first time in their lives'.[21] Attempts to curb unofficial strike activity saw the return of the political strike for the first time since the 1920s.[22] A series of one-day stoppages against the 1971 Industrial Relations Bill culminated in the TUC instructing its members to not comply with the Act by refusing to register themselves as trade unions when the Bill became law. Such action was reinforced by over 500 occupations and sit-ins that took place during this period.[23]

There was no necessary correlation between this rising tide of class struggle and the formation of an anti-racist consciousness in the working class. In fact, in those early years of intensifying class confrontation between 1968 and 1972, the white working class and its institutions remained resolutely indifferent to the struggles being waged by black workers against discriminatory practices as evidenced by their failure to confront everyday racism, Powellism and the resultant racist strikes by dockers and Smithfield porters, and state racism. The rank and file participants of the class struggles against exploitation rarely interpreted their campaigns as intersecting with the ongoing struggles of black workers against exploitation enveloped in oppression. Further, it appeared that events in the 1970s would proceed along the tracks laid down in the preceding decade with the newly elected Conservative government introducing a further Immigration Act in 1971 on the grounds that it would avert, once and for all, the 'legitimate fears' of 'our people' by assuring them that there would be 'no further large-scale immigration.'[24] The Act was even more restrictive than previous legislation, and effectively took away the right of black and Asian Commonwealth immigrants to settle by declaring that all Commonwealth citizens who were not patrials needed permission to enter Britain. Although such state racism was vigorously challenged by the black community[25] the reaction from the organised labour movement was noticeable only by its meekness: 'Insofar as the institutionalisation of racism by the state was concerned, the TUC had nothing to say.'[26]

When it comes to understanding the development of a current of working class anti-racism, crucial was the growing importance of socialist activists and stewards in the rising tide of class struggle. Over the course of the struggles waged between 1968 and 1972, it became more and more difficult to sustain the myth that workers and bosses shared some common national interest when one side was effectively forcing the other to pay for the crisis of British capitalism. As the old hegemony disintegrated, for the first time since the 1920s, workers found themselves increasingly drawn to the socialist left and their advocacy of militant collective action to combat attacks on working-class living standards.[27] As the strikes and other actions increased exponentially throughout 1972,[28] it signalled that workers were increasingly looking beyond the conventional tactics employed to defend working-class conditions during the high-point of welfare capitalism.

This growing synchronicity in ideological frame between the rank and file worker and socialist activists in this conjuncture of heightened class consciousness helped to begin the process of transforming the leadership of the trade union movement at all levels. It forced some traditional national trade union leaders to adopt a more militant class perspective, whilst others who refused to adapt to the changing relations of force were swept away in the maelstrom and replaced by left-wing leaders. Significant leftward swings in the leadership of several major trade unions took place during this period.[29] At the regional, district and branch level, it brought to positions of trade union influence a diverse layer of socialist activists, including those on the left of the Labour Party, members of the CPGB, as well as to a lesser extent representatives of the International Socialists. By the mid-1970s, it was estimated that 10 per cent of all trade union officials were Communists.[30] The CPGB was by now operating increasingly as a left-wing pressure group on the Labour Party. As well as securing important leadership positions within the trade union movement, this wave of industrial struggle had arrested its long-term decline in membership.[31] On a much smaller scale, various Trotskyist parties also saw significant increases in their membership.[32] The most significant of them, the IS, saw their organisation grow from around 1,000 members across 47 branches to around 3,500 members with significant roots in the working class.[33]

In summary, this rising arc of contentious class protests brought forth in its wake many socialist and sometimes Marxist activists to positions of influence throughout all rungs of the trade union movement. A generation of socialist and often Marxist, CPGB and New Left activists who had been gestating in the womb of British society for a decade or more now found themselves in a position of authority where they could shape and influence the direction of organised working-class politics, not just in the workplace, but also beyond.

From Rock Against Racism to Grunwick

Significantly, this layer of socialist activists that came to prominence in the early 1970s were on the whole more conscious of the dangers of racism undermining working-class solidarity and more willing to challenge it than socialist activists in previous waves of working-class insurgency in British history. Principally, the difference in position towards racism arose because this New Left, the 'class of 68', was shaped by a conjuncture marked by a unique set of relations of force – a world of imperial retreat where national liberation struggles waged by black and brown peoples had successfully undermined the domination of the non-white world by the white, and were bringing into question the powerful ideologies that had sustained such rule, including racism. Equally significant were the struggles against white supremacy being waged by African Americans and the subsequent rise of the black power movement which, when entwined with iconic figures like Muhammad Ali, Angela Davis and Malcolm X, and set to the soundtrack of Motown and Stax, had set the world alight in righteous indignation. And perhaps most important of all, were the domestic struggles against working class and elite racism that had been waged by Asian and Caribbean workers without any show of solidarity from the organised labour movement and its institutions since the mid-1960s.[34]

Socialist opinion by the early 1970s had been forced to concede that it had greatly underestimated the depth of racist sentiment within the British working class during the first phase of working-class collective action that broke out during the late 1960s.[35] With little working-class public to speak of, they had watched helpless from the sidelines the racist strikes inspired by Powellism and the failure of the organised labour movement to support the self-activity of black workers forced to resist such racism alone. However, by the mid-1970s, lessons had been learnt: the working class could ill-afford such racist divisions if it was to successfully resist employer and state attacks. The growing authority and power of these socialist activists that accompanied the formation of a stronger class identification was indispensable in helping to create a more favourable political terrain for the development of a united struggle against racism. The first indications of a shift in trade union political practice on racism was reflected in the growing pressure brought to bear by such socialist activists on the official structures of the trade union movement. Anti-racist motions were passed at regional and national union conferences, and eventually at the TUC annual conference itself.[36]

At the same time, the country was polarising, fast. The growing intersection of contradictions over Northern Ireland, black resistance and an increasingly class-conscious organised labour movement on the one hand, and the rise of the National Front (NF) on the other, provoked a powerful response from the state. A decisive shift in strategic direction was instigated towards a 'law and order society', affected through the construction and amplification of ever increasing moral panics and accompanying folk-devils.[37] Amidst this heightened atmosphere of social tension and crisis, the twin concerns associated with the black presence in Britain recurred over and over again: uncontrolled immigration and the problems arising from it.[38] When, in 1974, the Prime Minister Edward Heath called a general election around the theme of 'who governs Britain?', it was commonly understood in leftist folklore, that the people had replied 'not you, Ted'. There is no doubt that the rising wave of worker insurgency was crucial to securing the election of a Labour government on a more avowedly socialist programme than hitherto, including a commitment to introduce the Alternative Economic Strategy.[39] However, what is masked in such accounts is that the working class had bifurcated. Alongside the shift to the left amongst particularly well-organised sections of the working class, was a shift to the right amongst those less well-organised sections of the working class; many didn't just conjoin themselves to the Conservative Party, but increasingly also to the NF. The Conservatives actually polled more votes than Labour in the two general elections held in 1974 and the NF would see its share of the vote rise from scarcely 12,000 votes at the 1970 general election to 77,000 votes in the February 1974 general election, before almost doubling to 114,000 votes in the October 1974 election.[40] Significantly, as the events at Imperial Typewriters in Leicester in 1974 and elsewhere suggested, the NF was now increasingly drawing its support from the less well-organised sections of the manual white working class residing in ethnically mixed areas of residential settlement.

When Enoch Powell made a speech in April 1976 warning how Britain was 'still being eroded and hollowed out from within' by 'alien wedges', the NF again proved to be the beneficiary, securing almost 250,000 votes throughout the country, including 119,000 votes at the London County Council elections of 1977.[41] Increasingly concerned about continuing 'non-white' immigration and unsure about the Conservative Party's ability to arrest it or prevent the continuing drift to the left taking place under a Labour government, growing numbers of working-class Tories switched their allegiance to the Front. Although its membership had peaked in 1973 at between 14,000 and 20,000 members in the aftermath of the Ugandan Asian affair and concern at the wave of industrial militancy, it gained a further 5,000 members following the decision of the Labour government to admit the Malawi Asians in 1976.[42]

Buoyed by its electoral success and its ability to draw in growing numbers of angry young white men, the political repertoire of the NF diversified during the mid-1970s to encompass not only electoral contests but also attempts to mark out and reclaim territory that had been allegedly conceded to racialised minorities through the strategic deployment of graffiti, random violence and, increasingly, marches in ethnically diverse areas. This was clearly driven by the national socialist element of the Front which was in the ascendant within the leadership. Modelling themselves on the German National Socialists, they believed, according to Gerry Gable, veteran anti-fascist activist and co-founder of Searchlight, 'in Dr. Goebbels' maxim: who controls the streets will win the final victory'.[43] The aim was clear as it had been in 1920s Weimar Germany: to intimidate the racialised minority communities and their supporters amongst the socialist left.

Racist murders increased. And when Gurdip Singh Chaggar was stabbed to death by white youths in Southall, John Kingsley Read, leader of a small far-right organisation called the National Party, was reported to have commented 'One down, one million to go.' No part of British cultural or social life was immune from this rising arc of racist hate. Important cultural icons like David Bowie displayed an open affection for Nazism at the time.[44] Then, at a concert held in Birmingham in August 1976 – just a month after the racist murder of Gurdip Singh Chaggar – a heavily drunk Eric Clapton, renowned musician of blues, rock and jazz and a former member of the Yardbirds, Cream and Derek and the Dominos, made an explosive racist outburst declaring his support for Powell before calling on the audience to 'keep Britain white'.[45] This time the response was immediate. In September 1976, the photographer Red Saunders and designer Roger Huddle, along with four others, published an angry letter in key music weeklies including *Sounds, NME* and *Melody Maker*:

> When we read about Eric Clapton's Birmingham concert when he urged support for Enoch Powell, we nearly puked. Come on Eric ... you've been taking too much of that *Daily Express* stuff and you know you can't handle it. Own up. Half your music is black. You're rock music's biggest colonist ... We want to organise a rank and file movement against the racist poison in music ... P.S. Who shot the sheriff Eric? It sure as hell wasn't you![46]

Six hundred people wrote in to express their support and RAR was born.[47] David Widgery, one of the founders of RAR confirmed how the movement was 'inspired by a mixture of socialism, punk rock and common humanity'.[48] The intention was to change the political values of British youth, to use music as a means to transmit an anti-racist message to a young audience that wouldn't be inspired to take action listening to socialist speeches opposing racism. The necessity of such an initiative was confirmed by Red Saunders who described the mid-1970s as 'an emergency. People were being attacked and murdered ... We were music fans looking for a way for ordinary kids who loved black music to have a voice. Out of that came a youth campaign that wasn't about boring old-fashioned politics, but harnessed the energy of new sounds like punk and reggae.'[49] RAR's intentions were crystallised in the first issue of its fanzine, *Temporary Hoarding*, in which it declared:

> We want Rebel music, street music. Music that breaks down people's fear of one another. Crisis music. Now music. Music that knows who the real enemy is. Rock against racism. Love Music Hate Racism.[50]

Within three months of its formation this aim was given concrete expression with the first RAR event held at the Royal College of Art on 10 December 1976 with Carol Grimes headlining. This was quickly followed by further musical events involving Aswad, Steel Pulse and Matumbi.[51] RAR's growth was extraordinary moving rapidly in three years 'from a letter in the music press to a national organisation able to organise major outdoor festivals.'[52]

Significantly, the first breaches in the wall-to-wall racism faced by racialised minorities since the 1950s were now made. The national leadership of the trade union movement, driven by socialist activist pressure from below, had formally committed itself to challenging racism and fascism, and with RAR there emerged the first indications that white youth were also receptive to such a message. It signalled the beginning of a new-found confidence and desire amongst a small but growing element of the white community to join with those from racialised minority communities in actively challenging racism and fascism.

The Grunwick strike

A further politically potent response emanating from socialist activists was the effective mobilisation of the working class and trade unions in support of racialised minority workers striking against racism and poor working conditions. The most visible manifestation of such working-class solidarity and the rejection of racist ideologies took place between 1976 and 1978 during the Grunwick dispute.[53] Grunwick Film Processing Laboratories was a firm located in Willesden, north London, that developed and printed colour films. Employing around 440 people, mainly of Asian descent, the firm was notorious for the dreadful conditions under which workers were expected to labour. White workers were paid more than Asian workers and compulsory overtime was instituted without warning. Further, management engaged regularly in the racist harassment of the Asian workforce and particularly degrading was the timing of women's toilet breaks by the foreman overseeing the labour in the mail order department. The actual dispute was triggered when Jayaben Desai and her son Sunil refused to work overtime and resigned along with Devshi Bhudia, Chandrakant Patel, Bharet Patel and Suresh Ruparelia.[54] Jayaben Desai pointedly accused Grunwick bosses of running a zoo not a factory, and defiantly proclaimed 'But in a zoo there are many types of animals. Some are monkeys who dance on your finger-tips; others are lions who can bite your head off. We are those lions, Mr. Manager.'[55]

Mrs Desai then picketed the plant asking other workers to sign a petition demanding trade union recognition. In August 1976, when 137 mainly Asian women workers walked out of the plant following Desai's example and joined the picket line, the strike had begun. The strikers decided to establish a union and, after advice from the local Brent Trades Council and Tom Durkin, joined the Association of Professional, Executive and Computer Staff (APEX). Once they had become members, APEX immediately made the strike official and announced that strike pay would be given to the strikers. Grunwick's management responded by dismissing all the strikers. However, the strikers refused to concede, defiantly stating to the employer that: 'If you refuse to talk to us, we will turn off all the taps, one by one, until you have to.'[56] To achieve this objective, they required support from other groups of workers and even the black radical author, Ron Ramdin, is forced to concede that on this occasion, 'Support for the strike from sections of the British labour movement was quick and widespread.'[57]

At the 1976 Trades Union Congress (TUC) Annual Conference, Roy Grantham, General Secretary of APEX, called upon the trade union movement to lend its support to the strikers. He explicitly raised the issue of racism, arguing it was central to the exploitation that South Asian workers suffered. Similarly, Tom Jackson of the Union of Post Office Workers (UPW), pledged support and agreed to stop the delivery of mail coming in or out of Grunwick which would effectively prevent the business from operating. It was not only senior white trade unionists that offered support to the strikers but also large numbers of rank and file workers. Local people from the London Borough of Brent responded with 'donations from Milliner Park Ward, Rolls-Royce Works Committee, Express Dairies, Associated Automation (GEC), Transport and General Workers Union (TGWU), and the UPW Cricklewood Office Branch'.[58] Importantly, on 1 November 1976, the post office workers in the UPW stopped delivering Grunwick's mail. Despite the extension of such solidarity, a combination of management refusal to concede to the strikers' demands combined with the overly bureaucratic management of the dispute by the leadership of APEX, led the local strike committee to call on the support of the rank and file of the trade union movement to support a mass picket of the firm for one week in June 1977. The intention was to cause maximum disruption during Grunwick's busiest trading period. The call was not to go unheeded.

Mass picketing began in the week beginning 13 June 1977 with between 1,000 and 2,000 workers regularly in attendance. By the end of the week, there were 3,000 pickets noisily demonstrating outside the gates of Grunwick including amongst them miners from South Wales and Yorkshire – of whom the latter were led by Arthur Scargill.[59] On 23 June, two coachloads of coalminers from Barnsley drove through the night to join the picket line along with Scottish miners led by Mick McGahey. Alongside this, the picketing local post office workers continued to stop the delivery of mail coming in or out of Grunwick despite having their strike pay withdrawn by their union, the UPW. Contracted TGWU drivers, working for the police on picket duty at Grunwick refused to drive them into the firm's premises. The largest picket occurred on 11 July when an estimated 18,000 workers, feminists and anti-racists joined Desai and the strikers in an unprecedented show of solidarity.[60] Particularly significant was the solidarity action of the London dockers who, in 1968, had marched to the Houses of Parliament in support of Enoch. Less than a decade later, on 11 July 1977, amidst the wave of industrial militancy, there was a marked change in the attitudes of these same dockers towards black labour as demonstrated when 'the Royal Docks Shop Stewards' banner headed a mass picket of overwhelmingly white trade unionists in support of the predominately Asian workforce at Grunwicks'.[61]

What Grunwick crystallised above all was how, in the space of less than a decade, parts of the working class had undergone a dramatic, organic transformation in their political consciousness. From being attached to a narrow, sectionalist class identity that had sat comfortably within the dominant conceptions of race and nation, the more militant sections had moved to a position where their consciousness of class could no longer fit so neatly within such identifications. As the class struggle intensified, so such attachments came into increasing conflict with one another, and it was in that moment of conflict and change in the mid-1970s that the direct intervention of socialist activists was decisive in facilitating the expansion of a conception and language of class that could now encompass racialised minority workers as well. A process of black and white working-class formation was taking place, uneven, contradictory, but most definitely present in the crisis politics of 1970s Britain.

The Anti-Nazi League

By the summer of 1977, then, anti-fascist sentiment could no longer be seen as the preserve of the black community and white socialists as it had been for much of the previous decade. Instead, significant layers of opinion including many in the Labour Party as well as unaffiliated white youth and trade unionists were now keen to oppose the NF through collective action and demonstrations. The ANL was established in November 1977 as an organisational vehicle around which such activity could be developed. Although the SWP played an instrumental role in its formation and subsequent evolution, its aim was to construct the broadest possible coalition of radical forces in opposition to the National Front (NF).

This diversity in political opinion was reflected in the organisational structure of the League. The three executive positions of the League were occupied by Peter Hain (press officer), then a leading left-winger in the Labour Party with a strong anti-racist record; Ernie Roberts (treasurer), a left-wing Labour MP and deputy general secretary of the Amalgamated Union of Engineering Workers (AUEW); and Paul Holborow (organiser), a member of the Socialist Workers Party (SWP). Other members of the steering committee included a further four Labour MP's – Martin Flannery, Dennis Skinner, Audrey Wise and Neil Kinnock, a former Young Liberal Simon Hebditch, Maurice Ludmer of Searchlight, Miriam Karlin, an actress of British Jewish descent, and finally two members of the SWP – Nigel Harris and Jerry Fitzpatrick. In addition, the League received the support of a further 40 Labour MPs, including Tony Benn and Gwyneth Dunwoody, as well as Arthur Scargill of the National Union of Mineworkers (NUM) and Tariq Ali of the International Marxist Group (IMG). This mainly socialist coalition of anti-fascist forces was supplemented by a diverse range of 'sponsors' – high-profile personalities

who lent their support to the anti-fascist politics of the League. Amongst
the more prominent were football managers Terry Venables and Brian
Clough, writers Arnold Wesker and Keith Waterhouse, and actors Julie
Christie and Warren Mitchell, the latter renowned for playing the racist
character Alf Garnett in the sitcom *Till Death Us Do Part*.[62]

The ANL was officially launched in November 1977 at the House of
Commons. Its opening press release declared:

> For the first time since Mosley in the thirties there is the worrying prospect
> of a Nazi party gaining significant support in Britain ... The leaders,
> philosophy, and origins of the National Front and similar organisations
> followed directly from the Nazis in Germany ... They must not go
> unopposed. Ordinary voters must be made aware of the threat that lies
> behind the National Front. In every town, in every factory, in every school,
> on every housing estate, wherever the Nazis attempt to organise they must
> be countered.[63]

The coordinates for the confrontation between fascists and anti-fascists
that had been in the making for nearly a decade were now firmly set.
Over the next 18 months, between November 1977 and April 1979, racists
and anti-racists found themselves locked in a perpetual struggle with
each side adapting their repertoire of actions to accommodate, negotiate
and circumvent the other's activities. These racist and anti-racist forces
would battle it out on the streets of Britain, in elections and other fora
to determine whether Britain would accept its transformation into a
multi-ethnic society at ease with itself, or mutate into a society that
would demand the expulsion of black and brown Britons and thereby
recreate the mythical all-white Britain of far-right folklore. It would be no
exaggeration to claim that in this short period during the late 1970s, we
find condensed a decisive political struggle for the soul of Britain and the
kind of society it might become.

The ANL quickly built up a wide network of activists who helped
sustain a huge array of activities – both local and national – with the
primary aim of exposing the NF as fascist racists, equating their politics
with those of Nazi Germany and pointing out the consequences of
remaining indifferent to them – the genocide of 'racial inferiors' along
the lines of the death camps of Auschwitz and Bergen-Belsen and the
destruction of the organised labour movement. Fascist arguments about
black criminality, unemployment and repatriation were actively challenged
and blamed on the social system that perpetuated such wrongs: capitalism.
As well as confronting the ideological arguments of the NF, the ANL
counter-posed its own fragile embryonic vision of the alternative society
– one based on love not hate, multi-ethnic unity not racial division. This
was no more clearly evidenced than at the major carnivals it organised

alongside RAR throughout 1978 and 1979. The first, held on 30 April 1978 took place 130 years to the day that the Chartists had last united the working class in multi-ethnic solidarity.[64] It was a truly national gathering of anti-racists with over 40 coaches arriving from Glasgow, a whole train from Manchester and 15 coaches from Sheffield.[65]

The march to the carnival site at Victoria Park in East London was bold and uncompromising with giant papier mache models of Martin Webster and Adolf Hitler built by Peter Fluck and Roger Law – the makers of *Spitting Image* – leading the demonstrators through many of the NF strongholds in East London. At the carnival itself, the Clash, X-Ray Spex, Tom Robinson and Steel Pulse played to 80,000 people. Peter Hain, Vishnu Sharma of the Indian Workers' Association (IWA), Miriam Karlin and Ray Buckton spoke of the importance of tackling racism and fascism and the people chanted 'We're black, we're white, we're dynamite.' Raphael Samuel, one of the key members of the CPGB historians group, described Victoria Park as 'the most working-class demonstration I have been on, and one of the very few of my adult lifetime to have sensibly changed the climate of public opinion.'[66] The Victoria Park event was followed by carnivals in Manchester, Cardiff, Edinburgh, Harwich and Southampton, culminating in the second and biggest carnival in London held at Brockwell Park on 24 September 1978 with over 100,000 people in attendance. Sham 69 were the headline act, performing alongside them were Crisis, Inganda, RAS, The Ruts and others.[67]

These large events bringing together thousands of disparate individuals openly celebrated a multi-ethnic conception of British society. Slowly, incrementally, the ANL at these large collective gatherings and elsewhere was helping to generate a counter-hegemony, providing anti-racists and anti-fascists with the political and ideological armoury to more confidently go out and confront racism and fascism in their everyday lives. A vast plethora of local groups were set up in its slipstream, including Students Against the Nazis, Teachers Against the Nazis, School Kids Against the Nazis, Skateboarders Against the Nazis, Football Fans Against the Nazis – all with the aim of rejecting and often confronting racist and fascist ideas in these diverse sites. In February 1979, 200 people attended a Miners Against the Nazis conference held in Barnsley. Speakers included Arthur Scargill, television presenter Jonathan Dimbleby, Paul Holborow and Alex Biswas. The Port of London shop stewards committee voted to affiliate to the ANL, a remarkable achievement given what had occurred ten years previously. Such collective action was sending out a message to racialised minority communities – that there were white people prepared to join with black and brown people in their struggle against racism and fascism. The bifurcation of the working class, including on the grounds of racism, that had begun in 1973 began to accelerate throughout the late 1970s.

Ideologically solidifying opposition to the NF was important because running parallel to the Carnivals was the continuing need to mobilise the largest possible contingent wherever the NF sought to campaign and organise. Racist attacks didn't suddenly stop with the formation of the ANL. Altab Ali, a Bangladeshi clothing machinist from Wapping, was murdered just days after the first RAR festival held at Victoria Park. There were others too. Throughout 1978 and 1979, the ANL would mobilise its followers alongside those from the black community to oppose the activities of the NF. Such anti-fascist activity continued throughout the course of the general election campaign of May 1979 after the NF had announced its intention to organise a series of demonstrations through ethnically mixed areas as part of its strategy to stand in over 300 constituencies. In one demonstration in Southall, West London on 23 April 1979, amidst sustained fighting between the police and members of the ANL, IWA, People's Unite and the Southall Youth Movement, Blair Peach, teacher and ANL activist, was allegedly truncheoned to death by a member of the Special Patrol Group (SPG). Peach had come to Southall to demonstrate against the NF and their attempts to march through an area densely populated by those of Indian Sikh descent. A month later at the 1979 general election, the NF, despite standing in over 300 seats, managed to save only a handful of deposits with their national vote reduced to 1.3 per cent.

Conclusion

The ANL was undoubtedly one of the largest and most important social movements in post-war British history. It is estimated that between 1977 and 1979, around 250 ANL branches were established throughout the country with a membership of between 40,000 and 50,000. Fifty constituency Labour Party branches affiliated, along with 30 AUEW trade union branches, 25 trades councils, 13 shop stewards committees, 11 NUM lodges and similar numbers of affiliations from the TGWU, Civil and Public Servants Association (CPSA), Technical, Administrative and Supervisory Section (TASS), National Union of Journalists (NUJ), National Union of Teachers (NUT) and National Union of Public Employees (NUPE). Overall, approximately 9 million ANL leaflets were distributed and 750,000 badges were sold.[68]

A key question that we must pose in conclusion is did the ANL contribute to the decline of the NF? There cannot be a simple answer to this question. The replacement of Edward Heath, the arch enemy of the racist right in the Tory Party, by Margaret Thatcher, a leading representative of the

New Right in 1975, marked an important shift in Conservative politics, including their position on race, that was little appreciated at the time. In January 1978, Mrs Thatcher on Granada TV had claimed:

> I think people are really rather afraid that this country might be rather swamped by people with a different culture and, you know, the British character has done so much for democracy and law, and has done so much throughout the world, that if there is any fear that it might be swamped, people are going to be really rather hostile to those coming in.[69]

Such a statement amounted to a political dogwhistle inviting those disaffected Tories that had joined the NF in disgust at Heath's censure of Powell, to come home to their natural party of affiliation because the house had been put back in order.

Whilst this undoubtedly constituted the primary pull factor, equally important was the push factor that made those working-class, middle-class and Empire-loving Conservatives currently aligned with the NF realise that their concerns would be better served in the party of Margaret Thatcher – and that push factor was the ANL. When, in 1982, Peter Hain, one of the leaders of the ANL, brought a libel case against Martin Webster – one of the leaders of the NF – he recounted how Webster had claimed that:

> prior to 1977, the NF were unstoppable and he was well on the way to becoming Prime Minister. Then suddenly the Anti-Nazi League was everywhere and knocked hell out of them. It obviously still hurt. He said that the sheer presence of the ANL had made it impossible to get NF members on the streets, had dashed recruitment and cut away at their vote.[70]

It was precisely this capacity of the ANL to fashion, and then mobilise a community of anti-racists, of committed white anti-racists in particular, that undermined the NF, and forced many of the racist middle classes and deferential working-class Tories to retreat back into the Conservative Party. More broadly, it is highly unlikely that such a community of mainly working-class anti-racists would have emerged in the 1970s had it not been for the political radicalisation that took place amongst important sectors of the working class (including working-class youth) from the late 1960s. And key to bringing that class revolt into some kind of alignment with the struggle against racism were the mediating forces of the socialist left.

Notes

1 D. Widgery, *Beating Time: Riot 'n' Race 'n' Rock 'n' Roll* (London, Chatto & Windus, 1986), p. 112.
2 I. Wallerstein, 'New Revolts against the System', *New Left Review*, 18 (2002), pp. 33.

3 F. Lindop, 'Racism and the Working Class: Strikes in Support of Enoch Powell in 1968', *Labour History Review*, 66, 1 (2001), pp. 79–100.

4 S. Virdee, 'The Continuing Significance of Race', in A. Bloch and J. Solomos (eds), *Race and Ethnicity in the 21ˢᵗ Century* (Basingstoke: Palgrave Macmillan, 2010).

5 R. Miles and A. Phizacklea, *White Man's Country: Racism in British Politics* (London: Pluto Press, 1984).

6 Cited in J. Solomos and L. Back, *Race, Politics and Social Change* (London: Routledge, 1995), p. 54.

7 S. Hall, 'The Great Moving Right Show', in S. Hall and M. Jacques (eds), *The Politics of Thatcherism* (London: Lawrence & Wishart, 1983), p. 19; M. Barker, *The New Racism: Conservatives and the ideology of Tribe* (London: Junction Books, 1981).

8 Cited in J. Solomos, *Race and Racism in Contemporary Britain* (Basingstoke: Macmillan, 1993), p. 84.

9 Lindop, 'Racism and the Working Class', p. 91.

10 Ibid., p. 91.

11 Ibid., p. 92.

12 A. Sivanandan, *A Different Hunger: Writings on Black Resistance* (London: Pluto Press, 1982).

13 J. Wrench, 'Unequal Comrades: Trade Unions, Equal Opportunity and Racism', in R. Jenkins and J. Solomos (eds), *Racism and Equal Opportunity Policies in the 1980s* (Cambridge: Cambridge University Press, 1987), p. 166.

14 Sivanandan, *A Different Hunger*.

15 A. Sivanandan, *Communities of Resistance: Writings on Black Struggles for Socialism* (London: Verso, 1990).

16 J. McIlroy, *Trade Unions in Britain Today* (Manchester: Manchester University Press, 1995).

17 J. Eldridge, P. Cressey and J. MacInnes, *Industrial Sociology and Economic Crisis* (Hemel Hempstead: Harvester, 1991), p. 25.

18 McIlroy, *Trade Unions in Britain Today*.

19 J. Sheldrake, *Industrial Relations and Politics in Britain, 1880–1989* (London: Pinter, 1991).

20 K. Grint, *The Sociology of Work* (London: Polity, 1991), p. 172 (table 7).

21 J. Kelly, *Trade Unions and Socialist Politics* (London: Verso, 1988), p. 107.

22 Grint, *The Sociology of Work*.

23 Kelly, *Trade Unions and Socialist Politics*, pp. 108–9.

24 Cited in Miles and Phizacklea, *White Man's Country*, p. 80.

25 *The Times*, cited in D. Renton, *When We Touched the Sky: The Anti-Nazi League, 1977–81* (London: Clarion, 2006), p. 15.

26 Miles and Phizacklea, *White Man's Country*, p. 75.

27 J. Verberckmoes, 'The United Kingdom: Between Policy and Party', in P. Pasture, J. Verberckmoes and H. De Witte (eds), *The Lost Perspective? Trade Unions between Ideology and Social Action in the New Europe*, vol. 1 (Aldershot: Ashgate, 1996), p. 227.

28 R. Darlington, *The Dynamics of Workplace Unionism* (London: Mansell, 1994).

29 Kelly, *Trade Unions and Socialist Politics,* p. 109.
30 Verberckmoes, 'The United Kingdom'.
31 E. Smith, '"Class Before Race": British communism and the Place of Empire in Postwar Race Relations', *Science and Society,* 72, 4 (2008), pp. 455–81; E. Smith, '1968 – Too Little and Too Late? The Communist Party and Race Relations in the Late 1960s', *Critique,* 36, 3 (2008), pp. 363–84.
32 McIlroy, *Trade Unions in Britain Today,* p. 104.
33 I. Birchall, *The Smallest Mass Party in the World* (London: SWP, 1981).
34 S. Virdee, *Racism, Class and the Racialized Outsider* (Basingstoke: Palgrave Macmillan, 2014).
35 D. Widgery, *The Left in Britain, 1956–1968* (London: Penguin, 1976).
36 S. Virdee, 'A Marxist Critique of Black Radical Theories of Trade Union Racism', *Sociology,* 34, 2 (2000), pp. 545–65.
37 S. Hall, C. Critcher, T. Jefferson, J. Clarke and B. Roberts, *Policing the Crisis: Mugging, The State, and Law and Order* (Basingstoke: Macmillan, 1978).
38 Ibid., p. 299.
39 T. Benn, *Parliament, People and Power: Agenda for a New Society* (London: Verso, 1982).
40 S. Taylor, 'The National Front', in R. Miles and A. Phizacklea (eds), *Racism and Political Action in Britain* (London: Law Book Co., 1979), p. 134.
41 D. Renton, 'Guarding the Barricades', in N. Copsey and D. Renton (eds), *British Fascism, The Labour Movement and The State* (Basingstoke: Palgrave Macmillan, 2005), p. 1.
42 Messina, *Race and Party Competition in Britain* (Oxford: Clarendon Press, 1989), p. 112.
43 Renton, 'Guarding the Barricades', p. 21.
44 D. Buckley, *Strange Fascination – David Bowie: The Definitive Story* (London: Virgin, 2000), pp. 281–9.
45 R. Denselow, *When the Music Stopped: The Story of Political Pop* (London: Faber & Faber, 1989), pp. 138–9; see also E. Vulliamy, 'Blood and Glory', *The Observer,* 4 March 2007.
46 Widgery, *Beating Time,* p. 40.
47 Renton, *When We Touched the Sky,* p. 34.
48 Widgery, *Beating Time,* p. 8.
49 P. Sawyer, 'Redemption Songs', *New Statesman,* 23 April 2007.
50 Renton, 'Guarding the Barricades', p. 33.
51 Widgery, *Beating Time,* 56; Renton, *When We Touched the Sky,* pp. 34–5.
52 D. Widgery, *Preserving Disorder* (London: Pluto Press, 1989), pp. 119–20.
53 J. Rogaly, *Grunwick* (London: Penguin, 1977); A. Phizacklea and R. Miles, 'The Strike at Grunwick', *New Community,* 6, 3 (1978), pp. 268–78.
54 A. Wilson, *Finding a Voice: Asian Women in Britain* (London: Virago, 1978).
55 J. Lane, 'The Battle of Grunwick', *Workers Liberty* 50–1 (1978), https://archive.workersliberty.org/wlmags/w150/history.htm, accessed 2 June 2008.
56 Phizacklea and Miles, 'The Strike at Grunwick', 270.
57 R. Ramdin, *The Making of the Black Working Class in Britain* (Aldershot: Ashgate, 1987), p. 289.

58 Ibid., p. 292.
59 Rogaly, *Grunwick*, p. 178.
60 Ibid.
61 Virdee, 'A Marxist Critique of Black Radical Theories of Trade Union Racism', pp. 545–65.
62 Renton, *When We Touched the Sky*, pp. 80–1.
63 Ibid., p. 81.
64 Widgery, *Beating Time*, p. 82.
65 Ibid., p. 84.
66 Renton, *When We Touched the Sky*, p. 121.
67 Ibid., p. 132.
68 Ibid., p. 175.
69 Widgery, *Beating Time*, p. 14.
70 Ibid., p. 111.

12

Red Action – left-wing political pariah

Some observations regarding ideological apostasy and the discourse of proletarian resistance

Mark Hayes

It would be very easy to dismiss Red Action (RA) as a political irrelevance, especially since 'revolutionary' activism on the far left of the ideological spectrum in Britain has been characterised by an abundance of apparently similar, short-lived sectarian micro-groups. Red Action might easily be portrayed as a minuscule manifestation of the same genus – just another militant microbe in the sad story of socialist ephemera which, although achieving some notoriety in the 1980s and 1990s, followed an entirely predictable path toward political oblivion. Yet there is a significant sense in which such a dismissive approach would be inappropriate in this case because Red Action, despite its small size, managed, in some ways, to make a unique contribution to the politics of the far left in late twentieth-century Britain. Indeed it might be argued that there were elements of both theory and practice which warrant more sustained critical analysis.

There is no doubt that Red Action was an organisation which caused, and to some extent courted, controversy. The political positions adopted by Red Action precipitated as much concern and consternation on the left as it did in those quarters where hostility was entirely predictable. Red Action's leftist enemies were multifarious, and it would not be an exaggeration to say that the organisation was detested and derided by a variety of groups which, ostensibly at least, shared a similar position on the ideological axis. At the same time the media's reaction to Red Action's brand of uncompromising political praxis was a mixture of fear and fascination. As the *Observer* journalist Matt Seaton exclaimed after meeting prominent members in the mid-1990s, Red Action (RA) was a 'semi-legal, semi-paramilitary group who believe absolutely in the efficacy of political violence'.[1] Indeed Red Action's infamy was noted, somewhat sardonically, by its National Organiser in an internal Report: 'three or four years ago RA members would have been tickled by a mention in the *Leninist*. Today it does not come as a total surprise to be the subject of editorial comment in *The Times*'.[2] Red Action therefore managed to elicit an extraordinary reaction amongst a variety of activists, organisations and media, most of which ranged from hostile incredulity to vitriolic hatred. Therefore it is perhaps worth considering in more detail how and why such a tiny leftist pebble created so many political waves.

Red Action was formed late in 1981, principally by ex-members of the Socialist Workers' Party (SWP) who had been expelled for the venal sin of 'squadism'. In effect these members were politically excommunicated because they insisted upon adopting a more robust response to the fascist violence perpetrated against them. The spectacular electoral demise of the National Front (NF) in 1979 had convinced the leadership of the SWP that the Anti-Nazi League (ANL) had served its purpose and should be wound down. However, the fascists had not simply disappeared into the political ether – whilst some went on to pursue Strasserite fantasies as semi-clandestine 'political soldiers', others simply reverted to the traditional Hitlerite tactic of 'controlling the streets', which inevitably left some socialist activists vulnerable to attack. So the nucleus of what was to become Red Action was that section of the SWP who refused to accept that electoral performance was the only indices by which to measure fascist activity or success, and who therefore advocated a more proactive response to fascists, most of whom were intent on returning to a strategy of street level rebellion. The SWP Central Committee would not countenance such unilateral activity and individual members were expelled, although some jumped before they were pushed, whilst others left in solidarity with their comrades. It was an important moment. As National Organiser for Red Action Gary O'Shea says, 'the suspensions and expulsions were Kafkaesque and bizarre – I was suspended even though I was one of the few working-class shop stewards. By the time it happened we'd had enough anyway. We were starting to question everything. In the end they fabricated evidence against us. It was a purge. We also felt that culturally they didn't like us. They were dismissive of the working class'.[3]

So at its inception Red Action was product of what was considered to be the SWP's strategic failure to organise effectively against fascists, and a cultural antipathy toward working-class members. As National Treasurer Pete Coen says, 'we had a decision to make – melt away or form something else. There was lots going on politically and culturally and we had a presence so we refused to go away. It was all open to debate – no pre-determined outcomes apart from being left wing'.[4] Those in positions of responsibility within the SWP undoubtedly expected those who were ejected to accept their fate as political outcasts, but the small coterie of comrades in London coalesced into Red Action and became, as one activist infamously put it, "'the abortion that lived'".[5]

Initially the secrecy surrounding the embryonic organisation reflected the fact that Red Action sought neither recognition nor recruits, they were simply content to engage the fascist enemy wherever possible on a pragmatic basis.[6] However, a key moment for the group occurred on 10 June 1984 in London at an open air concert at Jubilee Gardens organised by the Greater London Council (GLC) against Tory cuts and unemployment. The Redskins were playing and around eighty NF skinheads attacked the crowd, which included women, children and families.[7] Red Action, it was felt, had to move beyond a defensive position and onto the offensive. The initial aim was to develop a mobile combat unit to defend the public meetings, gigs and paper sales of any left-wing organisation under threat of attack. At the same time there was a concerted effort to examine in more depth the processes which had precipitated the organisation's political emergence. That reflexive analysis was to produce a critique of the contemporary far left which defined, more precisely, the lines of demarcation between Red Action and its political progenitors.

So Red Action started out as a single-issue rapid response unit, but soon began to examine in greater detail the ideology of the other organisations on the far left. Slowly, principally via the *Bulletin*, a critique was constructed which, it was argued, helped explain not only why they had found themselves marginalised but, more importantly, why the 'revolutionary' left in Britain had singularly failed to make any real political impact. In more specific terms Leninist modes of organisation became the focus of critical attention in Red Action literature and, significantly, this critique was constructed upon a re-examination of the original democratic ideals of Marx and Engels. Those at the forefront of Red Action had become increasingly aware that it was the Leninist method, with its emphasis on the Bolshevik party paradigm and democratic centralism, which created the structural defects that in turn led to the sectarian utopianism of Trotskyist politics in the late 1970s and early 1980s. The degradation of democratic practice, in deference to the bureaucratic centralism of central committees, was seen as the inevitable outcome of a vanguard party model which produced a plethora of mutually antagonistic sects, each anxious to proclaim its credentials as the genuine article against competing imposters. It was, argued Red Action, a recipe for acrimonious inaction.

As a result Red Action explicitly rejected the idea of a top-heavy, vanguard leadership, which had been adopted by numerous Trotskyist parties. Experience appeared to confirm that, no matter how democratic the organisation was designed to be in theory, in practice the reality turned out to be an organisation dominated by an authoritarian, if not dictatorial, central committee. As Red Action member (and former Militant organiser) Steve West put it: 'there was no genuine democracy in other left-wing groups. I used to be a Militant full-timer and you were expected to follow the line or be re-educated. It was absolutely venomous at times'.[8] Indeed it was 'no secret that a number of the founding members of Red Action left the SWP precisely in protest against that organisation's bias in favour of centralism above democracy'.[9] In effect Red Action's critique of this element of revolutionary praxis endorsed the perspective of those earlier Marxist theorists like Rosa Luxemburg who saw the anti-democratic contradictions at an early stage. Hence the ideological orientation of Red Action was essentially Marxist but anti-Leninist, at least in terms of its opposition to democratic centralism.[10] In effect Red Action argued that Lenin's perspective on party organisation, which was always designed for a very specific set of historical circumstances (and which was predicated on the success of a European revolution), had been elevated to a matter of political principle by left-wing sects that, crucially, had no organic link with the working class. In the contemporary British context therefore, according to Red Action, the Leninist paradigm was essentially misapplied, and the claim to represent the interest of the working classes fundamentally fraudulent.

Following on from this, Trotskyism, with its theoretical emphasis on 'permanent revolution', was perceived as a distorted manifestation of Bolshevism. Ignoring or denying responsibility for the suppression at Kronstadt or the formation of the Cheka, was simply symptomatic of a similar tendency toward authoritarian forms of organisation. Even Trotsky's powerful (and legitimate) critique of Stalinism did not disqualify the weaknesses inherent in his proposals for political practice, which remained essentially Bolshevik in inspiration, and which evolved into a rigid political template adhered to with quasi-religious reverence by various left-wing sects. Red Action, therefore, argued that the working class had been very badly served by a variety of squabbling Trotskyist micro-groups. As the first issue of the *RA Bulletin* pointed out, the working class had absolutely no empathy for the left, and any group with real aspirations needed to begin by earning trust and respect in working-class areas.[11] The fact that so-called revolutionary groups were completely detached from the working class, with no institutional mechanism to facilitate its future participation, meant that such organisations were not fit for purpose – indeed, after a Red Action conference in 1988 it was concluded that 'not one single organisation on the left could be considered to be authentically revolutionary'.[12] This was a theme which would continue throughout Red Action's existence: 'without the means of practical application revolutionary ideas become, at best, pious aspirations. At worst it invites ridicule'.[13] As the 'We are Red Action' programme outlined:

> sectarian division on the left continues to be a comfort to a system which socialism promised to replace. Factions, whose immaculate programmes for party dictatorship result in the pursuit of goals exclusive to themselves, contribute nothing to the real movement of the working class, except to delay its political renaissance. In all essentials reactionary, they are socialists of the previous generation. This betrayal mocks the theory and practice of Marx and Engels, and the notion of independent working-class initiative.[14]

Although this perspective differentiated Red Action clearly from the older Bolshevik and Trotskyist positions, there was also a clear demarcation line with forms of anarchism too. The anarchist assumption that all forms of authority are potentially autocratic, and therefore need to be resisted, did not cut much ice in Red Action circles. Despite its legitimate ideological heritage and its desire to remain untainted by compromises, anarchism contained within it a fatal flaw, as Red Action explained:

> anarchism, which claims to be a libertarian alternative to Leninism, could never work. Anarchism means the principled opposition to the exercise of any authority. Accordingly even the most perfect democracy would be regarded by anarchism as authoritarian as it means the imposition of a social decision by a majority on a minority. The answer to bureaucratic authority is democratic authority not the abolition of authority.[15]

Red Action acknowledged that there would always be a leadership but the real point was to ensure accountability. So whilst tactical cooperation with anarchist groups was entirely possible, given a mutual emphasis on anti-capitalist de-centralisation, the prescriptive component of associated anarchist programmes was considered to be unrealistic. Red Action looked to Marx and Engels rather than Bakunin and Proudhon, reiterating on a number of occasions that the flag was staying red.[16]

Of course the emerging Red Action thesis was also constructed upon the premise, axiomatic within the organisation after the catastrophe of the miners' strike in 1984, that the Labour Party was not only irredeemably reformist, but also in the process of abandoning the working class. Although debates were conducted in *Red Action* before 1984 about whether it was acceptable to vote Labour,[17] the miners' strike was a watershed.[18] As Coen says, 'the Labour Party offered tangible gains in the early 1980s – we had an open mind but that changed after the miners' strike. After that I don't think a pro-Labour argument was viable'.[19] More controversially Red Action also questioned the capacity of the broader labour movement to deliver tangible benefits to workers. In essence it was felt that the trade union movement was no longer in a position to effectively represent the

aspirations of the majority of ordinary people. The Red Action contribution to the debate, conducted via *Open Polemic,* clearly illustrates its
position: 'due to the changing nature of capitalism, trade unionism as
the centrepiece of a working-class strategy for total social change has
to be dismissed. It is not that trade unionism is finished entirely, or that
workplace activity is counter-productive, but that its political relevance to
the working class will continue to diminish'.[20] According to Red Action,
'trade unions only work effectively when capitalism is working effectively.
In other words the "labour movement" offers no protection and is largely
irrelevant to those sections of the working class that need it the most'.[21]
In short, syndicalism as a strategy was never likely to work because
capitalism itself had been reconfigured in Britain, which had in turn altered
the position of the working class. Well-organised trade unions in heavy
industries like mining, shipbuilding and steel works were diminishing
rapidly, if not disappearing completely, leaving a residual public-sector
trade union movement to engage in special pleading over resources from
central government.[22] A trade union dominated labour movement was
finding it increasingly difficult to mobilise the masses, and was likely to
decline in relevance to the working class, who were increasingly disenfran-
chised and denied adequate representation in the workplace.

Nor was there any real salvation for the working class in looking abroad
for solutions – emulating more persuasive political paradigms around the
globe was not really a viable option. Within Red Action there was a strident
rejection of some of the 'actually existing' communist regimes, which were
perceived to be coercive, monolithic and dominated by unaccountable
bureaucratic elites.[23] It might also be noted that it was felt to be the
Leninist organisational model that, to some extent, pre-figured the disaster
of Stalinism, which was considered to be the antithesis of a genuinely
socialist society.[24] Across Europe the consequences of Stalinism for the
working class were deemed disastrous, and early critics like Victor Serge
were marshalled in Red Action publications to confirm the observation:
'Serge's greatest achievement is to show quite clearly the futility of trying
to build socialism by trying to use methods that are against socialist
principle.'[25]

Yet despite its trenchant critique of other left-wing groups, anarchism,
the labour movement and communist regimes, Red Action continued to
articulate a principled opposition to capitalism drawn directly from Marx.
Red Action emphasised the need for a new system of economic organisation
and public ownership of the means of production in order to facilitate
genuine equality and freedom. Thus Red Action still proclaimed its revolutionary socialist credentials and confirmed its adherence to the original
Marxist credo. Red Action's ideology has been described as 'libertarian

communism', which perhaps goes some way to explaining its distinctive theoretical position.[26] However it is extremely important to note that Red Action did not claim to be the answer to the problems it had identified. Its purpose was to ask difficult questions in the hope of precipitating a wider response, rather than providing all the solutions. Red Action was quite explicit on this point: 'we recognise that a revolutionary working-class party is necessary if capitalism is to be overthrown. We are not that party, neither are the groups which claim to be it ... we do not seek to imitate the traditional left, we seek to work in areas they neglect'.[27] The aim of Red Action was, rather modestly, to sustain the tradition of militant working-class activism and identify the weaknesses evident in other left-wing organisations which claimed to provide all the political answers.

Moreover, in a meaningful sense, Red Action set out to embrace and mobilise the working class. As one document put it, 'integration within general working-class culture is essential if the organisation is not to become detached from the class it represents ... A revolutionary socialist party must be composed of working-class members – anything else is a sham or a sect'.[28] Here again Red Action reverted back to Marx. In September 1990 *Red Action* carried an article entitled 'Blind Beauty' which, in deploying Marx's analysis, spoke of the working class as not only economically exploited but permanently maintained in a condition of servility. In this sense ordinary people were not only dispossessed in terms of material resources, but disarmed politically by being denied access to positions of political responsibility. Red Action adopted the view that the working class must be given the opportunity to determine its own destiny – they certainly did not require 'commissioned officers' from the middle classes to tell those in the ranks what do and how to behave. In this sense the Red Action agenda, much maligned though it was, mirrored the message of self-emancipation contained in the original writings of Marx and Engels. As O'Shea says,

> We challenged the left, for example through the *Leninist* and *Open Polemic*. We met them head-on theoretically. We went back to the original Marx and Engels. We discovered that there were all sorts of flaws in their arguments. They used texts fairly cynically to support their tactical requirements. They got it wrong. No intellectual rigour, no credibility at all. If you are going to use Marx the least you can do is read the relevant material.[29]

As Red Action concluded, any 'serious revolutionary organisation must be working class in instinct, character, composition and appeal'.[30] It is important to be clear on this point, given the criticisms that were invariably levelled at Red Action about 'workerism' and infatuation with the proletariat – this perspective was never intended to make a fetish of the

working class. Workers were no more intelligent, courageous or humanitarian than any other people – they were also as capable of being selfish,
ignorant and manipulated – but objective conditions dictated that they
were likely to be the critical dynamic driving progressive social change.

As a consequence of the political positions adopted by Red Action,
the model of organisation deployed internally was designed to invert the
fashionable top-down model of the pseudo-revolutionary left in order to
re-connect with ordinary people and liberate the vitality and imagination
of the working class itself. In short, 'power must flow democratically
and accountably from below'.[31] There would be no omnipotent central
committee, no closed meetings, and no unaccountable revolutionary cadre.
Red Action stated unequivocally that political pluralism should exist
within the organisation and that this was the only effective way of ensuring
that genuine debate, and indeed truth, would never be subordinated to
power.

As a result of Red Action's emphasis on the need for accountability,
internal governance was scrupulously democratic. The National Conference
was the sovereign body of the organisation, where all important strategic
and tactical decisions were made and where, significantly, the national
leadership had to argue from the floor with other delegates via the chair.
Each member received a single vote, and a majority was required to ratify
any proposal from the floor. This inevitably led to protracted debate,
but this was felt to be a price worth paying to secure transparency.[32] The
National Council was the body responsible for running the organisation
between conferences, making more routine logistical decisions, although
all regions could send representatives to National Council meetings.
This organisational framework, rudimentary though it undoubtedly was,
avoided the labyrinthine structures common to many groups on the left
and facilitated membership participation. Although overall membership
levels never exceeded more than a few hundred, active branches were
assembled in major metropolitan areas like London, Birmingham and
Glasgow. As Coen says, 'we had a branch and regional structure in key
areas. It was genuinely democratic. People were encouraged to debate and
ask questions'.[33] Moreover, as O'Shea points out, 'the membership was
overwhelmingly working class'.[34]

However, it is important to note that the organisation was not 'open'
in a conventional sense. Red Action members were inducted into the
organisation and had to serve a probationary period before becoming full
members. As Red Action put it, members were rigorously 'checked out'
and subject to a process of selection.[35] Although this might be construed as
compromising its position on openness and accountability, this procedure
was considered essential because of over-riding security considerations,

given the fact that the state had shown a very keen interest in Red Action from the very early stages of its development. Security was a persistent theme throughout the period of Red Action's existence, particularly given its orientation toward Ireland (see later), indeed any Red Action member arrested or questioned by the police or security forces had to inform the organisation, and failure to do so could precipitate disciplinary action. The emphasis therefore was on the quality rather than the quantity of members, which undoubtedly impacted negatively on the size and growth of the membership.

From a Red Action perspective, one of the key consequences of the fact that the left was composed of groups exogenous to the working class, was that fascists could portray themselves as a 'radical alternative' to a capitalist system which was clearly failing ordinary people. Here the need for a viable leftist group, rooted in working-class communities, was not only a necessity in order to sustain the legitimacy of socialist ideas, it was a considered a critical bulwark against fascism. Without an identifiably working-class socialist organisation, those communities would become vulnerable to fascist penetration since such ideas are more easily incubated in those residential areas where resources are meagre and progressive political aspirations have been seriously attenuated.

Anti-fascism was therefore a key component of the Red Action agenda, and in many ways Red Action was the catalyst which created Anti-Fascist Action (AFA), a fact acknowledged by most of the other participants.[36] AFA was formed on 28 July 1985 at Conway Hall in London, although formally launched in Liverpool in the following year. Initially AFA consisted of a variety of groups, such as the Newham Monitoring Project and *Searchlight*, along with numerous Labour and trade union affiliates, with a steering committee of eight elected people. As O'Shea says 'the first manifestation of AFA was very respectable, including liberal anti-racist groups'.[37] However, it soon became evident that some of those liberal elements were distinctly uneasy at the methods deployed to confront the fascists. As a consequence AFA split in 1989 and the re-launch clearly positioned the organisation as a street-level activist organisation which included, principally, Red Action (communist), the Direct Action Movement (anarcho-syndicalist) and Workers' Power (Trotskyist). There is no question that Red Action formed the most active nucleus within Anti-Fascist Action during this period. As Copsey puts it, 'confident of an increasingly receptive audience for militant anti-fascism, RA, which constituted the largest single group in AFA and comprised the majority of its active membership, seized the initiative'.[38] Gary O'Shea argues that, 'from 1989 AFA was run by an activist membership, which meant a stronger, more effective organisation'.[39] Henceforth AFA, and particularly

Red Action, deployed an unremitting ruthlessness in dealing with its ideological enemies on the extreme right.

The Red Action position clearly reflected the belief that although fascism was a clear and present danger to ethnic minorities it was, in essence, an anti-working class movement. This meant that all those who stood to lose under fascism should be actively engaged in the effort to fight it. In essence it would be a struggle conducted by members of the working class, irrespective of ethnicity. Importantly AFA aimed to be totally non-sectarian and democratic, its *only* objective being to oppose fascism physically and ideologically. As the *European Militant Anti-Fascist Network Manifesto* explained, anti-fascism was 'not the appropriate political arena for ideological debate: for unravelling historic rivalries between Stalinism and Trotskyism; Marxism and Anarchism ... We have a common enemy, and if the enemy is to be defeated then what unites us rather than what divides us must have primacy'.[40] Violence was deployed as an important tactic, but not a principle, and only part of a multi-faceted approach to anti-fascist practice. The magazine *Fighting Talk* was set up in 1991, and an attempt was made to mobilise people via various cultural and leisure activities such as Cable St. Beat, Unity Carnivals, Northern Network and Freedom of Movement. Football clubs were also the focus of considerable AFA activity (e.g. at Celtic and Manchester Utd) and AFA even produced a BBC Open Space video entitled *Fighting Talk*. So tactically AFA engaged in a wide range of methods in a variety of contexts. By 1990 AFA was clearly identified as the militant wing of the anti-fascist movement.[41] At its peak in the early 1990s AFA had four regions and around forty branches with particular areas of strength in London, Manchester, Birmingham and Glasgow.

However, although AFA was never simply a pretext for a punch-up there was a realistic acknowledgement that purely legal and peaceful methods, or a passive reliance upon state agencies, was unlikely to achieve the required results – physical confrontation was emphasised by Red Action and central to AFA's strategy. The tactics utilised were relatively straight-forward and the aim unambiguous – to destroy all semblance of fascist presence in public spaces – pubs, clubs, halls, streets – and to clear fascists out of working-class areas. It was Red Action that formed the hard core of AFA's 'stewards group', and its role was pivotal when engaging the fascists. The key to Red Action's operational activity within AFA was meticulous preparation and organisation. For example, knowledge of local geography, accurate intelligence and effective scouting were always deemed to be of crucial importance, briefings were given prior to mobilisation instructing people on how to behave in police custody, and advice was provided on which solicitors to use if charges were brought by the police.[42] Although some Red Action members spent long terms in jail for their activities, generally speaking the activists endorse the tactic of physical confrontation as an extremely effective short-term measure. As O'Shea argues, 'the idea that they controlled the streets was revealed as total nonsense. They couldn't handle us. The impact was immense and they never recovered'.[43] Occasionally Red Action activists even infiltrated the fascists themselves, as Patrick Muldowney explains:

> We went to Winchester for a lefty demo against the BNP [British National Party] but instead of marching we found the fascists in a local pub. They had come from London, Birmingham and elsewhere to attack the march. We just got chatting with them. At the right moment we turned on them. They were absolutely destroyed. And it wasn't just that they got physically beaten, we had completely out-manoeuvred them. It was reported in the local papers as a fight amongst the fascists – but they knew who we were. It was over for them and they weren't coming back.[44]

As Coen confirms, 'we re-claimed areas back from the fascists. The stewards group was very effective. When it came to mobilisations it had to be well organised ... you need to be careful when confronting the enemy, it has to be well controlled'.[45] The violence deployed was therefore disciplined and precisely focused, and the suggestion that Red Action was simply a football 'firm' or hooligan outfit is curtly dismissed by O'Shea: 'the idea that Red Action was a gang is a total nonsense. There was absolutely no bullying anywhere and it certainly did not seep into any other areas of Red Action's conduct'.[46]

It is worth elaborating upon this point given the controversy precipitated by this tactic. The violence was used for a very specific political purpose – it was never advocated as a means of inducing some kind of personal catharsis; neither was it a primitive eruption of visceral class rage; nor indeed was it the instinctive expression of a specifically working-class masculine identity.[47] It *was* an expression of community resistance and a realistic acknowledgement that, in general, fascism is about exerting prejudicial power and intimidating people. The first people thrown into the concentration camps under fascism would be communists, socialists, anarchists and trade unionists – this fact alone, it was felt, bestowed upon Red Action the moral right, indeed the obligation, to resist. It also recognised that a key part of fascist strategy was to 'control the streets' in order to 'march and grow' as the Nazis did in Germany prior to 1933. Red Action (and AFA) aimed to make that claim look ridiculous and thereby completely discredit them in the eyes of working-class communities.

It would be fair to say that the ruthlessness and brutality of the violence deployed, in what was effectively a clandestine turf-war waged in working-class communities across Britain, caused considerable consternation on the liberal left. Often the left and the liberal intelligentsia would talk of 'free speech', 'civil liberties' and the need to expose fascism to the light of democratic debate – rational people would, they argued, see through the half-truths and lies of fascist discourse. However, prioritising liberal freedom of speech above political reality would have constituted a categorical error because fascists sought simply to use freedom and democracy in order to destroy it. In any event, freedom of speech is a contingent liberty, and we all accept reasonable constraints upon our freedom of expression in order to respect others. Freedom of speech cannot be an absolute right in all circumstances and *everything* depends upon political circumstances and social consequences. Indeed it might be argued quite persuasively that liberal critics of physical force resistance were hypocritical because, unless they adopted an explicitly pacifist position, more or less everyone accepts that force is legitimate for particular purposes. Certainly it was particularly disingenuous for those liberals who endorsed the most brutal military interventions abroad to condemn, in moralistic tones, domestic anti-fascist violence. The liberal notion that 'violence never solves anything' was only ever selectively deployed by its advocates. The reality is that fascism is the political equivalent of plutonium and should be destroyed completely – there was, therefore, according to Red Action, no genuinely 'safe' way to engage with it at any level.

Red Action's success against the BNP and Combat 18 (C18) has been clearly reflected in the reaction of the fascists themselves; both Tim Hepple and Matthew Collins, for example, have provided detailed evidence of Red Action's impact.[48] Red Action was the only organisation that literally 'terrified' BNP thugs into capitulation and forced the BNP to alter its strategy.[49] By the mid-1990s it was clear that the fascists were being beaten off the streets and, in 1994, in an internal document written by Nick Griffin and Tony Lecomber, they pronounced there would be 'no more marches, meetings or punch-ups'. In effect the violent hooligan element within the BNP (Combat 18) were to be de-commissioned and the BNP opted for a Euro-Nationalist strategy of contesting elections and courting political 'respectability'. While C18 would continue to attract the fickle loyalties of football firms and political outcasts, eventually imploding as a consequence of state infiltration, the BNP was to make a concerted effort to enter the mainstream of British political life. Red Action (and AFA) had succeeded in driving the fascists off the streets and, as O'Shea says, 'directly the fascists threw in the towel we stopped'.[50]

However, the fact that Red Action was instrumental in deterring fascists when they were clearly intent on a policy of street-level insurrection has been the subject of some academic denigration. Nigel Copsey has argued that although 'militant anti-fascism left an indelible impression on the BNP',[51] he maintains that this brand of resistance was, in the final analysis, counter-productive.[52] Copsey asserts that 'far from destroying the BNP in a war of attrition, militant anti-fascism actually *encouraged* its modernisation ... militant anti-fascism, although perhaps successful in the short term, had a deleterious effect over the longer term'.[53] Such a thesis inevitably involves a degree of counter-factual guessing – who is to say whether, if left unopposed to control the streets, the BNP would not have earned the space to elect parliamentary representatives? How many more people would have suffered brutality at the hands of racist bullies? Copsey obviously prefers a typically liberal emphasis on 'moderate and coordinated campaigns' of community-based activism which prioritise the Labour Party.[54] Interestingly Red Action not only rejected this approach in the context of ongoing fascist violence, it explicitly refuted the multi-cultural assumptions of the liberal left which underpinned it. This was yet another reason why Red Action induced such contempt, and requires some explanation.

Throughout the period of its existence Red Action steadfastly refused to endorse the liberal agenda which prioritised gender, ethnicity and sexuality over class. Moreover, Red Action criticised the state-funded agencies of the multi-cultural establishment, stating unequivocally:

> to concede that race is the dominant motive force in society is to justify the political existence of the enemy for them. This theoretical displacement of class as the primary dynamic within society for one of race, gender or sexual orientation is nothing less than a fundamental betrayal and the fount of all our misfortunes ... it is the subversion of the progressive movement from within.[55]

According to O'Shea, 'identity politics is totally destructive to class unity. It's a point of principle for us because it is a right-wing idea that has been adopted by the left'.[56] As Coen explains, 'multi-culturalism elevates ethnicity over class. The capitalist system is perfectly happy to divide people along racial lines'.[57] Well aware of the controversial nature of such a critical view of a dominant liberal orthodoxy, Red Action persistently claimed that the 'celebration of diversity' position was, in essence, politically divisive, strategically counter-productive and, ultimately, self-defeating.[58] Gains made by minorities were, it was argued, achieved at the expense of working-class unity and advancement, and multi-culturalism was deemed to be inherently reactionary in that it prefigured the 'Balkanisation' of the working class. However, this did not mean that Red Action was unsympathetic to issues focused on gender, sexuality or race.[59] For example Red Action insisted that all questions of personal morality should be free from state interference and, moreover, 'it is axiomatic that any minorities, racial or sexual, must be defended when under attack. As part of a defensive formation the articulation and support for minority rights is understandable. But it is not the way forward'.[60] To forefront minority rights 'fragments any alliance, needlessly antagonises the neglected majority, and ultimately reinforces rivalries and institutionalises division'.[61] Politics thereby becomes an exercise in special pleading with the working class divided, which inevitably undermined the possibility of effective, unified action.

Although the assault on the multicultural consensus undoubtedly ruffled liberal feathers there was another area of Red Action activity which created an even greater furore, and that was its political and ideological orientation toward Ireland and, more specifically, its unconditional support for armed resistance by Irish Republicans. This controversial position was evident right from the very start, and the first issue of the *Bulletin* argued not only that the British working class had to come to terms with its imperial past, but observed that 'those who support armed liberation struggles in El Salvador, Zimbabwe, Vietnam and Angola fall strangely silent when the war is on their own doorstep and the guerrilla movement is fighting their own master, the British ruling class'.[62] It was a hypocrisy which Red Action never ceased to expose. Red Action saw Republicans as engaged in a war of national liberation, which had the potential (at least) to produce a progressive socialist outcome by fusing military, political and economic struggles. In effect Red Action not only endorsed the position held by Marx and Connolly about the need to deal with the 'national question' as a prelude to, or in conjunction with, any socialist aspirations, they paid tribute to those Republicans who were taking the fight to the British state.[63]

Throughout the period of its active existence Red Action supported local Irish activities and sustained practical political contact with Republican paramilitary organisations. Red Action believed that genuine revolutionary socialist groups should place Irish national liberation high on their agenda.[64] According to Red Action the liberal left in Britain had, in effect, abandoned the issue of 'Northern Ireland' when the struggle for civil liberties was transformed into an armed insurrection. Even the Trotskyist left, which had the habit of offering 'conditional support' for Republicanism, was decidedly equivocal when it came to the use of armalites and semtex. As West explains, 'in the post war era you could tell the quality of the left in relation to certain key areas – Ireland was a critical issue and the left ignored it'.[65] Red Action, on the other hand, resolved to offer unwavering support. In *Red Action* interviews were conducted with Republican volunteers, and the regular column 'Dispatches from a War

Zone' was penned by a member of the Irish National Liberation Army (INLA).[66] Headlines such as 'IRA [Irish Republican Army]/INLA: Why We Support Them', 'Why We Say "Up the IRA"' and 'IRA Call the Shots: Britain Bombed to the Negotiating Table', indicated an explicit allegiance consistently held.[67] O'Shea elaborates:

> There was a war in Ireland, an armed insurrection against the state, and we decided to contribute in whatever way we could. It was a litmus test for the left. When Bobby Sands died he was put on the back page of the SWP paper! That tells you everything you need to know about them. We were for the IRA against the common enemy. We knew who the good guys were. We were instrumental in the Saoirse campaign to support Irish prisoners. If you weren't interested in Ireland you weren't a revolutionary. Simple.[68]

As Coen confirms, 'the commitment to Ireland was ideological. The Republican movement was doing things we approved of so we supported it. We were close to the IRSP in the early days, but gravitated toward Sinn Fein as the struggle developed because it was felt to be more productive'.[69] Red Action delegations were sent regularly to Belfast, and members actively participated in Republican events (demonstrations, marches, funerals), since it was felt that much could be learned from Sinn Fein in terms of its organic connection to Nationalist working-class communities in Ireland.[70]

For some in Red Action the act of visiting the Sinn Fein or the Irish Republican Socialist Party (IRSP) HQ in Belfast, or participating as a steward for Bloody Sunday demonstrations, or perhaps attending meetings at the Camden Irish Centre, were enough to indicate a political commitment.[71] However, for others the contribution was more practical and extensive, as illustrated by the activities of Pat Hayes and Liam Heffernan, who were jailed for their activities as volunteers in the Republican movement. When Pat Hayes addressed the jury at the Old Bailey in his summation, which referred to (among other things) the colonial history of Ireland and the moral obligation of armed resistance, most Red Action members (many of whom had Irish family connections) would have concurred. Moreover, when Hayes concluded that 'the issue of the accuracy or inaccuracy of the prosecution case is not one I am interested in challenging. I am a volunteer in the Irish Republican Army. I have no criminal charges to answer', the demarcation line between the conventional 'revolutionary' left and Red Action appeared to be a chasm.[72] To the national media, the liberal intelligentsia and, indeed, most of the left, the arrest of the volunteers was shocking and sensational. To those in Red Action, however, there was no ideological or political Rubicon to be crossed between active revolutionary socialism and armed Republicanism because they were self-evidently part of the same struggle for emancipation. Red Action was clearly different, as Birchall points out, it was 'a frame of reference definitely more Irish Republican than British labour movement'.[73]

Given Red Action's critique of the revolutionary left, its rejection of the Leninist party model, Trotskyist practice and anarchist ideology, and considering its rejection of the Labour Party and the trade union movement as instruments of social reform, and if we add to this its vehement rejection of liberal multi-culturalism along with its (albeit under-developed) critique of global communist alternatives, it is easy to see how accusations of apostasy (or nihilism) could gain credence. However, it is important to acknowledge the limited purpose of the organisation and the narrow policy areas upon which it focused. In these particular areas, most notably regarding fascism and Ireland, it is possible to conclude that Red Action's intervention was significant and meaningful. Yet the enduring importance of Red Action might lie elsewhere, as a consequence of its underlying emphasis on proletarian palingenesis – it was an organisation that simply refused to abandon its attachment to, and belief in, the working class. From the Red Action perspective the working class was to be engaged, mobilised and deployed rather than patronised, marginalised and misled. Crucially, Red Action saw ordinary working people as possessing the potential for positive agency in the political process, rather than being passive receptors for the pre-packaged plans of the major political parties and/or so-called revolutionary groups. Ordinary working people were encouraged to participate and play a role beyond the ballot box, even if that entailed the judicious deployment of political violence. This aspect of Red Action's legacy is critical, because there can be no socialism without the eradication of deference toward those deemed to be socially superior and destined to rule. De-subordination is part of the very essence of socialism, and Red Action's assertive (even aggressive) prioritisation of working-class identity and agency made it an organisation which, in taking its revolutionary aspirations seriously, punched well above its weight.[74]

In conclusion, although it would be relatively easy to dismiss Red Action as constituting little more than a peripheral manifestation of revolutionary left-wing politics during a period of substantive social transformation toward new post-industrial realities – a political relic unable to adapt to the new neoliberal, pluralist, post-modern political world – such a perspective would be fundamentally misconceived. A more carefully considered analysis reveals not only an extraordinary degree of practical commitment amongst activists, but a political position that reflected a relatively high level of theoretical sophistication, distinctive elements of which deserve much closer scrutiny as examples of 'best practice', especially for those on the left who stubbornly refuse to relinquish their commitment to the ideas of working-class emancipation and egalitarian social transformation.

Notes

1 M. Seaton, 'Charge of the New Red Brigades', *Independent*, 29 January 1995.
2 *Red Action Newsletter* (1993). See also, for example, Michael Gove, 'Red Flag Flies Again' *Times*, 15 January 2002.
3 Gary O'Shea, National Organiser, Red Action, interview, 25 June 2012.
4 Steve Coen, National Treasurer, Red Action, interview, 25 June 2012.
5 Cited in M. McNamara and M. Piggott, 'Interview with RA', *Blitz*, June 1998.
6 See S. Birchall, *Beating the Fascists: The Untold Story of Anti-Fascist Action* (London: Freedom Press, 2010), p. 89.
7 Ibid., p. 98.
8 Steve West, member of Red Action, interview 25 June 2012.
9 *Red Action*, spring (1991).
10 See 'Marx v Lenin', *Red Action*, 55 (undated).
11 *Red Action*, 1, February (1982).
12 *Red Action*, April–May (1992).
13 *Red Action*, 74, spring (1997).
14 *Red Action*, summer (1994).
15 Ibid, and 'Anarchism and the Invisible Legions', *Red Action*, 56 (undated).
16 See *Red Action*, 56 (undated).
17 See *Red Action* (special election issue 1983).
18 See 'Dig Deep for the Miners' and 'Scabs Are Scum', *Red Action*, 12 (undated).
19 S. Coen, interview.
20 *Red Action Newsletter*, September–October (1995).
21 *Red Action Newsletter*, January–February (1996).
22 See 'Realism or Collaboration: The Changing Face of Trade Union Sell-Outs', *Red Action*, 32, April (1987).
23 *Red Action*, 28, November (1986).
24 *Red Action*, September–October (1991).
25 *Red Action*, 16, February (1985).
26 N. Copsey, *Anti-Fascism in Britain* (Basingstoke: Macmillan, 2000), p. 164.
27 *Red Action*, 32, April (1987); 4, July (1982).
28 *Red Action*, spring (1991).
29 G. O'Shea, interview.
30 *Red Action*, September (1990).
31 *Red Action*, Spring (1991).
32 See *Red Action Internal Affairs*, August (1999).
33 S. Coen, interview.
34 G. O'Shea, interview.
35 *Red Action Newsletter*, January (1997).
36 See K. Bullstreet, *Bash the Fash: Anti-Fascist Recollections, 1984–93* (London: Kate Sharpley Library, 2001), p. 3.
37 G. O'Shea, interview.
38 N. Copsey, 'From Direct Action to Community Action: The Changing Dynamics of Anti-Fascist Opposition', in N. Copsey and G. Macklin (eds),

British National Party: Contemporary Perspectives (London, Routledge, 2011), p. 126.

39 G. O'Shea, interview.

40 *European Militant Anti-Fascist Network Manifesto* (undated).

41 M. Hayes and P. Aylward, 'Anti-Fascist Action: Radical Resistance or Rent-a-Mob?', *Soundings*, 14 (2000), pp. 53–62.

42 Birchall, *Beating the Fascists*.

43 G. O'Shea, interview.

44 Patrick Muldowney, Member Red Action, interview, 25 June 2012.

45 S. Coen, interview.

46 G. O'Shea, interview.

47 Hayes and Aylward, 'Anti-Fascist Action', pp. 53–62.

48 See T. Hepple, *At War with Society* (London: Searchlight, 1993); M. Collins, *Hate: My Life in the British Far Right* (London: Biteback Publishing, 2011).

49 Birchall, *Beating the Fascists*, p. 387.

50 G. O'Shea, interview.

51 Copsey, *Anti-Fascism in Britain*, p. 128.

52 Ibid., p. 130.

53 Ibid., pp. 130 and 137.

54 Ibid.

55 *Red Action*, August–September (1988).

56 G. O'Shea, interview.

57 S. Coen, interview.

58 See *Red Action*, 3, 5 (1999); 4, 11 (2001).

59 See *Red Action*, 38, January (1988); 40, March (1999).

60 See *Red Action*, 32, April (1987); *Red Action Agenda National Meeting* (1999).

61 *Red Action Agenda National Meeting* (1999); 'Race or Class? Fatal Distraction', *Red Action*, 3, 6 (1999).

62 *Red Action*, 1 (1982).

63 See *Red Action*, 2, April (1982); 3, May (1982).

64 *Red Action Newsletter*, July–August (1995).

65 S. West, interview.

66 See 'Inside the Maze', *Red Action*, 64, December (1992).

67 *Red Action*, 14, September–October (1984); 35, October (1987); 69, autumn (1994). Also issue 53 (undated).

68 G. O'Shea, interview; *Red Action*, 72, autumn–winter (1995) and 73, spring (1996).

69 S. Coen, interview.

70 See 'Building Sinn Fein in South Belfast: The Lessons for Red Action', *Red Action National Conference Document* (2000).

71 *Red Action*, 3, 6 (1999).

72 *Red Action*, summer (1994).

73 Birchall, *Beating the Fascists*, p. 328; Seaton. 'Charge of the New Red Brigades'.

74 Some members of Red Action went on to pursue such ideas via the Independent Working Class Association (IWCA).

13

Anti-fascism in Britain, 1997–2012

David Renton

Anti-fascism is along with anti-militarism one of the most successful campaigns with which the left in Britain has been associated: key moments, such as the Battles of Olympia (1934), Cable Street (1936) or Lewisham (1977) were events at which the activities of the left forced themselves into the news, and through which whole generations of activists came into the movement. They played a key part in limiting the ability of British fascists to grow. That is not to say, however, that anti-fascism has always been successful or easy; part of the story also involves long periods of attrition, during which anti-fascism had little obvious success at all.

1997

Seasoned anti-fascists viewed New Labour's victory at the 1997 general election with scepticism. The previous Labour government had provided a favourable context for the National Front (NF), whose rapid growth under Wilson and Callaghan had been halted by the success of the Anti-Nazi League (ANL) between 1977 and 1979.[1] By 1997, Britain's largest fascist party, John Tyndall's British National Party (BNP), was in a robust position and was able to stand a record 56 candidates in that year's general election. The party had the recent memory of electoral success, chiefly Derek Beackon's victory at a council by-election on the Isle of Dogs in 1992. Beackon had been defeated in a further local election the year following; but the architects of his success, including Tony Lecomber, who had developed the BNP's 'Rights for Whites' strategy, remained in the organisation. This continuity was marked by the BNP's concentration on East London in its 1997 general election campaign, in which its two best results were 3,350 votes in Bethnal Green and Bow (7.5 per cent) and 2,849 votes in Poplar and Canning Town (7.3 per cent). Finally, while the exact misdeeds of New Labour could not have been predicted in advance, long before election night it was clear that Tony Blair was the most right-wing leader in the history of the Labour Party and had a particular line in grandiose, nationalistic rhetoric ('third way', 'a thousand days to prepare for a thousand years') that came close at times to echoing the language of the interwar fascists. This rhetorical fascism-lite was encapsulated in Blair's choreographed arrival at Downing Street, where he was welcomed by a crowd of Labour Party supporters, waving Union Jacks, with no red flags to be seen. Given that New Labour was destined to disappoint, given that the Tories were weak and that Labour faced no serious electoral competition to its left, it was easy to predict that the BNP would flourish. But while there were plenty of anti-fascists who stood with Paul Foot in regarding Blair's triumph with a combination of 'joyful anticipation' and 'pervasive unease', and several for whom the unease eclipsed any optimism at all, few would have predicted the difficulties anti-fascists were about to face.[2]

1997–2001

Between 1997 and 2001, the BNP grew noticeably, albeit without achieving the electoral breakthroughs which were to follow later. A key moment was the October 1999 election for leader in which Nick Griffin, previously of the National Front (c.1977–89) and the International Third Position (1989–90), and a BNP member since 1995, ousted the party's founder John Tyndall (previously the chairman of the National Front), with 70 per cent of the vote out of just under 1,500 BNP members voting. Griffin then won 4.25 of the vote in a by-election in West Bromwich in winter 2000. Reports reached anti-fascists of BNP public meetings in the North West and Yorkshire attended by several hundred people at a time.

The largest anti-fascist network was the ANL, backed by the Socialist Workers Party (SWP) and supported by several hundred union branches, and able to draw on the SWP's own network of then around 8-10,000 members in around 200 or so branches. Led by the SWP's Julie Waterson, the ANL had a steering committee comprising MPs and trade unionists. The ANL sent several hundred supporters to a demonstration of 50,000 against the Front National at Strasbourg in March 1997. It organised a conference on the threat of Euro-fascism in September 1997 with speakers from Germany and France, and there were ANL-sponsored delegations to Auschwitz.[3] Within Britain, a central focus of the ANL's activity was confronting the NF, which attempted marches in Dover in 1997 and 1998 and in Sunderland in 2001. In general, these events saw mobilisations of around 60–100 people by the NF, and around 4–5 times that number of anti-fascists.[4] In 1999, the ANL supported protests against the London nail bomber David Copeland, including outside the Admiral Duncan pub in Soho. Yet this same period saw a reduction in the number of ANL supporters and by 2000–1, it was noticeable that even at high-profile London-wide mobilisations, the ANL was capable of turning out just 500–1000 supporters: less than half of what would have been expected at comparable events eight years earlier.

The most dramatic indication of the League's weakness came on 7 July 2001, when ANL stewards lost control of an anti-NF demonstration in Bradford, after which several hundred people rioted against the NF and the police. Some 200 participants were convicted of public order offences and the total sentences handed down exceeded 600 years.[5] One reason why the ANL had not been able to control the rioters is that it lacked a sufficient network of supporters in Bradford to prevent the riot or to protect the community from legal reprisal afterwards. Indeed Bradford was only one of several race riots that summer, with the BNP sponsoring anti-Asian riots in Oldham and Burnley. While these riots boosted the BNP and fuelled the campaign of their leader Nick Griffin who was then standing for election in Oldham, the ANL was criticised by other anti-fascists for chasing unsuccessfully after street confrontations with the NF who were marginal and for having no strategy to deal with the BNP which had chosen to prioritise elections over the street.

The relative eclipse of the ANL was matched by the decline of Anti-Fascist Action (AFA). At its early-1990s heyday, compared to the ANL, AFA had a much smaller inner-core (the ex-Trotskyists of Red Action (RA), probably never more than 200 strong), but a more diffuse periphery of several hundred and previously (c.1992) up to a thousand anarchists, syndicalists and semi-'independent' anti-fascist activists. The difficulty was keeping the core and the periphery in synch. AFA's magazine *Fighting Talk* boasted 30 local groups in September 1997,[6] but by 2001 AFA had expelled its branches in Leeds and Huddersfield, claimed no more than four 'regions', and barely existed any more as a national network.

Anti-Fascist Action was well-known on the left for its endlessly upbeat, self-promotional tone, in which every intervention resulted in victory. Its rivals among other anti-fascist networks were portrayed as idiotic, its enemies (the police and the BNP) as cowardly, weak and stupid. Unfortunately, while there are now several excellent studies of AFA at its peak, which go some way to explaining the initiatives which AFA got right (e.g. its physical routing of Combat 18 at Waterloo station in 1992), there still has been no explanation of what then went wrong after 1997.

In Sean Birchall's semi-official history of AFA, *Beating the Fascists: The Untold Story of Anti-Fascist Action,*[7] AFA's difficulties are alluded to only indirectly. Birchall describes how in 1995 AFA published a 'seminal' document, *Filling the Vacuum*,[8] predicting that 'the election of Labour will be a massive shot in the arm for the far-right' and arguing that the only way to defeat the BNP in Britain's working-class communities would be by 'out-radicalising them', i.e. by establishing a 'political wing' that would have a presence in every community and displace the BNP by offering a far more consistent hostility to every aspect of the status quo.[9] Birchall's story ends abruptly in 1995; several years prior to AFA's actual demise.

The result of the new political approach set out in *Filling the Vacuum* was the creation of the Independent Working Class Association (IWCA), which was formed in October 1995. The announcement of the IWCA, and RA's determination to win support for its strategy from people outside its ranks, saw RA deprioritise AFA, which showed after 1995 fewer and fewer signs of independent existence. The last issue of its magazine *Fighting Talk* appeared in May 2001. AFA itself had barely been seen in public for two years.

Dave Hann and Steve Tilzey's book *No Retreat* is similar to Sean Birchall's, in that most of the account is given over to the various victories of AFA, especially in Manchester where the two authors were based. Hann is, however, more critical of the politics of *Filling the Vacuum*, which he saw as RA imposing itself on AFA:

> AFA groups were for the first time being asked to accept a political programme based on the political philosophy of one particular organisation within it ... If Red Action wanted to build a grassroots, community-based organisation then good luck to them, I didn't see why AFA should be expected to become that organisation, which was basically the hidden agenda behind the Red Action/London AFA proposals.[10]

Searchlight magazine continued, as it had for more than two decades, to expose the British far-right, gathering intelligence and largely leaving the terrains of mass mobilisation and electoral work to others. Its former editor Gerry Gable had handed the reins on to younger editors, Steve Silver and Nick Lowles. There were also various occasional contributors and regional allies, the two most important of which were Paul Meszaros in Bradford and Mike Luft in Oldham.

Finally the last of the 'big beasts' of 1990s anti-fascism,[11] the Anti-Racist Alliance, which had been set up in 1991 as a black-led campaign against both institutional racism and fascism, had morphed in the middle of the 1990s into the National Assembly Against Racism (NAAR). Three features marked NAAR out compared to the other organisations on the far left: the first was a greater prioritisation of hostility to institutional racism rather than the activities of the far-right; the second was a 'community organisation' approach to hosting political events (which meant, at its worst, lengthy rallies burdened by an excess of speakers); the third was the dominance of NAAR by the small Trotskyist group Socialist Action (this in turn meant prioritising Ken Livingstone and tailing a Labour Party 'left').

2001–5

Between 2001 and 2005, the BNP enjoyed sustained electoral success. The process began in the aftermath of the Macpherson report, whose findings of institutional racism in the police were accepted by the force with considerable ill-grace, and with the widely publicised remarks of Chief Superintendent Eric Hewitt, the head of the Oldham police division, who told the press in January of 2001 that over the previous 12 months, his force had investigated 572 racial incidents, and that 60 per cent of the victims had been white.[12] The situation escalated further the next month when 76-year-old war veteran Walter Chamberlain was shown on national television, his face beaten raw in what appeared to be a racist attack (although his family denied there was any racial content to the incident).[13] In March 2001, the NF attempted to march through Oldham. Anti-fascists organised protest meetings of 350 and then 500 people, and a counter-demonstration 1,000-strong. Members of the BNP and the NF organised further marches on 5 and 27 May.[14] Following the third march, the far-right gangs refused to disperse, but congregated in Oldham's pubs, waiting for trouble. Clashes between black and white youths saw the police then intervene decisively against the former. The majority of Oldham's white residents (who formed more than four-fifths of the local population) blamed 'Asians' rather than the far-right for the trouble, and 16 per cent of voters backed the BNP in that spring's general election.

Over the next four years, the BNP was able to maintain the momentum caused by this initial breakthrough. In local elections in 2002, the BNP stood in 66 wards, winning votes of between 10 and 20 per cent in 19 of them and seeing three of its candidates elected in Burnley. A total of 13 BNP councillors were elected, from 221 candidates, in 2003. The following year the BNP took four seats in Bradford and three in Epping Forest and 14 altogether. In the 2005 general election, the BNP, which contested 119 seats, took 192,850 votes in total, very roughly four times more votes than it had secured in 2001.[15]

Meanwhile, the BNP was not just growing in terms of votes but also in terms of membership. The 2005 accounts reported total BNP membership of 6,502 and a party income of £672,246, mainly from membership fees.[16] The first of these figures represented roughly double the party's claimed membership count in 1999, and four times as many as had actually voted in the 1999 leadership contest.

While the BNP's electoral success could hardly have been welcomed by any anti-fascist worthy of the name, for Red Action in particular there must have been a modest, grim feeling of satisfaction. This was the future about which they had been warning since the mid-1990s. What then of the IWCA, their proposed new shield? Alongside the BNP's growth Labour's second term also saw a brief period of electoral success for the IWCA, including the election of a first councillor Stuart Craft in Oxford in 2002, and votes of over 20 per cent in council wards that year in Islington, Hackney and Havering, followed by 22 per cent the following year in another London council election. An IWCA candidate, Lorna Reid, won 2.1 per cent of second preference votes in the 2004 mayoral elections in London. Reid was outvoted 3 to 1 by the BNP candidate Julian Leppert, who himself came within just 3,000 votes of the main far-left candidate, Lindsey German of Respect.

Yet while Reid's vote was impressive, the IWCA was showing every sign of geographical containment. Its contingent of Oxford County councillors increased to three in 2004. In 2005, however, the organisation stood no candidates outside Oxford. Moreover, while Oxford IWCA was able to increase its total number of candidates to 5, none were elected, with Labour enjoying a dramatic general election 'bounce'. Even Sean Birchall's consistently upbeat history of AFA admits that the IWCA was 'fast disappearing in the BNP's wing mirrors'.[17]

AFA's publications were pitched at an audience of disaffected white workers, football fans and working-class punks. It was proclaimed that this audience was instinctively anti-Labour. But Labour's hold on trade unionists' sympathies remained constant through Blair's honeymoon. Anti-Fascist Action's intended audience remained Labourist or lost interest in politics. Moreover, within the Red Action core, there was a further 'inner core', of trusted activists with usually a shared history going back to the ANL 'mark 1' of 1977–79. By 2007, few in this group were under 40; they were getting old for the physical confrontations at which AFA excelled. Red Action's leaders stood AFA down rather than hand the network on to a younger generation who had not lived through the same experiences.

After RA's turn to elections, the next sign of a change of approach by anti-fascists in response to the BNP's rise was the launch in autumn 2002 of Love Music Hate Racism (LMHR). Led for several years by Lee Billingham, LMHR took its name from the manifesto published in the first (1977) issue of the Rock Against Racism fanzine *Temporary Hoarding*: 'We want Rebel music, street music. Music that breaks down people's fear of one another. Crisis music. Now Music. Music that knows who the real enemy is. Rock against racism. Love music hate racism.'[18] LMHR copied much of the RAR template save for the addition of new musical genres, hip hop, indie, drum 'n' bass, grime to the original RAR pantheon of rock, punk and reggae. Love Music Hate Racism held its first gig in Burnley, following the BNP victories there in local elections, with Chumbawamba playing, following that with a Carnival in Manchester in September 2002, with Ms Dynamite and Billy Bragg.[19]

The creation of LMHR was followed a year later by the setting up of Unite Against Fascism, a merger of the ANL and the NAAR, who provided the alliance's two national secretaries, Weyman Bennett (ANL) and Sabby Dhallu (NAAR). United Against Fascism (UAF), which had been several months in the planning, was publicly launched in the North West in January 2004, at a 500-strong meeting in Manchester. Two weeks later, the BNP demonstrated outside the headquarters of the Commission for Racial Equality and the National Union of Journalists (NUJ). The BNP reported that 100 of its supporters turned out. The real figure was just 37.[20] Outside the NUJ, they looked like a small, bedraggled mob. The stunt, ironically, increased the numbers signing up for the new anti-fascist coalition. The National Union of Journalists, whose members are usually expected to report both sides of any story, had been wary of being seen as partisan. But, under attack from the BNP, it affiliated to Unite Against Fascism.

From the launch of UAF, there were tensions between the SWP/NAAR and *Searchlight*. The latter complained that they were being marginalised within UAF. They suggested that the SWP's main allies in UAF, Socialist Action, were biased against them. Socialist Action's belief that anti-fascism had to be black-led, Steve Silver argued, inevitably resulted in hostility to *Searchlight*, whose two editors and former editor were each white. At least two of these three were also Jews, with Gable and Silver claiming that supporters of Unite Against Fascism criticised them behind their backs as 'Zionists' (i.e. used anti-Semitic code-words against them).

There were other issues at stake in the deepening row between *Searchlight* and UAF. Gable and Silver were shaped by their former membership and active membership (respectively) of the Communist Party, while Lowles worked closely with John Cruddas of the Labour 'centre-left' and MP of the BNP target-seat Dagenham and Rainham. Long before UAF had been established, Searchlight had had the backing of several unions, chiefly the general unions GMB and TGWU (later UNITE) in which Old Labour, Communist Party-influenced and right-wing Labour factions ('broad lefts') battled for supremacy with barely a challenger from the far left. Paul Mackney the General Secretary of the lecturers union Natfhe (from 2006, University and College Union: UCU) had secured a mandate from the TUC General Council to take a leading responsibility for anti-fascist work, but his political background was one Gable or Silver would have considered 'Trotskyist' (he was a former member of the SWP's predecessor the International Socialists). Gable, Silver and Lowles wanted to split from UAF, but did not want to be seen in the trade union movement as the protagonists of division.[21]

After *Searchlight* eventually left UAF, in June 2005, it created a national organisation Hope not Hate (HnH), which was intended to be a counterpart to UAF, i.e. a mass membership anti-fascist organisation capable of challenging the BNP at election time and whenever it organised. For some time *Searchlight* had been cultivating the remnants, such as there were, of the country's anti-fascist 'independents', i.e. the two dozen or so local groups with 'Together' in their name or 'Unite' or 'CARF' (Campaign Against Racism and Fascism) that had held together, generally with the backing of their trades council, from previous unity ventures of the early 1990s or before, and *Searchlight* had positioned itself as the protector of the local knowledge of these networks.[22] HnH would offer these groups the skills of its journalists, and of *Searchlight*'s own research knowledge, to assist in putting together locally titled tabloid newspapers running exposés of the fascist past or political inadequacy of BNP candidates. *Searchlight* found distributors of the newsletters, either from the local groups, or from the unions affiliated to Trade Union Friends of Searchlight.

Hope not Hate saw itself as the purveyor of anti-fascist expertise, not merely information-gathering about fascists but using computer software to build up databases of BNP members and anti-fascist voters. In the years following the anti-war mobilisations of 2003 (led by the SWP-sponsored Stop the War Coalition) which had seen Muslims and non-Muslims march together against the Iraq War, *Searchlight* (in common with the majority of mainstream opinion in Britain, but in contrast to the majority of the left) preferred to see Islamists and fascists as two parallel sets of extremists. Faced with BNP claims that black groups received funding from the state, or that black people were involved in crime, or that Muslim men were paedophiles, Nick Lowles criticised UAF for insisting that there was no basis at all to these arguments. 'Grooming is a real not a perceived problem', he countered, 'It is pointless denying some predominantly ethnic minority communities receive more funding than their white neighbours because, again, they clearly do.'[23] Unite Against Fascism in turn accused *Searchlight* of making concessions to racist myths. Lowles responded by threatening to sue UAF:

> I have committed the last 19 years of my life to Searchlight and the anti-fascist cause. I got involved because my mother is from Mauritius and as a young child I experienced racism towards her when I was growing up

in Hounslow, West London. I have no problem with a debate over strategy but to insinuate that I pander to racism, that I am some sort of racist or even worse some sort of closet fascist is reprehensible. And I will not tolerate it.[24]

Despite their differences, UAF and HnH did have an impact on the far right. The success of anti-fascists could be traced in a number of high-profile defections from the BNP, including Robin Evans (former BNP councillor in Blackburn) in 2003 and Maureen Stowe (former councillor in Blackburn) in 2004. Most important was the way in which the BNP was forced to ratchet down the predictions it was making of its own future success. In spring 2003, the party boasted that it would stand 1,000 candidates in the next local elections. This figure was talked down to 600 by the start of 2004. The actual number of BNP candidates was under 400. In the 2005 general election, the BNP obtained votes of 8–10 per cent in around a dozen constituencies. But in only three seats did it break 10 per cent. This was less dramatic progress than would have been predicted in 2002 or 2003.

2005–10

For the first four years of New Labour's third term, the pattern of the second term continued with the BNP seemingly doing ever better in elections. In 2006, its biggest gains were in Barking and Dagenham, where it took 11 of the 13 seats it contested, becoming the second party on the council and the BNP increased its total number of councillors to 46. In 2007, although the BNP won 9 new council seats, it also lost 8 sitting councillors, leading to a net gain of just 1. In 2008, the BNP gained 13 new council seats, taking it to 55 councillors. In 2009, Nick Griffin and Andrew Brons of the BNP were elected to the European Parliament, and the BNP made a net gain of 3 seats taking it to a peak of 58 local councillors altogether.

Griffin's successful bid to become an MEP raised the profile of the BNP enormously; he became a panellist on the BBC television programme *Question Time* and the press published a number of profiles of him, not all of them unfavourable. The sympathy extended even to the aftermath of *Question Time*, during which Griffin received a number of hostile questions from the audience, and appeared nervous and incoherent, and it was unclear how most viewers would respond to his performance. The *Daily Mail* in particular blamed Griffin's negative reception on hostile questions selected by the BBC and suggested he had been unfairly treated. The *Guardian* complained that the *Mail* had published a faked document doctored by its journalists or the BNP.[25]

The risk of Griffin's success in the European elections galvanised the left, creating a wider audience for anti-fascist organisation than at any time since Derek Beackon's election for the BNP at Tower Hamlets in

1993–94. *Searchlight* claimed to have delivered 3.4 million leaflets across the country in the two months leading up to the 2009 European election. In the North West alone, the magazine reported to have mobilised no fewer than 1,200 supporters, delivering on average more than a thousand leaflets each: as great a concentration of resources as that of any of the political parties who had contested the same elections.

Griffin's success also had the effect of destabilising his own party: it increased his prominence within the group but despite the BNP's electoral success, he was bitterly unpopular within his party. He was widely perceived as weak and indecisive, and as a chancer: someone who used the group to push himself personally, often in quite tawdry money-making schemes. There had already been leadership challenges to him (Colin Auty and Colin Jackson in 2007) and more were to follow.

Meanwhile, in June 2009 (i.e. the very month of Griffin's election as an MEP), a rival far-right organisation the English Defence League (EDL) was founded, as a street-fighting Islamophobic group. The EDL came out of events in Luton in March 2009 when a return-home event by the Royal Anglian Regiment was opposed by a tiny number of Muslims organised by the group Islam4UK. A mixture of football hooligans and fascists attacked them, and there were further anti-Islamic demonstrations in Luton on 13 April and 24 May 2009.[26] The EDL eschewed elections in favour of direct confrontation. Although it was funded by a millionaire 'Alan Lake' (really Alan Ayling, who worked for the European Bank for Reconstruction and Development) it seemed to lack the money-grabbing of Griffin's inner circle.[27]

The greater public role of the BNP, and the EDL's emphasis on marches, swung attention back to UAF, which since AFA's demise had been almost the only exponent of street-level anti-fascism. Hope not Hate called for a general ban on marches, those of the EDL in particular and inevitably those of UAF also, as the only power available to the police was to ban all protests in an area, pro- or anti-EDL.

In August 2009, the BNP held a Red White and Blue 'festival' at Codnor in Derbyshire. Around 1,500 demonstrators opposed it. The press described a few hundred BNP members huddling to keep each other warm, while demonstrators sang 'what shall do with the BNP … string 'em up like Mussolini'. Shortly afterwards the BNP announced that it would not hold an event at Codnor again.

The EDL organised online rather than in branches, with seemingly little interest in ideology or funding. The EDL would meet at a central point (usually a pub) in advance of a pre-publicised 'static assembly' at the centre of a town. The police would allow the supporters of the EDL to get very drunk. They would then escort them on what was in effect a march to their final destination. If unopposed, the EDL would sing such ditties as 'Allah is a paedo', and in all probability try to attack a local shop or two. Eventually the police would get fed up and a skirmish of sorts would occur. Afterwards, the police would escort the supporters of the EDL back to the train station. Around the set piece events, smaller numbers of EDL supporters would attempt racist stunts, ranging from placing pigs heads outside mosques to occupying mosque minarets.

Unite Against Fascism opposed these events. Through 2009–10, a number of anti-fascists (not just Hope not Hate, but other voices from the Labour centre and right) criticised UAF for seeking physical confrontation with the EDL. The supporters of the EDL were generally younger than their counterparts in UAF, and many of them, being used to fighting at or around football matches, were better prepared for physical confrontation. In 2009, 2010 and until summer 2011, the UAF and EDL numbers were usually broadly even. UAF did not have such a weight of numbers that it could simply sweep the EDL off the streets. UAF was accused of being irresponsible with its supporters in taking them into battles for which they were not ready. The most coherent statement of this opposition to street marches came from Nigel Copsey, a one-time supporter of AFA and the author of *Anti-Fascism in Britain*:

> If the EDL win on the street, this will heavily contribute to its glamour. Socialist Workers Party students playing at street fighters behind Muslim kids playing up to a script of extremist youth – this will only 'feed the EDL narrative'. The obvious danger is that if anyone is seriously injured or even killed as a result of EDL protest/counter-protest, the potential for radicalisation on both sides – 'cumulative radicalisation' – will increase significantly. Deny the EDL the 'oxygen of publicity' by minimising the potential for violent confrontation, and the chances are that the EDL will lose its standing, glamour, credibility and interest amongst the hardcore hooligan element.[28]

2010–12

Ostensibly the pattern of the 2010 general election was of further but uneven growth for the BNP, consistent with the party's fortunes generally since 1997.[29] The BNP increased its number of candidates to 326, winning a total of 514,819 votes. Both of these figures were around three times higher than in 2010: i.e. the BNP had achieved a geographical dispersal of its vote without seeing any decline in its average support. Yet what gives the lie to something that might otherwise have seemed the consolidation of the far-right vote, was the distinct failure of the BNP in its target seats. In Barking, the BNP was defending 12 seats, and had high hopes of taking control of the local council. Nick Griffin gave his backing to this ambition by standing for the parliamentary seat. He secured 6,600 votes or 14.6 per cent of the poll: nearly 2 per cent down on the BNP's result in 2010. All 12 of the BNP's Barking councillors were defeated, as were 26 of the 28 incumbent BNP local councillors nationally. Defeat in Barking was mirrored by defeat in Stoke, the BNP's second target seat, where the BNP councillors ended up tied in fourth alongside the Liberal Democrats. 'When the results came in', the journalist and historian of the BNP Daniel Trilling writes, 'they signalled a rout'.[30]

Much of the BNP's defeat can be put down to the activity of local anti-fascists. In Barking for example, the UAF full-timer was Alys Zaerin, who seven years earlier had been one of the school students who struck against the Iraq war. UAF organised 13 days of action, and gave out over 200,000 leaflets in the seat.[31] HnH also produced a similar volume of material, which means that the average voter would have received around 9 leaflets inviting them not to vote for the BNP.

Anti-fascists were helped by the resurgence of a previously dormant Labour vote, in traditional Labour constituencies, motivated no doubt by fear at the prospect of a Conservative election victory. The BNP was not the only party to lose out in East London. Respect, previously victorious in Tower Hamlets, was also defeated, as was the Christian People's Alliance, which had held three councillors in Canning.

The demise continued in 2011 and 2012, with the majority of BNP councillors losing their seats, and the party shrinking after the 2012 elections to a rump of just 3 elected councillors: Sharon Wilkinson on Lancashire County Council, Brian Parker in Pendle and Catherine Duffy in Charnwood. Electoral decline highlighted Griffin's personal unpopularity. In 2011 and 2012, Griffin had to face election challenges from within the BNP; first from Eddy Butler (previously a BNP's election strategist) and then from Andrew Brons (the BNP's second MEP), with Griffin surviving the latter's challenge by just 9 votes. The total number of BNP members voting, at just over 2,300, was only 50 per cent up on the 1999 internal elections in which Griffin had ousted Tyndall, and this figure gives a far truer indication of the BNP's actual membership than its claimed total of around 14,000 members.

As for the EDL, through 2010 and until about summer 2011, this group continued to show every sign of continued growth. A number of former BNP members were attracted to it, including its leader 'Tommy Robinson' (Stephen Yaxley-Lennon), as well as local activists Chris Renton (no relation), Davy Cooling and Richard Price. Major EDL mobilisations in 2010 alone included Stoke-on-Trent (January), central London (March), Bolton (March), Dudley (April), Aylesbury (May), Dudley (May),

Newcastle (May), Cardiff and Swansea (June), East London (June), Dudley (July), Bradford (August) and Leicester (October).

In *Coming Down the Road*, Billy Blake's insider history of the EDL, several of these events are portrayed as victories for the right. This, for example, is Blake's account of the EDL procession entering Bolton's Victoria Square in March 2010:

> These were the forgotten people, the sons and daughters of old England, here to reclaim their birthright. A mass of coloured flags filled the square, as it was reclaimed in the name of the English people. Here were the descendants of people who built the modern world, their battle flag rich with exotic names from far flung shores. Now more familiar sounding names were being added, Birmingham, Manchester, Leeds, London and now Bolton. There were well over 1500 of them, all chanting in unison and drowning out the chants of the anti-fascists. It was pure, crude and brutal Anglo-Saxon defiance.[32]

I was standing in Victoria Square at 2pm when the EDL arrived; and while the UAF presence outnumbered the EDL around 3:2, anti-fascists had by this point spent two hours fighting with the police while the EDL arrived fresh from the pub with a police escort. I have no doubt that Blake accurately reflects most EDL supporters' feeling that the day was turning out better for them than they could have hoped.

At Bolton, the vast majority of the 74 arrests were of anti-fascists, and UAF organisers Weyman Bennett and Rhetta Moran were both originally arrested and investigated for conspiracy to commit public disorder (an offence potentially carrying several years' imprisonment). It was only afterwards, as a result of a lengthy legal battle, that the anti-fascists began to rescue the situation, with the majority of anti-fascists being acquitted following trials, and two Greater Manchester police officers facing criminal charges of attempting to pervert the course of justice after making witness statements in which they accused Alan Clough, an anti-fascist in his sixties, of assaulting them, when the police's own video evidence showed they had hit him.[33]

The next major conflict came at Bradford in August 2010. Unite Against Fascism initially sought to mobilise against the EDL directly, with *Socialist Worker* running a front-page interview with a former member of the Bradford 12,[34] Tariq Mehmood: 'The EDL is riding on an anti-Islamic wave – a set of racist ideas that are a necessary component of the "war on terror". The EDL must be confronted, both in ideas and a battle for the streets. If the streets are lost, we will never win the battle of ideas.'[35] However, Bradford proved especially difficult terrain for UAF. The memory of defeat in 2001 was still fresh. *Searchlight* meanwhile had had a group in the city since even before its split with UAF and won a majority of Labour councillors to its position that there should be a ban on all demonstrations including UAF's. Nick Lowles explained his position to *Searchlight*'s readers as follows:

> No EDL protest has actually been stopped by a counter-demonstration so the argument about No Platform does not hold. In almost every instance the EDL has held its static protest regardless of the actions of anti-fascists. More worryingly, some have led to disorder … We also question the impact counter-demonstrations have on local people. Unfortunately much of the media coverage of earlier protests has presented a scene of two groups of extremists. This has especially been the case when there has been disorder or large-scale arrests of anti-EDL protests. The media coverage in Birmingham, Bolton and Manchester presented the anti-EDL protests in a negative light – hardly the best way to win hearts and minds of local people.[36]

Under pressure, Unite Against Fascism limited its plans to organising an anti-EDL musical event, 'We Are Bradford', in the city's Exchange Square, with somewhere between 1000 and 1500 people attending. UAF did not confront the EDL, although some anti-fascists (probably around 300 altogether) broke away in the hope of doing so.[37] The EDL themselves turned out around 1,000 people, and there followed a lengthy stand-off, with the EDL throwing sticks and bottles and, in at least one case, flares at anti-fascists, before turning on their own stewards.

On 5 February 2011, the EDL were able to pull off a march of about 2,500 people in Luton, one of its largest mobilisations to date. The event was, however, challenged by anti-fascists, who initially occupied Luton train station preventing the EDL from congregating, and then held Luton's Park Square and Bury Park. Blake's *Coming Down the Road* paints a vivid picture of the EDL as a movement in slow decline from this point onwards. Part of the problem lay in the EDL's initial claims to novelty as a single-issue anti-Islamist movement. While this enabled the EDL to pose as free of the British far-right's historic taint of Nazism, the individuals who were pushed forward to personify the EDL's 'newness' (including Roberta Moore of the EDL's 'Jewish division' and Guramit Singh a Sikh) were bitterly unpopular with the EDL's rank and file members, a significant portion of whom had come through one or other of the BNP, Combat 18 or the National Front. Opposition from the left opened up another fault-line between those who wanted to keep the EDL a single-issue campaign and those who just wanted to attack 'communists'. In autumn 2011 Blake wrote, 'the EDL is in disarray, too many people want a slice of the action'.[38]

In September 2011 the EDL announced a march through the East End. Despite making it a national mobilisation only around 600 people turned up. Tommy Robinson was arrested along with around 60 other EDL members. Some of the same rows that had previously dogged the anti-fascist side resurfaced, in particular as to whether the left should call for bans on the EDL. In the end, the Home Secretary did ban all public processions in the area, but this was ignored on both sides: the EDL were, as ever, escorted through the streets by the police to their supposedly 'static' assembly point. Finding this occupied by anti-fascists, who outnumbered them by around four or five to one, and without assistance from the police, they dispersed, leaving the streets free to UAF for a half-mile victory procession.

Finally, in August 2012, the EDL attempted to march through Walthamstow, but were prevented by a crowd of around 4,000 anti-fascists, who occupied the junction of Hoe Street and Forest Road, blocking the planned EDL march route. The EDL leaders Tommy Robinson and Kevin Caroll were separated from their supporters and ended the day in a fierce row with one another. The EDL then tried to reclaim the initiative by proposing a return to Walthamstow two months later, but realising that Unite Against Fascism was mobilising in similar numbers to before, they cancelled their event, taking just 60 people to stand berating tourists outside parliament.[39] The EDL even had to endure the humiliation of Nick Griffin telling the world, through the BNP's You Tube channel, that 'Walthamstow Two' would be a disaster, 'a counterproductive battle than cannot be won'.

> We are up against far stronger opponents than we can muster. We are outnumbered, out-financed, out-mediaed and outgunned in every possible way. So if we go up against our far more powerful opponents on their grounds, if we give them advance notice that we are coming, if we become so predictable that they will be able to bring out their big guns, we will lose.[40]

At this point, anti-fascists could at last draw breath and feel that after a difficult fifteen years the conflict was finally moving in the right direction.

Notes

1 D. Renton, *When We Touched the Sky: The Anti-Nazi League, 1977–81* (Cheltenham: New Clarion Press, 2006), pp. 156–8.

2 P. Foot, 'Socialism and Democracy', *Socialist Review*, April (1997), pp. 11–14.

3 There had been a similar event in March 1982, see Renton, *When We Touched the Sky*, p. 166.

4 J. Sweeney, 'Tea and Loathing on Dover Seafront', *Observer*, 16 November 1997.

5 'Heroes of the Riots Praised by Judge', [Bradford] *Telegraph and Argus*, 4 March 2008.

6 *Fighting Talk*, 17, p. 2.

7 S. Birchall, *Beating the Fascists: The Untold Story of Anti-Fascist Action* (London: Freedom Press, 2010).

8 The text is online at http://libcom.org/library/filling-vacuum-london-afa, accessed 11 November 2012.

9 Birchall, *Beating the Fascists*, p. 390.

10 D. Hann and S. Tilzey, *No Retreat: The Secret War between Britain's Anti-Fascists and the Far-Right* (Lytham: Milo, 2003), p. 267.

11 The Socialist Party (previously Militant) organised its own anti-fascist 'united front', Youth Against Racism in Europe, which mobilised for the Welling demonstration in 1993, but was less visible after 1997. Some former supporters of Militant later worked with former AFA supporters in a further group, No Platform.

12 'Asians "Behind Most Racial Violence"', *BBC News*, 9 February 2001, http://news.bbc.co.uk/2/hi/uk_news/1160552.stm, accessed 11 November 2012.

13 'War Veteran in "Racist" Attack', *BBC News*, 24 April 2001, http://news.bbc.co.uk/2/hi/uk_news/1294021.stm, accessed 11 November 2012.

14 'When Frustration Erupts', *Guardian*, 28 May 2001, http://www.theguardian.com/uk/2001/may/28/race.politics, accessed 11 November 2012.

15 'Electoral performance of the British National Party in the UK', House of Commons Library, 15 May 2009.

16 *Searchlight*, 22 December 2007.

17 Birchall, *Beating the Fascists,* p. 403.

18 Renton, *When We Touched the Sky*, p. 33.

19 M. Smith, 'Ten Years of Loving Music and Hating Racism', *Socialist Review*, July (2012), http://www.socialistreview.org.uk/article.php?articlenumber=12058, accessed 11 November 2012.

20 As counted by the author.

21 At this point, I was a national equality official of the lecturers' union UCU (and one of 2–3 UCU representatives on the steering committee of UAF) and previously a regular contributor to *Searchlight* magazine. I attended a final attempted reconciliation meeting between Paul Mackney, Gerry Gable and Steve Silver.

22 The concluding words of Nigel Copsey's *Anti-Fascism in Britain* (Basingstoke: Palgrave, 2000), p. 188 give a flavour of how *Searchlight* liked to present itself to the trade union movement between *c*.1997 and *c*.2005: 'As *Searchlight* has now recognised, any collective anti-fascist response must be rooted firmly in the local community. That is the practical lesson for anti-fascists today. Whether it will be accepted by all remains to be seen.'

23 N. Lowles, 'Tackling Taboo Issues', *Searchlight*, April (2005), pp. 14–15.

24 N. Lowles, 9 September 2009, www.radicalactivistnewham.org.uk/Letter_to_Steering_Committee.pdf, accessed 11 November 2012.

25 'It's Question Time for the *Daily Mail*', *Guardian*, 26 October 2009, http://www.theguardian.com/media/mediamonkeyblog/2009/oct/26/question-time-daily-mail-nick-griffin, accessed 11 November 2012.

26 M. Smith, 'The English Defence League: The Organ-Grinder's Monkey', in H. Mahamdallie (ed.), *Defending Multiculturalism: A Guide for the Movement* (London: Bookmarks, 2011), pp. 179–90.

27 T. Patey, 'Bank Suspends Manager over EDL links', *Morning Star*, 1 February 2012.

28 N. Copsey, *The English Defence League: Challenging Our Country and Our Values of Social Inclusion, Fairness and Equality* (London: Faith Matters, 2010).

29 The only group of anti-fascists to read the 2010 election result as a victory for the BNP was the Independent Working Class Alliance, who described the BNP's vote in the following terms: 'not only are they no longer a small party, they are still a growing party with momentum behind them'. 'If this is failure, what would success look like?', www.iwca.info/?p=10153, accessed 11 November 2012.

30 D. Trilling, *Bloody Nasty People: The Rise of Britain's Far Right* (London: Verso, 2012), p. 181.

31 A. Zaerin, 'How the BNP was Beaten in Barking', *Socialist Review*, June (2010), http://www.socialistreview.org.uk/article.php?articlenumber=11295, accessed 11 November 2012.

32 B. Blake, *EDL: Coming Down the Road* (Birmingham: VHC Publishing, 2012), pp. 88–91.

33 H. Carter, 'Police Officers to Face Magistrates after Protester's Arrest at Anti-EDL rally', *Guardian*, 4 September 2012, http://www.theguardian.com/uk/2012/sep/04/manchester-police-summonses-perverting-justice, accessed 11 November 2012.

34 Twelve activists were charged in 1981 with possession of explosives and conspiracy. Their defence was that they had stockpiled molotov cocktails to prevent racist attacks. They were sensationally acquitted.

35 *Socialist Worker*, 14 August 2010.

36 N. Lowles, 'The Case Against a Counter-demo', *Searchlight*, August (2010), www.hopenothate.org.uk/features/articles/28/the-case-against-a-counter-demo, accessed 11 November 2012. In 2011, there was a split within the *Searchlight* organising group. Control of *Searchlight* magazine returned to Gerry Gable, its former editor, who reversed the magazine's previous line. S. Gable, 'To Ban or Not to Ban', *Searchlight*, March (2012), www.searchlightmagazine.com/blogs/searchlight-blog/to-ban-or-not-to-ban, accessed 11 November 2012.

37 D. Hann, *Physical Resistance Or, A Hundred Years of Anti-Fascism* (London: Zero Books, 2012), p. 378.

38 Blake, *Going Down the Road*, p. 259.

39 In *Physical Resistance*, David Hann suggests that where UAF was unwilling to confront the EDL the initiative passed to 'Antifa', i.e. class struggle anarchists. While there were always anarchists at every large mobilisation against the EDL, there are only a few examples where they represented a major component of the anti-fascist crowds. This was the case at Brighton in June 2012 (where much of the organising was done by UK Uncut and Smash EDO) and to a certain extent at Bristol a month later.

40 www.youtube.com/watch?v=emdqfnL887U, accessed 11 November 2012.

Index

Index